REVOLUTION AND RED TAPE

REVOLUTION AND RED TAPE

The French Ministerial Bureaucracy 1770–1850

By
CLIVE H. CHURCH

CLARENDON PRESS · OXFORD
1981

Oxford University Press, Walton Street, Oxford OX2 6DP

OXFORD   LONDON   GLASGOW
NEW YORK   TORONTO   MELBOURNE   WELLINGTON
KUALA LUMPUR   SINGAPORE   HONG KONG   TOKYO
DELHI   BOMBAY   CALCUTTA   MADRAS   KARACHI
NAIROBI   DAR ES SALAAM   CAPE TOWN

Published in the United States
by Oxford University Press, New York

British Library Cataloguing in Publication Data

Church, Clive H
    Revolution and red tape.
    1. France – Politics and government – 18th century
    2. France – Politics and government – 1789–1900
    I. Title
    354'.44'0009   JN2369   80–41147

    ISBN 0–19–822562–8

Phototypesetting by Parkway Group, London and Abingdon
Printed in Great Britain at the University Press, Oxford,
by Eric Buckley, Printer to the University.

To my mother, who began it all;
To Christine, who first thought it might happen;
To Margaret, without whom it never would have happened.

'Our best and most divine knowledge
is intended for action; and those
may justly be accounted barren
studies which do not conduce to
practice as their proper end.'

John Wilkins, *Mathematical Magick*,
(London, 1648) p. 2.

PREFACE

This study has its origins, both distant and recent, in research for a University of London doctorate on 'The Organisation and Personnel of French Central Government under the Directory' supervised by the late Alfred Cobban. After a while it was subsumed in a much wider-ranging investigation of the growth of French administration since the Middle Ages. This in turn got caught up in the toils of various publishers and their reaction to the economic crisis of the seventies, with the result that after an unconscionably long time the present study has returned to something closer to its original starting point than might otherwise have been the case. However, the basic analysis is now set in the wider context which it needs for a fuller understanding of its significance.

This investigation of the development of a bureaucracy in a precise period, that of the revolutionary era in France, is also much closer to what Alfred Cobban had always urged. The fact that it has taken such a circuitous route to finish up following his advice is a sign of the value of that advice. This, is of course, only part of the debt I owe to his inspiration, encouragement, and criticism. Much of the credit for any such virtues as the present study possesses belongs to his initial impulse, while its detours and failings, like the opinions expressed in it, are my responsibility. I should also mention my gratitude to Muriel Cobban for her interest and support in recent years. I hope she will feel it is an adequate recompense for these debts.

In the course of time I have contracted innumerable other debts of an institutional as well as a personal nature. Where people are concerned all the members of the French History Seminar at the Institute of Historical Research during the early sixties and the several generations of students who have all listened to sermons on the true meaning and significance of bureaucracy have contributed more than they may have realized.

Many scholars in other fields, beginning with Gerald Aylmer, have done more to convince me of the value of theoretical approaches to the historian of administration than may appear here. I must also thank Pierre Legendre of the Université de Paris I for his help and encouragement on many occasions, notably in 1975, which made the writing of earlier versions of the present book immeasurably easier and agreeable. Similarly, I owe a great deal to the many other French scholars who have dealt so patiently with my queries or provided so much inspiration over the years. I hope they will also regard this book as an acceptable way of expressing my thanks.

I must also thank Brian Dalby, then of the University of Lancaster Computer Laboratory, and his colleagues for help in processing some of my data on personnel. In Lancaster I have always been grateful for the sympathetic and unflinching support of Joe Shennan and the School of European Studies in the last few years, and particularly for the amazing patience and kindness of Mrs Janet Howarth, the Departmental Secretary, especially when typing the final draft. Again, I must also acknowledge the support, interest, and friendship of John Heywood, now of Trinity College, Dublin, which has always meant a great deal. Finally on the personal level I owe more to Penny Hull and her family—who always provided a second home in Paris for a wandering scholar—than I had any right to expect.

I have also accumulated a large number of debts of a more institutional kind. To the Central Research Fund of the University of London, the Centre Nationale de la Recherche Scientifique in Paris, Trinity College, Dublin, the University of Lancaster, the Ministère des Affaires Étrangères and the British Academy I owe my sincerest thanks for the many grants and scholarships which have enabled me to spend so much time in France, often with my family. Similarly, I am grateful to the Departments of French and History in the University of Lancaster, along with the School of European Studies, for facilitating the sabbatical leave and other periods of absence in France which made the research possible. I must also thank the editors of those periodicals in which articles of mine have appeared for allowing me to draw on that material here. Lastly, but by no means least, I owe an equal debt to all the archives, libraries, and other research centres—such as the Service de Recherches Juridiques Comparatives of the CNRS—both in Britain and in France, who have received me so willingly and helpfully. In particular, the Archives Nationales, the Archives Historiques de la Guerre, the Service Historique de la Marine, and the Archives des Affaires Étrangères all have a special place in my affections, for without their willingness to break their own regulations, the original research on which this study is based could never have been carried out.

Finally, I owe a great deal to my wife and family, both for their tolerance of the absences, preoccupations, and enforced residences abroad which made up the trials of bureaucracy for them. In the case of my wife in particular, I owe much help in the preparation, typing, and correction of many parts and drafts of this book. I hope that they too will feel that this is an adequate means of thanks for bearing with me during a gestation period, which must often have seemed both longer and likely to be less rewarding than that leading to Brahms's First Symphony, a parallel which has always been a consolation to me.

Lancaster Autumn 1978

CONTENTS

FIGURES AND TABLES

Figures

Statistical Tables

ABBREVIATIONS

AAE	*Archives des Affaires Etrangères* (Quai d'Orsay)
AD	*Archives départementales*
AESC	*Annales. Économies, sociétés, civilisations*
AHG	*Archives Historiques de la Guerre* (Vincennes)
AHM	*Archives Historiques de la Marine* (Vincennes)
AHRF	*Annales Historiques de la Révolution Française*
AN	*Archives Nationales* (Paris)
ASQ	*Administrative Science Quarterly*
BL	*British Library* (Croker Collection)
CSSH	*Comparative Studies in Society and History*
ESR	*European Studies Review*
FHS	*French Historical Studies*
RA	*Revue administrative*
RH	*Revue historique*
RHDFE	*Revue historique du droit français et étranger*
RHMC	*Revue d'histoire moderne et contemporaine*

CHAPTER I: THE FRENCH MINISTRIES AND THEIR SETTING

'As a flood spreads wider and wider, the water becomes dirtier and dirtier. So the Revolution evaporates and leaves behind only the slime of a new bureaucracy. The chains of tormented mankind are made out of red tape.'[1] Kafka speaks for many in his belief that bureaucracy is a bad thing in itself, which always intensifies with a revolution. No matter that revolutionaries think of themselves as liberators they seem to end up by increasing the amount of officialdom and red tape. So just as bureaucracy is always under attack, so there are continuing complaints about the way revolutionary movements degenerate into even more monolithic bureaucracies than those they replaced.[2] Criticism of bureaucracy is a constant theme in European history. As Sauvy says 'des phrases citées sous Charles IX pourraient, à peine transposés être mises aujourd'hui dans la bouche d'une pamphletaire soviétique'.[3] One is left wondering why, if bureaucracy is held to be so universally bad, people continue to make such use of it, whether in revolutionary or in less tense times.

France seems to enjoy a special place in the history of bureaucracy. This is partly because of the supposed early appearance of bureaucracy there, partly because of the parallel tradition of virulent criticism of administration, and partly because of the power and stability displayed by French bureaucracy in face of repeated revolutions and crises. According to Philip Williams, 'long before she had democratic institutions, France possessed an exceptionally capable, self-confident, powerful and centralised bureaucracy'.[4] France is also the home of one the most powerful of anti-bureaucratic images, *Messieurs les ronds-de-cuir*, as satirized by Courteline. Moreover, although their verdicts have not always been in agreement either with each other or with the facts, many authorities have accepted the gist of de Tocqueville's argument that the early development of bureaucracy led to a granite-like administrative continuity in France. So although France experienced not only the first and greatest of the liberal revolutions at the end of the eighteenth century but also a whole series of subsequent upheavals, the administration is said to have survived them all unscathed. It is claimed that the French bureaucracy first passed largely unchanged from the Ancien Régime to the post-Revolutionary era and then assimilated all other social and political changes. The Fifth Republic, for instance, is said to have seen a fusion between *haute administration* and Gaullism, producing a technocratic *république des fonctionnaires*.[5] This is perhaps one reason why, although the French have been the foremost critics of their own administration, they have also been avid seekers of positions within it. As one writer puts it 'le Français est donc publiquement anti-fonctionnaire. Ceci-dit, il faut également savoir que le plupart des Français desirent que leurs enfants soient des fonctionnaires, parce que le fonctionnaire est tout puissant.'[6] This striking ambiguity brings one back to the suspicion that criticisms of bureaucracy are not all they seem.

Yet if France is a test case both of bureaucratization, especially in a period of revolutionary change, and of the ambiguities of public hostility to administration, there has been little real research on the development of bureaucracy in France. There has been much talk of the continuing evils of bureaucracy, but that is not the same thing. So myths continue to go unchallenged and unexplored. The fact that people agree that in France, above all other countries, bureaucracy is a vital if regrettable issue, and yet do nothing to investigate it, is surely revealing. Similarly the intertwining of bureaucracy and revolution in France is a commonplace. Yet it has never been systematically explored. De Tocqueville has been accepted as a final answer rather than as a starting-point for research. As a result there is much still to be discovered both about bureaucracy and about the way it should be studied in a historical setting.

At the beginning of this century historians and political scientists pointed out how much was even then unknown about quite basic facets of French administration. This situation has been somewhat remedied since. Yet even in 1968, the year of a self-confessed revolt against the strait-jacket of the Napoleonic state, it could be said that 'il n'existe pas d'histoire de l'administration française; seules existent quelques monographies dispersées, beaucoup des romans de mœurs et d'essais, mais aucun tableau d'ensemble de la realité administrative dans toute sa complexité'.[7] There have, in fact, been a number of studies of separate agencies, of variable quality. There are also a large number of treatises on the history of 'institutions' and of administrative law. However, the history of administrative personnel and procedures, of the civil service in the English sense of the word, remains to be written.

To suggest that the reason for French timidity and neglect in the study of administration is due to a lack of methodological rigour and modernity is a patronizing half truth.[8] The task is far from easy in itself. The French division of research between conservative faculties of law and arts faculties suspicious of the state perhaps stood at the origin of the neglect. With the explosion of knowledge and the growth of the social sciences this became cumulative and self-perpetuating. Only in recent years have the social sciences been utilized in administrative studies in France. One offshoot of the emergence of 'la science administrative' has been much soul-searching about the need for a new and self-contained discipline of 'administrative history' to provide a parallel methodology for the study of administration in the past.[9] So far this movement has offered only prospectuses and lists of sources. This suggests that its roots lie more in the antiquarian interest of some administrative bodies for their own past than in the development of theoretical approaches to administration. In any case a separate discipline of any kind risks becoming yet another barrier in the way of the historical study of French administration. To be fair, historians proper have not made a great contribution to this, even though they often use the term bureaucracy somewhat loosely. Where the Revolution is concerned there are a dozen local studies for every one of an administrative agency. And when bureaucracy is discussed in the context of revolution it tends to be the question of how far the former was politicized which monopolizes attention.

Such lacunae are a reminder of some of the other difficulties facing the student of French adminstration. A study of French administration in its totality over a long period of time is impossible at present, at least for the lone research worker. Even a short-term study is open to the charge that the administration was too large, too lacking in homogenity, and too unknown to be grasped in its entirety. The sources, moreover, do not always exist for such a study, particularly one which wishes to answer the questions central to modern social science approaches to bureaucracy. One reason for myths about administration is that the easiest available sources are those which denigrate bureaucracy.

A further difficulty is the total lack of certainty as to what bureaucracy actually means. It has been defined as 'taking measures'.[10] But red tape cannot exist in isolation. Taking measures is what people do. Bureaucracy is a matter of men. And although the semantics of the term are somewhat contradictory, it is used here to denote a group of officials with specific characteristics. Obviously, many authorities have considered bureaucracy in such terms before this. Unfortunately, there is a problem about their choice of administrative men for study. The administration in France has a number of layers and strands. Very often it is the elective or nominated nexus of government which has been described as bureaucratic. Even when people like Armstrong study paid administrators who work to such political figures they have tended to concentrate on the élite few, and to ignore what the French call the *basse administration*.[11] Although the former are the more powerful, they cannot function without the latter, Moreover, as will become clear, much of the complexity of development of administration across the revolutionary era is only explicable in terms of the interplay between the two levels of administrative personnel. The social basis of recruitment to the two levels, which is the question which obsesses much research into administration today, was often fundamentally different.

This concentration on small and not always typical elements of the civil service is another reason, like the problems arising from the sources, for the prevalence of myth over research in our understanding of bureaucratization. Here it is very definitely not the political level of the administration which is at issue. Interest focuses on the professional administration, and on the rank and file at that, those who have been called the workers rather than the policy-makers.[12] For many Frenchmen such a concentration on the *basse administration* will no doubt seen regrettable and a misunderstanding of the real nature of French administration. Those foreigners who have suffered on the other side of the grill in a French office may be more able to appreciate the point. Admittedly there is a danger of 'tout comprendre, c'est tout pardonner' in such an approach. Yet the *basse administration* is the most neglected area of all in terms of the history of administration.

The problem of scope again poses itself here. Even during the revolutionary era there were a large number of corps of employees who went through somewhat different processes of development. Because the arguments about administrative continuity place such stress on centralization in France, the centre is the obvious place to start. Hence the study looks at the staff of the Administrations centrales, the clerical core of the ministries, which are one of the key elements in the administrative structure as a whole. Such an investigation cannot be conducted in a vacuum. All too often French writers have offered a somewhat mythical history of administration because they assume that things can be explained either in terms of laws and government enactment or of organizational structures. Politicians are particularly prone to imagine that structural changes will of themselves solve all administrative problems. Structures are important, and figure largely in the sources, but they too need to be seen in a wider framework.[13] Partly this involves seeing the ministries as part of the general development of France and its government in the revolutionary era.

The ambiguity of critiques of bureaucracy also demands that the ministries should be seen in the public arena, so that as well as tracing the interrelationships between the ministerial bureaucracy and the phases of the Revolution, this study looks at the nature of the debate on the bureaucracy at the time. It is to be hoped that this will bring to light some of the roots of the obsessive love–hate relationship the French have with their administration. At least it will provide one case study of a bureaucracy in a revolutionary era, and show the complicated and changing way in which the various revolutionary regimes handled the problems thrown up by the bureaucracy's adaption to the overthrow of the old order. It makes no claim to be a proper history of the Revolution as a whole, nor even of revolutionary institutions in the widest sense. Nor does it seek to provide a precise demonstration of the working of the Administrations centrales in their many fields of activity. It simply tries to trace something of the history of the French civil service, particularly its ministerial elements, and to place it in its social and political context at a crucial time in its development.

Too much should not be read into this. The lessons of the ministries are not necessarily applicable to the administration as a whole. None the less, with these reservations a basically empirical study, using such insights from other disciplines as are appropriate to fill in the many gaps, even on this limited scale, can hope to do five things. Firstly, it can show exactly how one French bureaucracy did develop over the revolutionary divide, thereby throwing some new light on the de Toqueville thesis. Secondly, it can show exactly what happened to a bureaucracy in a revolutionary situation, and whether it expanded as Kafka and others suggest. In fact the French Revolution was a unique conglomeration of circumstances, and the way the administration drew on the Ancien Régime personnel is a different story from that often told. It is not very likely to be repeated elsewhere today. Similarly, the Revolution changed the nature of red tape rather than simply expanding it.

A third aim is to show the bureaucracy in context. While it would not be accurate to call this a political history of bureaucracy, it does appear that there is more to be gained from seeing the civil service as a participant in the political arena than as a matter of structures and regulations alone. This links with the fourth point. Such a study can show that it is possible to analyse the growth of the civil service without resorting to the creation of a separate discipline. However, it does also show that there is something to be gained from adopting a fairly rigorous approach to problems of definition. Finally, it can hope to shed some light on how far the failure of criticisms of bureaucracy to bring about desired changes is due to the ambiguity which the French even then had about their administration.

Even this is not free of problems. Thus to talk of the Administrations centrales as a whole is to endow them with a unity and a uniformity which they did not have. They also have a variety of facets to their existence: legal and statutory, social and organizational. There is another difficulty over the precise choice of period. The revolutionary era was a long and rich one, and it is not possible satisfactorily to study it all in depth. The focus is therefore on the Directorial era when the ministries had just emerged from their first and major experience of bureaucratization. They then settled down into something close to the shape they were to adopt for the first half of the nineteenth century. Moreover, although the period has been singled out as one in which bureaucracy reached grotesque proportions, the Directory —whatever its other faults—proved to be a regime which was more adept than most in dealing rationally, if in an embarrassed way, with the new bureaucracy. This is perhaps why it is often claimed to be a key period in bureaucratization.[14] Like many other myths about a regime which has been as much neglected as maligned by historians, it does point to a basic truth about its achievements. The way the Directory created an amalgam of Ancien Régime and revolutionary administration by reinserting the new revolutionary bureaucracy within the old ministerial framework was, in fact, essential to the consolidation of the former. It is also a process about which, as Godechot says, we know even less than normal in Directorial historiography.

Concentration on any one period tends to throw its achievements into too sharp relief. And as a previous study of the Directory alone showed, it is very difficult to extract the regime from the Revolution as a whole. Unless one broadens the focus to other phases of the Revolution it is hard to see what the Directorial era's true significance was both for the administration itself, and for its public standing. To give balance and an archival foundation to the wider setting, this study has been extended to cover the period 1770 to 1850. This gives both adequate scope for assessing the Directorial contribution to administrative change, and for seeing the relationship between bureaucracy and revolution as a whole. It also coincides roughly with the periods in which Directorial civil servants actually worked in administration. This enables one to avoid the need to carry out similar analyses of personnel to that with which the study originally started. The study of Directorial personnel tells one much about administrative life at other phases of the revolutionary era. So this basic picture has been compared with other samples, sometimes drawn down the rich source of the

Ministry of War, in order to illustrate the changing nature of ministerial recruitment.[15]

The story could be taken a long way back in time, since the French administration has long roots, albeit not the bureaucratic ones sometimes suggested. However, by the late eighteenth century the administration had reached a turning-point. The structure of government as it then was, was not such as to allow real moderization, and an examination of the failure of reform attempts and of the nature of the ministries in the reign of Louis XVI makes this fairly clear. Even the Constitutional Monarchy failed to effect more than minor changes in the nature of the ministries. With the radical republic the ministries were first bureaucratized and then replaced by new bodies. They were, as has already been observed, reunited under the Directory. Here the narrative gives way to a detailed analysis of the structures, personnel, and socio-political situation of the slowly crystallizing bureaucracy. The Revolution was far from over in 1799, and there was room for Bonaparte to complete the consolidation of bureaucracy by reforming the structures and the leadership within which it worked. The relationship between him and the bureaucracy was more complex, and less a matter of dictatorship, than is usually suggested. However, there was still a good deal of reticence about the position of the new bureaucracy. It was left to the regimes which followed the Empire, notably the July Monarchy, to complete the process by formally recognizing the bureaucracy as a participant in government and in politics. Even so, the recognition was not accompanied by substantive action. The problems of revolutionary bureaucracy were by no means at an end in 1848.

This process of bureaucratization under the radical republic, consolidation under the Directory and under Napoleon, and recognition under the constitutional monarchies is less straightforward than is often allowed. One of de Toqueville's contemporaries saw the history of French administration as a dramatic and geometric progression from feudal chaos to modern unity: 'tumulteuse, multiple à l'origine, elle devient régulière, uniforme'.[16] In fact, French administration and its central core did not progress directly from the simplicities of the Middle Ages to the complexities of today. They followed a more winding and circuitous route. That people should have adopted de

Tocqueville in a facile manner, and thought that this was not so, is due to a lack of care about definitions and concepts.

De Tocqueville only used the word 'bureaucracy' twice, and then without making clear what he meant by it.[17] His main interest was in the structure of government, and with the jurisdiction of superior officials within that structure. At that level there obviously was great continuity over the revolutionary era. For him the Revolution *par excellence* was the Constituent Assembly. If, however, one looks more closely at the next stage of the Revolution there is much more of a case for the creative role of the Revolution. This is particularly so if one considers what happened at the subaltern level and the way in which administration was actually carried out. The disposition of personnel, together with the centre of gravity and the ethos of administration all changed markedly after the Revolution. However, even revolutions cannot make something out of nothing. The new administration was built from pieces provided by the old order. At the level which de Tocqueville ignored, the radical republic produced a building as different from that of the Ancien Régime as is the new from the old Euston. Then after the initial bureaucratization of the late nineties things often slipped back to something nearer what they had been before the Revolution of 1789. The revolutionary discontinuity is thereby concealed from view. The appearance of continuity is also unfairly reinforced by the fact that each generation goes through a similar cycle in its relations with administration. So the discussion of administrative problems is repetitive not cumulative.

In other words de Tocqueville was both right and wrong. For although France had a strong, complicated, and centralized administrative structure before the Revolution just as it did after, the former was dominated by superior officials and the patrimonial characteristics deriving from the way they had begun as, and indeed still remained, direct servants of the king. Although the administration had some bureaucratic dimensions it cannot fairly be called bureaucratic as it can after the Revolution. This is a reminder of the confusion which has arisen from failing to distinguish between different kinds of administrators and different kinds of administration.

Since the last war all public servants in France have been

known as *fonctionnaires* but previously, and especially in the last century, a *fonctionnaire* meant someone exercising a political role, authority, and responsibility in his own right. Such officials, elected or nominated, were very clearly distinguished from *employés*, the subaltern officials who worked for them, 'espèce de rouages inaperçus qui font mouvoir la machine administrative'.[18] They had no political role and few privileges and perks. Whereas some people in the Revolution felt that an employee should always be salaried, *fonctionnaires* were often deemed not to need a salary, the concept of the citizen–functionary as it has been called. And while France has always had *fonctionnaires*, whether elective or nominated administrators, it was only with the radical revolution that she acquired a truly bureaucratic army of employees. Similarly it was only then that the employees began to exercise an influence which could balance that of the *fonctionnaires*. Even then the influence was for a long time merely informal. It may not always be possible to distinguish the two classes but their existence is not to be denied.

It is the change in the position of the employees that marks the real discontinuity between old and new in French bureaucracy. In talking of bureaucracy, however, one comes up against another problem of definition. Bureaucracy is a doubly ambiguous term. It is used both as a noun and as an adjective. It is also used as a pejorative and, as is the case here, as a precise and descriptive term. For although there has been much debate about the value of using concepts from other disciplines in history, and about the nature of his concept, there is little doubt but that Max Weber's definition of bureaucracy is the most stimulating one available to historians. And since, as critics now point out reproachfully, it is based on close observation of the nineteenth-century scene, it is also the closest to the realities of early nineteenth-century French administration. Indeed, some authorities claim it is still the best guide to understanding recent changes in ministerial organization in France.[19]

Weber's ideal type of bureaucracy is a specific form of administration which is a direct outgrowth of the nature of authority in the polity.[20] Administration can and does exist in all ages and countries as an intermediary between government and governed. Bureaucracy however comes into being only with the rational and legal authority of the modern state. Basically for Weber a

bureaucracy is a formal establishment of professional administrators, organized on rational lines, to carry out the wishes of a
superior political will.[21] Since it is an 'ideal type' one should not
of course assume that every characteristic will always be present
in every bureaucracy, nor that the list of criteria is exclusive and
permanent. Institutions can be bureaucratic in some dimensions
and not in others, and the distribution and intensity of bureaucratic characteristics may well change with time. Again, it is
probably impossible to be wholly consistent in using this one
concept of bureaucracy in analysis, just as it is hard to always
distinguish clearly between functionaries and employees. None
the less, the two distinctions are essential to understanding the
changes which took place in French administration in the
revolutionary era, and to gauging to which category particular
administrations belong.[22] The use of the Weberian view of
bureaucracy, however, does not mean simply being tricked by
hindsight into believing that modern administrative science
knows best. Much recent work stresses the differences between
countries and their administrations, and would respect the
individuality of a past administration.

The adoption of the concept does help to resolve the thorny
question of when bureaucracy first emerged in France.[23] For
not only has the Directory been singled out as the time when
bureaucracy emerged, but so has nearly every other phase in
French history, from the Renaissance right through to the late
nineteenth century. Such contradictory opinions are proof of
the problems of definition both of bureaucracy and of growth.
Bureaucracy has thus been taken to mean men, legislative
controls, and government structures by different writers. Most
have considered its emergence as an immediate, deplorable,
and irreversible phase of administrative history, rather than as
something more gradual and complex.

Using the Weberian definition as a guide, at most one can say
that there were anticipations of bureaucracy in France from the
seventeenth century onwards when a new nexus of government
was superimposed on the venal officers inherited from the
Middle Ages. There is no case for seeing the venal officers
themselves as bureaucrats.[24] By the eighteenth century there is
evidence of further bureaucratization, at least in the field
services. Yet the changes that took place then were, as has

already been argued, quantitatively and qualitatively less than those which took place after 1793.[25] Significantly, it was at this time that the term bureaucracy really took root in France, even though semantically and concretely it was always an ambiguous idea.[26] With the experience of total war the Republic felt it had to set aside a service which remained true to its courtly and patrimonial origins if it was to increase the power and standing of the administration to enable it to cope with the military crisis. As well as extending and reordering its operations, it introduced a growing number of employees. And though these were drawn from the central and especially the field services of the old order, this was the crucial transformation. Where there had been administration, by 1794 there was bureaucracy.

Though later regimes were sometimes to backtrack on this, the initial bureaucratization was never fully reversed, and there was always an internal dynamic and self-conciousness to the bureaucracy which was hard to ignore.[27] Yet if the initial bureaucratization was a sharp and sudden matter, the transformation of the ministries was actually a much longer drawn-out process of metamorphosis from the administration of the Ancien Régime.[28] Concentration on the initial phase thus leads one to underestimate both the debt to the past and the extent of future problems. Admittedly the radical revolution was needed to transform the chrysalis into an adolescent bureaucracy, but it needed the larva to be able to do this. And adolescence is not the same as adulthood. All three phases of development need to be remembered when thinking of the emergence of bureaucracy in France.

One reason why discussions of the relationship between revolution and bureaucracy in France have been relatively unsatisfactory is that the former has too often been looked at as a simple 'bloc'. In fact it went through several phases of its own, as has already been suggested. It was the second phase of the Revolution which produced the new form of domination that produced the change from a 'fonctionnairocracy' to a bureaucracy. This is in line with recent analyses of revolution as complex processes rather than single-shot upheavals or even simple series of stages.[29] In such a process violence does not necessarily rise to a crescendo with the seizure of power, but can often escalate as the revolutionary movement seeks to extend its control to the peripheries, after the seizure of power at the centre.

If this is so, relationships between bureaucracy and revolution are not likely to be decided at the outset. They are even less likely to be a simple matter of the replacement of one set of officials by another. The question which obsessed politicians at the time in France—and which has worried historians too—is to what extent they could rely on the political loyalty of the bureaucracy after the Revolution. Whichever faction was in power tended to believe that the bureaucracy was peopled solely by its political opponents. And if, as has been suggested, the Revolution did lead to a major change in the nature of French administration one would expect that something like this would have happened. The take-over of the administration should, for instance, have led to its being peopled with Jacobins. In fact, it was fear of continuing royalist predominance that really worried the revolutionaries. This may suggest that they were more aware of the way the new bureaucracy was woven out of fragments from the Ancien Régime administration than they are sometimes given credit for. Their mistake, and it is one which has been followed by some historians, was to assume that officials are politically motivated. This was probably not the case. The question of political loyalty was of rather minor significance at the time.

Overall the revolutionary government probably forced people to accept the reality of the Revolution, even if not committing them to any particular revolutionary party. Once this was done the bureaucracy seems to have surmounted many of the upheavals implicit in the revolutionary process. It thereby justified Weber's view, that 'even in the case of revolution by force or of occupation by an enemy the bureaucratic machine will normally continue to function just as it had for the last legal government'.[30] This was because its motives were material rather than ideological. Of course this seemed a major threat to many revolutionaries for whom loyalty to the movement was all. They might have agreed with those who see the main problem of bureaucracy not as its susceptibility to reactionary ideals but the fact that 'rather than working to continue the revolutionary process, the new bureaucrats tend to work to maintain the bureaucracy itself'.[31] In so doing they corrupt the movement by disinterest and not by subversion.

The real issue is thus not a matter of politics but the more general problem of the control of bureaucracy, which faces orthodox as well as revolutionary regimes. The French revolutionaries' political obsessions and the ambiguous attitude towards the state generally prevalent in France actually hindered attempts to direct the bureaucracy in the way they wanted. Their concentration on political liaisons prevented them developing effective coercive controls, while their hostility to bureaucracy in general tended to prevent them, at least until the time of the Directory, from controlling the bureaucracy by offering it concessions. They also failed to realize that whatever their internal dynamic bureaucracies are usually produced by external stimuli, so that bureaucracy is there to some extent because it is necessary.[32] Here again they failed to get the best out of the civil service. Their hesitation, however, is understandable. The gradualness of the transition in administration up till 1793 probably emphazied the legacy from the past, both generally and where the ministries in particular were concerned. That legacy went back to the earliest days of the monarch in some ways. And though it is arguable that the *basse administration* had a functional attitude to the monarchy even before the revolution, it is not surprising that the revolutionaries emphazied the links which bound it to the monarchy. As pioneers in dealing with bureaucracy during a revolutionary crisis they can hardly be blamed for not having today's understanding of the problem.

Since the revolutionaries' attitude to the administration was shaped by the latter's monarchical past, just as were the problems of the administration itself at that time, it is necessary to trace the way in which the administration did evolve up to the mid-eighteenth century. This evolution again owed much to external forces, notably political ones.[33] Even in the earliest times when the monarchy was overwhelmingly a personal matter, the king needed some kind of administrative assistance to carry out his will. The story of the evolution of French central government is in part a search for a reliable set of servants. After the fall of the Roman Empire, from which little was handed on, the monarchy was feudal and government was not a recognized activity.[34] The king was a justiciar and administration was carried out by grand officers, barons, and estate managers, who never amounted to a real administrative class.[35]

All this changed with the 'royal revolution' of the late thirteenth and early fourteenth centuries. The expansion of the royal domain, and the new international role of the monarchy, combined with the increasing wealth and complexity of society to demand something more than mere estate management.[36] This was provided by the new breed of lawyers from the recently annexed southern provinces who brought with them ideas of royal *puissance* derived from Roman Law. Court officers, nobles, *prévots*, and *baillis* were thus superseded by new corps of trained lawyers staffing sophisticated new institutions of government and administration. This officer class, though by no means bureaucratic, proved fairly loyal at first and helped the monarchy to survive the trials and tribulations which beset it in the late fourteenth and early fifteenth centuries.[37] Whether its independence was enough to deserve the polity being called a *Standestaat* is, on the other hand, open to doubt.[38]

In any case the monarchy was rebuilt by Louis XI after the end of the Hundred Years War on the foundations provided by the *officier* class. The restored monarchy adopted a more authoritarian and, above all, a more fiscalist stance.[39] The officer class, however, was institutionalized as bodies like the Grand Conseil went out of court and venality set in, thereby beginning an era of clashes between the king and the officer corporations. As the monarchy once again faced a critical political situation at home and abroad, the need arose for a new and more reliable body of royal servants. Here again, however, there was never any thought of doing away with the existing officer class.[40] It was merely exploited and superseded, so that the solidity of the sixteenth-century monarchy was largely superficial.[41] The absolute monarchy had to cope with a disaffected populace, a dissident old nobility, and a discontented officer class.[42]

To deal with the combination of social unrest and political turmoil, the so called century of 'civil war between 1559 and 1661', the monarchy inveigled French society into a new alliance with the state, which is now known as the Ancien Régime.[43] As a result of this process, the officers went beyond institutionalization, to attain nobility and administrative inaction. For the king bypassed them and divided them into conflicting groups, from amongst which he extracted trusted dynasties to whom he entrusted a new nexus of government formed by the *Maîtres des Requêtes* and the *Conseillers d'État,* acting through the royal council and the Intendancies. These 'trusties' were more of a tribe than a bureaucracy.[44] They were further outflanked by the emerging ministers who represented an even more trusted new elite. Under Richelieu and Mazarin the conciliar network was the key although the system of Intendants was extended. Yet if the very different nature of *commissaires* were made clear, the *officiers* were still partly used, for instance as *sub-délégués*.[45] Under Louis XIV increasing use was made of the ministers, who helped to take the power of the state to new heights, and thus the functional role of the officers was further reduced.[46] This was not done wholly consciously, as the hesitations over permanent Intendancies and the establishment of *sub-délégués* shows.[47] It was basically the result of the demands of war. On the other hand, it was deliberately paralleled at the centre in 1661 with the demotion of the Chancellor and the increased reliance on the ministers.[48]

As Louis XIV's *Grand Commis* were *fonctionnaires* drawn from a limited number of dynasties, who adopted a very personal working style, they were not bureaucrats. However they did in the long run build up the power of the ministerial departments. For it was the *Grands Commis* who bestowed power on the bureaux and not vice versa. In the later years of the reign, when Colbert and his generation had died, his successors were faced with even greater problems. Since many of them were lesser men, owing their position to birth rather than to ability, they relied on their clerks. So the period after 1690 saw an institutionalization of government, but also a partial militarization, and fleetingly, even an attempt to introduce venality into the efficient part of government. So the emergence of a putative new layer of servants on whom the Crown could rely was never carried to its logical conclusion. The relationships between such elites remained confused. As a result there were few initiatives in government at the end of the reign.[49]

Because of the institutionalization there was little structural change in government in the eighteenth century. The Polysynodie was an ineffective challenge to the new machine on the part of sections of the *noblesse d'épée*.[50] Thereafter, despite some initial hesitations the old nobility had to resort to subverting the machine by infiltrating themselves into the ministries at the expense of the old dynasties. The officers increasingly failed either to execute their old roles or to perform the new services required in a changing environment, and were further outflanked by increases in the power of the intendants and the development of some new technical services, based on more modern administrative principles.[51] Needless to say they did not accept this without complaint.

The unease of the *noblesse de la robe*, together with the lack of royal leadership and an increased conflict over places as inflation undermined the system of venality, had disastrous effects on administration. The adoption of routine procedures and declining efficiency were, according to some authorities, its dominant characteristics.[52] The newer elements in the administration were swamped by the decorative ones. The *noblesse de la robe* became increasingly active politically, while the attractions of ennobling office remained as strong as ever. On the one hand this subverted the newest elements of government while together with the associated financial problems, it also sapped the effectiveness of government as a whole. Elements such as the ministries were thus still very much in the grip of the social ethos created by the monarchy to solve the administrative problems of an earlier age. So although they had emerged as part of the attempt to create yet another class of reliable state servants, they remained only a tiny caste within the old structure.

Despite the gradual resolution of problems of functional responsibilty amongst them in the early eighteenth century, the staffs of the ministries remained very much the offshoot of personal royal power that they had always been.[53] Emerging as confidential clerks under Philip IV in the wake of the breakdown of government by *grands officiers*, the ministers had risen to the rank of *secrétaires des finances et des commandements* from the late fourteenth century, a status which often conferred nobility on them. Because of the long tenure and abilities of Florimond Robertet in the early sixteenth century they developed an even greater political and administrative role, at the expense of the Parlements.[54] In 1547 they divided up responsibilities for the affairs of the provinces between them and twelve years later they were elevated to the rank of *Secrétaires d'État* with a seat on the royal council. So Sutherland can observe that 'where the

King and a secretary were—even on a battle field—there was the government'.[55] Their new role caused immense antagonism and to save them from further abuse they were suspended by Henri III in 1588.

Restored under Henri IV they began to exchange provincial responsibilities for more functional ones, so that some authorities claim to be able to see the origins of particular ministries in these years. However, close examination of their roles under the Cardinals shows both how personal a matter this all was, and how limited were their rights to control matters apparently in their brief.[56] None the less, from the late sixteenth century it was formally recognized that they needed assistance to carry out their growing tasks, and they were entitled to one senior clerk (or *Premier Commis*) and six ordinary clerks.[57] Even as late as the time of Colbert some departments were still under this establishment, and even when, as with Louvois the demands of war forced the employment of up to twenty clerks divided into bureaux corresponding to the various functions of a ministry, the clerks were very different from modern bureaucrats. The ordinary clerks were all clients of the Minister and there was virtually no continuity between different tenures, as each minister brought in his own clients. The *Premiers Commis* were neither professional civil servants, any more than were their juniors, nor were they really administrators at all. More often than not in the early days they were putative ministers themselves, waiting for the *charge* to come their way. Even under Louis XIV by when specialization and professionalization had made some impact on the ministries, the *Premiers Commis* played a political role and often acted for their ministers in their absence. In the following century they proved very hard to dismiss and were paid by fees and bribes, proving their own claim to be a kind of *officier*.[58] Although they inhabited a structure which was more sophisticated and rational than that which had prevailed a hundred years before, their position was still ambiguous and patrimonial, and their future development as uncertain as that of the administration as a whole.

As well as being socially regressive the administration also had a number of structural problems.[59] For despite its development in the seventeenth century, there were still many structural confusions and uncertainties in the eighteenth century. The king remained in theory at the centre of government, but increasingly the machine worked without him, even though its members remained *commensaux du roi*, revocable at will in theory. The conciliar apparatus still existed, but the real process of decision-making had been transferred to the ministers, first acting individually and increasingly as a corporate body.[60] The Conseil Royal de Commerce never met and the Conseils de Dépêches and des Finances were merely facades for the decisions of the *Controleur Général*, his *Intendants des Finances*, and other ministers and high officials. The Conseil d'État Privé, Finances et Direction continued to play a role as a nursery of administrative talent and a supreme court for administrative law but even so its greatest days were behind it. Arrêts du Conseil in fact increasingly were simply departmental decisions.

The ministerial departments however were still limited in their status and operation by the conciliar screen. They were also hampered by the way they got sucked into court politics, even though the Royal Household no longer played a real administrative role. Similarly, their decisions often had to be registered through the Parlements and other sovereign courts which could hold them up. Moreover, their own divisions of functions and standing did not make their tasks any easier. The ministries were variegated bodies enjoying differing titles and status. Although in theory the Chancellor was the most senior, his department was very small and composed largely of venal dignitaries such as the *chauffe-cires*, and his administrative role was negligible. And at times even his dignities could be taken away and entrusted to a *Garde des Sceaux*. The senior *Secrétariat d'État* was that for Foreign Affairs. Yet this too was a small department and one of the most liable to involvement in court life, despite its expertise and its slow development of technical services. The real power in government was, of course, the *Contrôleur Général*. Even though he was not a minister and had for long needed a Secretary of State to counter-sign his acts, his influence was paramount because of his relationships with the Intendants and his powers of financial control. His staff made up half the total number then involved in the central administration, although many of them were again venal officials such as the *Intendants de Commerce*. Overall his bureaux were more of an anarchy than a modern administrative service.

The rise of the Contrôle Général had stripped the secretariats of their old responsibility for affairs in various parts of France, save in the case of the frontier provinces where the Ministry of War exercised some authority. As a result the vestigial interest in internal administration was increasingly centred in the Ministry for the Royal Household which, in the 1750s, was separated from the Admiralty and reunited with the Hugenots Portfolio. It also took over some responsibility for Paris from the War Office, although the *Lieutenant Général de Police de Paris* was even more influential. Yet although in theory it took on some of the characteristics of a Ministry of the Interior, its staff was small and its standing somewhat low. When a separate portfolio for economic affairs was created for Bertin, for instance, there was never any thought of attaching it to the Household department. The two service ministries were amongst the largest secretariats and had developed a number of technical services, although their internal structure was subject to quite frequent changes. There were also struggles for power between clerks and serving officers.

On the surface this may sound like a set of departments moving towards a fairly rational division of labour, but in fact, as Bosher observes, ministerial services were really very disordered. There was great overlapping of functions, unclear divisions of responsibility, and a general lack of internal control. For although the concept of 'public' official emerged at this time, many of those who worked in the departments actually owned their offices and were not subject to ministerial control. And even though there was no States General the ministries found that the sovereign financial courts which were meant to exercise some control over royal expenditure and activity rarely did so, allowing many services to slip further towards the world of venality and business. So whatever progress the ministries made tended to be cancelled out by the twofold confusion from which they suffered, within their own organizations and in their relationships with other bodies.

At the local level the problem was similar. For although it is generally assumed that power and communications ran directly from Versailles to the Intendants, the reality was rather different. The Intendant was not a prefect and faced many problems which the latter was spared. Thus he did not control all local emanations of central services. Nor was his authority unchallenged. He had often to negotiate with the provincial estates, the Parlement or other sovereign court, the governors, and the officer corporations. Their pull was so great that some authorities have discerned a move from upholding the royal will, to one of subservience to privileged interests, especially with the Crown failing to support them as it had previously done.[61] His freedom of action was often limited by such dealings and by the fact that although his administrative services, notably the Secretary of the Intendance, began to develop, he was still reliant on officers to get many things done. This involved him in an increasing number of jurisdictional conflicts, which although they developed the administrative law provision, inhibited more positive action.[62] So there was little improvement in the mad mosaic of fiscal, legal, and administrative jurisdictions into which France was divided, all of which enjoyed rights and jurisdiction. Many of them, like the *Receveurs-Général*, also served as bankers and thereby subverted legitimate chains of authority.[63] There was also a great deal of confusion between such old services, still marked by the older roles of the monarchy, and the new technical services such as the Maréchaussée, the Fermes, and the Ponts et Chaussées some of which employed thousands of men, some of whom were close to bureaucracy.[64] Finally, the Ancien Régime continually failed to resolve the problem of municipal government which had fallen into the hands of self-perpetuating corporations of officers.

At all levels then the modern elements in the royal administration were embedded in a web of archaism which not merely inhibited their day-to-day operation, but also made it increasingly difficult for them to break out of the strait-jacket. Since the eighteenth century saw a growing tendency to the strengthening of the web of social and political privilege and interest, the middle of the eighteenth century was a turning-point. Was the administration to accept the returning control of venality and patrimonialism or not? Although the problem was not always seen in these terms it did dog the middle of the century, threatening all the confused attempts made through recent centuries to create new groups of royal servants who would prove more reliable than the officers, of whom the ministerial staffs were one.

The question was largely avoided by Louis XV until the last years of his reign when the Brittany crisis with the Parlements brought it home to him.[65] Hence the early seventies saw an attempt to rationalize the whole structure of the Ancien Régime. Unfortunately the social liaisons created by Louis XIV proved too strong for his successor. And although the early years of Louis XVI saw a number of attempts to ameliorate some of the worst of the administrative shortcomings, it became increasingly apparent that without the full support of government—that is without a change in 'domination' as Weber would put it—this would not succeed. The changes themselves became of increasingly political significance as the crisis of the monarchy deepened. So far perhaps the first time the civil service began to figure in the political arena. Unfortunately the prevailing ideas tended to inhibit necessary reforms, because the administration was seen so much as a monarchical creation. The fact that the monarchy had created the problems of the administration as well was overlooked. It was this position of *les commensaux du roi* which hindered the modernization of the ministries. The monarchy never resolved this problem. Indeed it was overwhelmed by it in the end. Even in the reformed guise created by the Constitutional Monarchy, the administration did not change all that much, partly because the same unhelpful ideas were carried over from the age of reform. Bureaucracy almost existed as much in the eyes of its critics as it did in reality. Opposition to red tape was from the start a useful rallying-cry for politicians. So the late eighteenth-century central administrations were caught up in a variety of complicated settings as will, and can only, be explained by a more detailed historial analysis.[66]

CHAPTER II: ACROSS THE
REVOLUTIONARY DIVIDE, 1771–1792

Towards the end of the eighteenth century the French administration had reached a turning-point. Its modern elements
were cancelled out by a renewed challenge from the old social
élites of the Ancien`Régime. The *officier* class in particular,
having seen its institutional status subverted in the seventeenth
century, was not satisfied by the compensation provided by
social promotion, and in alliance with the *noblesse d'épée*, began
to renew its pressure for administrative and political power. Its
weapons in this so called 'feudal reaction' were partly the
traditional magnetic attraction of noble status and partly the
new intellectual critiques of the time.[1] This change of mood and
direction was to make impossible further movement towards
bureaucratization.[2]

If there were elements of bureaucracy in the technical field
services and the lower echelons of the ministries, these were
neither fully developed nor powerful enough to outweigh the
effects of the new social pressures. Moreover, prevailing attitudes
to the administration remained paradoxical and limiting. For
although one English observer could claim that 'an entire
revolution in the form of government is looked forward to with
the greatest eagerness' the *officiers* and their allies had the
gravest reservations about such changes.[3] The rising middle
classes and the nobility often wanted reform in general, and
administrative modernization in particular, on intellectual
grounds. Yet, on political grounds they also opposed administrative reform in case it undermined property rights and
strenghtened the royal 'despotism' which they so disliked. And
while they differed on future forms of government, the élites
could unite in opposition to the Crown. They were also able to
enlist the support of public opinion at large in this opposition,
for whatever popular attitudes were to royal authority and

privilege, government taxation and control was felt to be oppressive.

So while the problems of administration may have been more clearly identified, the royal reform movement did not succeed in bringing the central administration closer to modernity. This can be seen both in the case of a typical ministerial department and more generally. The effort at reform was undermined by the way economic crisis lent credence to the privileged orders' opposition to royal authority together with the insidious pull of privilege itself, which led to the take-over of many ministerial and provincial positions by the nobility. At the same time, the insufficiency of prevailing ideas on the means of restructuring and controlling administrative services thwarted both Crown and opposition policies. And so strong were these ideas that even when the events of 1789 brought a change in domination and so broke the hold of privilege on administration, the central administration was not at once allowed to develop freely. As far as the significantly scant sources for the period allow one to judge, the central administrations were not really remodelled until 1791 when the radical revolution began to make itself felt.

The impact of the Revolution was thus, in some respects, a delayed one. 1789 unceremoniously removed the old *officier* class and many of the existing administrative structures and practices. Yet it left the employees behind, as uncared for as before, and the continuing suspicion of administration meant that their problems were no nearer solution than they had been in 1770. So while the structures of government changed greatly many other things remained unchanged in the world of administration, despite the energies expended on destroying institutions, purging leading personnel, and devising sophisticated judicial controls. In fact some things remained unchanged because of these energies, as when the premature winding-up of some services demanded an actual increase in administrative manpower. Despite the changes brought about by the Revolution then there was continuity between the last phase of the Ancien Régime and the Constitutional Monarchy in administrative matters, notably in the absence of operational ideas on regulating the day-to-day realities of administrative life. And, as the War Office shows, there were also significant personnel currents which were to effect the evolution of the civil service.

The relationship of revolution and bureaucracy was thus a matter of men and not just of abstractions. The Revolution built on what the Ancien Régime had done, although it did not always use those elements of administration where bureaucratization was most advanced. Moreover, whatever they claimed, the early revolutionaries were still too close to the social ethos of the Ancien Régime, if not to its actual institutions, to be able to complete the process of modernization which they began in 1789. The social ethos thus marked the central administration over the revolutionary divide, as did the effects of the royal reform campaign. Questions about the nature of administration, its role, and the means to control it were continually posed but rarely resolved. It was left to the radical revolution to come up with new approaches to the administration and to complete the second task of the Revolution, that of positive construction. Yet even then, the old ideas and the old preference for government by *fonctionnaires* lingered on.

In 1770 all this lay in the future. At that time administration was seen as less of a problem than politics. The long-drawn-out conflicts over Brittany, taxation, and Jansenism finally came to a head in the Falkland Islands crisis of 1770.[4] The refusal of the Parlements to accept the royal discipline that flowed from this forced a reluctant Maupeau to set them aside. The death of Louis XV helped, however, to prevent this from turning into a major breach in the old venal and social order. Yet the royal *coup* and its subsequent partial reversal by Louis XVI served notice on the opposition, both that there was still a possibility that the Crown could sweep them aside and reinforce its position through a renovated system of government, and that the Crown could be swayed by resistance and force. This classic combination of coercion and cowardice was a further incitement to the disobedience already plaguing the polity.[5]

Adminstrative reform was not unrelated to all this. Even minor technical changes in the administration often served only to alarm the opposition further, reinforcing their belief that the real danger to France lay in royal despotism operating openly through a reinforced state apparatus instead of behind a conciliar screen.[6] This attitude, which was to have long-term implications, in the short term blocked royally sponsored change. The Crown lost the political initiative it had briefly recaptured at the end of Louis XV's reign while the noble reaction gathered pace. The administration was eventually forced to make its own attempts at reform from inside, but it was too tightly bound by the old order for this to go very far.

It would be wrong to think, however, that there had ever been any deliberate effort by the Crown to make the administration take any particular road, whether to full bureaucratization or backwards to enhanced venality. There were merely a variety of often ineffective efforts, much affected by the political crisis, to remedy specific problems which had arisen inside the administration. Such alterations as followed were usually limited in nature.[7] They sought the best of both worlds by remodelling tactical points while preserving the strategic social structure in which the administration was operated. As the two were often incompatible the alterations were frequently short-lived and insubstantial. Sometimes, moreover, the changes led to a relapse into patrimonialism, as the increasing pace of issue of patents of nobility to senior ministerial employees shows.[8] So while the *Premiers Commis* of the reign of Louis XVI may have been more specialized and qualified than their predecessors they were far from exempt from contagion by the social ethos of the times. Thus Henin of the Foreign Office was *Sécretaire du Cabinet* to Louis XVI. In the Ministry of War senior men like Lelu and Ponteney were rewarded not merely with *Commissaire des Guerre* status but also allowed to hold venal office as, in the latter's case, as *Trésorier de le Généralité de Paris*.[9] One junior clerk, Henri Colmar, was able to invest his prematurely taken pension in a venal office in the *Capitainerie* of Versailles in 1779. So, if power did devolve one rung down the central hierarchy, as many critrics were convinced it had, it only devolved on people who were the mirror image of their ministerial masters, who had themselves fallen into the hands of privilege.

At the local level the failure of the municipal reform project of Laverdy in 1765 and the consequent restoration of municipal offices also testifies to the all-pervading influence of privilege. It also shows the difficulties of combining the kinds of improvement desired by some reformers with the existing style of administration. As Bordes shows, the greater the technical expertise of the Intendants, the lower was their political standing.[10] All this points to the fact that despite the encomiums somtimes heaped on it, the administration actually possessed only a very limited dynamic of its own and needed the external stimuli stressed by Weber for change. In the seventies and eighties the regime made an effort to mediate the growing, though still inchoate, demand for reform but its efforts proved counter-productive. They tended to stimulate the growing criticism of the administration from the outside. And at times during the pre-Revolution period the Crown even had to accept attempts to subject the administration to a new kind of control. It was out of this crisis that the early talk of 'bureaucracy' developed. The term administration then came to signify 'la service public et son personnel' rather than just a mode of activity.[11] So to a certain extent the development of the term was part of a political battle rather than the result of any objective analysis. Bureaucracy thus became for some people an adjunct of despotism. Attitudes towards the administration depended on attitudes towards the Crown.

How this worked out in practice can be seen if one looks first at the way in which the over-all structure of government changed after 1770 and then at the evolution of the ministries, both in general and more particularly at the special case of the War Office. Such examinations also help to bring out the precise nature of the continuity between the era of reform and the first phase of the Revolution. In principle the over-all structure of the machinery of state did not alter during the reign of Louis XVI. The Crown continued to exercise its authority through the complicated conciliar mechanism and in conjunction with a vast range of judicial, ecclesiastical, and provincial corporations, as well as more directly through ministers, field services, and the *Intendents*.[12] However, there was some attempt to simplify this structure and make it more amenable to royal control. For instance, the prohibition on ordinary courts hearing administrative cases was reinforced.[13] Similarly, bodies like the Chambre des Comptes and Monnaies were reduced in number. Large economies were made in the Royal Household and some unnecessary branches of the Council, and the fiscal system were suppressed along with the remaining military *grands officiers*. In the Conciliar reform of 1787 a number of Councils were consolidated into the new Conseil Royal des Finances et Commerce and a large number of its standing committees or bureaux were pruned.[14] In the financial services royal authority was made more effective by Necker's attempts to unite the many royal treasuries into one strictly controlled central deposit and to replace some of the venal officers and *fermes* involved with Régies of salaried officials, as in the postal and saltpetre services. The same desire to limit private enterprise in government can be seen in the substitution of nominated Directors for private contractors in some of the army's logistical services, and the utilization of *savants* in the field of agriculture and commerce.

At the same time the Crown had also to divest itself of some powers through the Six Acts of Turgot and Vergennes's free trade treaties. This can also be seen in the hesitant introduction of provincial and other assemblies. So while individuals like Necker were very active and although there was some improvement in the provision of administrative jurisdiction at the heart of the system, there was no consistent attempt to change its basic features, as Maupeau had eventually come to desire.[15]

There was slightly more movement inside the major administrative *corps* themselves, where specialization continued, both amongst field services and ministries. There was also a greater interest in the problem of controlling such *corps*, particularly where Necker was concerned. In services like the maréchausée, the ponts et chaussées, the reformed Ingénieurs Geographes Militaires of 1777, and the Inspecteurs des Mines of 1781 the trend towards more complex, coherent, and even bureaucratic administration continued.[16]

The Ferme Générale is a good example of this. It employed thousands of so-called *buralists* and technicians who were leased out to the *Fermiers Généraux en masse* while remaining a permanent property of the king's. The Crown came to exercise increasingly direct control of their activities. In some ways they were bureaucratic in that they had a strict staff hierarchy, complicated and rigid regulations, detailed personnel records, and from 1768 a contributory pension fund. On the other hand promotion by merit or by seniority was limited by the great gulf between ordinary employees and the *préposés*, directors, and controllers. The latter needed large financial resources to meet the bond required of them by the state, and were recruited by patronage. The lower grades included collectors, guards, and clerks. Even here many were the personal appointees of individual officers and not established members of the Fermes. As time went on recruitment to the lower grades became more difficult as the disparities between the two groups increased. So although the Fermes like the ponts et chaussées and the Intendancies contained people who were 'prototypes of the modern fonctionnaire', they were still inside institutions which retained many non-bureaucratic traits.[17]

Whatever their precise characteristics the government was very concerned about the existence of such bodies. Trusted officials like the *Premiers Commis* of the Contrôle Général were given increased powers of audit and inspection as part of Necker's attempt to replace private *comptables*, often themselves financiers, by a better defined financial system 'composed solely of capable functionaries devoted to the public good'.[18] Similarly, the ministers became ever more heads of departments, more concerned with controlling the services placed at their disposition than with claiming a place on the Conseil d'en haut. The meetings of the ministers continued to develop so that with the tensions of the times ministers could no longer be professionals as before but became, again quoting Bosher, 'political to a degree'.[10] The Contrôle also came to occupy a very special position, in this, to some extent undermining the other ministries. A further barrier to rational administrative organization was thus created. This obviously also militated against any moves away from prevailing norms, so that Necker and services like the Fermes were odd men out. The growing liaisons of society and the administrative élite found in the Ministry of War were in the end more typical and significant.

The politicization of ministers increased the concern of the opposition and also made it necessary to revive the position of Prime Minister, so as to reconcile competing departmental imperialisms and co-ordinate policy. The position of *Chef du Conseil Royal des Finances* provided an opportune constitutional niche for a post which, although vital, often came into conflict with traditions of ministerial independence. One aspect of this which did lapse at this time is the old secretarial responsibility for all the affairs of named provinces. This had been applied in theory to Bertin's department but in reality it was all dealt with by the Contrôle Général under the cover of the nominal responsibility of the Maison du Roi secretariat.[20] Some 40 per cent of the business transacted for the Council by the latter was actually executed by the former. Even the War Office had to refer non-military matters relating to frontier provinces to the Contrôle.

The loss of these attributions did not prevent an expansion in ministerial staffs from under 400 in the fifties to about 670 by the late eighties, of whom well over a third were in the Contrôle.[21] With the exception of the defence ministries the other departments were small, the Maison du Roi still only having about 30 clerks, as did that of Bertin, while the Chancery had even fewer. Bertin's staff, even with the Contrôle's attempt to limit its operation, proved insufficient to handle the business for which he was responsible so that long delays developed.[22] This does not seem to have been a problem in the defence ministries, or even in the Ministry of Foreign Affairs which had, perhaps significantly, grown as fast as any other department in the last quarter of a century of the Ancien Régime. One reason that a department like the Chancery could manage on so few staff was that it had lost control of the vital work of censorship. This had been transferred to the *Lieutenance Général de Police* where over a hundred and seventy people were employed to carry out the work, even though the Chancery had been able to manage with many fewer earlier in the century when censorship had been perhaps more active.

The department of the Royal Household, despite the smallness of its staff, was divided up into some ten sections. These were entrusted to the control of some of the most highly paid officials in any of the ministries like Petigny de Saint Romain who had an immense income of 47,250 *livres* derived from fees, grants, and honours as well as from his basic salary.[23] Petigny, who was born in 1738, had served for thirteen years in the partly patrimonial post of *Secrétaire de Sceau* in the Chancery before he transferred to the Maison du Roi in about 1778. His juniors were far less well paid, although they could include people like Desloseaux who had entered the Ministry when he was 19 in 1753 after a period in the Domaines service. He too received about 40 per cent of his earnings from pensions, including one of 1,299 *livres* paid in compensation for a place of *femme de chambre*, promised to his wife on their marriage by Madame Victoire, the sister of Louis XVI, but never made good. The structure of the

Ministry was also marked by courtly origins although it had moved closer to an orthodox Ministry of the Interior after 1750 in obtaining control of Paris and police affairs, together with the provincial responsibilities entrusted to Bertin. These had previously been briefly transferred to the Ministry of Foreign Affairs. The ten sections thus included offices for provincial administration in general, the affairs of Paris, various archival bureaux, a secretariat, and of course a section for dealing with the administration of the Royal Household itself.

Bertin's department itself was also an interesting and paradoxical combination of the old and the new. It was set up largely to reward and to retain an effective royal servant but it also came to reflect the more technical role towards which the monarchy was trying to move. Bertin was made responsible for trade, transport, mining, lotteries, and various aspects of agriculture. Yet its staff were divided into an unbalanced set of four offices. These dealt with agriculture, mining, and postal communications; provincial affairs; stud farms; and secretarial matters respectively. However, it was not the fallibility of its internal structure that ended the experiment, but the play of vested interest. The Contrôle Général resented the loss of authority and refused to provide it with either the financial backing or the freedom of action which Bertin needed.

Similarly, despite the ramshackle nature of its structure the Contrôle Général was able to dominate the whole range of government activity, even including foreign affairs on occasions. Whereas most of the other departments of state had a relatively simple structure of bureaux and a few attached services, the Contrôle was a rambling agglomeration of commissions, services, semi-independent functionaries, and others, all held more or less together by a small and still very personal team of clerks who gathered around the *Contrôleur* himself and the *Premier Commis* of the department—who himself controlled 7 bureaux employing 46 men at a cost of over 210,000 *livres* per annum.[24] Necker's attempt to rationalize this by replacing the *Intendents des Finances*—the most important of the independent posts in the department—with *Premier Commis*—of whom there were 50 in any case—and an advisory committee was short-lived. Even though the *Intendents* after 1781 did not regain the whole of their powers, their re-establishment marked the continuing triumph of venal *fonctionnaires* within the most important ministry.

The *Premiers Commis* in the Contrôle, for all that they were *commissaires* and not *officiers*, were not appointed in a very rational manner, any more than those in the Ministry of Foreign Affairs where these *commensaux du roi* became so important as to depress the standing of the growing number of ordinary clerks.[25] The latter were often recruited now by the *Premiers Commis* from families with traditions of ministerial service rather than from the diplomatic corps as before. This patronage, however, failed to procure any real security so that they had the disadvantages of both patrimonial and bureaucratic systems. The *Premier Commis* on the other hand could look forward to nobility, and in Vergennes's time, to forming virtually a policy-making *troika* with the Minister. Henin and Rayneval thus lived comfortable, elegant, cultured, and very well-connected lives in Versailles as nobles and courtiers as well as civil servants. The *Premiers Commis* of the Contrôle also possessed venal offices and expected to act as financiers themselves.

Their colleagues in the Admiralty, on the other hand, slightly lost ground to the serving officers, rivals who were brought in over their heads to direct the four major sections into which the Ministry was divided, a policy which was supported by the junior staff.[26] The results can be seen in the ordinance of 1785 which provided for a formal structure of *Commis en Second*, *Commis Ordinaire*, and *Expeditionnaire*, and allowed for promotion after three years in a grade, together with other benefits. However, although structural rationalization here weakened the *Premiers Commis*, whereas in Affaires Étrangères the creation of the two great political directions served to strengthen them, it did not dispossess them or prevent them from resisting further changes. So all that happened was that the Ministry was swollen by the influx of naval officers. This is typical both of the dilemma of the Ancien Régime administration and of its attempt at solving it. It also reflected the increasing tendency for *Premiers Commis* themselves to become favoured and quasi-venal *fonctionnaires*. Similarly, the structures of administration did not make any lasting escape from the confusion prevailing at mid-century.

All this is very apparent in the relatively rich sources of the Ministry of War, one of the largest and most homogeneous departments, therefore as likely as any to have been bureaucratic.[27] The special role of the *Premier Commis* stands out very clearly, as does the problem of evolving some kind of a *statut des fonctionnaires* in that kind of environment. There were problems too with serving officers and the kind of people recruited by the Ancien Régime. What one finds very often is Bosher's 'combination of aristocracy and private business'.[28] The structure of the Ministry was highly fluid since the political importance of the Ministry made it attractive and each incumbent felt that he alone knew how to organize its bureaux. As a result its staff grew from 85, split into 12 sections in 1745, to 180 in 18 sections by 1771. By then it was becoming unmanageable since many of its new staff were low-paid and insecure quasi-auxiliaries.

So first Belle-Isle, and more significantly Saint Germain in his ordinances of the summer of 1776, tried to solve the problem. The latter halved the number of bureaux and cut the staff to 105, while at the same time continuing to raise salaries to realistic levels.[29] He also laid down one of the first personnel regulations of the Ancien Régime, which included a code of good conduct and the first official hierarchy. This ranged from *Chef de Bureau* (formerly *Premier Commis*) at 15,000 *livres* per annum, through three grades of *commis ordinaire* at 5, 2, and 1,000 *livres* respectively, to *élève* at 600 *livres*. It was expected that sinecures would be abolished or surrendered, and that in future entry to the ministry would only be after satisfactory performance as a trainee. Special pensions and gratifications would have to be surrendered, and *Premiers Commis* would have to buy the *charge* of *Commissaire des Guerres* and wear its uniform.

With the exception of the last, this is very close to modern ideas of a bureaucratic career pattern, and significantly it came from an outsider. Saint Germain had spent much of his life in foreign service. It was to be unsuccessful, even though the Minister was supported by Guibert, one of the leading military reformers of the time.[30] There is no evidence that clerks surrendered their pensions or chose between War Office posts and sinecures, though some of them did gain the additional honour of becoming a *Commissaire des Guerres*. This had not been unknown in the past, and in any case it was typical of the Ancien Régime that it should not rely on militarization and venalization in order to control its civil servants.

As a result of this failure and the outbreak of the War of

American Independence the inflation of numbers and costs continued, there being nearly 200 employees in 10 bureaux by 1787. Ségur and Guibert reduced this the following year but this was soon reversed and further attempts to keep the Ministry to a reasonable size and structure continued into the Revolution.[31] Where structure was concerned they had some success, especially under Saint Germain, for although the precise organization he ordained changed, its general principles survived into the Revolution. By then there were bureaux for provincial affairs; officers and 'graces'; funds and personnel; artillery and engineering; supplies; discipline and correspondence, and the geographical study section: the Dépôt Général de la Guerre.

However, if one looks at the way the work of a bureau such as that Fonds was actually organized, the limits to rationality were only too apparent.[32] There was only a higgledy-piggledy division of tasks among the clerks, and most of them were weighed down with routine work so that there was virtually no provision for budgetry control. Moreover, the salaries paid, especially to Melin, the head of the bureau—who was to be executed in 1794—were drawn from a variety of courtly sources, including the Contrôle in which he was concurrently employed. His very attractive but honorific rewards were a long way from the Weberian condition of dependence on salary.

Since the names and roles of employees varied according to the department and to the time in question, this rough guide has been devised to facilitate analysis of administrative hierarchies. It is based mainly on salaries and positions current in the second half of the Directory. These are broadly comparable to those prevalent at all other periods covered by the study except the inflationary phase of the Revolution.

Obviously not all the employees of the bureau, let alone of the Ministry as a whole, enjoyed this kind of facility. Indeed from the analysis of some 350 clerks who are known to have served between 1771 and 1789, for two-thirds of whom there is some information, the difference between the élite and the mass is very clear.[33] It seems as though the ratio between senior and junior staff was of the order of 1–2.5 which shows that there were a fair number of senior *fonctionnaires* with a few, rather separate, clerks attached to them. The overwhelming majority in both classes thus came from the towns. Some 11 per cent were

TABLE I: TITLES AND RANKS USED IN THE MINISTRIES

Grade I	Salary 4800–8000 frs. p.a. plus: Secrétaire Général, Directeur, Chef de Division, and Premier Commis, etc.
Grade II	Salary 3200–6000 frs. p.a.: Chef de Bureau, Sous-Chef de Division, Chef-Adjoint, and Membre du Conseil, etc.
Grade III	Salary 2700–5600 frs. p.a.: Sous-Chef, Secrétaire, Adjoint, and Caissier, etc.
Grade IV	Salary 2700–4800 frs. p.a.: Rédacteur, Commis Principal, Secrétaire Commis, and Employé Principal, etc.
Grade V	Salary 2000–6000 frs. p.a.: Traducteur, Examinateur, Ingénieur, and Dessinateur, etc.
Grade VI	Salary 1000–3000 frs. p.a.: Commis d'ordre. Enregistreur, Analyseur, and Commis, etc.
Grade VII	Salary 1000–2500 frs. p.a.: Exéditionnaires of all classes, etc.
Grade VIII	Salary 1000–1400 frs. p.a.: Surnuméraire, Auxiliaire, Elève, and Aspirant, etc.
Grade IX	Salary 700–1200 frs. p.a.: Garçons, Timbreurs, and Huissiers, etc.
Grade X	Salary 200–1800 frs. p.a.: Portier, Concierge, Jardinier, and Homme à Peine, etc.

born in Versailles, a further 8 per cent in Paris, and the rest coming from all over the kingdom, save that the future departments of the Moselle and the Haute-Marne supplied five clerks each. Overall, there seem to have been slightly fewer southerners than was later to be the case and also slightly fewer from the Channel coast, but otherwise the pattern is very close to that found in the revolutionary era. The concentration of recruits from Champagne and Alsace is probably to be explained by the Ministry's vestigial responsibilities in those areas.

Of those for whom the information is available, about 40 per cent were born before 1730 and a further 40 per cent between 1730 and 1750, as compared with only 29 per cent between 1750 and 1770. This suggests a fairly mature service, in which men tended to live and die. What information there is on the age of entry shows that 39 per cent entered before they were twenty.

Even more entered administrative service in general before that age. This is significantly younger than during the Directory for instance. The Ministry thus recruited most of its clerks young, so that a fifth had no other employment before their entry, and supplemented them with a further 18 per cent recruited from venal, local, or field service. Only one man entered the Ministry duing the life of Louis XIV and only a handful before 1730 whereas 12 per cent joined between 1730 and 1750, 30 per cent between 1750 and 1770, and the remaining 50 per cent there-after. This was not the steadily increasing pattern that is at first sight suggested since the over-all figures conceal very high peaks of recruitment during the Seven Years War and even more markedly during the American War of Independence. It was probably then that the Ministry had to recruit those with some administrative service rather than untrained youths.

Information on their social standing is much more elusive. Virtually all seemed to have lived in Versailles, to have been married, with an average of one point six children, and to have had virtually no financial resources other than their salaries, although this must be treated with caution. Similarly, there is little evidence of formal education although a few clerks had been trained in the law. The impression is of a group of people whose social position was determined by their occupation rather than the other way round. This is reinforced if one turns to their social origins, using the categories devised by Adeline Daumard as a base, since these show—admittedly on a very small sample —that four-fifths of those whose father's occupation is known were born into administrative families, mostly connected with the Ministry of War.[34] There were also a few sons of venal officers, some employees of the Maison du Roi, and one or two other subaltern royal agents. Only three came from noble back-grounds, along with about half a dozen from *rentier* stock and the law respectively. The scanty evidence on marriage patterns does not suggest the prestigious marriage alliances that some *Premiers Commis* were able to make. Marriage within the circle of the Ministry or into that of minor domestics of the Royal Household was more common. This tendency to departmental inbreeding is very marked, with 60 per cent of those on whom information is available having at least one relative in the bureaux and almost a fifth more than one, the father–son relationship having been the most common.

The Ministry seems to have been more socially homogeneous than was Affaires Étrangères. Its leadership was more technical in nature and slightly less elevated socially, although still very clearly distinguished from the rank and file. In some ways it was closer to bureaucracy in that its staff were less venal and less *fonctionnaire* orientated than elsewhere, but none the less, they were still dominated by family relationships and possessiveness, and did include a minority of quite wealthy clerks. Often private resources were needed, as people requisitioned by the Ministry were poorly paid and could lose by the transfer, which perhaps explains the rarity of such transfers. Appointment to the Ministry was much more related to finding a first job or to patronage, very rarely it would seem to sheer economic need. The pull of tradition, family, and patronage is also visible in the mode of appointment. Over half the cases for which information is available involved a relative, while a quarter were protégés of a minister or courtier. All of this goes to show how even quite humble employees were caught up in the social network of the Ancien Régime and would have been lost without its support, given the deficiencies in the career pattern.

The Ministry seems to have offered a somewhat unattractive career and might have been in difficulties had it not been for the support of such traditions. The majority of its staff started out at the bottom of the scale, as many as 14 per cent in fact beginning as unpaid supernumeraries with salaries inferior to 2,500 *livres*.[35] This was not compensated for by rapid promotion. Twenty-nine per cent achieved no promotion at all, though this includes the few who were recruited at the top of the scale, and 4 per cent were demoted. Of those who did achieve promotion, very few penetrated to the heights of becoming a *fonctionnaire*. Thirty per cent managed to rise four grades and 9 per cent were promoted to other services, which was perhaps better than in the revolutionary era. None the less the possibilities were limited and had to be waited for, often over long and painful years. Certainly the range of terminal salaries was wider than those at entry, but the majority still earned less than 2,500 *livres* per annum at the end of their careers, and this despite rapid inflation.

It was presumably these social prospects and the hopes of welfare which were the attraction rather than mere gain. The relative freedom with which pensions were accorded ties in with this. Moreover, 30 per cent of those who are known to have benefited from such pensions, usually during their careers as well as after, received up to 2,500 *livres* and a fifth more than this. So security of income was lifelong, and extended to families as well, even if the pensions scheme was not as well organized as in the Fermes. They were based, as a *Premier Commis* in Affaires Étrangères said, on 'des décisions particulières au bas des mémoires ou rapports successivement presentés, au Roi par le ministre'.[36]

Another major source of security and reward came from the payment of special bonuses or *gratifications*. These ranged from repayment of legitimate expenses, such as costs incurred in travelling with the court on one of its expeditions, postage, or learning a language abroad, to rewards for special duties and the reimbursement of costs incurred in private life. The first category was akin to modern university merit increments for special work or to remedy anomalies in pay relativities, while the second could include marriage, sickness and bereavement grants, and, more rarely, help with housing and rent.

Finally, there were the various honours that clerks could gain: exemption from taxation, monopolies of printing French treaties, accession to sinecures such as the 900 *livres* paid to the ' clerk to the garrison of Brouage, clerical posts in the households of royal princes, nominal places as *valets de chambre* to the king, and, most commonly, the auxiliary posts of *secrétaire-interprète* to a foreign regiment in French service and *Commissaire des Guerres*. Although less striking than in some other areas, these honours did confer social esteem and security on their holders. Many people came to count on them as did Charlot, head of the Bureau des Grâces between 1723 and 1776, who, in addition to a salary of 18,000 *livres* per annum, largely reversible to his family, and a pension of 14,000 *livres*, demanded exemption from the *taille*, large *gratifications*, the ribbon of the order of S. Michel, and all 'autres franchises qui peuvent resulter de mon état de Premier Commis du Secrétaire d'État de la Guerre'. Although few could aspire quite so high, all could hope for something, particularly in time of need.

It was this hope which made a career in the Ministry both attractive and fundamentally dependent on its non-bureaucratic qualities. In an age in which fortunes could fluctuate wildly, the bounty flowing from being a *commensal du roi* was not lightly to be rejected. The staff thus depended on their relatively close contact with the Crown to see them through any crises. The thought of this must have consoled them during the somewhat impoverished years of waiting and in the face of the constant possibility of dismissal for corruption or for the sake of economy. The years of waiting could be very long given the early entry and the tendency to fill many top posts from outside. Over half the entire sample served for more than 15 years and 8 per cent for more than 40, the rest being spaced out between, saved for the unusually low figure of 10 per cent who stayed for only 3 years. Moreover, many had also served in other administrative service, so that over a half of the entire group had actually served the state for more than 20 years. Service could thus be for life, and even with the Revolution it was not till 1821 that the last of the group left the Ministry and others remained in the wider reaches of the civil service till as late as 1836. Obviously the Revolution did upset the pattern since while only 77 employees left in the seventies, 127 went in the eighties, nearly 40 per cent of them in 1789 alone, and a further 100 in the nineties. However, many went into other spheres of administration, where 1815 saw most of them leave the civil service.

Politics was a minor cause of such departures.[37] Of those on whom information is available, 8 per cent died in office, 1.5 per cent resigned because of ill health and other personal reasons, 8 per cent transferred to other services, 16.6 per cent had to leave because of varying administrative shake-ups such as the ministerial reorganizations already referred to, and 23 per cent retired normally. Only 1.4 per cent were dismissed for incapacity, as many again for personal political reasons, and 5.7 per cent because of general political shake-ups. These ratios also hold good for those who remained in the civil service on leaving the Ministry.

On leaving the Ministry a third retired at once, a sixth went into other administrative service, and a twelfth died almost at once, reinforcing the impression of a career which was little more than informalized venality for the lucky ones. That luck often required patronage and even humble clerks were able to enlist the support of powerful patrons like Polignac, so that the figure of 17 per cent for those who benefited from such patronage is probably an underestimate. Certainly, such patronage is more significant than pure politics, although the two often overlapped, especially in the appointment of *Premiers Commis*. Ministers played a large role as patrons, as was notably the case with Montbarey, and the death or retirement of a minister could often disrupt promised rewards. The individual Minister thus had a marked effect on the personnel of his department as well as on its structure, playing a decisive role in deciding who should enter the charmed circle of rewards which was the real aim of most of the staff.

Thus, to exemplify the general case, a clerk like Lemoine owed his entry to the Ministry solely to the fact the he was Puysegur's godchild. The Minister used him as an auxiliary in his private secretariat and when he left office Lemoine had to solicit a grant to enable him to return home.[38] Puysegur's secretary, Adrien Daverton, was even luckier being able to stay in office and to receive grants to facilitate removal. These were examples of the kind of relief to which employees looked forward. Similarly when in 1788 the house in Saint-Dizier, a property on which Durup de Baleine was dependent for much needed extra income, burned down, the department bailed him out with a gratification as they were morally obliged to do, having brought him from a post in Toulon which had paid twice what the state offered.

Again Claude Géant, a *père de famille nombreuse*, and *Premier Commis* of the Artillery Bureau, was regularly given aid as for example when his wife was ill in 1786. Even Antoine Denniée who was to be one of the most distinguished members of the military civil service under the Empire and the Restoration, and who was a *Garde de la Porte du Roi* as well as a clerk and *Élève Commissaire des Guerres* of ten years' standing needed aid that same year to help him support his wife and two children. Others like Fautrier, who had left a judicial post in the provinces to take a place in the War Office, were less fortunate. He had to serve for eighteen months as a supernumerary and never in fact gained the kind of support he had obviously counted on. Only in 1790 did he get some help with the costs of his daughter's marriage.

All this does not lead one to accept recent suggestions that the

Ancien Régime produced both the bureaucratic state and also the means whereby it could be subordinated to the wishes of society.[39] The War Office was not merely not bureaucratic— and if it was not then undoubtedly the smaller Administrations centrales are most unlikely to have been—but all the evidence suggests that it actually depended for its proper functioning on its honorific and patrimonial traits, since these made up for its lack of bureaucratic development. Similarly, there was no satisfactory means of control. Obviously the Ministry was nearer to bureaucracy in 1790 than it had been in 1760, but not markedly so. The failure of Bertin's department as well as of the attempted reorganizations inside the Ministry of War show the continuing barrier to further specialization.

If the personnel of the administration were not venal, many of those at the centre owned sinecures of which they could not easily be dispossessed.[40] Their salaries were also a small part of their incomes and in some cases were paid as part of office expenses or from levies on provincial towns. The growing stress on expertise and careers was balanced by patronage, family tradition, and dependence on *gratifications*. It was even more threatened by the tendency of the ministerial élite to cut themselves off from their juniors so as to establish themselves as *fonctionnaires* in competition with other such groups.[41] The breakthrough to bureaucratization was not achieved because 'the aristrocratic society of the Ancien Regime inevitably undermined all general laws and regulations, because privileges, *graces*, favours and marks of distinction consisted in personal exemptions and exceptions'.

Moreover, neither society nor government was able to exercise very purposive control of the administration. Reform was not easily imposed from outside as Saint Germain found, and it had to grow internally first. Such attempts as there were to regulate the *cursus honorum* inside the ministries were transitory, and were countermanded by social pressures. They do not suggest that the administration itself was any more capable of bringing about its own reform than was the Crown. There were therefore large gaps in both the system of internal discipline and in that of administrative law.[42] The *Intendents* and the *Conseil* exercised a limited administrative jurisdiction, but it was somewhat undefined and took no account of the bureaux. Nor was the

Crown always able either to enforce it so as to provide a proper central control of local and field services. The ministries were not organized to do this. As Ymbert remarked, it was 'la révolution [qui] a conduit le gouvernement à résaisir partout de cette action, et elle a ouvert sur tous les points, des contrôles à cet immense personnel d'agents et d'employés qui dissimulait autrefois le système de fermage et d'enterprise'.[43]

Yet even this limited progress towards the administrative Rubicon had frightened the opposition to the Crown, putting them on their guard against further reforms. It also stimulated general public criticism of the administration. For whatever modern verdicts about the precise nature of the changes through which it went, contemporaries do seem to have believed that it had changed drastically. Thus while in the fifties and sixties Grimm and Gournai had railed against any kind of legislative interference in society, by the eighties people were more concerned with the illicit influence of administration and of clerks inside it.[44] Such complaints had two themes, first that the administration was corrupt and self-seeking, peopled by 'des simples aventuriers, sans mœurs, sans talens, qui après avoir dissipé dans les plaisirs d'une vie crapuleuse et dissolué le petit patrimoine de leurs pères, ont trouvé dans les liason de leur libertinage d'infâmes protectrices qui leur ont procuré, auprès des gens en place, un accès que des honnêtes citoyens n'ont pu obtenir'. There was an element of truth in this, as the War Office suggests, but it was magnified by the fact that some elements of public opinion in general were rapidly developing a more advanced concept of public service than was prevalent amongst the main beneficiaries of the Ancien Régime.

The second complaint centred on the excessive authority acquired by the administration as a whole, irrespective of grade or service, and which seemed to be subject to no constitutional or other restraint as to the burdens they could impose on the public. Jacques Peuchet summed this up when he said:

la burocratie [sic] est gouvernement lorsque, par un abus aussi bizarre qu'incroyable, de bureaux faits pour jouer un rôle subalterne, elle s'érige en magistrat, exempte tel ou tel de la soumission des lois ou assujettit les citoyens à des obligations qu'elles desavouent: elle est administration lorsque des commis stupides ou corrompus s'érigent en ministres, font de la fortune publique l'objet de leurs speculations particulières, changent, reforment; altèrent les meilleurs règlements ou arrêtent des articles, etc. Elle est commandement lorsque les agents du pouvoir souverain vont prendre l'ordre des hommes incompetent pour le donner, soit par rapport aux opérations militaires ou à l'execution d'ordres arbitraires. Ce genre d'abus règne depuis les premiers bureaux de l'état, jusque dans ceux de la politique qui sont le resumé, et pour ainsi dire, l'âme du système despotique qui nous gouverne depuis si longtemps.[45]

Peuchet wanted to combat both old and new abuses through a formal commission or regulation, but this was not to be, either then or during the Revolution since few shared his insight into the mechanics of administration. The complaints simply grew more emphatic and resentful, as did the solutions, but with little real effect until about 1795.

Because of the growth of criticism the administration was brought much more into politics during the period following the failure of the *coup* of 1770. Louis XVI then looked to Turgot and Necker but never really supported them against the storm of opposition which was caused, for instance, by the publication of the *Compte Rendu*, the annexation of the financial power of the Ministries of War and of the Navy, and Necker's other reforms.[46] Hence the new few years saw little attempt to carry on his work either with the administration or generally. Indeed many of his reforms were reversed as a result of wartime financial stringency. Abuses continued unrectified, and may have increased as the growing strength of the opposition tended to favour the honorific tendencies inside the administration as with the *Intendents des Finances*. It is less common nowadays, however, to suggest that the provincial *Intendents* were captured by the aristocratic opposition as a result of feudal reaction.[47] The royal failure to maintain the impetus gave the initiative to the opposition so that policies were spasmodic and uncoordinated, undermined by chronic shortage of money and by the way Louis XVI's lack of will had strewn the way to the scaffold with the political corpses of would-be Straffords. Concern for administrative reform continued both inside and outside the service but there was no real campaign and increasingly little royal participation.

When the financial bubble finally burst, government policy was in the hands of Calonne, a loyal servant of the Crown but also a pillar of the venal order.[48] His reform programme in 1786 summed up the best fiscal and representional thinking of the time. It also set itself firmly against any social and administrative modernization beyond tax reform. This point was taken up by the Assembly of Notables who were aware of the extent to which the economic crisis was linked to the failure of the venal accountants. They also suspected that they already bore a large enough tax burden.[49] In other words, even the success of Calonne's programme would not have led to the kind of change produced by the Revolution.

In the event Calonne was dismissed mainly because of his own tactical political errors. His successor, Lomonie de Brienne, was more interested in administrative reform but neither this nor the concessions he made in the course of implementing Calonne's programme endeared him to the opposition. Indeed his simplification of court, councils, commercial, and financial administration, not to mention the Ministry of War, of which his brother was a reforming minister, further increased the opposition's antagonism.[50] They feared that any more strengthening of administration would facilitate royal resistance to the introduction of representative government, with which they now sought to complete their increasingly violent assault on the absolute monarchy. In their view for instance the size of the *Contrôle Genérale* bureaus was already dangerously large.[51] The Crown, being so criticized and ill obeyed, abandoned the administration. The latter was left to the tender mercies of an opposition reinforced by the sanction of election, and to any internal changes it might make.[52]

There is an element of truth in Antoine's dictum that it was the administrative monarchy that killed the monarchy, in so far as it was obviously a grievance in the 1780s.[53] The fact that it remained administrative rather than bureaucratic annoyed some people and also robbed the king of the strength which a bureaucratic administration might have offered him *in extremis*. This was not, however, the only cause of the fall of the monarchy. Moreover, if there had not been an administrative revolution in the late eighteenth century as de Tocqueville liked to suggest there had been some change.[54] But to fully blossom, the trees of the old administration, to use Schweitzer's aphorism, really had to wait on a basic change of principle. The Ancien Régime had inched its way to a more simplified and centralized structure as well as beginning the development of administrative law, but in doing so it had had to leave untouched all the things which held it together: patrimonialism, venality, interest, and property. It was not able to resolve the ultimate dilemma of social privileges and exception on which it had deliberately been built in the first place.[55]

Yet if the Ancien Régime was in 1789 a barrier to change this was not widely recognized. When the Revolution came few were prepared for it, and even fewer could have predicted it. With the defeat of Lomonie de Brienne and the agreement to call the Estates General the aristocratic opposition seemed in late 1788 to have victory in their grasp.[56] But to gain their real end, an institutional veto over public affairs, they had to declare their hand and come out from behind the fiction of the united opposition to royal 'tyranny'. Their declarations on the form that the States General should take were quite unacceptable to liberal and middle-class elements in the opposition. These believed both in the reality of royal tyranny and in the rectitude of real representative government, such as had been talked about during the conflict with the Crown.

Their answer to administrative oppression was to make administration the task of the citizenry and its representatives. They used the electoral machinery and the States General itself to show their resolute hostility to the Crown and to the privileged orders. Finally they cut the gordian knot of the future of the Ancien Régime by the declaration of the National Assembly. Then, in uneasy conjunction with popular militancy in July and August 1789, they consolidated and imposed their solution on the upper classes and the rest of the country.

Although the popular militancy was a shadow on the horizon, the Constituents had the field to themselves for a while. They were able to create the new state of their choice, and to do away with the administrative institutions and practices of which they so much disapproved. As Dunn says 'the only revolutionary achievement is the creation of a new order'.[57] The Constituents were able to take up the criticisms of the old administration, and carry them further, once having disposed of the social foundations of the Ancien Régime on 4 August. It was the Revolution, through what Hoselitz calls 'the sacrifice of the

bourgeoisie' which broke the intimate liaison between administration and social structure. The crucial log jam was broken.
The whole administrative setting with which the ministries
worked was also destroyed.

Yet this did not have quite the immediate results that might
have been expected. The Revolution did not at once produce a
major and positive change in the actual nature of the administration, its working, its control, or its role, as will become
clear. What it did do was to produce a sharper view of what
administration should be. This view, which owed much to the
Ancien Régime, was, in the short run, to impede a real transformation and, in the long run was to dominate French thinking
about bureaucracy. The administration gained no new freedom
under the Constituents. Their conservative views on administration thus led to more administrative continuity with the old
order than they really wanted. It was, however, a continuity of a
less creative kind than de Tocqueville realized and rested on
contradiction, not the simple inheritance he assumed.

Here again it is perhaps wrong to attribute too much of a
conscious administrative strategy of the Constituents. They
were certainly no more successful at restructuring or controlling
the administration than the old monarchy had been. This was
despite, or perhaps because of, the idealized view of administration which they held. This view, like the administration
itself, was to survive into the next phase of the Revolution. The
continuance of the administration and its fundamental role in
the creation of the new bureaucracy was far from what the
Constituents wanted. They deplored a situation in which, as
they saw it, 'le citoyen n'est rien [et] le commis gouverne' just as
they deplored royal despotism. This latter produced an
obsessional fear of the royalist political opinions of clerks.[58]
Such negative attitudes were probably more influential in
shaping their approach to the administration than more positive
desires to reorganize it along lines acceptable to the Enlightment
as a public duty and service.[59] Hence before looking at what
actually happened to administration these ideas need to be
explored.

The Constituents' view of what administration should be was
that it represented the execution of the will of the sovereign
people by duly appointed citizens holding 'une charge civique'

under the general surveillance of the king. In other words, their conception was of a *citoyen–fonctionnaire* or a magistrate in the old Roman sense. The bureaux and the old *gens du roi* were unpopular, and at heart many of the Constituents could see no need for technicians and clerks. As Van Berkel remarks, 'sans doute, les représentants aux Etats Généraux ont-ils consideré qu'il suffirait de supprimer l'emploi d'Intendent, si unaniment honni, pour que soit tranchée la question administrative'. Their idea was an administrative system in which the state did less, and did it infinitely more simply. Indeed it is hardly going too far to suggest that in theory the Constituents saw absolutely no need for administration in the modern sense of a body of men and measures to ensure that the will of the executive is turned into concrete action. They rather give the impression that they believed that merely posting the latest laws on a convenient tree would automatically lead to these being implemented and obeyed. Cloots said 'le peuple n'exige de ses administrateurs que du pain et le *Bulletin*. Nous saurons bien nous procurer le reste sans que le gouvernement s'en mêle.'

This should have led to supreme neglect of administration once offending structures had gone, but because of their intense fear of the power and political orientation of the administration the Constituents could never leave well alone. They subjected the administration to close scrutiny and regulation, and overestimating the ease with which men and institutions can be reformed, and underestimating their own tendency to recognize reality by turning to the administration to get things done, ending up by getting the worst of all worlds.[60]

Where power was concerned they failed to appreciate both that their legislative proposals in fact reinforced the machinery of state with new responsibilities and that, as Moleville reminded them 'les despenses de l'administration sont infiniment plus considerables dans une république que dans une monarchie, parce qu'il est necessaire d'y employer un plus grand nombre d'agens'.[61] Instead they occupied themselves with worrying about the ministers. As Billaud-Varennes urged in a pamphlet in 1790 'plus de Ministres ou point de grace'.[62] This hostility was intensified by the fact that the ministers were central to the constitutional debates of the time. It ultimately helped to defeat Mirabeau's ideas on responsible government and left the ministers in an ambivalent position, subject to continual suspicion and niggling controls.[63] At times this hostility extended to officials in general, as when Rey suggested a 5 per cent levy on their salaries as part of a tax reform. Lamy went even further, and though accepting that clerks were 'l'âme des differents administrations' required them to be 'responsible' for their actions in the same penal way as were ministers.[64] He would have agreed with Lamarque that 'the time when *premiers commis* did the duties of legislators is past' so that by laws and cuts in salaries their role should be reduced to a minimum.

The Constituents' hostility to the administration was not based on principled objections to its power alone. There was also a strong current of party political feeling involved. They feared the administration because too many of its members had been appointed by politically unreliable ministers. The latter might also have been attracted by the spoils rather than by the chance of serving the public good. All this made officials morally and politically undesirable. The lust for spoils gave clerks a vested interest in the old order. One critic called them 'les premiers nourris dans l'ancien régime, entichés de vils dépre- dations: ces égoistes sont dangereux, au point d'être aussi audacieux pour gagner les bons patriotes'.[65] Instead of trying to counteract such tendencies by offering countervailing forms of security the revolutionaries preferred inquisitorial approach, sometimes inspectors and, in the case of Saint Just, by wholesale disestablishment of the civil service.[66]

Such political suspicions deepened as the Counter-Revolution developed. Clerks came to be regarded as uniformly reactionary. If they had not actually been chosen for their political views then they had been chosen at random, which was equally as bad. They were therefore required to act in ways which would have put a successful Caesar's wife to shame. This did not still the vociferous demand for purges which, especially after the spring of 1792, became almost the only technique used to control the civil service. Unfortunately, although all revol- utionary opinion was agreed on the need to replace parasites and enemies of the new order by men of proven ability and loyalty, there was no agreement on who fell into which category. Hence, as is often the case with such purges the administration was both held back and endowed with a sense of grievance about the injustices inherent in the purge.[67] So one purge tended to breed another, even though they were often what has been called 'épurations de convenance' rather than more brutal changes. Moreover, the unsettled situation of the Revolution also tended to induce continual self-purging as people felt it wiser to leave rather than risk being ejected. However, it would not be wise to overlook the fact that there were always more people seeking jobs than were being ejected. The purges and the creation of new institutions thus enabled many employees of field services to aspire to the hitherto closed central administrations. In the case of the Ministry of Marine this could often mean moving from a clerical job in one of the ports, as had Jean Pierre Deschamps, a Parisian in his thirties who was called to the Ministry in 1792 and stayed there till 1814.[68] Purges were thus often self-defeating and contradictory but, as has already been suggested, the negative and obsessional attitudes adopted towards the administration prevented the Constitutents from resorting to the simple idea of interviewing prospective clerks as did the elected officials of the Loir-et-Cher in 1791.[69]

At the same time some of the structural changes made by the Constitutents had consequences other than those they had intended. Thus their first bold stroke of abolishing venality and liquidating the national debt forced them to create new bodies to deal with the consequent paper work. These included the Direction Générale de la Liquidation which initially employed a staff which by itself was half the size of the Ministries as a whole.[70] Similarly the nationalization of Church lands produced the Caisse de l'Extraordinaire while the attempt to institute proper accounting procedures for the state was dogged by the ever burgeoning problem of war accounts, so that the Commission de Comptabilité Intermédiaire had to be added to the Bureau Générale de la Comptabilité, the ancestor of the Cour des Comptes.

This matter shows that the Constitutents' use of the administrative machine was affected by factors other than their rather negative suspicion of its authority and political reliability. So although they were not well situated for exercising the kind of control of the administration which they would have liked, and although they chose to use means which were basically external to the administration, rather than working from the inside as would now be the case, there were at least five ways in which they tried to control it and link it to their ideals and constitutional systems.

To begin with there was a ceaseless attempt to legislate the vestiges of the old order out of administration. Hence Louis XVI was made to say in November 1789, apropos of the abolition of *étrennes* or payments in kind that:

tout fonction publique est un devoir; que tous les agens de l'administration doivent à la chose publique leur travaux et leurs soins; que les Ministres nécessaires, ils n'ont ni faveur ni préférence à accorder, par conséquent aucun droit à une reconnaissance particulière; considérant encore qu'il importe à la régénération des mœurs, autant qu'à l'économie des finances . . . d'anéantir le trafic de corruption et de venalité que se faisait sous le nom de Étrennes, etc.[71]

Secondly, given their belief that 'publicité est la sauvegarde du peuple', from the *Livre Rouge* onward the Assembly required the administration to be open to public scrutiny. They also demanded that members of the public should always be received with courtesy when they called at the bureaux.[72] Thirdly, they were also determined that nobody should be able to influence the administration by bringing superior authority to bear on it. So between December 1789 and October 1790 the judiciary was banned from hearing cases connected with the administration.[73] In this the idea of separation of powers was reinforced by the fear of interference by such bodies as the Parlements. Their adherence to past attitudes thus coincided with their belief in the virtue of unpaid, elected *fonctionnnaires*. In theory any administrative misdemeanours these might commit was to be reviewed by the immediately superior administrative authority. But in practice nothing was done to make a reality of this. In the Seine-et-Marne, however, an advisory Conseil de Jurisprudence was set up to advise on such matters.

Similar weaknesses can also be seen in another of the Constitutents' beliefs, that organizations could be controlled by tampering with their internal structures. There was thus a detailed and mechanistic attempt to restructure the departments of state. Every minister was therefore encouraged to 'simplify' the organization of his bureaux as soon as he took up office.[74] Essential posts were suppressed with one breath and re-established, along with consultative committees, with the next. The logic of this was visible only to the reorganizer. It testified, as Bosher says, to the Constituents' belief in the perfectability of organizations but it did not noticeably increase the efficiency of the civil service.

Finally, the Constituents relied on direct parliamentary and constitutional controls.[75] Thus the Ministers were made responsible to the Assembly which also defined their functions in an abstract way. Similarly, the mass of legislation affecting the ministries was never codified and cannot have been an effective means of control. The evolving constitution also had a very literal view of the executive role. It existed to execute laws and nothing else. And save for certain sensitive areas like the treasury and specific appointments, the Assembly was willing to allow the king to supervise it.[76] The king was provided with no special means of doing this. He was financed by a Civil List and advised by a Council of State which consisted purely and simply of departmental ministers, serviced by a small staff. So at the time when its function in administrative law ought to have been developed, in line with the Constitutents' own objection to judicial interference, all its judicial powers were made inoperative after May 1791 and the positions of *Maîtres des Requêtes* and *Conseillers d'État* were abolished. All decisions were supposed to be taken through the Council but in reality no thought was given as to how it should exercise its duties of surveillance of the administration.

Locally the various directories and nominated administrations enjoyed a considerable degree of autonomy as a result, although they were subject to royal *tutelle*. The Gendarmerie Nationale when it was created in February 1791 was placed specifically under the direction of the Ministry of War.[77] In both cases such control was purely epistolary. However, financial pressure led to some other form of control when in 1790 the legislature established nominal control of the costs and salaries of ministerial bureaux.[78] The Flight to Varennes also increased the fundamental hostility to the administration and led to a whole new series of edicts, insisting that officials must be subject to an oath of allegiance and to a salary ceiling of 12,000 *livres*. The names of all those receiving state salaries were also to be published.

The summation of parliamentary and constitutional control came with the long-delayed organic law on the executive of 27 April–24 May 1791. By the time it was finally promulgated, and ideas of creating 6 Directors-General inside the Ministry of the Interior and of splitting colonial administration from the Admiralty had been rejected, the ministerial structure had already changed a considerable amount. The law confirmed the reorganization of the Conseil d'État and restated the ministers' responsibility to the Assembly. It also indicated the ways in which the ministers could be sued. It laid down their duties, significantly, by detailing the laws which the six ministries were supposed to execute. Thus the Department of Justice, formerly the Chancery, was required to execute laws on the sanctioning of legal decrees and to pass relevant correspondence on to the Commissioner of the Appeal Court. How this was to be done was nowhere specified. The only reference to the bureaux was the provision that service within them was dependent on taking the oath of allegiance. Thus none of the parliamentary and constitutional controls really got past the point of assuming that enunciating and publicizing laws was all that was needed by way of administration under the new order. And all in all, the Constituent Assembly, the first generation of revolutionaries failed to use the opportunities open to them to develop the administration. The fears and hatreds of the Ancien Régime, combined with the technical failings in their primarily external-ist attempts to define administrative control, to impede real transformation.

This somewhat surprising stance, which was to be just as firmly ingrained in the next generation of revolutionary leaders, did not of course prevent all change in the administration. Their ideas may have blinded the revolutionaries, but they did not blind the administration in the real world. This was not merely because some of their ideas and practices of adminis-trative control tended to achieve results which had not been expected. The realities of administrative life did, in fact, impinge on Ministers and others at times, so that some changes were made. In other words, while not wishing the means of an active administration they did will the end of the successful implemen-tation of a whole range of new laws. However, the first two years of the Revolution were a period of rather limited change, which explains why it is so hard to find hard evidence of any kind. This quiescence was partly political. From the autumn of 1789 it looked as if the Revolution was not going to go any farther so that administrative change was not really necessary. And the political pressures on the executive tended to discourage them from any provocative initiatives. Departments thus remained very small and continued to function much as they had previously. Moreover, in the winter of 1789–90 they had to move from Versailles to Paris and find new homes there, a process which seems to have used up more energy and resources.[79]

It was therefore the summer of 1790 before change was really possible. It was then that the first changes in the old ministerial structure were made. This happened, however, after the suppression of the *gabelles*, the *aides*, and the *fermes*. This meant not merely the ending of various forms of fiscal exploitation but also the winding-up of the *régies* which had collected them, thereby throwing thousands of employees out of work.[80] The Constituents recognized that their services deserved a pension or a place in a new organization between July 1790 and March 1791 but as pensions were small, long delayed, and highly unreliable, pressure built up for continuing employment. It was on this pool of trained labour that the Ministries in their limited recruitment of the Constitutional Monarchy were to draw. The pattern was to be repeated later when some of the bodies set up in 1789–90 or 1793–4 were themselves to become redundant. New waves of employees were released on to the market.

And though this was not welcomed by the legislators, as it conflicted with their administrative ideals, it is doubtful whether the Revolution could have achieved many of its ends without it.[81] These northern Frenchmen, who had received some education and who had found niches in the field services of the old regime had a trained incapacity for other forms of employment and sought what security they could find in continuing in administrative service. Very often many of them had lost financially by the Revolution which had already effectively destroyed investments in *rentes* and similar things. Although in some respects the Revolution brought a career open to talents it also brought about demotion and demolition of existing careers. So even though some clerks were happy to attend the Federation in 1790 or to denounce their minister for peculation, as happened to Claret de Fleurieu in the spring of 1791, others kept their distance and began to think increasingly of their own interests. Perhaps the first evidence of this came in a petition of January 1791.[82]

This reservoir of staff was the one to which the ministries automatically turned when their changing structures and political positions began to create new vacancies. Such structural changes also had considerable implications for Ancien Régime staff who found themselves moved from one service to another with what must have been unpleasant rapidity. On 5 June 1790 the first major changes in ministerial structure came with the transfer of some duties like responsibility for the States General from the Contrôle Général to the Maison du Roi which, in August was rechristened the Ministry of the Interior.[83] The Contrôle Générale retained its old sprawling structure with over 300 clerks divided into a very loose divisional structure which seemed to have no great logic about it.[84] There were divisions for the Fermes, for welfare and public works, lands and resources, taxation, accounts, and significantly provincial assemblies which were under the control of Tarbé, the future Finance Minister. The split between the *Premiers Commis* and the ordinary clerks was still very marked as the latter, probably because of the salary cuts imposed early in the year, had average salaries of 2,000 *livres* per annum and less. The influence of the Ancien Régime can be seen in the fact that the low salaries were offset to some extent by quite large *gratifications* which could be paid to certain bureaux. These could amount to anything between 20 and 40 per cent of the salary bill for junior clerks.

The Contrôle Générale, for all that in Necker's time it was officially called simply the Administration des Finances, was obviously exposed to change because it was so dominant in the Ancien Régime, functioning as it had both as a mechanism of financial control and as the overseer of the majority of social, economic, and administrative activities in the country. However, in the first instance, transfer of duties to the Maison du Roi raised some problems because it meant bestowing critical powers on a department still very closely linked to the king himself. At this stage the Maison du Roi was still very small and reflected its eighteenth-century history and role, being divided into sections responsible for the Household, Paris (including clerical and noble affairs), papers of previous administrations, and two provincial affairs bureaux (to one of which benefices and Hugenot affairs were still attached). Interestingly, the department seems to have maintained separate secretariats in Versailles and Paris, another proof of links with king and past. Not merely did the bureaus keep their highly paid *Premiers Commis*, but the example of Petigny de Saint Romain's provincial affairs bureau shows that the staff as a whole were still very close to the old order.[85] There was only one new, and young, appointee. The remaining eight employees had an average age of fifty and had served for an average of thirteen years in the Maison du Roi, and often in other bodies as well. They represented an almost totally homogeneous team which may have been able to adapt because of the changes through which they had gone previously, but who were almost bound to arouse the suspicion of revolutionary politicians like Desmoulins and Brissot.[86]

With the wholesale change of Ministers at the end of 1790 when men more sympathetic to the Revolution replaced the royalists like Champion de Cicé, Luzerne, and Saint Priest the pace of change again speeded up. Thus Duport Dutertre who took over the Ministry of Justice began to transform the old Chancery into a more modern department based on civil, criminal, and general jurisprudential sections, supported by a secretariat and a special bureau for prison affairs.[87] This later gave way to a more complicated and significant structure with a ministerial cabinet, and advisory committee on jurisprudence, secretarial bureaux, the basic legal departments, and a number of sections dealing with the ratification and dispatch of legislation to the provinces. This was reflected in a rise in its staff from thirty to eighty.

In the spring of 1791 the king finally ratified the changes in the status of the old Maison du Roi department, which was to be a prelude to the general reorganization of the ministries of 27 April–25 May 1791. This was to see major transfer of functions from the Ministry of Public Contributions as it was now called. The latter was left with taxation, national lands, the budget, and local government finance and the *assignats,* a mute testimony to its demotion. The Interior gained mines, trade, public works, hospitals, and agriculture to add to its old duties. At the same time tasks such as education, elections, and civil administration had already come its way, and the process was completed by the transfer of the remaining independent provincial affairs bureau from the Ministry of War early in April 1791 in anticipation of the new law.[88] The basic transfer was no doubt eased by the fact that Delessart was for a while both Minister of Finance and Minister of the Interior. It was Delessart who began to cope with the problems it posed for the latter in October 1791 when he introduced a half-way-house organization between the old order and later formulations.[89] His structure retained a geographical division of duty between three of the six divisions into which the Ministry was divided. Two of these specialized almost entirely in correspondence with departments while the third dealt with the Paris region, together with police and clerical affairs. The other three divisions dealt with education, public works, and trade respectively, though to say merely this gives too flattering an impression of the rationality of their functions.

Delessart was well aware of the burden of correspondence with all of the eighty-three departments on his staff just as were the Constituents. But whereas they tried to meet the problem in a mechanical way, he sought to ensure that his staff were appropriate to the new tasks and worked in a way consonant with the new situation in France. He kept most of the old *Premiers Commis* but many others were retired to make way for new appointments. And it is also notable that the scale of *gratifications* paid was considerably less than that which had been prevalent in the Contrôle Général a few months before. It was presumably such appointments which made the legislatures introduce new demands for printed statements of all ministerial employees in the autumn of 1791 just as they had earlier tried to ensure that nobody who had been pensioned off should receive a salary as well. They were no doubt aware that the number of central employees was beginning to creep beyond the levels of 1788 but although this may have frightened them, especially in the aftermath of Varennes, it was often their own doing. Thus the Minister of Justice had to complain to the Finance Committee in the spring of 1791 of the way his department had been overloaded by work arising from the sale of Church lands.[90] He had been forced to take on extra temporary help without going through all the requisite formalities. On the other hand, with the exception of the creation of a rudimentary general staff in

December 1791 there was less change in the War Office.[91]

Such changes of course did have implications for the clerks working within the slowly evolving departments. The Interior thus contained men who, like Remy Fleurigeon and Julien Henri Sausseret, had come from the Contrôle Général.[92] The former had once served under Bertin, an experience which no doubt aided him to adjust to the transition demanded by the Revolution, since his transfer to the Interior earned him promotion to *Sous-Chef*. The latter had also been in the Intendance des Flandres before his entry to the Contrôle in 1783. In the Interior they were joined by Jean Dominique Laprime, a Versaillais who after working as a *procureur*'s clerk in the Chatelet joined the War Office where he served in its provincial affairs bureaux until October 1791, sometime later than one would have expected his transfer. Others were less fortunate and found themselves pensioned off—or found it expedient to opt for retirement before it became strictly necessary. The War Office was full of such people as Joseph François Gau de Voves.[93] Born in Strasburg in 1748, he had entered the War Office in February 1769, and rose to be *Commissaire des Guerres* and Director of the Accounts Bureau before he retired in October 1791. His retirement was only to last until Thermidor after which he was often recalled to administrative service and also to political life.

His pension was granted without any trouble whereas others had to wait, sometimes till 1794, for their cases to be settled. Others found, as did François Hipolyte Lelu, that the Ministry could actually not manage without them, so that they went on working often without pay, for some months afterwards. In Lelu's case frontier defences were his speciality. The Ministry, in fact, seems to have been very short of money to pension people off, although it was still able to recruit auxiliaries. Thus Julien Adrien Hervet, a fifty-year-old *Commissaire des Guerres* with thirty-seven-years' service in the Nominations Bureau of the Ministry was told by the Minister in October 1791 that all the monies allocated by the Assembly for retirement had been used up on pensions to those whose jobs had been wound up. Hervet, who wished to retire on health grounds, was invited to stay on the active strength at an increased salary until pension funds were available. Grumbling about the way his section had been unfairly treated and his seniority and family connections in the Ministry ignored, Hervet had to stay on for a further year. And even then it may well have been the case that his pension was insufficient to support him—a very common phenomenon—as he returned to service in the later nineties. Others saw *gratifications* and pensions granted in the last years of the Ancien Régime suspended, although there are still cases of people being rewarded with decorations and treating their posts as a form of property.[94]

The transition to a new form of civil service life was fraught with many other difficulties too. The slowly expanding departments also needed new buildings in Paris.[95] These were not always easy to find. They could be coveted by other departments, while permission and finance for installation was often hard to extract from the committees of the Legislative Assembly.[96] And once alterations started, the fabric could prove to be unreliable as happened in the case of the Bureau de Comptabilité. If few field services were created at this time other central services shared the problems of the ministries.[97] Local government was probably even more affected. Whereas there was a carry-over in all cases amongst the ministries the vast majority of departments had to start from scratch, since the Intendant's bureaux were either far distant or too unpopular to use because, as in Lorraine, they had charged for their services. This may have impelled more innovation than at the centre. Certainly it seems as though they were quicker to formalize the way their clerks worked.[98] The majority of departments set up bureaux for Taxation, Police affairs, Domaines, and Public Works, sometimes Agricultural, economic, welfare, and Military matters along with the normal accounting, archival, and secretarial bureaux.

However, in the Loir-et-Cher they did not go as far towards specialization as was the case at the centre. For although each *chef de bureau* had specified aides it was laid down that no employee could refuse to work in another area if the pressure of work demanded it. This decision caused some trouble over differentials. Because of the lack of alternative employment local authorities faced even more pressure for employment, which forced them to take more care over appointments, looking for patriotism, handwriting, and details of previous employment. One would-be archivist in the Cher offered to do the job for 200 *livres* per annum less than his rival and in the Oise people were willing to work free in order to secure a place. As Van Berkel says many departments therefore came to presume on their bureaux and especially on the Secretaries-General, who became as influential as those of the old Intendancies in some cases. This pressure for places may, indeed, have led some departments to copy the old services even though, in principle, they disapproved of them.

However, neither centrally nor locally can one estimate the degree of change brought about by the Revolution on the basis of organizational structures and personnel pressures alone. The way the administration worked is also significant. At the centre the relative absence of specific regulations on the subject implies that the ministries continued to work much as before whereas in some of the departments the new order led to somewhat rigorous norms, frowning on most absences and treating employment as a civic duty to which clerks were obliged to sacrifice their leisure when necessary. The change in ministers late in 1790 led to some changes in the style with which departments worked. Delessart thus in March 1791 complained about the variety and unsuitability of some of the terms of address and signature used.[99] He reported that the king had decided that 'une forme simple, degagé de tout cérémonial et parfaitement analogue à L'Esprit et aux principes de la Constitution serait généralement preferée'. Another problem seems to have been adjusting to the new locations of adminstrative authority in the provinces.

All this points to the fact that the basic concern of the ministries at this stage was with correspondence, whether with local authorities or the legislature. It was more a case of handling the flow of paper than devising new policy initiatives. Thus in the Admiralty about this time a *Mémoire sur le travail* begins with the arrival of mail in the secretariat where it was opened, listed in a register of incoming pieces, and then distributed to the relevant divisions for replies or reports.[100] Within each division the *chef* redistributed them with his comments to his subordinates and checked their draft answers. The instructions go on to lay down in great detail the differing methods which the various divisions used for filing their work, some putting minutes of replies on the letter, other keeping them together by a numbering system. This speaks of a certain *naïveté* about the importance of paper although the evidence suggests that it also conceals some-what the more positive and specialist roles which were slowly emerging.

In the Ministry of Justice early in 1792 this can be seen quite clearly.[101] The Ministry was one of the first to appoint a Secretary-General, a post then held by one Duveyrier, who was entrusted with over-all responsibility for the whole department. Like his successors in the Ministry of Marine, Duveyrier read and distributed all incoming letters and pieces, of which there were about two hundred per day. He was entitled to make decisions on matters of day-to-day administration and was the Minister's main adviser on critical matters in the fields of criminal and civil law. Moreover, because the Ministry could only function as a team, he was an indispensible link between the ministers and the various sections, a fact which was, by implication not now recognized in his salary after the recent reductions ordered by the Constituent.

The Minister was also assisted by an advisory judicial com-mittee of four lawyers who found it necessary to meet every day of the week in order to look at the points of law thrown up by the Ministry's work, picking out those which had to be referred to the Assembly for decision and those on which the Minister was competent to decide. On the latter they prepared briefs for him. They also checked applications for leave to appeal. In all this they were assisted by a Secretary and a number of clerks who were responsible for filing and checking material for the correct terminology, tasks which required extra assistance because of a backlog of decisions. The same was true in the Bureau de Redaction where extra help had been brought in even though the established staff had been working longer hours than was formally required of them. The bureau was headed by one Leroy who was in charge of a semi-collegiate group of employees called *Secrétaires de Correspondance* each of whom had their own speciality. Leroy distributed the correspondence amongst them and checked their work as well as looking after his own area and generally aiding the Secretary-General. The *Secrétaires*, most of whom were new appointments, dealt with all administrative correspondence with local authorities on the running of the courts, leaving the ordinary employees to deal with the courts themselves. One of them, Pierre Bressant, a former attaché to the Chancery who had joined the department in the previous spring, was responsible for going through the work of the department to précis everything for the Secretary-General and to point out areas on which the law was insufficient so that the Minister could report on it to the Assembly.[102]

As in the Marine a great deal of work involved filing, hence there was a bureau of Enregistrement, headed by Jean Baptiste Rigollet, a former *Contrôleur des Fermes*, who had joined the department a year before and was to remain there until 1798. His task was to register and distribute mail while Louis Jouffroy, another new appointment at this time, a Thionviller from the Aides, was responsible for following up all incoming business and ensuring that the staff did what they were required to do. The actual distribution of mail, of course, was left to a senior *garçon de bureau*, while the Minister had a private secretary to aid him, Jean Baptiste Dalmassy, a former lawyer from Langres who entered the Ministry as *Chef de Contentieux* in 1787 and was to retire in 1811 when he was only fifty-one. The existence of a reservoir of administrative talent is very evident in this case.

A great deal of the Ministry's work at this stage was concerned with the processing of the many laws passed by the legislatures and communicating them to local authorities, a task very much in line with the revolutionaries basic idea of administration. Hence Toussaint Le Roux headed the *Bureau du Sceau* which dealt with all formal appointments, notably to the courts, and personnel matters. Le Roux had in fact been in the Ministry from April 1769 but left in August 1792, presumably because of the *coup*. However, after a surprising period in which he served on a sectional committee and in the police administration he returned to the Ministry for a second stint as head of its archives in 1796–9. The *Envoi des Lois* bureau, which was eventually to become a separate service, was responsible for receiving laws, setting them in print, proof reading them, printing them, dispatching them to local authorities, and dealing with the queries which arose. General oversight of this was exercised by P. J. B. Broyard, a forty-eight-year-old former *avocat au Chatelet* who had been taken on in December 1790, while each of the clerks had specific responsibilities, for instance proof-reading and looking after equipment.

Formal receipt of laws from the Assembly was handled by a

separate Bureau du Sanction et des Archives du Sceau headed by Louis Rondonneau, an Orleannais who had entered the department in 1789 after a period in the Contrôle, and was to become a major collector of and expert on revolutionary legislation. His section provided for printing all laws in the appropriate forms and depositing them in national and other archives. The head of the ministerial archive section itself was a *Commis Principal* called Mathieu François Barrier, a Parisian of thirty-two who had entered the department in March 1791 after working for an Academician in an unspecified capacity. Much of the section's work arose from the sale of church and other lands and, as has already been noted, this required extra staff. This had helped to increase the costs of the ministry in a way which was not forseen when they had been calculated by the Assembly at just under 200,000 *livres*. This was less than half the allowance for departments like the Interior and the War Office. All told the costs of the ministries came to over 2,250,000 *livres* which, given that the old Conseil d'État in 1790 had cost nearly 600,000 *livres,* was not excessive.[103] And though the revolutionaries regretted even such restrained expenditures and additions they were also the first to complain when essential services like the Admiralty came to admit that they were two years behind in dealing with crucial personnel business.[104] They were also not behindhand in increasing both their own staff and those, like the Treasury, which came under their direct control. They also demanded by the law of 2 October 1791 that the bureaux of the central administration should never cease operating.

Despite their reservations about the necessity and rectitude of administration, the early politicians thus worked the ministries fairly hard. Reality broke through especially in areas where there was only a limited carry-over from the past. The resulting pattern was reasonably efficient, if often rather hidebound, because of the continuing belief that administration should play a basically clerical role. Generally, however, there had by the end of 1791 been relatively little disturbance in the structures and personnel of the old order. And with one major exception it had been internal transfers, and recruitment of new personnel which had been most notable in terms of personnel change. Even where employees of the old ministries did lose their jobs this was done in a relatively civilized and unpolitical way, with premature retirement being the most usual way of proceeding. To judge from the Ministry of Justice, especially after the fall of Duport in March 1792, this was to change in 1792, although the printing of staff lists may have had a hand in this as well. In any case it was from 1792 that the old *Premiers Commis* were removed, along with many of the newcomers recruited in 1790–1 who were suspect to the Girondin ministers of the next phase of the Revolution.

By the end of 1791 the ministries seem to have had a staff of roughly the same size as in 1788.[105] The apparent stability at about 670 clerks, however, concealed both an initial fall in numbers after 1789, as the War Office had continued its attempts to restrict its staffing, and a considerable redistribution amongst the departments. In 1788 the Contrôle had dominated the scene, and its numbers seem to have risen into 1790. However, by 1791 it had lost over half its effectives, partly to the Interior which had grown fivefold, and partly because of the winding-up of the old field services for which it had been responsible. The Chancery had also grown greatly, whereas the external departments had all declined somewhat. The apparent continuity thus conceals a marked shift in both the role and the nature of the ministries in the early stages of the Revolution, although had the attitudes of the politicians been different even greater change might have resulted. With the gathering crisis and the absorption of the legacy from the old order things began to change markedly in 1792. By the late spring numbers rose to something like 800, with the military departments really making the difference.[106] By then because of continuing economy drives the cost of the new establishment was still much the same. It appears that average salaries were only about 2,500 *livres* per year owing to the expulsion of some of the old *premiers commis* and the imposition of a legal maximum on salaries which was ultimately fixed at 8,000 *livres*.

Structural changes inside the ministries were equally patchy and variable. The Interior as a whole had changed drastically but some of its new divisions were able to endure largely unchanged until quite late in 1792.[107] Thus its sixth division remained basically a litter of small bureaux inherited from the Contrôle dealing with various commercial and liquidation functions. The Ministry of Foreign Affairs had also maintained much of its old structure with two basic political divisions, supplemented by various administrative services. If the Justice department changed fairly constantly because it was so new, its two major divisions for civil and criminal law correspondence were to enjoy a long run. The Ministry of War had also left its 1789 form far behind except in the division of general administration where Gau inherited most of Melin's functions, although with many other services added. Yet only a sixth of the staff in post in 1791 had not been there in 1789.

Under Narbonne the War Office was to continue an uncertain path towards a more functional structure.[108] By the beginning of 1792 this had involved four large divisions: Administration, Inspection, Correspondence, and Artillery with Engineering, together with advisory committees, a secretariat, and the Dépôt. The large divisions may have been copied from the Duc de Castries's reform in the Admiralty in the eighties which had gone in the same direction, though paradoxically this was to be abandoned during the Revolution because of the fear of the power enjoyed by their heads. It was replaced in the time of Moleville by a complicated structure involving 116 staff and 20 bureaux. It is also interesting to note that Dumouriez's arrival at the Ministry of Foreign Affairs also coincided with the replacement of the two large political divisions by half a dozen geographically based ones, staffed largely by newcomers.

Even more radical changes had of course been made in the other domestic department. The old Contrôle at first retained its old mess of 18 services, save for the Fermes, the Treasury, and the Aides, until the transfers to the Interior in the late summer of 1790. By 1792 the new department had a staff of 136 divided into 10 fairly specialized sections, including 4 regionally based bureaux for direct taxes, a great change from the once mighty Ministry of the old monarchy. Like the Ministry of War, however, it had held on to many of its most qualified officials.

The administration then, though battered by the demolition of certain field services and decapitated by the dismissal of some of its old élite and the reorganization of the rest, still retained many of its old characteristics. It had also preserved a modicum of its erstwhile freedom from too much state interference at least until 1792. Both regimes had wanted to reform the administration and to subject it to new legal controls. yet neither had the mechanism nor the force to make a positive reality of their wishes. Change had been therefore spasmodic, uncertain, and limited to specific instances under the Ancien Régime because of the political and social conflicts of the time.

The revolutionaries had added the further complication of parliamentary regulation and intense political suspicion. They did not want the administration to remain at all free and no doubt wished to improve on the Ancien Régime's handling of it but their nostrums were often more counter-productive. Moreover, despite their desire to make a fresh start they inherited more of the ideas and of the social ethos of the past than they realized. So although their regulations were apparently much wider in their application they were too abstract and too many to make quite the impact intended.

Both regimes thus bypassed obstacles rather than removing them. The revolutionaries particularly refused to make any allowance for 'interest' and preferred to rely on heavy-handed and niggling controls, such as that of 19 September–2 October 1791 on the printing of lists of ministerial employees. The employees remained largely uncared for. Such controls, moreover, were too late, too generalized, and too dependent on an assumption of human perfection to be easily enforceable. Then at times the revolutionaries were forced to face up to their need for the civil service, as well as to its rights—for instance over pensions—and to its potential as a pressure group.[109] For whatever the politicians liked to think about ideal government, lower down the scale many people were still drawn to state employment, particularly in the uncertain economic climate of 1791–2. The limited consistency in the Constituents' policy towards the administration was further undermined as their political foundations crumbled away, just as those of Louis XVI had done before.

The Constitutional Monarchy thus had roughly the same kind of civil service as that of the 1780s. In a way, despite the Revolution and the consequent flurry of legislation, it still remained in limbo. Its future prospects were perhaps less than they might have been because of the illusions of the reformers.[110] For although it had not been destroyed either by the timid reforms of the 1770s and 1780s or by the drastic changes of the early 1790s, notably the amputation of some of its limbs and its extraction from its old venal cocoon, it still had a half-unconstitutional status. There were no general rules regarding its operation and no detailed discussion of its role in the constitution, such discussion being regarded as almost improper. Again, although the individual ministries were beginning to change, France still lacked proper means of co-ordinating the various branches just as it had done before the Revolution. What was significant, despite this failure to solve problems already visible long since, was the way in which the ministries remained the dominant element in the government as they had been throughout the century. The Revolution, however, in ironing out the differences of structure and standing amongst them, had begun to remove the *Premiers Commis*, leaving the way clear for the next level of employees to make themselves really felt when the time was ripe.

Finally, the civil service of the two regimes was similar in terms of manpower. If anything that of Constitutional Monarchy was at times smaller than its predecessors because the suppressions of 1789 had not been fully cancelled out by the new initiatives. The people involved were also much the same. The fact that so many of them had been recruited in periods of reform, either directly into the ministries in 1775–85 or from the field services between 1789–91, must have made it easier for them to adjust to the new situation. For not merely were they experienced—and experienced in some of the problems of reform at least—but they were also quite young. In terms of personnel the legacy of the old to the new order was thus a continuous and rich one.

Obviously there had been many changes, even in the field of personnel. The employees of the Constitutional Monarchy were no longer half-court personages.[111] They were state servants, directly linked to the leadership of the state, and expected to defend the national interest. They also worked within a structure which was different in three main ways. It no longer had to co-operate with a second venal sphere of government; the services needed to carry out its roles had been in part taken away from direct executive control and entrusted to elective bodies; and its central cortex had taken the first steps towards a major rationalization. Moreover, ministries were decreasingly likely to be dependent on honorific oil for lubricating their works.

The ministers themselves had had their already large political role considerably enhanced by the Revolution. So it was obviously going to be more difficult for them to immerse themselves in the business of administration as they had done before with the result that, as was also happening at the local level, they would have to look increasingly to their bureaux for advice and information. By 1792 this had not yet really taken place, and no doubt the employees of the time were holding their breath waiting to see which way things would turn out, whether they could keep their remaining honours or whether something wholly new would be required. Similarly, it was still an open question as to whether the general role of the administration was to change so that it became a real means to power, able to attract the resources it needed to enable it to channel national efforts, and with a more rational relationship to the state. It was thus a static and somewhat unstable situation, a kind of lull before the storm.

In fact the storm was going to sweep most of the remains of the Ancien Régime away with it, but despite this and notwithstanding its failure to reform itself when it had the chance, the old order should not be overlooked. It had helped France to survive earlier crises and, inside the armoured corselet which had been developed for this purpose, it had generated a lively central administrative core and large and capable field services. But these were still inside the old structure and still, in the last resort, posited on their continuance. As even de Tocqueville admitted, 'ces fonctionnaires si puissants étaient pourtant éclipsés par les restes de l'ancienne aristocratie féodale, et comme perdus au milieu de l'éclat qu'elle jetait encore; c'est ce qui fait que, le leur temps même, on les voyait à peine quoique leur main fût déjà partout'.[112] The inheritance from the Ancien Régime could, however, be a barrier to innovation as the activities of ministers with little to build on shows. Even though this was not what the revolutionaries actually wanted the changes in domination they brought about proved more positive than the negative continuity with the Ancien Régime. As Baecheler says of such changes 'la forme prise par cette réalisation reste profondément originale et irreductible à toute rationalisation retrospective'. Bureaucratization and professionalization were indeed still only in their initial stages within the absolutism of

Louis XVI. Without the Revolution and especially without the Revolution from 1792–4, the administration could not have broken free of this situation.

This fact must be set against the justified tributes which were paid from both sides of the revolutionary political divide to the administration of the old order. Senac de Meilhan, for instance, said that:

Il y avait dans l'administration de la France, une force intérieure, qui luttait contre la dissipation, l'ignorance et l'impérité, et qui provenait de l'application, de l'expérience et des lumières des Agens subalternes du gouvernement. On a dit pour critiquer leur influence, que le Gouvernement Français était bureaucratique. Mais dans le perpetual changement de Ministres, qui a signalé les règnes de Louis XV et Louis XVI, it était heureux pour l'état qu'il y eût des hommes permanens dans leurs postes, et à portée de guider ces ministres ephémères, et des les prémunir contre la seduction des novateurs, l'enthousiasme et l'artifice des gens à projets.[113]

Certainly the administration was not bureaucratic. As a result of this and other factors its potential had not been fully realized, even by 1792. Had de Tocqueville looked a little further ahead in the Revolution he might have seen how much change was necessary to realize that potential. Up until then, however, there was continuity in men, in position, and in impetus although this continuity was neither so positive nor so conscious as he suggested. Neither the reforming monarchy nor the Constitutional Monarchy then, despite all appearances and claims to the contrary, had sufficient momentum to produce a bureaucratic central administration.

CHAPTER III: THE RADICAL REVOLUTION AND THE MAKING OF THE BUREAUCRACY, 1792–1795

Early in 1792 the central administration had begun to change more drastically than at any time in the previous three years. This was simply a prelude to an even more far-reaching transformation over the next three years of revolutionary turmoil. Whereas the Constitutional Monarchy had suddenly destroyed the bases of the Ancien Régime, both generally and within some of the ministries, it had been unable to complete the process of modernization. It had more clearly identified many of the problems of the nature, role, and control of the administration which had been visible since the 1770s, but it had not really solved them. The Republic was to provide some of the answers. So with equal suddenness the next phase of the Revolution was to see the laying of the foundations of the modern bureaucratic state.[1] For although they still clung to many of the ideals of administration by the *citoyen—fonctionnaire* the political élites of the First Republic found that, to enable the nation to surmount the crises of the revolutionary climacteric, they had to use the administration in a completely new way on a totally new scale.

The process in 1792–3 began with the establishment of the Republic and the completion of the ministerial changes which had begun in 1792. Then came the crucial stage with the creation of a wholesale new state organization by the *gouvernement révolutionnaire* of 1793–4, in the shadow of which the new bureaucracy finally emerged. It was to be partially accepted and consolidated under the Thermidorians in 1794–5. Yet few people seem, either then or now, to have realized the way the radical republic, and particularly the system of the Year II, created a fully fledged bureaucracy out of the existing administrative structures.[2] In some ways the nature of the administration was more visible in the late eighties and early nineties than in the hand-to-mouth days of the Terror. And even though it was debated anew in the somewhat calmer days after Thermidor, historians have continued to lose sight of it against the more dramatic backdrop of the revolutionary government.

This lack of awareness of the qualitative and quantitative changes undergone by the administration under the radical republic is also due, in part, to a continuity of ideas with earlier times. For although what was increasingly at issue was the question of how to mobilize and control the body politic of bureaucracy, the revolutionaries persisted in seeing the problem as one of eradicating a malignant tumour.[3] In other words, their main concern was to root out possible political subversion inside the bureaucracy. The Thermidorians began hesitatingly to correct this imbalance, but there remained much for the Directory to do in this context, as in other areas of administrative development.

That the revolutionaries of 1792–4 allowed the bureaucracy to develop despite their continuing fears of its unreliability was due to the increasing exigencies of the situation in which they found themselves. From the spring of 1792 the revolutionary situation in France began to develop apace, with increasing violence at home and the beginnings of war on the frontiers. As the Revolution moved from what has been called its libertarian 'reversal of legality' to the absolutist 'new orientation' arising from the Jacobin determination to resist the new challenges, the administration was caught up in the general rush.[4] Particularly between the autumn of 1793, when a concrete change in the exercise of sovereignty began with the consolidation of the *gouvernement révolutionnaire*, and the summer of 1794 when the process was to some extent halted, there was a massive increase in the scale and intensity of state operation, which could only be supported by bureaucratization—in Weber's sense of the term —on a large scale. It was thus that the process of administrative modernization was completed.

The regime of the Year II was positive and emphatic in its dealings with administration. It completed the demolition of old structures, revised and vastly expanded the personnel of the government machine, and thrust on them new styles and modes of operation. The traumas of foreign and internal war, which their ideology and their supporters insisted must be overcome, left them no alternative but to overcome their suspicions of the executive. Like people before and since, they found they needed the bureaucracy, even though they neither liked it nor came to terms with the difficulties of controlling it.

In other words the regime of the Year II represented a new form of domination, and as Weber argued it must, this in turn called forth its own new form of administration. The imposition of new tasks removed the inhibitions on modernization carried over from the Ancien Régime. The bureaucracy thus emerged as the pendant of the rational modern state, based on popular sovereignty incarnated in a dynamic government. The creation of the new state was the product of total war against most of Europe, together with civil war and rebellion at home, and popular militancy unleashed by food crises and growing political consciousness. 'Le gouvernement révolutionnaire a été une organisation de guerre *et* une organisation de l'ordre', as Pertué has said.[5] The revolutionary government was driven by the desire for national and self-preservation to create a massive bureaucracy to second its own agents in the task of enforcing all the controls and means of mobilization needed for transformation and victory over its enemies and allies. No half-hearted measures would have sufficed. It had to be all or nothing.

Such internal factors as there were in the movement of the administration towards bureaucracy were both secondary and themselves largely dependent on the exigencies of the situation. Had it not been for that the revolutionaries would not have allowed things to develop to a state in which it could be said that the Republic was 'envahi par la papasserie, que la multiplication des bureaux et de commis ne suffit plus à résorber'.[6] This conflicted totally with beliefs in both direct democracy and of 'little government' by elected *fonctionnaires*. The administration, had it had the potential to do so, which it did not, could never have foisted this on the politicians and *sans-culottes* without the revolutionary crisis. It was this which forced the men of the Year II to live in an uneasy love–hate relationship with the new bureaucracy, and to realize, as did the Commission des Administrations Civiles in Floréal II that if they paid better they could demand more work from men who were patriots but who were also family men in an age of high food prices.[7] They should not be like the Ancien Régime and economize at the expense of lower-grade employees.

The bureaucracy, which was thus allowed to emerge, probably rose to a strength of some 250,000 or five times the total size of the effective non-venal administration in 1788. The central core itself rose as Figure I shows, from under 700 before the Revolution to about 6,000, an 850 per cent increase over 1788. Moreover, these huge numbers of employees enjoyed a new power and standing as well as working in a radically different structure. Their social status was probably less than under the Ancien Régime and their local roots weaker, but they represented a rising social and political group. For whereas under the Constitutional Monarchy they had been servants of a state whose authority was weak and contested, now they served an omnipotent and self-confident state. This was in fact recognized by de Tocqueville when he said that the Revolution produced:

un pouvoir central immense qui a attiré et englouti dans sa unité toutes les parcelles d'autorite et d'influence qui étaient auparavant dispersée dans une foule de pouvoirs secondaires, d'ordres, de classes, de familles et d'individus, et comme éparpillées dans tout le corps semblable. On n'avait pas vu dans le monde un pouvoir semblable. On n'avait pas vu dans le monde un pouvoir semblable depuis la chute de l'Empire Romain.[8]

The men who shared and supported this authority were thus no longer courtly functionaries or clerks personally dependent on such luminaries, but modern bureaucrats in a condition of impersonal dependence on the state. The old élites had gone and with them the remaining traces of venality and patrimonial status. Civil servants were thus left in a rational hierarchy which applied throughout and not just in the lower echelons of certain departments. The radical revolution, therefore, not merely created bureaucratization in an abstract sense, but also in the way it provided a golden opportunity for such hitherto depressed cadres to rise. Thus War Office employees demoted by Brienne were able to secure new posts and promotion.[9]

The structure within which they worked was also very different. This was particularly so in 1794, when there was a wholesale reconstruction of the central agencies in addition to the creation of a whole range of new local and field services. All of this

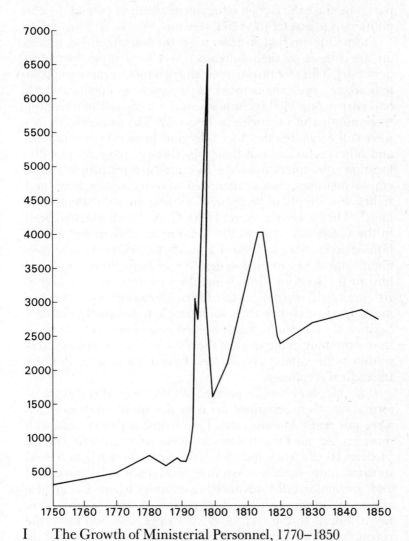

I   The Growth of Ministerial Personnel, 1770–1850

demanded new attitudes and styles of behaviour from employees. Those who had transferred from the Ancien Régime, as many had, found themselves faced with a far greater pressure of work and with new structural constraints. Moreover, they found that more authority and responsibility was thrust on them by the revolutionary government, partly so as to get things done, and partly because the faction struggles made it less possible for the politicians to master their civil servants.

The politicians had, in order to get the machine going, to take on all comers to their bureaux. As Caron says, 'quant au personnel, il fut recruté progressivement à mésure que s'amplifiat le besogne', since the network of patronage and politics which had earlier provided recruits was quite incapable of filling the huge number of vacancies in 1793–4.[10] The gainers from this were still very often the Ancien Régime field service employees and others who had lost their jobs through the economic dislocation consequent upon the Revolution. Such people sought employment not, as was often said, in order to gain power and riches, but simply to keep alive by using the only talents they had.[11] Thus a former *avocat* like M. G. A. Treuil who had been in the *Contentieux service* of the Aides from 1788, passed into its liquidation service in 1790–1 and, after a period of unemployment, into the Commission des Arts et Agriculture which led him to the Interior, from which he was to retire as a *Chef de Bureau* in 1815 when in his late fifties. Despite the resentment of many good revolutionaries, such people were usually welcome because they brought much-needed experience with them, so that something of the spirit of the old administration was transmitted to the fundamentally new bureaucracy called forth by the radical revolution.

It should, however, be pointed out that even after this transformation, there remained areas of the administration which were not really bureaucratic. Like British industry, and with more excuse, the French Revolution has paid a price for being a pioneer. Its efficiency and effectiveness have been left far behind by later, more socially orientated, revolutions in industrialized and technologically advanced countries, where far greater effects on administration were possible. Such resources were not available to the men of 1793–4 since, as Cobb says, 'the revolutionary government did not have loud speakers to put up on trees and telegraph poles, nor could it keep the population mobilised in perpetual fetes'.[12] It was not equipped to carry out a parody of 1984. Indeed some parts of France were often untouched by the Revolution for months on end.

One must therefore expect to find not merely continuities, but also that things were left undone, which today would be done quite automatically. So it was with the bureaucracy. It may have been one of the first of its kind but it was by no means the ultimate in bureaucratization. Not every institution could be remodelled in a year or so, not every official would respond to the new situation in which he found himself, and even·when changes were made they were not always pushed to the limit. Nor were they sufficiently firmly based to last very long. The events of the Year II meant the triumph of bureaucracy. They did not mean that the process of bureaucratization was complete and final. However, it did produce a civil service which was not the red-taped disaster area some people like to think: 'des bureaux que les épurations révolutionnaires renouvelées depuis 1792 privent de traditions, d'archives bien souvent et d'employés compétents'. The inheritance from the past counter-balanced the worst of the revolutionary ravages.

Implicit in all this is the view of revolution as not just an isolated outburst but, as has already been suggested, as a dynamic process involving the replacement of one monopoly by another.[13] In this case the process had its roots in the revolutionary situation of the mid-eighties which led to it becoming one of the first examples of quasi-permanent revolution. The implications of the maximum intensity of the process for bureaucracy deserve further consideration. It has, in fact, been suggested that revolutions in general are phenomena that invariably increase bureaucracy, and that Weber's belief that bureaucracy could survive revolution unchanged, was unfounded. As Kamenka puts it, 'every great revolution has destroyed the state apparatus which it found. After much vacillation and experimentation, every revolution has set another apparatus in its place, in most cases quite different from the one destroyed, for the changes in the state order which a revolution produces are no less important than the changes in the social order.'[14] This has in turn been challenged, but if revolution is indeed a process involving the replacement of one power by another, analysis needs to go beyond mere questions of continuity.

It would seem to follow that if revolution is a process basically concerned with changes in the monopoly of power inside a society, then any new regime in a successful revolution must be stronger than the one it overthrew, and hence it is more likely to be bureaucratic.[15] As Edwards says, 'there is not less government during a revolution, there is more government. Not only are there more laws, but these laws are enforced with a thoroughness quite unknown in ordinary times.'[16] Revolutions in other words compel bureaucratization by multiplying rules, by intensifying political suspicion, and by interfering inside with administration as well as in society at large. Yet if government gets bigger during a period of revolution it does not necessarily have to be bureaucratic or totally divorced from the old administration. Much depends on the nature of the revolution in question. Whereas an administration will respond, as was the case in Year II, to a major change, it does not follow that it must thereafter respond to every minor change in the political climate.[17] Even the initial stages of the Revolution of 1789 failed wholly to transform the administration. Similarly, the relationship will depend on the administration and on the revolution in question. It is regrettable that the French Revolution, which has been the basis for so many theories of revolution, has so rarely been studied or understood by many of the theorists concerned. Like most things in human life the relationship between revolution and bureaucracy during the French Revolution, as indeed in any major revolution, is a highly individual and complex thing.

In any case up until about 1791 it might well have seemed that the Revolution was not going much further and that the administration was therefore unlikely to develop bureaucratic tendencies. It was, after all, only in 1790–1 that the ministries began to adjust themselves to the new order in a meaningful way, as when Duport-Dutertre took over the Ministry of Justice and proceeded to replace the relics of the old Chancery by a new organization.[18] This later gave way to an arrangement involving a cabinet, as has already been seen. Save for the Ministry of Justice and that of Affaires Étrangères, however, structural changes and the importation of new personnel did not get very far before 1791–2. Most ministries, even that of the Interior, tended to rely on Ancien Régime staff of one kind or another at this stage. And many of those in posts in 1792 had a good chance of staying there for some years, whereas those who were to be brought in during the factional struggles of 1792–3 were to be less fortunate.[19] For although in these years the ministries did undergo considerable change, as often as not this was for political as much as purely organizational reasons. The effect of the Jacobin–Girondin struggles was to change the leadership of the ministries with brutal frequency. This may have inhibited the gradual move towards more systematic internal structures of divisions and bureaux.

The political crisis begun by the war in the spring of 1792 not merely started to speed up structural change, but also brought the first major challenge to the security of the staff through the string of purges which the crisis unleashed. Although attention usually focuses on the *sans-culotte* input it may in fact have been this period which actually saw the most draconian purges and controls. The economic crisis was also less influential than it was to become as a recruitment factor. The first of these was staged by Dumouriez in the Ministry of Foreign Affairs that spring, and was to be followed by those by Roland and Pache in the War Office and the Interior respectively after 10 August.[20]

The purges obviously led to the introduction of new men who were often regarded as being little better than those they had replaced by the increasingly radical revolutionary temper. Therefore such purges became almost self-perpetuating, one influx having to be balanced by another. As Goyard said, the Revolution then brought in 'un système exagérément mobilisateur' which made for instability both in the sense of counterbalancing purges and in enhancing the tendency to 'épuration permanente' amongst staff.[21] And although the purges were intended to enhance commitment to cause and efficiency they probably enhanced inertia by making clerks too afraid of making mistakes of commission.

Very often too, these purges were done rather privately so that their results were not publicized. People rarely trusted them and came to demand the printing of lists of the dates of birth, services, and emoluments of the ministerial staff for consideration by the Assembly. Purges thus gave a boost to another means of control. At the same time ministers were required to present a formal report on their tenure of office within a fortnight of leaving it. They were also made personally responsible for crimes against the stage during the emergency. The conflict between the *Feuillants* and the *Brissotins* over the war, was partly fought out over the possession of ministerial portfolios. This led to 19 men holding 24 portfolios between April and August 1792, some 44 per cent of all such holders during the Constitutional Monarchy. Such instability left the staffs doubly leaderless and reduced some departments to virtual impotence.[22] It also continued the tendency visible from the 1770s for ministries to be significant for their cabinet role rather than for the administrative base they had provided since the death of Louis XIV.

This growing political concern over the ministries was a reflection of the way the war had made politics increasingly radical and bitter. The disastrous start to the war and the king's refusal to tolerate his *Brissotin* ministers helped to strengthen the republican movement which showed itself first on 20 June, and then—amid fears of a royal *coup* in alliance with the *Brissotins* —on 10 August. The Convention was immediately summoned, but, in the interim, power was entrusted to a Conseil Exécutif Provisoire, which was another name for the ministers, who thereby recovered some of the authority they had lost during the summer. The Council was allowed to suspend any officials it chose and officials were ordered to stay at their posts, to send out its own agents, and to enforce stringent regulations on the publication of detailed statements of the pay and working arrangements of the civil service.[23]

Such prescripts were apparently unsuccessful since they had to be repeated, but the reaction to the fall of the monarchy is interesting for two reasons. Firstly, it cleared the way for the theoretical bases of a new form of domination. It also showed that in a time of crisis the politicians could not manage without the civil service, which they had been busily harassing. Therefore they ought to have made some allowance for its needs. As L. E. Sedillez observed in the Legislative Assembly shortly before the fall of the monarchy:

Quant au patriotisme, il faut le résérver pour les grands événements: beaucoup des hommes se dévourent, hasarderont leur vie pour des instans prompts et rapides; sachez en user et vous ferez de grandes choses, mais le sacrifice habituel et journalier de tous ses moments, de toutes ses aises, de tous ses goûts, n'y comptez pas messieurs, ce sacrifice n'est pas dans la nature de l'homme. L'interêt seul est le résort de tous les jours; employez-le avec confiance, il ne vous manquera jamais.[24]

Unfortunately, it was to be some time before this advice was fully accepted, and for long the revolutionaries continued to ignore the civil service's economic, material, and career needs, preferring to demand total self-sacrifice to the *res publica*.

This was particularly notable during the winter of 1792–3 when the initial threat of invasion had passed. It left behind a further bitter internal struggly between the Jacobins and the Girondins, in which the latter's influence on the ministries was an issue. The conflict was basically fought out over the question of what should happen to the king, and the Girondins found themselves in an increasingly weak and ambiguous position, so that the publication of their lengthy constitution was a somewhat unreal exercise.[25] However, it is worth noting that the document did provide some recognition of the role of field service employees, since local government officials were only allowed to deal with them through a special commissioner. However, the bulk of the constitution was more concerned with protecting the citizen against the state than with helping the administration.

This hostility remained very much in evidence during the spring of 1793, partly because of the Conseil Exécutif's powers and liaison with the Girondins. From the end of 1792 it therefore came under increasing control from the Convention, while its functions were partly taken over by the various committees of the legislature, a process which led to the creation, in April, of the Comité de Salut Public.[26] The latter began to impinge on all the other committees and on the administration, where since 28 October 1791 the committees had been entitled to investigate the bureaux of any organization within their remit. The Convention continued to issue regulations on the administration, making the level of salaries public knowledge and subject to government control for instance, and also trying to ensure that the administration properly executed legislation agains the *émigrés*.[27] With the ending of the string of victories of the winter, the subsequent treason of Dumouriez, and the acute grain shortage, the administration was drawn even further into politics. The Convention responded to the crisis and to the demands of the popular movement in Paris by the *lévée* of 300,000 men, the establishment of the revolutionary tribunal and the revolutionary committees, and the dispatch of *représentants en mission* to the provinces. The reluctance of the *Gironde* to accept such measures and its desire to break the sections increased popular distrust both of them and the administration.[28]

New criticism of the latter's royalist and authoritarian inclinations was heard, while in the Ministry of War Bouchotte recalled many of those radicals dismissed by Beurnonville.[29] Then on 20 March the Convention ordered ministers to produce definitive lists of the names, duties, and background of their employees. As before, this failed to produce any immediate response and the demand was reiterated on 8 and 18 April, while on 28 April the Conseil Exécutif was collectively taken to task for such delay. Even so, it was only on 14 May that permission could be given to print all the information then available for the Convention. The motives behind this enquiry were overwhelmingly political: the fear that ministers, even men as left wing as Bouchotte, might be infiltrating counter-revolutionaries into the bureaux at what was proving to be a particularly delicate time. Hence the Jacobin Club demanded monthly statements of changes in the staffing of the Ministry of War, while the Commune and the sections demanded to share in the process of investigation. Such pressures do not merely show how tense the situation was becoming but also how difficult it was, even for someone as well disposed to the idea as was Bouchotte, to carry out and report on a purge. It was proof of the way in which the Girondins' rearguard action was preventing any resolution of the problems facing the Republic.[30]

In the event, when on the 21 May the War Office presented its returns, the Convention had other things on its mind and took little note of them. For the historian, on the other hand, the returns are an essential source for showing how far the ministries had developed along the road to bureaucratization since the Republic had been declared.[31] They also help to make up for the fact that no such similar 'photograph' of the ministries exists for the crucial expansion which was to follow. Although, since the respondents were apt to gloss over difficulties in their past, the returns have to be treated with a certain caution. However, they do provide an insight into both the way in which the structures of the Administrations Centrales had developed, and into the kind of people who were being used to staff them, at a moment when public opinion was more than usually convinced that they were all royalists.

The ministries by then had a staff which numbered some 1,250 in all.[32] This was nearly double the figure for 1788 and almost more than half as large again as in 1791–2, which shows that the rate of expansion was quickening. The staffs were also grouped slightly more simply and rationally amongst divisions and specialized bureaus. The most extreme specialization was to be found in the Ministry of Foreign Affairs where discussion of policy was spread between six bureaus each responsible for a well-defined geographical region, although this was not without its disadvantages. The Ministry for the Navy and Colonies had settled down into six divisions less complex than before: Ports and Arsenals, Provisions and Supplies, Navigation and Seamen, Funds and 'Invalides', Colonies, and Officers respectively. The War Office had experienced greater change and complexity. Pache had split it into two very large Directions Générales, for Personnel and Materials, but this had proved unworkable and later ministers had, with varying degrees of enthusiasm, returned to a more orthodox structure. At the end of May 1793 there were six divisions, each headed by an *Adjoint* who enjoyed greater standing and autonomy than ordinary *Chefs de Division*. They dealt with Accounts, Supplies and Buildings, Artillery and Engineering, Troops and Discipline, Movements and the National Guard, and Officers; and they were supported by a Secretariat. Significantly the largest division was that dealing with Supplies and Buildings which suggests that the Ministry was coming to deal with routine administration. Strategy and policy would presumably be passed to the Comité de Salut Public around which all the geographical services of the ministries were then being centralized.

There was less development in the ministries orientated towards the domestic scene.[33] The Interior had changed most, dropping the geographical separation of local affairs which were now concentrated into one of five divisions. The others: prisons, funds, and clergy; education and the arts; public works; and food and trade, were supported by secretarial and correspondence bureaus. The Ministry of Contributions, however, preserved its complex and largely geographical structure, and relied very heavily on staff drawn from the Ancien Régime, whereas the Ministry of Justice had a large number of new men as temporary employees. It was divided into a large and complicated secretariat, together with the kind of annexed services which had developed in 1791–2. The over-all pattern then, is that of a rationalized and expanded version of that found in 1791, save for the fact that the increasing numbers were sometimes being used for routine tasks and not for policy-making. In structural terms then the ministries had not yet broken out of their earlier framework.

This concentration on routine and the slippage of power away from the ministers possibly explains why there is such limited documentation provided on the staff. The vague and often ignored categories laid down by the Convention may also have been responsible. The staff were primarily northerners, nearly half having been born in the Seine and the Seine-et-Oise, with the rest coming in more or less equal numbers from the departments to the north-east of a line from the Jura to the base of the Cotentin, with a slight bias towards the Seine and the Marne valleys. The majority were mature men, over half being aged between twenty-four and forty-four, with a median age of thirty-four.[34] The well-established departments like Contributions had the highest proportion of older men, and, with the Interior and Foreign Affairs, also of those who had joined the ministries before the Revolution. Overall a quarter had joined before the Revolution and as many again between 1789 and August 1792, together with nearly a third in late 1792 and a further quarter in early 1793, which shows that the pace of recruitment had only increased very gradually.[35]

The exact time when individual ministries had begun to recruit largely depended on their own histories, but the Ministry of Finance at least drew not on new men, but on those who had already served in the administration. Only one in ten entered administrative service in general during the Revolution, while over half had joined it before 1779. The median date for entry was 1781. The evidence from the same department suggests that they had on average about eight years' service, involving such services as the Civil List, the Treasury, the Intendancies, the various fiscal field services, and the Provincial Assemblies. The remainder, moreover, were far from being young idlers since some volunteered for the army when they could have claimed exemption and many of them came from the law or other professions where they would have received a not irrelevant training.

The number who came from administrations or professions which had fallen on bad days suggests that political motives for recruitment were not very important. Indeed even where patronage is involved it turns out very often to have been that of a section head who would be in a position to judge the competence of the applicant. Their experience, however, was a little limited and not very technical in nature, so that the median position was that of a junior clerk at about 2,000 *livres* per annum. The need to work close to one's home is also another factor which comes through as strongly as any political motivation.[36] This is not to say that there were not odd and dubious characters, such as I. Agasse of Affaires Étrangères who was executed for passing forged cheques, but the majority were ordinary men. This was not because they were militants who had become bureaucrats, but because they were the product of long administrative service. Again, much of the patronage was simply personal, as with Danton's friendly appointment of two teenagers from Arcis-sur-Aube to humble positions in the Ministry of Justice. Indeed, this kind of thing was more common than political appointment to the still exiguous senior levels.

Rather than the 'patriots sans travail' whom Herlaut, and to a lesser extent Caritey, have seen as the basis of the new civil service, Mme Bernadin's very nuanced account is more accurate.[37] Herlaut is right to stress unemployment, but wrong to play down the importance of prior experience and qualifications. The truth was more banal than either Herlaut's emphasis on political motives or Walter's picture of totally haphazard recruitment.[38] The first major expansion of the ministerial services, had, quite naturally, pulled in those most committed to working in administration and who then were unable to find it elsewhere. Mere unemployment was less of a source of recruitment. Generally the Revolution increased the proportion of entrants with administrative experience. As one technical adviser remarked to the *Commissaire de l'Institution Publique* a little later 'en administration les sentiments qu'inspirent les individus ne font qu'une partie de la garantie que l'on peut desirer'.[39]

Such a pattern of recruitment drew in men like J. A. Hervet, an *Ingénieur Géographe Militaire* who was pensioned off on the suppression of the *corps* in 1791. Two years later, when his pension became worthless he moved into the museum at Versailles, a step to a new career which was eventually to bring him into the War Office again.[40] Similarly, there was an ex-soldier Bocher, whose investment in a military office failed, driving him to the Ministry, and J. J. Chovot who had served in both the War Office and the Admiralty before the Revolution. He took the chance offered him in 1793 to leave his post as *Secrétaire Général* of the Seine-et-Oise to return to the Ministry of War as a *Premier Commis*. So although it was beginning to modernize under the pressure of events, it was still basically the service of 1788–92, though somewhat modified. The major transformation was still to come.

In the summer of 1793, however, the civil service and, to a lesser extent, the Revolution in some ways marked time. The crises facing the Revolution intensified, but there was no agreement amongst the forces which brought about the 31 May as to how resistance could best be organized. None the less, the crises were sufficient to divert the Convention's attention away from the civil service and no real action was taken on the results produced by the *enquête* of May 1793.[41] To some extent this was also due to the slowly dawning realization that in order to surmount the crises facing it, the Revolution actually needed the administration. Faction struggles could not always take predominance over national need. Hence even apparently political appointments could contain an element of recommendation by merit in them, as did some nominations by Pache.

Hence despite the continuation of threatening gestures by the *sans-culottes* and the Convention, officials were given some security against interference, were allowed greater access to the armies, and were permitted to recruit such subordinates as they chose. However, in principle the revolutionaries remained deeply suspicious of the civil service, whose members were felt to need purging and the possession of an acceptable *carte de civisme*, since as one section observed 'il faut dans le ministère plus de probité que connaissances scientifiques, plus de patriotisme que de la machiavellianisme des tyrans'.[42] The potentially unsettling effects of this insistence on adherence to a momentarily dominant party line seems to have escaped them. Their attempts to settle the pension situation in July 1793 were undermined by technical failings and gathering inflation. The revised constitution of June 1793 testifies to this continuing lack of esteem, with its provisions that all officials were to be elected and that there could be no security of tenure or immunity of any sort.[43] Similarly, the ministers were to be downgraded to mere *agents en chef* of an elected executive council. In addition they were to be subjected to stringent penal controls. Locally, administrators were forbidden to be *receveurs du droits d'enregistrement*, not merely because this form of pluralism prevented wide democratic distribution of jobs, but significantly, because one could not be 'surveillant et surveillé en même temps'.

The real changes in both the administration and the Revolution as a whole came after the *journées* of 3 and 4 September. It was in September that the creation of the revolutionary government began in earnest. Though its creation was a long-drawn-out process, the style of government at once became more organized and more dynamic. This did not mean that the Jacobin leadership of the Convention gave way to all the demands of the *sans-culottes*, including the call for a purge of the administration and the replacement of *muscadins* and other unreliable elements by trustworthy and needy members of their own ranks.[44] The new government wished to be its own master. So despite the agreement to impose a general Maximum, to establish the *armées révolutionnaires*, the Commission des Subsistances, and other new bodies, there was no general purge, though there were radical changes in the Ministry of War. Moreover, the exercise of direct democracy was itself controlled, so that the revolutionary government had its hands free to mobilize national resources so as to defend the Revolution in the way they saw fit. Their way necessitated building up the administration.[45]

The institutions through which this was to be done were often already in existence, as were the initial laws of the Terror, but they were uncoordinated and incomplete, and enjoyed a somewhat ambiguous legal standing because of the constitution of 1793. This was resolved by the degrees of 10 October and 4 December. The former declared that the government should be 'revolutionary', in Robespierre's sense of the word, until peace was achieved. In the interim, it subjected the whole range of ministerial activity to the Comité de Salut Public in order to overcome the alleged inertia of the state machine.[46]

The second sprang from the problems later experienced at the local level, for whereas the Comité was able to centralize power in Paris, structures outside were at first less easy to co-ordinate. As Billaud-Varenne said in launching this 'constitution of the Terror' on 14 Frimaire, 'en gouvernement, comme en mécanique, tout ce que n'est point combiné avec précision, tant pour le nombre que pour l'étendue, n'obtient qu'un jeu embarrassée, et occassione des brisemens à l'infini'.[47] The law provided for a better exercise of authority, partly through the *Bulletin des Lois* and partly through the increased supervisory role over the districts, communes, *agents nationaux*, and revolutionary committees to whom power was entrusted, by the *représentants en mission* and especially by the Comité de Salut Public. The deputies *en mission* were empowered to denounce or to remove recalcitrant officials. The latter with their employees—who were specifically denied any public character or status—were warned against exceeding the laws or their own powers. Officials were also forced to report regularly to Paris, and made to accept the authority of local revolutionary committees and of the new legislation on state employment which was to be codified into a special penal statute. This was never drafted, let alone promulgated, but the idea showed that there had been some movement towards recognizing the role of employees in government, albeit in a limited and grudging way.

Although one should not exaggerate its powers, the revolutionary government as it developed through the winter of 1793–4 was probably the most active and forceful government which France had known up to the time of its emergence. Local authorities remained as recalcitrant as ever, mountain areas remained as difficult of access and as unaware of the wishes of Paris as ever, and the play of individualism amongst the members of the various authorities was consistently provoking, but none the less the countryside was better policed and the will of the government far more effectively enforced than had been the case even in the days of Louis XIV.[48]

Backed by the threat of the Terror in all its manifestations, not to mention the support of a million-strong army and an active network of militant 'party' and local organs, the state was able to mobilize the resources of the country as never before. As indeed was necessary if it was to resist the onslaught of the more or less united armies of half Europe and the manifold challenges to its authority at home. Hardly any aspect of social life was left untouched by the new initiatives and controls deriving from the Convention and its committees. The role played by deputies, committees, clubs, *agents nationaux*, sections, and the other revolutionary organs in making this activity possible has often been stressed as has the take-over of religion and education. What has been less emphasized is the extent to which, as the *loi 14 Frimaire* implies, all this was dependent not only on militants and *fonctionnaires* but also on a whole host of minor technical and administrative personnel who were absolutely essential for handling the array of new tasks which the revolutionary government took upon itself.

Both for the provision of relief payments to soldiers' families and the negotiation of contracts to buy food for the towns as well as the supply of assistance to *représentants en mission* the revolutionary government needed a civil service base to enable them to carry out their functions and aims.[49] So too did local government. The decline in the growth of the bureaux of the Meurthe was reversed by the imposition of the revolutionary government. Decisions taken in Paris and urgent tasks in the field could not of themselves be put into practice. They needed executives, advisers, controllers, and inspectors for this to be done properly. And even if many of the tasks involved were routine and mechanical, the very size of the operation meant that there was room for some initiative and some influence in policy-making. So despite their many reservations about the administration, the leaders of the revolutionary government were willing to trust their employees to act, freeing them from arrest by over-zealous sectional committees, and freeing them from National Guard duties because 'il faut que la Machine roule sans interruption et sans secousses', and the leadership sought to impart 'toute l'activité possible' so as to 'faire marcher la machine'.[50]

The extent to which the revolutionary government depended on a bureaucratic infrastructure can be seen, not merely in the way in which the new field and local services which the *loi 14*

Frimaire set out to co-ordinate had developed, but even in the central organs of co-ordination, and notably in the Comité de Salut Public itself.[51] This epitomizes the general process of bureaucratization. At 1793 drew to a close, the recapture of Toulon and the crucial victory over the Vendéans at Savernay meant that the support of the *sans-culottes* was becoming more of an embarrassment than a necessity, so the Comité was busily engaged in strengthening its own position and limiting that of rivals such as the *sans-culottes*. The committee had begun life with a small office staff patterned on that of the Conseil Exécutif, but this soon proved inadequate and by the summer of 1793 some twenty-six *secrétaires-commis* were employed in taking, filing, and dispatching minutes. The committee rapidly became much more than a correspondence centre and the secretaries, under first Desforgues and then J. B. Pierre, a protégé of Guyton de Morveau, not merely followed the members of the committee in dividing themselves into sections for dealing with the ministries, other statutory bodies, and the army and navy respectively, but also started directly supervising such things as the arms manufactures themselves.

By the end of the year there were over a hundred staff, plus a good number of couriers attached to the various sections, and control of such a machine needed someone of greater ability than a mere clerk—'an intelligent patriot of great merit' as Robespierre put it. The committee turned first to Charles Julien de Carentan, a former professor who had been Secretary-General of the Basses-Pyrénées and a military agent.[52] When he had to be dismissed in the autumn for peculation while on a mission to the armies of Mainz and of the Vendée, they turned—after a short interregnum when Pierre and André Aubusson, an ex-dragoon who had worked for the correspondence committee of the Convention, ran the bureaux together—to Saint-Cyr Nugues. He was a twenty-three-year-old *Toulousain* who had been *aide-commissaire des guerres et chef des bureaux* to the Army of the Pyrenees. He took over from Carentan as Director-General of the bureaux on 21 November 1793 on the recommendation of Julien de Toulouse, and presumably of Barère, who seems to have been his patron and may well have also sponsored his predecessor. Nugues was to serve in this unique and totally forgotten post until after Thermidor, following which he embarked on a triumphant career on the army staff. Throughout his later life he never seems to have mentioned his earlier *Montagnard* and *Salut Public* role which must have made him one of the most powerful men in France, albeit one of the least known.

By the time he took up his post the staff had already grown to about 80 and its salary bill to some 15,000 *livres* per month, for a day from 7 a.m. to 10 a.m. and from 7 p.m. to 10 p.m. Individual salaries ranged from 1,500 to 3,000 *livres* per annum. Within four months the number of staff had risen to 250, within six it had reached nearly 400, and in Thermidor II it attained a peak of 523. By then the salary bill had rocketed to 111,000 *livres* per month, representing a salary range of only 2,050 *livres* to 2,650 *livres*. The largely secretarial organization was maintained until the turn of 1794. This involved major bureaux for secretarial affairs, arrears in correspondence, communication with *représentents en missions*, translations, design, and archives. There were also small sections for war, diplomacy, naval affairs, and rather larger ones for military logistical services such as arms, powder, heavy artillery, and side arms, together with other services such as that for 'action du gouvernement révolutionnaire' and the execution of revolutionary laws.

By Floréal the structure had left behind its secretarial roots and was divided into four broad areas: the Secretariat, which included specialized bureaux for war, food supplies, finances, public works, the navy, and diplomacy, with 88 employees; police affairs, including *indigents*, detainees, and the famous *bureau de police générale* which had 18 of the area's 65 employees; revolutionary action with 106 staff divided into 6 bureaux; and supervision of the war effort with 91 employees in 7 bureaux. In addition there were some 34 couriers and *garçons de bureau*. By Thermidor it was the military bureaux which had grown most, with the Bureau de la Guerre doubling to 62 staff under Saint-Just's leadership. The Subsistances and police sections had also increased, with the latter now counting 50 employees, whereas the revolutionary government division had declined somewhat, suggesting that consolidation may have been achieved by then. Thereafter, despite a temporary drop in numbers, the organization became even more streamlined, although its power was diminished.

The creation of this huge staff shows exactly how the process of bureaucratization occurred in the Year II, as well as explaining how the Comité was able to dominate the revolutionary government as a whole. The process is similarly visible in the Comité de Sûreté Générale and the other committees which played a large part in the central direction of the revolutionary government. The former had acquired 112 staff by Pluviose II and between Floréal and Fructidor reached a peak of 150 who cost 44,000 *livres* per month.[53] The staff were strictly controlled by the Director, a well-known political figure in Bugnaître. They were divided into a Bureau Central which fed information to four regional bureaux and an *agènce générale* which dealt with affairs relating to the political élite. These bureaux initiated action which was then overseen by the largest section of all, the *bureau de l'exécution des ordres*, or by a section for arrears of work. A number of other committees of the Convention acquired not inconsiderable staffs of their own in order to play a certain role in the supervision of government activity in such fields as agriculture, finance, public works, education, and especially war.[54] By the spring of 1794 the Convention's committees had 500 clerks, of whom 58 per cent were in the two major committees, and by Floréal this had risen to 750, with 72 per cent in the major committees. Their real expansion was still to come.

None the less, the network of conventional committees and their staffs already played a crucial role in decision-making and in controlling the revolutionary government, almost forming a counter-bureaucracy to ensure surveillance of the ministerial bureaucracy. It gave the Comité de Salut Public some of the strength necessary not merely to run the war effort but also to deal with factional challenges to its growing monopoly of power. It similarly aided the attempt to ensure the reliability of the whole new machinery of government. This led to the establishment of the Bureau de Police Générale on 27 Germinal II, a move which through the boundary disputes it unleashed helped more to undermine than to control the structure of government by executing that 'censure des fonctionnaires' which Saint-Just sought.[55] The bureau was a reflection of the general concern about the recruitment of people whose primary loyalty was to their careers rather than to the Republic and who thus produced that 'sclérose bureaucratique' which moved Saint-Just to claim that 'la révolution est glacée'. In fact, the bureau, which was allegedly headed by a protégé of Saint-Just called Lejeune, did not function properly until Messidor. Even then its encroachment on the autonomy of the Sûreté Générale was more psychological than physical. Similarly, it was not very effective in controlling or purging the officialdom to the growth of which it was a significant testimony.

The Comité de Salut Public in fact found that its desire to impart movement to its new bureaucratic machine often conflicted with its desire to control it, and the former had to take precedence in the crisis.[56] So it had to free its agents from too many restraints and, when it introduced a *surveillant* to check on the exactitude of the employees in their commissions they soon found this counter-productive. Attempts to reduce staffing in central bureaux and to transfer responsibility to the field merely meant there were insufficient employees to exercise necessary control over local authority operations. The very magnitude of the revolutionary government's activities meant that they needed many hands to carry them through. They also needed larger numbers at the centre to try and oversee and control them.

The assembling of as many as 1,800 staff in the Ministry of War, in particular, was therefore widely feared, since the existence of such concentrations of personnel and power could give too many levers to bureaupathology and to *Hébertistes* and *Dantonistes* in the Interior as well as impeding the authority of the Comité.[57] It was therefore basically to facilitate the expansion of the latter that Carnot and others wanted the ministries replaced by bodies modelled upon, and very much subordinate to, the Committee. Hence on 12 Germinal, they were replaced by twelve more specialized executive commissions, each controlled by a Commissioner and a number of *Adjoints* and subject to stringent legislative and committee control. Since Contributions Publiques, Affaires Étrangères, and the Admiralty were left virtually unscathed, the political motivation stands out clearly in the division of the War Office between the Commission pour l'organisation et mouvement des armées de terre and six other commissions. The latter also absorbed elements of the

Interior's work, along with the Commission des Administrations Civiles, Police, et Tribunaux which also consumed the luckless Ministry of Justice.

In themselves, even though their establishment may initially have involved a cut of up to 60 per cent in the ministerial staffs, the commissions still constituted a dense network working for the Comité and the other supervisory organs. At first they employed perhaps 1,200 staff and later so many more that one contemporary estimated that there were between 15,000 and 21,000 staff, so that 'tout marchait bien avant le 12 Germinal, depuis rien se fait'.[58] The machine, even allowing for exaggeration, had obviously become immensely costly, complicated, and perhaps even unproductive. However, if it had probably no more than doubled in size since its creation, the very fact of having twelve separate bodies instead of six created problems of co-ordination. The Commission des Travaux Publics thus reported that it had to deal with every one of the other eleven, since it was responsible for court buildings, the upkeep of monuments, river works, mines, hospitals, the transport of building materials, land purchases, defence works, port installations, powder magazines, and even frontier posts.[59] And though the Comité de Salut Public tried to funnel all intercommission dealing through the *commissaires* it is doubtful if this was ever possible. It is not surprising that Herman on 22 Germinal found 'une certaine morgue, une certaine hauteur' in his bureaux as they no doubt found the public a distraction from an ever growing burden of work and communications problems.

In internal structure the commissions varied, with some like Revenus Nationaux, Relations Extérieurs, and Marine et Colonies changing little but their title, while those carved out of the Intérieur, and to a lesser extent from the Ministère de la Guerre, being radically new and altered.[60] Thus both Armes et Poudres and Administrations Civiles drew largely on the ministries from which they emerged for their *chefs* and divisions, while there was very little carry over from the Intérieur to the new Commissions de l'Instruction Publique and des Travaux Publics. With the partial exception of Armes et Poudres and Revenus Nationaux the commissions so far mentioned formed one unitary and fairly large organization responsible for making and executing decisions on the areas within their purview.

The remaining commissions, however, formed a small clerical core which acted as a co-ordinating centre for a variety of executive agencies which actually carried out many of the tasks for which the commission was responsible, somewhat on the Scandinavian pattern of public administration. The Commission du Commerce et des Approvisionnements, for example, had 10, rising to 80 or 90, staff of its own together with some 8 agencies, for varying forms of trade and price controls, with between 1,000 and 1,500 employees. This added a further complicating element to the new core of the administration. The reorganization of central government on these new and eventually much enlarged lines was a slow but relatively untroubled process thanks both to the careful way the Comité de Salut Public defined functions and to the efficiency of the administration itself. One piece of evidence for this is the fact that two-sevenths of those who held office as *Commissaires* or *Adjoints* were promoted direct from the ranks of the new bureaucracy, and overall, after the initial appointments of Robespierrists like Herman, Fleuriot-Lescot, and Payan, there were twice as many administrative appointments as political ones.

Even more numerous than this burgeoning central core of government, were the vast new field services which developed to underline the authority of the Comité and to help consolidate the revolution at home and abroad. Unfortunately even less is known about them than about the executive commissions. There seem to have been four main areas of growth, the largest being in the military field.[61] The huge armies, and to a lesser extent the navy, required hospitals, magazines, barracks, artillery parks, munitions, provision for the wounded and pensioned, and above all a mass of transport facilities for men, munitions, equipment, and food. All these services required thousands upon thousands of civilian employees: factory workers, guards, drivers, storekeepers, craftsmen, and, of course, clerks and inspectors.

The second major group were employed in the equally vital task of supplying the armies and towns with food. Agricultural development, price control, trading arrangements, and financial management all demanded a further horde of inspectors, accountants, clerks, and drivers to enforce the Maximum and collect, process, and distribute food. The third group consisted of employees in those financial services which had survived the destruction of the Ancien Régime: *enregistrement et domaines*, customs, and the *assignats*. The last group included all those in technical services such as the posts, the *gendarmerie*, the *cadastre*, archives, and printing, all of which required a certain number of personnel to perform valuable services for the government. People such as these, as has already been suggested, did as much to ensure that the revolutionary government actually worked as did the elective officials, popular societies, and militants and deputies from Paris. Their function may have been secondary, but they were none the less indispensable.

The effect of such expansion was to make the Comité de Salut Public's task of controlling and co-ordinating the government machine increasingly difficult. At the same time expansion completed the process of bureaucratization of the machine. The Comité tried to defend its position in a number of ways: by establishing new branches of its own bureaux such as the *bureau de l'action révolutionnaire*, limiting the right of employees in the machine to correspond amongst themselves rather than through their *commissaires* or via the committee, and above all by trying to insist that the civil service was fully republicanized. State employees were to use only republican language, to deal politely and promptly with the public, and to resolve problems arising from the massive inflow of correspondence, which was the life blood of the revolutionary government, as soon as possible.[62] But one has the impression that the process of bureaucratization was too far advanced for so slight a campaign to have much chance of reversing it. The new bureaucracy, both central and local, was so large, so powerful and active, so hierarchical and centralized, and so much staffed by people committed more to administrative employment than to faction politics that even a government as powerful as that of the Year II was hardly able to estimate its size, let alone utilize it for specific political ends.

It is virtually impossible to say at present how big the new bureaucracy actually was, since so little attention has been paid to its development. Some authorities have suggested that anything between 30,000 and 90,000 new jobs were created by the Terror.[63] Certainly there must have been at least 13,000 officials and employees in Paris alone, and probably more than 15,000, of which the commissions would have counted for about a quarter. Outside, there could have been 250,000 or perhaps even 300,000 if one includes elected officials, field, local, and military employees. It is obviously true that, 'pour appliquer la loi, la Convention fait appel à une bureaucratie omnipotente, infiniment plus redoutable que celle dont les hommes de 1789 avaient décrété l'abolition'.[64] Its authority sprang not merely from its size but also from both its manifold activities and from its increasingly bureaucratic characteristics. The new bureaucracy was active in a far wider area than its predecessors. The justiciar and fiscalist state gave way in the eighteenth century to a more administrative role, and during the brief life of the *gouvernement révolutionnaire* it sought to be omnipotent.

It was also much more consciously hierarchical, both in the way *la tutelle administrative* was developed by the Comité and also in its internal organization. A good example of this is the sevenfold system of grades laid down by the Comité in Thermidor II for the staff of the executive commissions, which ranged from copyists at 1,200 *livres* per annum to *Chefs* at 6,000 *livres* per annum.[65] Similarly, there was some kind of hierarchy amongst the different branches of the state machine, with the committees of the Convention at the top. The commissions provided coordination not merely for other central administrations dependent on them, but also for local and field services. The ensemble of state services represented a much more deliberate effort to provide France with the basic tools for her administrative functions than had been seen before. Although little was known about this new machine then, as now, it does seem to have been more rational and objective than even a few months previously. It was also more centralized than before, not merely because of the Comité de Salut Public, but also because of the imposition of a new and large central bureaucracy over the old services, and the new political controls. This upset the old balance between *fonctionnaires* and employees, making the former dependent on both political leaders and civil service expertise, although few people seem to have been aware of the change.

The role of expertise for example has rarely been appreciated. Yet there was, as has already been implied, room for a creative role for the civil service. One Commissioner of Transport in fact refused to regard his employees as mere 'agents d'exécution' and upgraded them so as to recognize the fact that he could not himself even sign the 1,100 documents issued every day by the department.[66] His fear was that the low salaries and fiscal constraints imposed on the commissions would prevent them from recruiting the calibre of employee needed. To give one example, the Commission de l'Instruction Publique had, as part of its responsibility for establishing republican institutions, inherited an active role in dealing with the property left behind by *émigrés* and by the Church. This began as early as 1791 and was in the hands of Antoine Grandjean Fauchy.[67] Born at Chasselors (Saône-et-Loire) about 1759, and the son of a propriétaire–cultivateur, he came to Paris in 1776. Within three years as allegedly a *licencié et agrégé* he was in the Balance du Commerce administration where he stayed until 1787 when he transferred to the Intendancy of Caen, remaining in charge there after the flight of the Intendant. This seems to have won him a place in the new education section of the reformed Ministry of the Interior where he was to stay until the late nineties. He classed himself as a republican and philosopher and was engaged under the Directory on a translation of Aristotle's *Politics*.

His ability was recognized by the Ministry both in promoting him to *Chef de Bureau* and in allowing him a larger degree of initiative. His main responsibility was for accounts but he was also responsible for liaison with the Commission Temporaire des Arts and for devising and implementing a policy to secure for the Republic materials of educational and cultural value from sequestrated and redundant properties. His role in this is evidenced by the fact that it was to him that experts in the field habitually wrote rather than to his hierarchical superiors. And although he kept his political record relatively clean by joining in the denunciation of one of his divisional heads, Le Gracieux, an ex-Treasury official and henchman of Payan and Fouquier-Tinville at Thermidor, he symbolizes the potential for an active and not uncreative role based on some kind of technical and administrative expertise latent in the new bureaucracy.

The men who provided this expertise were perhaps more of a corps than before, since they all now worked for the same master, the state, albeit with differing degrees of directness.

They all worked within much the same structural pattern of divisions and bureaux, and more importantly, they were part of bodies which in the case of the commissions were very much an amalgam of varying services and recruits. Because of the economic situation and the revolutionary attitude to public service, they could only be salaried and could not own their posts. They were also subject to new disciplinary norms and controls. Moreover, they could show very modern attitudes when claiming the provision of furniture and clocks for their offices.

They worked even more than ever before through written records. These began to proliferate at almost geometric rates from 1793 onwards, as the archives still testify. On one level the authorities sought to regularize these by instituting a formulary for appropriate republican usages and also by adopting new ways of distributing, filing, and registering papers.[68] In the Marine Commission the *Chefs* and *Sous-Chefs* distributed the mail, leaving the *Commis Principaux* to do the actual drafting. Each day's cases and each *decadi*'s work were subject to rigorous checks as 'la surveillance n'est rien, si l'ordre le plus exact ne règne pas dans le travail'. Their aim was to be able to provide the Comité de Salut Public with whatever information and advice it might need, on the spot. They wished to avoid the arrears experienced by other departments.

To some extent this could be resolved by employing more people, but some departments began to try and resolve the problem by the imposition of complex regulations on how the bureaux should function. In the Commission des Revenus Nationaux on 30 Floréal II an extremely complicated document was issued.[69] It was posited on a kind of one-sided contract between an administration which owed its employees justice in return for an ardent attachment to revolutionary ideals coupled with total dedication to their duties. They were required to work from 9 a.m. to 4 p.m. together with any evenings when the pressure of work demanded an extra session. Each bureau in turn was to provide a skeleton team from 10 to 2 on each *decadi*. The Bureau des Depêches was required to be open virtually non-stop, including every evening from 4 to 9. Those who were down for evening work were grudgingly allowed a lunch-break. Normally meal breaks and leave of all kinds were very much frowned on. All absences from the bureau needed notification or investigation. Even performance of National Guard duty was closely watched in this case.

Once in the bureaux clerks were required to work to a carefully devised pattern which was to be uniform across all divisions. All mail was to be opened by the Commissioner or his Adjutant, and then sent for registration in the Secretariat before being circulated to the divisions. These had to sign a receipt for all papers they received, as well as entering up all the pieces in registers of their own with a call-number entered in a different colour ink. Each piece was then put in a file and apportioned to a relevant sub-section where the *Chef* would, seemingly, prepare draft minutes in a specified form. Such minutes were then sent in a divisional file to the Commissioner for his approval. If this was forthcoming the *Chef de Division* would receive them back to make fair copies and précis for the files. The *Commis d'Ordre* of each division then took the finished letters and reports first for the Commissioner's signature and then to the mail room. Clerks were warned to respond immediately to any enquiry from Salut Public which had a register of its own and to deal with each affair as it arose and not to cumulate letters. The *gardiens* had orders to keep the public out except between 1 p.m. and 3 p.m. when the *chefs* alone would receive them. For the rest the work of the bureaucracy was to be carried on by silent application.

However, there were dimensions in which bureaucratization of the administration was only partly, or somewhat insecurely, achieved. The hierarchical structure was only in its infancy and the career pattern implicit in such hierarchies was devoid of guarantee. The increased promotion and pension prospects offered by the enlarged administration were rendered insecure in the extreme by the economic and political conditions of the Revolution. Similarly, regulations such as that imposed by Revenus Nationaux were often transitory and partial, and there was no consistency in either personnel policy or the general standing of the new bureaucracy. Moreover, the new realities were still veiled beneath the reservations and incomprehensions with which the revolutionaries regarded the administration.

Yet despite all this the crucial and irreversible steps towards bureaucratization had been taken and from then on the problem was how to consolidate the new administration. Consolidation is something which is, by definition, virtually impossible in a time of revolution. Indeed, even during the Thermidorian period, the process of expansion was another sign of the extent to which the administration was indispensable to the Revolution. As a result of this it gained practical freedom from the worst of the carping hostility with which it was regarded. This autonomy, like the relative a-politicization forced on the bureaucracy by factional struggles, was also to prove irrevocable, at least in the short term. So the changes brought about by the Revolution were merely to be the first of many for the new bureaucracy.

The revolutionaries were aware that the administration had changed and in a direction of which they did not much approve. Therefore, even though in some ways it was against their own best interests, they continued to watch uneasily and censoriously over it.[70] *Surveillants* or Inspectors were appointed to watch over the political actions of the staff and ensure that regulations on attendance and correct dealings with the public were enforced, while a further battery of controls was rushed through to satisfy the continuing stories of the political and literal illiteracy of the new bureaucrats. The Comité de Salut Public thus expected to approve all appointments and on 30 Germinal II decreed that nobody should be employed without submitting a curriculum vitae and some evidence of patriotism.[71] These controls also included demands that officials should always accept the public in their offices, should be paid only by salary, and should be liable to dismissal if they continued working in enemy-occupied areas. Similarly, recruiting those liable to military service into their bureaux, or failing to execute decisions of the Convention, led to ejection.

The need for such controls is usually attributed to the effects of political recruitment, typified by the way the Comité de Salut Public considered drawing up a list of reliable potential office-holders. Hanriot reinforced this approach when he informed the *armées révolutionnaires* that: 'Je suis bien aisé d'aviser mes frères d'armes que toutes les places sont à la disposition du gouvernement; le gouvernement actuel, qui est révolutionnaire, qui veut le bien de tous, va jusque dans les greniers chercher les pauvres et purs sans-culottes et leur dit: "Venez occuper cette place, la patrie vous y appelle." ' But the situation was not quite as simple as this might appear. Indeed in talking of 'poor' patriots Hanriot himself reminds one that it was more often economic dislocation, intensified at this time by the way the Maximum pressed on profit margins, than party spirit that led people to seek administrative employment.[72] Administrative posts gave people some assurance of a salary and of conditions which were better than those available on the open market. The feeling of making some kind of contribution to the new order was usually subordinate to this.

Moreover, the pressures under which the *gouvernement révolutionnaire* and its many agencies worked did not allow them to be too scrupulous about the motives and qualifications of the staff they employed, since delay in recruitment could mean delay in the war effort. In any case, one wonders whether, given the scale of expansion, there were enough patriots available to take up the vacancies. Even where militants did enter the civil service their activities could either lead to their becoming an embarrassment to their superiors, so that they were fired, or to themselves. In this case, as has often been emphasized, they cut themselves off from their political roots and became docile instruments of government. The dangers that this posed to political groups was vigorously pointed out to the Jacobins by Lachevardière amongst others. Ironically he himself was to become Secretary-General of the Ministry of Police under the Directory and a Consul under the Empire. As a militant in the Halle aux Bleds he said to the club's members, 'Restons Jacobins et ne soyons point Ministres. Notre société est une société d'opinions et ne peut jamais devienne un corps politique que donne des homes aux autorités constituées.'[73] Obviously political colouring and motivation did exist but it was less frequent than other rarely cited motives, while it was often inextricably mixed up with personal advantage, nepotism, and other things as well.

The more subtle fears voiced by Lachevardière were, in any case, not those which worried most revolutionary politicians. Their anxiety was caused by extremists whether of the left or especially of the right. In fact, although there were arrests of people like Champagneux in the autumn of 1793 as Rolandists or Federalists, there were few real cases of royalism. It was probably too dangerous to be an outspoken royalist, while the war probably made many employees more favourable to the Republic than they might have been. Again, although the records of the Commission de l'Instruction Publique show a number of people with connections with Payan, its first, Robespierrist commissioner, and a few militants, only Payan and two senior aides were removed at Thermidor.[74] This was partly because many as in the Administrations civiles commission were appointed by ministers and not by politicians or by sections; and partly because even these appointments had some technical reasons behind them as well. Hence, J. V. Dumas, a former administrator of the Drôme and member of a surveillance committee and P. Garicot, once of the Comité Révolutionnaires in the *Unité* section, seem to have kept their jobs.

Certainly the War Office pension files suggest that the Comité de Salut Public was willing to restore capable clerks dismissed by Pache and others, as it did with Devaux d'Huguesville. And on 8 Vendémiaire III it decided to make good the salary of any clerk who had been unjustly or illegally imprisoned prior to Thermidor.[75] In fact even before then the *Comité* had interfered to free Clement de Ris, who was then in the Commission de l'Instruction Publique, from arrest by over-zealous sectionaries seeking to influence the administration in their own interest. In any case the tendency to *auto-épurations* made it difficult for the bureaucracy to become too much of a refuge for the persecuted.

The limitations of the case for the political domination of the bureaucracy, which such intervention by the Comité de Salut Public implies, also appear clearly if one analyses the two most commonly cited instances. The first is the *Hébertiste* entrenchment in the Ministry of War, where despite the stress placed on it by Herlaut and others, the fact appears to be that certain *chefs de division*—Ronsin, Sijas, Xavier Audouin, and Vincent—were *Hébertistes*. After that the evidence is inconclusive to say the least. Herlaut lists only a few names, and admits that Vincent's influence only became effective after the *journées* of September.[76] He also shows that this influence was resisted inside the Ministry right up till the time that Bouchotte broke with Vincent. Moreover, Herlaut emphasizes the role of the Comité de Vérification —a twelve-strong body set up to provide a comfortable niche for favoured *Hérbertistes* and to facilitate a purge of right-wing elements in the Ministry—but this was resisted by the *Adjoints* and proved ineffective. Again, as Soboul points out, not all the staff reacted to the dismissal of Vincent and the associated purge, which in any case only involved 20 people out of something like 1,800. There is also evidence in Herlaut that even at their height the *Hébertistes* were unable to eliminate what they saw as a right-wing cell in the Ministry.

It rather seems that the actual number of *Hébertistes* in the Ministry was quite small. In any case what really alarmed people was the implications of possible *Hébertiste* influence. As Bouchotte himself said of his critics, to make him responsible for the politics of hundreds of clerks was merely to demonstrate their total lack of understanding of the realities of politics and of administration. Even Herlaut admits that many of the attacks on the civil service were either exaggerated or motivated by a desire on the part of its detractors to gain places for themselves.

The second example is equally unconvincing. It has often been claimed that within the new bureaucracy there was a group of dedicated counter-revolutionaries working to mitigate the effects of the Terror and especially to save the innocent from the guillotine.[77] This had been said even of the bureaux of the Comité itself. The head of the police section, Alexis Lejeune, the son of a *cultivateur* in the Soissonais, who had been a sergeant of *Chasseurs* before he was invalided out into the Ministry of Foreign Affairs from where he was selected by Saint-Just to run the crucial new bureau, and a one-time rake called Charles de la Bussière, both claimed to have saved lives. The former pretended to have delayed cases so that they never reached the Tribunal, while the latter boasted that he abstracted incriminating dossiers, notably those of the actors in the Coméde Française, and dumped nine hundred sets of papers in the river, thus preventing the prosecution of those to whom the dossier referred. Attractive though such stories are, they fit neither the evidence of Ording, nor the lists of employees of the committee. The latter show La Bussière in a different post from that which he claimed, and so the whole affair must be treated with some reserve. Paris was, after all, apparently full of active and lifelong royalists, after the Restoration. Even if both instances were true, they would tend to cancel each other out, rather than prove that the administration had one uniform political colouring. However, since they refer only to a tiny proportion of those employed in the administration at that stage, it would be unwise to rationalize from them, even if they were true.

A further argument for the lack of political involvement in the administration comes from a consideration of the turnover of personnel during the Revolution. It has often been suggested, by Napoleon amongst others, that the Revolution meant a massive turn-out, with ambitious and often incompetent new men saying 'allez-vous-en' to the old guard.[78] This was not really so. The expansion of jobs was enough to make such a turn-out largely unnecessary, although the status of individual jobs probably fell in the process. When reorganization or political suspicion led to a man losing a job in one sphere, he could usually get one in another, as did Lejeune, who retired as a senior administrator in the customs service under the Restoration. Furthermore, one has to allow for natural wastage, which was often very high even during the Ancien Régime. Admittedly in some cases, in the very early years of the Revolution, a large number of people took the opportunity to retire early, or were encouraged to do so, because of incompatibilities with the new order.

Although it is not necessarily typical, the example of the Ministry of War is instructive. It seems that 19 per cent of those in posts in 1788 served right through the revolutionary era, while 60 per cent left for the normal reasons of transfer, retirement, and, of course, natural deaths. So only 21 per cent were dismissed for political reasons. Moreover, such dismissals were often only temporary and the people concerned soon found themselves back in the War Office. In any case, this figure is probably no higher than would have been the case with the partly political reorganizations of the Ancien Régime, and suggests a higher degree of continuity than was sometimes found in old institutions like the Conseil du Roi.

It was the new entrants of 1792–4 who tended to be short-lived members of the new bureaucracy. This was mainly because it became necesary to thin it down once the military crisis was over. Moreover, the old hands tended to get the top jobs by the late nineties, even though by then they made up only a seventeenth of the total ministerial staff of that time. Many of those recruited between 1789–91 or between 1792–4 who remained in service by 1800 were themselves former employees of Ancien Régime institutions other than the ministry. In other words it was the old *Premiers Commis*, who, like the other Ancien Régime administrative élites, paid the price of the purges, rather than the rank and file. Given this situation, it is hardly surprising that the frequent controls and purges failed either to unearth many political appointees or to curtail the practical autonomy enjoyed by the administration.

The *coup* of 9–10 Thermidor did not really interrupt either this concern for a probably non-existent politicization in the administration, or the process of bureaucratization. Its effects were not sufficient to bring about a major change in the pattern of domination, because, although there were questions of policy involved in the *coup*, in the last resort it was more a *coup d'état* than a real revolution.[79]

It was not, despite some claims to the contrary, really aimed at the bureaucracy. Perhaps by drawing off some militants the bureaucracy may have undermined Robespierre's popular strength, but it is also possible that the *coup* itself may have prevented Robespierre and the Comité de Salut Public in general from developing the real administrative statute and strategy presaged by the decree on the clerical hierarchy of the commissions promulgated early in Thermidor.[80] In other words the overthrow of the Robespierrists meant a partial loss of momentum in efforts to control the bureaucracy, and a partial loss of expertise in government circles as well. As a result, the political autonomy of the administration may well have been increased by the *coup*, rather than diminished as many leading Thermidorians came to expect. Hence, Thermidor marked a new stage in the transformation of the bureaucracy, one which had forward links as well as backward ones.

Certainly the *coup* made consolidation more difficult, since it enabled the expansion of the bureaucracy to continue, although with the difference that its growth was now a function of government weakness rather than of government strength, as had been the case before. The continuing crisis in which the revolution found itself obviously played a part in this. The Thermidorian period was thus linked more closely to the phase of revolutionary creativity than to Directorial consolidation as far as the administration was concerned. Obviously it played a lesser part save where control and supply were concerned, but the situation of the two periods was very similar even if it was the former which was ultimately decisive. None the less, after an initial period in which the government rather lost its way over the administration, it eventually came to appreciate where the great Comité had been heading, and tried, albeit rather too late in the day, to follow in its footsteps. In so doing it left the Directory a rich legacy to utilize.

Yet if the Thermidorians came to detest the new administration they were as unsuccessful as their predecessors in their attempt to control it. There were three main reasons why they failed in this. To begin with, although the desire was sincere, it was still somewhat naïve. Because of the *coup*, little was known of the structure of the administration. What they did find out was all too quickly forgotten since they had no permanent means of exercising or following up their theoretical authority over the administration. Secondly, their attack could never be pushed home consistently since the Convention too often changed its mind for somewhat frivolous reasons or was diverted from the problem of administrative reform by new political crises. Moreover, although they agreed in principle that reform was necessary there was little or no agreement on the details of possible reforms. Finally, because of the decentralization brought about by the *coup*, they were just as dependent on the civil service as their predecessors, and could not really afford to disturb it by radical changes. They were therefore restricted to hoping it would wither away of its own accord and to changing minor elements of its structure under the pressure of events, rather than through a properly conceived programme of administrative reform.

At first the Thermidorians' fear of the administration was merely that which had prevailed beforehand, magnified by the new concern that it might contain secret Robespierrists who could nullify their changed policies. So at first they merely wanted a new purge and sought to establish the structural outlines of the administration as a preliminary. Gradually, however, they were pushed towards a more general scaling-down of the revolutinary government, as in the *loi de 7 Fructidor* which transferred much of the supervisory role of the old Comité de Salut Public to the sixteen reorganized committees of the legislature, notably those for Législation and Finances. As a result the staff of the Conventional committees rose to 1,115 in Vendémiaire III, and ultimately to 1,260 by Ventôse III by when only half the total was employed by the two old committees of government, while the Comité de Législation had acquired a staff of over two hundred. The new system did not, however, prove very effective, despite the accompanying barrage of regulations and controls on the staff, and proved to be a prelude to more radical changes in the pattern of government.[81] The *loi 7 Fructidor* did, howver, impel some changes inside the central core of the administration, as with the reorganization of the staff of the Comité de Salut Public into new sections for war industries, the armies, trade industry, and diplomacy, the latter involving the absorption of much of the work of the Commission des Relations Extérieures.[82]

Partly because of the failure of this early attempt at 'deconcentration' the bureaucracy continued to expand numerically during the Year III—not because of the desire of former victims of Robespierre or of members of the *jeunesse dorée* to seek their reward—but because of the relaxation of central control.[83] The Comité de Salut Public after an initial drop thus rose to nearly 500 by the early spring, divided now into 25 grades. Despite the simplification of such bodies as the Commission du Commerce et des Approvisionnements, which was downgraded to dealing simply with food supplies in January 1795, criticism of the administration grew accordingly. A leader in the *Moniteur* demanded that superfluous clerks should be redeployed to productive work in field or factory. The belief that the bureaux were full of young draft dodgers, supporters of Robespierre or of the king, imbued with an arrogant disdain for the public, was quasi-universal.

By the winter of 1794–5, therefore, there was a powerful movement for a major reform of an administration which seemed to many members of the middle classes and to Thermidorian politicians to be too powerful, too costly, too large, too cumbrous, and too inimical to free enterprise in general.[84] It had therefore to be prevented from devouring the Revolution which had created it. This seems to have been regarded as true at both central and local levels. Hence the Meurthe was, for instance, to see a new scaling-down of the size of its own staff, while the Parisian campaign was gathering momentum. This first consistent movement for administrative reform also drew strength from the growing desire to return to normal constitutional government, and the attack on the bureaucracy became part and parcel of this. The onslaught was initially unleashed in Brumaire when Barère and Audouin both called for organic laws to be drafted in order to make the constitution of 1793 operative.[85] Coming from such a quarter the idea did not get very far, but on 13 Frimaire III, after a very hostile debate on the transport administration, Thibaudeau was able to take up part of Barère's plans by moving the establishment of a Commission des Seize to consider the whole structure of government. Yet though few people were willing to defend the bureaucracy, and a majority agreed that a major reform was necessary, the various factions, even inside the commission itself, could not agree on a new form of government. Hence the commission petered out after investigating the general structure of the executive arm. Neither this nor the various decrees passed at that time in an attempt to reduce the administration both in terms of numbers and the salaries it paid out and to remove ex-terrorists and other enemies of the Convention were enough to satisfy the opposition to the existing government and to its administration.[86]

Hence on 11 Ventôse Freron renewed the call for organic laws to be drafted and a new committee of seven was created in place of the now redundant Seize to consider the question. Under the pressure of outside events it was decided to draft such laws and yet a third body, the Commission des Onze, was created to draft them. This posed the question of what should happen to the government, on whose failings the Convention was agreed, in the interim. Thibaudeau persistently urged the strengthening of the Comité de Salut Public but this was too reminiscent of the Year II, and the project for provisional reform was eventually dropped. Similarly, the risings of Germinal and especially Prairial led the Onze to drop the idea of organic laws and to draft a wholly new constitution. These two decisions ended any change of a major reconstruction of the administration. None the less public response to the call for thoughts on possible organic laws showed that a few people were still aware of how urgent it was to remedy a situation in which the real vice was that 'plus les employés principaux et secondaires sont nombreux plus la marche des choses est entravé. Moins il se fait d'opérations utiles, moins il y a de véritable responsabilité.'[87]

There were some structural changes all the same. The new Commission des Approvisionnements was wound up in Fructidor, as was that of Armes, Poudres, et Mines. Transports, Postes, et Messageries similarly vanished in Prairial. Some minor changes also too place in Travaux Publics and Instruction Publique, while the abolition of the latter was once considered. The two major committees of government also changed, with Sureté Générale loosing staff whereas Salut Public reached a new peak of 525 employees as the result of its absorption of the old *service de commerce* and the creation of a new central information service.[88] Such changes were, even with the creation of the École Polytechnique, however, a poor reward for all the efforts put into administrative reform. Probably much of the failure was due not only to the weaknesses of the Convention, but also to the sheer scale and complexity of the problems involved in administrative reform.[89]

However, under the pressure of financial stringency more drastic cuts were made in the new establishments, particularly at local level where many people felt they had become grossly inflated. The *loi 29 Prairial III* ordered a cut of a third in central staffs, and demanded that departmental staffs be cut back to the level prevailing in 1791.[90] The reductions were to fall on the untalented, the illiterate, the young, those who had escaped productive work, and those who had opposed the Revolution. Those remaining were guaranteed cost-of-living supplements a few days later. The laws were applied locally but it is not clear whether the cuts were ever made centrally. There was also legislation on the political role of the administration, which in an atmosphere stirred by three risings, continued to exercise the politicians. Yet on 16 Fructidor III the civil courts were again refused permission to take cognizance of administrative acts, which reinforces one's impression of the inconsistency of the Convention. Perhaps because of this, public opinion seems to have been largely unaware of the progress made in trimming the administration down to size, so that the criticism was just the same at the end of the reform movement as at its beginning.[91]

The new threat from the right which developed towards the

end of the Year III caused an even more marked return to old complaints, as well as presenting new problems for the Revolution. The decision of the majority of the Convention to ensure their own continuance in power as a guarantee against a possible restoration undermined the basic premise of the new constitution, that of harmony between the new Directory and the local notables. It therefore prompted the rising of 13 Vendémiaire and threw into prominence the technical failings of the constitution.[92] None the less, the very brave decision to persevere with the new order was taken. The Thermidorians also allowed the administraiton to continue, even though they thought they saw its hand in the rising of Vendémiaire, which rekindled all their traditional fears of political permeation of the bureaucracy. Hence, they set up another wide-ranging enquiry into the political behaviour of the central administration, though this too failed to turn up what was expected of it before it collapsed through the contradictory assumptions on which it was based.

They were no more successful in this then, than in their attempts at restructing and controlling the bureaucracy. However, they did make some progress in administrative law and in recognizing the reality of the bureaucracy's existence, and particularly in dealing with its economic problems. They made no attempt to destroy it, allowing the process of creation to continue. On the other hand they were unable to complete the process of endowing the administration with Weberian characteristics which had begun in Year II, or to find it a recognized place in the scheme of things. For although the Commission des Onze partly had its roots in a concern for administrative reform, and although it took the crucial step of restoring the old ministerial framework in the new constitution, it did not make any real mention of the bureaucracy in the new draft, thereby leaving the latter in a kind of constitutional limbo. This gap between the Thermidorians' rhetoric and expectations and their realizations meant that it was left to the Directory to bestow stability, consistency, and control on the bureaucracy. Their failure to grasp fully the need to recognize the role of 'interest' in dealing with the civil service meant that they could not go beyond the achievements of the Year II, to which they were, in the last resort, so closely tied.[93]

If the revolutionary government was the mother of the new bureaucracy, then the Thermidorians were perhaps the father of it, standing somewhat ineffectually by as the period of labour comes to an end. It was left to the Directory to play the midwife and to cut the umbilical cord which bound the bureaucracy to its mother, enabling it to grow up as a force in its own right. It was to be consolidated by the Directory, and then at one and the same time be curbed and reinforced under Bonaparte before being passed on with all its problems and potential to the changing circumstances of the nineteenth and early twentieth centuries. Yet without the Year II it might never have been so.

After the men of 1789 had removed the old carapace of patrimonialism, and those of 1791 had provided a new polity within which it had to work, the men of 1793, under the impact of war, rebellion, and social and political militancy, brought a transformed administration into being to support the new totalitarian nation state. Despite the fact that they disapproved of the changes that took place in the administration they allowed it to be transformed in numbers, style, and role, becoming a more or less fully fledged bureaucracy. Hence though its contacts with the Ancien Régime were never lost, the element of change is perhaps greater than that of continuity. The new bureaucracy was vastly different both from the courtly administration of the old monarchy with its barely veiled venality, and from the uneasy amalgam of old and new found between 1790 and 1792. Yet because revolution is a process rather than an instant, each phase of the revolution played its part in the development of the bureaucracy, though obviously not every stage had the same impact.[94] The first phase was disruptive and the second more constructive. However, there was still insufficient stability for consolidation and insufficient good will for full public recognition of the bureaucracy. This was to come gradually in later years. So though the process was cumulative, it was the Year II that led to France acquiring 'a bureaucratic organization without parallel in eighteenth century Europe'.[95]

CHAPTER IV: THE DIRECTORY AND THE NEW BUREAUCRACY 1795–1799

Because the years from 1793 to 1795 were so exceptional, the French administration became a bureaucracy. At the same time, the exceptional nature of the period also prevented the bureaucracy, once created, from developing normally. The Directory was therefore the first government to come to power at a time when it was possible for the bureaucracy to acquire stability and consistency. Since the Directory was also the first government to go beyond the somewhat hand-to-mouth approach of its predecessors and develop anything resembling a proper administrative strategy, this is precisely what happened. Because of the time and conditions of its lifetime, and also because of its attitudes, the Directory was able to go a long way towards consolidating the new bureaucracy. It gradually pared the latter's size down to a level more appropriate to more normal times, and simplified its structure, largely by implementing the decision to revive the traditional pattern of ministries. It also refined the bureaucracy's operation through closer and more realistic methods of control. These came to recognize the role of 'interest' within the bureaucracy, and largely confirmed the latter in its more or less a-political stance.[1]

In other words, by stripping away the 'accident' and leaving the 'substance', the Directory created a refined bureaucracy which could be used by successive regimes. In so doing the regime helped it to acquire some of the Weberian characteristics which were still lacking. This does not mean that under the Directory France suffered from what has been called 'une prolifération bureaucratique' for as well as being reduced in size the bureaucracy never quite escaped from the constitutional limbo into which it fell during the Year III.[2] Nor did it succeed in obtaining any real public respect or understanding. Once the

worst of the revolutionary turmoil was over, the basic characteristics of the new bureaucracy were more consistent and
visible. Therefore, after generally examining the changes which
the passage of time and the evolution of Directorial policy
brought about, it is possible to analyse in more depth, the
structure, organization, and socio-political role of the new
bureaucracy.[3] For had the Directory, like the Thermidorians,
not been consistently willing to accept the bureaucracy, then
the whole development and character of the administration
might have been different, not merely under the Directory but
even in later years. So a consideration of the Directory and its
policies is a vital prerequisite for understanding the ministerial
bureaucracy in France.

The Directory was a regime whose roots lay in the problems
of the second half of the Year III, but at the same time, because
of the desires of both the authors of the constitutions and of the
first Directors, it was a regime which inherited many other
legacies. In administration the Directory selected and defined
those elements of Ancien Régime and revolutionary practice
which, after further developments at the hands of Napoleon,
were to be viable in the nineteenth century. This preservation of
administrative continuity was closely connected with the resuscitation of the old ministerial framework, on to which the bureaucracy was welded anew after the experiments of Germinal II.[4]
This renewed attachment, along with the greater political
stability, the consequent lessening of attempts to purge the
administration, and the more sympathetic approach adopted
by the Directory had much to do with this consolidation. So did
the Directory's pressing need to economize, which was probably
the major motive behind its remodelling of the administration,
and its more intelligent efforts at controlling it. As a result, by
1799 the bureaucracy was too well entrenched to be greatly
disturbed, although Bonaparte's reign was greatly to affect its
authority and efficiency.

It was never inevitable, of course, that this would be the case.
The revolutionary situation continued well into the Consulate,
so that the era of the Directory was very much a period of
choice. It was not a bourgeois aberration on the highroad from
democracy to dictatorship, but a vital phase in French development in which the nation might have taken a number of courses.

The period from 1795 to 9 has been much ignored or undervalued both by theorists of revolution and by historians. The former have been too ready to write it off as a banal return to normality. Yet although this is in many ways true, it does not follow that the return to normality was either easy or uninteresting.[5] The Revolution was by no means over, and the Directory was far from having the *tabula rasa* which is so often implied by criticisms of its achievements particularly in economic terms.

Historians have all too often treated the Directory as a period or a society, marked by both corruption and social regression, rather than what it really was, a political organization: no stronger and often weaker than other regimes of the time.[6] It was a political élite, entrenched in central government and controlling the constitutional structure of the nation.[7] Because of the withdrawal of middle-class support after 13 Vendémiaire, it was forced to rely on the grudging support of local government, the efforts of self-seeking and unreliable politicians, together with the army and the administration in its attempts to secure its ends.[8] Its aim was not self-aggrandizement or self-enrichment, but the preservation of what it felt to be the revolutionary settlement, that is to say the gains of 1789 inside a republican framework as desired and guaranteed by the Thermidorian political élite. This had to be done despite the unpropitious inheritance from the immediate revolutionary past: the weaknesses in the constitution, the economic and social crisis, the new social tensions, the lack of food and employment, the bitter political passions, the religious controversies, the continuing way, and the lack of public order and authority.[9]

To say that the Directory was a regime which failed because it was not a tool of the bourgeoisie and because the Revolution was still in progress, is to fly in the face of much conventional wisdom.[10] Yet the conventional wisdom is riddled with contradictions and has led to the neglect of many aspects of the Directory's activities, including the key one of administration.[11] The Directory cannot claim reforms of a startling novelty or rigorous application, but it did much to tidy up the situation left by the Revolution. This administrative and legislative effort was, as has been pointed out by Clemendot and others, rather more successful than the purely political side of the Directory's work.

This is not to say the Directory was synonymous with or dominated by the bureaucracy. The monopoly of power created by the Revolution was still breaking up and complaints like those of Necker who said in 1796 that 'l'administration est tout' and Pelet de Lozère who argued that 'il faut enfin secouer le joug de cette bureaucratie dispendieuse qui a ruiné les finances de l'état' were directed less at the Directory than at the way in which the state, having moved to a quasi-omnipotent role, failed to convince people that its new position was a somewhat uncertain one.[12] The Directory paradoxically was imbued with much the same ideas, but its heritage from the past and its general approach to matters of governance forced it to act differently. It is doubtful, however, whether the Directory at any time formally and fully considered what role the bureaucracy as a whole should play, and how it should be managed. The problems arising from the almost total lack of resources at the time of its installation, and the low level of consciousness of matters organizational make this very unlikely.

The Directory's attitude to the bureaucracy has to be deduced from its acts, and these relate to constituent elements of the bureaucracy rather than to the corps as a whole. It was also conditioned by other concerns than the purely administrative, by the desire to improve the material conditions of social life announced in its initial proclamation for instance, in which there was no specific reference to the administration.[13] The Directory's administrative strategy was also derived from the constitution, particularly since the Directors themselves and a suspicious public expected obedience to every jot and tittle of its three hundred and seventy-seven articles. This denied the government some of the latitude available to the Thermidorians, even though it retained much discretionary authority.[14] The constitution, despite its origins in the Thermidorian campaign for administrative reform, really marked no great advance on what had gone before as far as the administration was concerned. Its division of government into thought and action and its reliance on minor irritants for administrative control did little justice to the aspirations of the men of the Year III or to the needs of the administration.

Public opinion singled out the political bases of the constitution as being its weak link by the hostile votes at the referendum, but there were other technical failings.[15] In addition to the lethargic provision for revision, the lack of flexibility in law-making, and the rigid separation of executive and legislature, which denied the Directory both control of the Treasury and proper liaison with the Councils, the constitution also carried the checks and balances into the executive arm. The constitution still envisaged the administration as being mainly composed of elected *fonctionnaires* although the Secretariat and the Treasury were mentioned. So the technical disadvantages were not cancelled out by any gains in status.

However, some people did see the administrative establishments implied by the implementation of the various sections of the constitution, and J. B. Say went as far as to claim that it would re-establish 'l'ancienne bureaucratie de Versailles'. Hence, although there was a clear chain of command, an insistence that all officials must be salaried and not venal, and a provision for nomination by the Directory, the constitution was only marginally more suited to running a state in which the bureaucracy was an important element, than previous documents had been. On the other hand, in general terms the constitution was probably no less successful than some of its rivals, and the regime did last longer—and with greater stability in some ways—than other regimes in the revolutionary era.

The Directory had four kinds of powers relevant to the administration granted to it by the constitution. Firstly, came the general requirement to see to the execution of all laws, which gave it considerable regulatory powers over certain areas of the administration. Then specific tasks were entrusted to the executive by the constitution. These included the right of nomination to many posts, direction of the armies, the right of censure and intervention in local government, the appointment of ministers, and the regulation of the judiciary. Next came the pre-eminent responsibility for taking all actions necessary to maintain internal and external security. The third power was the authority it enjoyed to issue executory and regulatory *arrêtés* on laws and fields of activity for which it was responsible, which would be binding on administrative bodies. Finally, it had large discretionary powers of more or less direct action through its subaltern agents, and notably the ministers and the local *commissaires du Directoire Exécutif.*

Then again, the Directors' attitudes were affected by their view of themselves as the chief magistrates of the 'First Republic' of Europe. This was a position of some dignity, which demanded both the maintenance of a prestigious Directorial palace employing some 150 domestic staff and taking up 30 per cent of their private budget, and a policy of somewhat overheated republicanism in order to bring home the glories of the Republic to a disenchanted population. Similarly, it also grew out of the Directors' own views of the weaknesses of the constitution, and notably the need for a strong, clear-sighted, central authority which would prevent the dissipation of power, whether to other bodies or into the minutiae of day-to-day routine.[16] François de Neufchâteau drew from the past an appreciation for the logic behind the reforms of Prairial and Messidor III as well as a belief that a few well-paid and capable clerks were a great deal more use than a large number of inept and poorly paid ones. The ministers, too, had a certain number of ideas of their own which the gaps in the constitution enabled them to act upon.

Finally, one must not overlook the political concerns of the Directory which led it both to a create a Ministry of Police to control Paris and the emerging Counter-Revolution, and to insist on the patriotism of its ministers and clerks. The latter was most prominent on the left. Dubois-Crancé made it plain as Minister of War in 1799 when he said that:

Un employé doit être instruit, laborieux et ami de la chose publique. Celui qui aurait la première de ces qualités sans les autres, doît être renvoyés irrévocablement. Un zèle ardent supplie quelquefois aux talens distinguées; rien ne supplie aux virtus républicains.

Ne croyez, cependant, que je pense qu'il suffire d'être ami de la constitution pour occuper des postes difficiles; il faut encore être en état de remplir sa place. C'est le seul moyen de servir la république avec succés.

Les conditions que j'impose sont faciles à atteindre; la révolution au commencement de sa course, a rencontré des hommes qui servaient dans l'Ancien Régime, sans en avoir contracté les mauvaises habitudes. Ils étaient républicains sous la tyrannie. Ces hommes sont précieux. Le génie de la liberté a fait plus; il a créé des hommes extraordinaire; il a développé des talens que le despotisme rendait nuls. C'est sur ceux ci que vous devez particulièrement vous fixer.

Cette double classe d'hommes, une fois réunie, sans mélange, vous verrez bientôt, disparaître dans le travail, cet arrière que tue l'administration et le crédit public.[17]

It is interesting that even a left-wing minister, during a period of neo-Jacobin ascendancy, was forced to concede that the old stereotypes were self-defeating and that administrative capacity was virtually as important, if not more so, than political loyalty. Similarly, he recognized that both the old and the new orders had produced capable civil servants who were capable of combining into a new administrative élite. Again, although politics often figured in public expressions of policy, it was administrative and especially financial considerations which really produced action, both generally and in specific institutions.

Given this variety of influence and motives for the Directory's administrative strategy, it would be unwise to expect too much consistency or to assume that the Directory always liked the policies forced on it by circumstances. As a weak regime the Directors felt the need for a bureaucracy, and saw both humanity and self-interest in treating it sensibly, but no doubt they would have preferred to handle it more roughly. Again, although their predilection was for *laissez-faire*, circumstances forced them gradually to become more interventionist, as well as more humane and flexible than the Councils with whom they had to work. So although they accepted the pressing need for economy, they also saw the need to maintain useful institutions such as the Agence des Poids et Mesures, whereas the Cinq Cents felt that redundancy was an end in itself.

Government policy also came up against the fact that the bureaucracy was so big and valuable that neither its needs nor its costs could be ignored. So the Directory had to seek to reduce state administrative overheads, while at the same time maintaining efficiency through organizational rather than political reforms. Policy of course was by no means uniform or successful. It varied from department to department and when, for instance, the Directory intervened in the running of diplomacy it left the Ministry of External Relations with very little to do.[18] At the same time it failed to support Ramel in his attempts at reform, involved the clerks of the Interior in politics at Floréal, and

sowed confusion from time to time by oscillating between opposing attitudes. Notwithstanding these limitations, the fact that
the Directory had four years to develop its strategy meant that it
did have a significant impact.

The Directory was probably most concerned with the administration in the early months of its existence when the transition
between two quite different constitutional systems coincided
with the paroxysm of the social and economic crises to make the
support of the administration absolutely essential. Partly
because of this there was a broad measure of agreement between
the government and the Councils on the measures necessary to
establish the new constitutional system and to preserve the
state from bankruptcy. This lasted until the election of the
second legislature in the spring of 1797. However, although
there was agreement on the need to economize, there were
subtle differences from the start in the way the two branches of
government actually sought to implement economies. Policy
towards the administration was therefore the result of a constant
dialogue between the Councils and the Directory.

The Directory wanted to strengthen government, so that it
was simpler, more efficient, free from corruption, officiousness,
and disloyalty, and above all, cheaper. As well as being urgently
necessary to ensure that government could be carried on, such
changes also represented a positive value in themselves. It was
to be hoped that such an attitude might also serve as an example
to the rest of society. To achieve this reduction in costs, complexity, and unreliability five things were imperative. There
had to be structural reforms, better techniques of administrative
practice, centralized control of the machinery of state and its
finances, republicanization to its cadres, and again, above all,
strict economy at all levels.

The state machine was regarded as inherently expensive, and
as an area in which it was particularly easy for the government
to make cuts, whether by abolishing redundant services inherited from the revolutionary government or by refusing to set
up costly new organs. Such a policy would also make government less complicated and parasitic, by improving internal
communications and freeing people for more productive work.
It could also lead to greater efficiency amongst civil servants
who often slowed down or stopped their work in protest against

the abysmally low salaries which were all that the very size of the bureaucracy allowed the government to pay them. The staff were also thought to give themselves over to dissipation, intrigue, patronage, and especially *sollicitation* because of this situation. So they should also be encouraged to use the republican calendar and the term *citoyen* rather than *monsieur*, and to treat the people, the fountain-head of republican sovereignty, with proper respect. If they could be persuaded to do this and also work more efficiently, then they could be guaranteed an adequate salary, subject to government control, not merely of salary levels, but also of appointments and work norms.

There was little disagreement between this analysis and that of such spokesmen on administrative matters in the Councils as Thibault and Camus. They too were rigidly opposed to the continuing existence of bodies whose work had been completed. But they took this a little further than the Directory, and likewise their suspicions of those who worked in them and the salaries they were paid. Reluctantly they were willing to authorize higher salaries during the inflationary crisis of 1796, but even then they sought reductions wherever possible, and refused to accept the Directory's belief in the value of paying an adequate salary to ensure efficiency and loyalty. The Councils also wanted to control things like pensions, finance, and state buildings themselves. So they differed on the implementation of centralized controls of the administration as well as in putting abstract economy above efficency and humanity.[19]

With the increase in right-wing membership in the Councils after the elections of 1797, distrust of the executive revived, and the relative harmony gave way to harassment of the Directory and of the administration. Harmony of a kind was re-established by the *coup* of 18 Fructidor. Afterwards the Councils were largely excluded from administrative affairs for a while. The bureaucracy was also allowed more autonomy, not because of any change of heart, since its occasional interventions showed that the Directory still held to its original diagnosis, but because the changing financial and political situation made penal controls less necessary.

The events of Floréal did not change this situation, but the *coup* of 30 Prairial destroyed the Directory's dominance in the administrative field, and began an open season for legislative hunting of the executive and its agents. Financial considerations again became predominant, along with renewed political suspicion of both high functionaries and ordinary employees. The Directory had to accept irrational and self-defeating intervention in the administration, along with the reintroduction of political tests and recruitment. So the last months of the regime were not a terribly happy time for the bureaucracy. It may well have been the way that the Prairialists undid many of the earlier Directorial achievements in the management of the administration that led them to accept Brumaire with so little demur. None the less, the Directory's general approach to the bureaucracy had proved reasonably effective in its time. A closer examination of the way its policy evolved, in each of the five areas it believed important, shows something of the effects the regime had on the bureaucracy.

At the beginning of the period it had been economy which had made the most impact both on the bureaucracy and on other facets of Directorial policy. The chaos consequent upon setting up the new order prevented any positive attempt to deal with the administration until 2 Frimaire IV, when the Directory urged the largest possible reductions in ministerial staffs. At the same time the *Cinq Cents* were asked to consider the clerks left jobless by the suppression of revolutinary institutions, thereby securing a gratuity of three months' salary for those with a clean political record and no new job in sight.[20] Five days later it was decided that salaries, paid in terms of varying quantities of wheat, should be converted into cash at the rate of 60 *livres* per *quintal*, and all other salaries should be increased to thirty times their face value in 1790. Set scales of pay running from 3,000 to 12,000*livres* per month in the capital and proportionately less in the provinces were also promulgated as a further means of ensuring that the state's salary bill did not bankrupt it. The same desire for economy can be seen in the proclamation of 6 Nivôse and other acts which halted the distribution of clothes and other goods, with the exception of foodstuffs, to civil servants. Legislation also insisted on reductions in local government staffs, and tried to control ministerial expenditure by insisting on the submission of pay sheets to the Directory prior to payment.

Yet despite these measures the government still had to pay

some 86,000,000 *livres* per annum in supplemetary food allowances to officials and others. An attempt to end this practice early in Pluviôse was foiled by public outcry and the rations were re-established on 24 Pluviôse. The compensation granted to dismissed officials also proved insufficient because of inflation and the government received many complaints on the subject. The Councils' belief that the cost of providing adequate compensation outweighed the claims of the administration on the government led to the first clash between executive and legislature over the administration. The Councils went ahead and abolished all remaining revolutionary commissions and agencies as from 1 Germinal, as well as replacing the remaining instances where salaries were calculated in terms of wheat. They also pressurized the Directory over the number of buildings used by the government and over the size of their own bureaux.[21]

Before the dispute could be resolved the whole basis of government finance was changed by the introduction of the *mandat territorial*. In the administrative field this led to the replacement of free food rations by price concessions for the civil service and other specially recognized categories such as *indigents*.[22] At first the less well paid amongst the civil service were allowed to buy one *livre* of bread a day for each member of their family at a quarter of the normal rate. This concession was soon extended to virtually all officials while the lowest paid were allowed to buy their allowance at only a twelfth of the going rate.

At the same time the law of 17 Germinal and the consequent Directorial *arrêté* of 29 Germinal made all salaries payable in *mandats* according to new scales. These were based on pre-inflationary salaries and ran from 900 francs per annum for a *garçon de bureau* to 8,000 francs per annum for a *chef de division*, with an average of 3,000 francs. Initially, two-thirds was to be paid in *mandats* and the remainder in *assignats* at the official rate of thirty per *franc mandat*. The rate was soon improved, but the weakness of the new currency and the continued use of *assignats* meant that salaries were still virtually worthless. Supplements to salaries had therefore to be paid in Prairial. The Directory had also to go back to the Councils for a new solution since the net result of this second attempt at normalization of salaries seems to have been that clerks either stopped work in protest

against the evaporation of their pay, or deserted to more rewarding jobs. This threatened administrative chaos, but the Councils
were slow to act, and a further supplement had to be paid at the
end of Prairial to tide staff over.

When the Councils eventually got round to the question,
Camus was willing to pay tribute to the steadfastness in adversity
shown by the administration. Yet since he saw speculation
rather than the level of salaries as the root cause—contrary to
the Directorial stress on the salaries themselves—the Councils
were only willing to concede a further supplement of two months'
salary, and then only to those employed since before 1 Germinal.[23]
This provision had later to be waived by the Directory after the
Minister of Justice had unwittingly paid it to all his staff. The
supplement was again paid on 24 Messidor but the Councils
refused to go any further. They refused to pay officials directly
in wheat received in lieu of taxes, and a compromise project was
rejected in the Upper House when Johannot pointed out that
the resultant salaries would be lower than those actually paid.
So it was not until 18 Thermidor that the Councils finally
agreed that half of official salaries could be paid in what,
calculated on the basis of a *quintal* per ten francs of annual
salary, leaving the remaining half to be paid in *mandats* at face
value. This decision created as many problems as it solved
because of the gathering depreciation of the *mandat*. Moreover,
the long-drawn-out arguments over salaries also prevented
proper discussion of proposals to increase salaries in order to
attract better recruits and to reduce differentials between the
seven grades of pay into which the service was then divided.

Because of their greater concern for the efficiency and welfare
of the administration the Directors had consistently pushed for
legislation on an adequate salary scheme, responsive to the cost
of living. They had then to pay the resulting increases, and this
conflicted with their need to economize.[24] They tried to make
good their losses by cutting down elsewhere. For instance, they
made employees responsible for providing their own office equipment, out of a monthly allowance of three francs. They also
sought the same ends by refusing subsidized food to all but the
indigent after 15 Fructidor—a less harsh move than might
appear, given the return to coin and the good harvest that
year—by dismissing more central staff with only a month's

salary as indemnity, and by insisting on a ceiling on ministerial budgets.

However, the collapse of the *mandat* undermined all their efforts, loath though they were to admit it. Hence on 2 Nivôse V they grudgingly allowed all salaries to be paid in coin rather than in food or notes, in order to ensure that the administration's loyalty could be secured by finally guaranteeing it an adequate recompense.[25] This last argument seems to have been the one which persuaded the Councils to grant the Directory's long-standing request. Even then they coupled the concession with the abolition of all supplementary payments and the reassertion of legislative control of salaries. This meant that the latter had to be whittled down to a level one-sixth above half their former face value when they were paid in hard cash. The average permissible salary was then cut from 3,000 francs to 1,750 francs per annum, thereby removing much of the benefit which might have accrued from deflation. The range of permissible salaries being thus fixed, the increasing resources of the ministries could not be used to improve them save in exceptional circumstances.

This continuing concentration on basic financial and economic questions failed to assure the administration of an adequate standard of living, and also distracted attention from equally vital facets of administrative reform. Given the confusion into which the transition to the new constitutional order threw the government, something had to be done. A start was made in Frimaire IV when the Directory ordered the ministers to report on the state of their departments and to submit weekly reports on subsequent developments and notably on the redistribution of duties previously handled by organs of the revolutionary government which had to be wound up.[26] The aim of the Directory in this field, as expressed in its circular of 2 Nivôse, was severe economy. It sought this especially by preventing any new establishment or expense, the setting of a good example of exactitude and probity amongst the top echelons of the civil service, and the removal of all supporters of factions along with all those who were corrupt or useless. The Directory intended to check that such things were done by means of close scrutiny of the detailed statements on the organization of ministries. These were called for at this time with the intention that they would be the basis for continuing intervention in matters affecting ministerial structures.

The Directory also inherited the traditional suspicion of the behaviour and motives of its staff, as its proclamation of 5 Nivôse on administrative retrenchment and austerity shows. Its opposition to new establishments had obvious limits, as the Councils were quick to point out, although without much effect over the creation of the Ministry of Police. Yet though some deputies thought that this would make the government still more powerful and complicated, the Directory was able to steer it through the Councils, showing that what mattered to it was not new establishments *per se* but only unnecessary ones. The Directory also continued to intervene in the administrative process, partly in an attempt to stop leakages of information, even though this somewhat infringed ministerial independence.

Once the salary question was on the road to solution the Directory was able to turn more purposefully to questions of structural reform. For instance, it tried to reduce the staff of the Ministry of War by two-thirds as part of a policy of putting the military on something closer to a peacetime footing, which obviously had considerable implications for the Ministry.[27] In the light of the continuing need for economy the government also introduced a simplified system of correspondence inside the administration, hoping that this would lead to widespread redundancies. similarly, they consolidated the agencies responsible for liquidating state debts into one much reduced body, and called on the ministers to reform all their bureaux and observe the strictest budgetary control. Other things like free lodging, over-lavish provision of furniture and fittings, and the toleration of practices such as the private legal consultancy undertaken by the staff of the Ministry of Justice were all theoretically brought to an end.

At the same time, the Directory was also concerned with another of its major interests in the administration, the republicanization of its cadres so as to bring them into line with the ideas of the new regime. From the beginning the traditional fear of royalist permeation of the bureaux had been visible, and the Minister of War was ordered to weed out political malcontents early in 1796. As far as circumstances allowed, the Directory also took a close interest in civilian and military appointments.[28]

However, although Lagarde was ordered to circulate the decisions of the Commission des Dix-Sept and the ministers were told to follow its recommendations, in practice the Directory was more flexible and open-minded than its public pronouncements suggest. It allowed the ministers to use their own judgement about the Commission's findings, and reversed a number of the latter's decisions when the victims appealed to it.

As well as being more realistic than the politicians who had drawn up the report the Directory was probably more concerned by other problems of behaviour in the bureaux, notably by the question of access to administrative departments. Ideally it wanted open access for the public, but the Directory soon found it necessary to take action against those who abused the right and sought or 'solicited' favours from government employees. It was particularly alarmed by the prior or illegal communication of official decisions. Yet despite its efforts against both 'solliciteurs' and clerks, the leakages continued, probably because of the underpayment of civil servants.[29]

In theory access was restricted to specific times and places. Poor rather than rich clients were to be given preference, and all formal communications with outside parties were to be in writing. Similarly, clerks were warned against wandering off from their posts in search of saleable information from other quarters, while the growing habit of employing professional lobbyists to bring pressure on the administration was strongly attacked by the Directory. This and the question of whether people were using state employment to avoid military service seem to have concerned the First Directory most. However, it did get around to worrying again about the possible presence of extremists of both left and right in the bureaux during the winter of 1796–7, although La Revellière claims to have believed such attacks to be much exaggerated.[30]

If the very obvious repetition of Directorial prohibitions suggests that its mandates were not always very successful, it is probable that the way it kept hammering away at the same themes did eventually have some effect. This would not have been true of other shorter-lived regimes which used the same techniques. Hence by the time the new legislators took up their seats the Directory had gone some way towards consolidating the bureaucracy. This had been done by achieving a relatively

successful change-over from the revolutionary to the constitutional order, by regularizing the payment and level of salaries,
and by doing a little to eliminate some of the abuses in organizational and administrative behaviour. This was no mean achievement, given both the contradictory ideas and forces which
underlay Directorial policies, and the unpropitious background
against which the Directory had to work. It is another ground
for allowing, with the liberal historiographical tradition, that
the first phase of the Directory was not bereft of honest if
undistinguished achievement.

This was not, however, conceded at the time. The left, always
cool towards the Directory, became increasingly hostile because
of the post-Babeuvist repression.[31] Though the Directory thus
moved towards the right neither this nor the grudging concessions towards Catholicism could prevent the far right from
winning a sweeping victory in the elections of 1797 when very
few left-wing republicans and even fewer ex-*conventionnels* were
re-elected. The new *tiers* although it may not really have been
royalist in any objective sense, was certainly diametrically
opposed to the government on matters such as religion, foreign
policy, and civil liberties, while its very existence encouraged
the forces of reaction. Faced with this dual threat, and more
particularly with legislation on *émigrés* and refractory priests
which seemed to threaten the land settlement, the Directory
was forced to move back towards the left, sponsoring the Cercles
Constitutionnels and resisting the pressure for a change in the
ministerial team on 26 Messidor.

Yet if they were able to turn the tables on the Clichy group—
as the leaders of the new majority were called—by replacing
the ministers whom they found least congenial, they were unable
to make the Councils accept such projects as a central body for
the collection of direct taxes.[32] The new majority regarded the
administration, regardless of its precise condition or of Directorial policy, as simply another stick with which they could beat
the regime. Hence the new salary scales were rejected, not
because of the technical defects which were admittedly revealed
in the debate, but because they transgressed parliamentary
rights over the administration. They also went on to arrogate
control of pensions to themselves. Some deputies wanted to
restrict Directorial patronage inside the administration by

promulgating an organic law on officials and their role. They also demanded that the Directory provide detailed ministerial accounts, thereby further infringing what little autonomy the ministers had, and placing a further barrier in the way of administrative efficiency.

So while they were thus engaged in harassing the Directory and its administration, they failed to deal with the recurring problems of salaries over which they had many complaints. Yet they took no action, and the Treasury over which they had sole control, never seemed to have any money available for salaries. For this they were criticized not merely by the Directorial press but also by one of the more enlightened of their own number, Laffon-Ladébat, who was afterwards to be deported to Guyana. He observed that:

le devoir du gouvèrnement était de simplifier le travail, de réunir dans les bureaux les hommes qui y sont les plus propres, et de n'en avoir que le nombre nécessaire; mais aussi il doit leur assurer un traitement qui satisfasse à leurs besoins, qui les attache à leurs places, et les mette à l'abri de la corruption, que si ce traitement est inférieur au salaire qui peut procurer un industrie ordinaire, il n'aura bientôt plus que des hommes incapables, inassidus, dégoutés et auprès des quels pourrait réussir l'intrigue qui veille sans cesse aux portes des bureaux, pour épier le moment de corrompre; et d'ailleurs si la détresse de nos finances exige une diminuation dans les traitements leur extrême modicité ne ferait que d'accroître nos embarras, par le rélâchement général qu'il produisait dans toutes les parties de l'administration.[33]

Similarly, the majority achieved very little in terms of administrative reform. The Directory did suppress its own print shop, and considered doing away with all its secretarial bureaux. There were also some economies in the Treasury. The majority preferred to denounce the Ministry of External Relations and to repeal the law banning political suspects from public office, further undermining the government's control of the administration.

The new majority may not have deliberately organized a royalist plot but the behaviour of some of its supporters gave the impression that it was doing so. Such a political threat, allied to the constant harassment of the Directory's financial, colonial, diplomatic, and administrative powers and policies, led the uneasy majority of Barras, Reubell, and Le Reveillière to stage their *coup* in conjunction with the army on 18 Fructidor.[34] Although Bonaparte was later to criticize the triumvirate for not going far enough, this 'surprisingly effective yet bloodless way' of removing the opposition, did produce a legislature more committed to the republican ideal and led to a certain increase in government authority.

This authority was used to try and remedy the financial situation which had been allowed to deteriorate by the pre-Fructidor majority, once more with unhappy effects for salaries in the civil service. This was done by partially repudiating the national debt. At the same time the Directory broke off negotiations with England and took stern action against *émigrés*, non-juring priests, and the press. Where the administration was concerned, it reaffirmed that suspects and those who had not taken an oath of loyalty could not hold public office, but it did not press its political grievances very hard in this field. It was more concerned to give the ministers greater freedom of action, to re-establish the security of salaries, and to continue with its general campaign against abuses.

There is, however, some suggestion that there was a substantial purge of some of the ministries, running into hundreds in the case of the War Office alone.[35] It is true that in the last days of the Year V the Directory did order all its ministers to present detailed reports on the personnel of their departments as a preliminary first to revoking all those guilty of immorality, venality, and uncivic conduct—an interesting choice for the aftermath of an allegedly anti-royalist *coup*—and then to present monthly reports on all changes in staffing. This instruction was repeated before all of the reports were forthcoming, but the Directory took no action on them when they were presented. Nor did it discipline the Ministries of External Relations and the Navy which failed to provide them. All told, the evidence implies that there was no major upheaval in the ministries as a result of Fructidor.

The reports, handwritten and listing the surnames, Christian names, residences, and careers of the staff before and during the Revolution and with special attention to the 13 Vendémiaire, reveal little political activity.[36] Thus the column for 'Observations' in the Ministry of Justice's returns contains only two routine entries for nearly two hundred employees. The returns show a staff of some 1,700 between the 7 ministries.

In most cases the evidence suggests changes before rather than after the *coup*. The Ministries of Justice and War remained static after 18 Fructidor, with the latter loosing only three clerks in the first month for which a return was made to the Directory, and only one of these was actually dismissed for *incivisme*. The Ministries of External Relations, the Interior, and the Navy all seem to have grown over the next few months. The last in particular would have found it hard to change since there had been large-scale reorganizations in both Germinal and Messidor V in which many clerks were retired on organizational and economic grounds, thereby bringing about a notable diminution of the over-all strength of the Ministries. Only the Ministry of Police seems to have made a major cut in its staff at this time, being reduced from 244 to 206, while the Cabinet Historique et Topographique was severely handled because of its dependence on Carnot.[37]

There were some cases of political dismissal, such as that of Augustin Mollien, a cousin of the future minister. He was a former lawyer, then in his third year in the *Contentieux* section of the Ministry of External Relations, who was arrested because his brother was suspected of working for one of the opposition papers proscribed after the *coup*. Even though a long interrogation revealed nothing it was felt too risky to keep him in the administration. This does not prove that he was a royalist. Indeed, the heads of department in the Interior after carrying out their own investigations, emphatically insisted on the loyalty of their staff during Vendémiaire and Fructidor, pointing out that all dismissals had been for reasons of economy, so that those involved could be reinstated if an occasion presented itself.

The returns suggest a bureaucracy which was on the way to becoming non-political. Other sources show that there were other good reasons for changing the internal structure of ministries, so that where politics did have an impact after Fructidor, it was in bringing in new, politically favoured men, rather than dismissing old hands. However, such arrivals were not all that numerous. An analysis of the Ministry of Police a few months later shows that the whole of the Year VI, let alone the period immediately after the *coup*, did not produce an unusually large number of new and lasting appointments. It is difficult to avoid the conclusion that the *coup* failed to disturb a bureaucracy which was smaller, more homogeneous, more streamlined, and, above all, more experienced than before.

It may well have been a realization of this fact that made the Second Directory unwilling to do more than make a symbolic gesture towards a purge, thereby setting aside the question of the bureaucracy's political stance. Of course the new regime, still uncertain of its position despite the support of the army, may also have felt its need of the bureaucracy more keenly. It certainly went on to rule more effectively and administratively after the *coup*, as Lucas points out.[38] It opened discussion with the Ministry of War on ways of raising loans on the Paris money market so as to pay ministerial officials and alleviate 'la pénible position de plusieurs pères de familles, utiles par leur travail au gouvernement'. They were owed up to five months' salary or were paid all too often in worthless scrip.[39] Perhaps significantly, even before the reports were received, the Directory was giving less attention to the politics of the civil service and much more to what it apparently considered its real problems, which were those of efficiency and general honesty.

Thus the ministers were ordered to ensure that all *arrêtés* and communications from the Directory were dispatched to the provinces within twenty-four hours of their receipt, and to render a report on their handling of their departments every *décade*.[40] The administration as a whole was repeatedly warned about peculation and other abuses. On 25 Frimaire VI the Directory again found it necessary to urge complete confidentiality and secrecy. It followed this upon 9 Nivôse with a new regulation laying down the hours which should be worked in the bureaux, the times at which the public were to be admitted, and the importance of not communicating government business to outsiders.

This last, like admonitions to use the revolutionary calendar, was probably more honoured in the breach than the observance. Hence a new regulation had to be issued in Vendémiaire VII insisting on a seven-hour working day, statutory punishments for absenteeism, and the obligation of employees to provide their own supplies and equipment. Some attempt was made to enforce this later that year when ministers were instructed to provide the government with a new list of their employees and to open dossiers on all their staff. To judge by the present state of the personnel records of the ministries, it is doubtful if this was ever done, save perhaps in the Secretariat-General. It was not until the late 1840s that real personnel dossiers began to appear in most ministries.

Similarly, the Directory did not really capitalize on the new authority it enjoyed after Fructidor to push through any major structural changes in the administration, although in theory this was always one of its main preoccupations. Indeed, they were actually unable to persuade the post-Fructidorian legislature to accept Ramel's proposal for an eighth ministry of national estates and resources which he felt necessary to relieve the burden on the Ministry of Finance.[41] He claimed that the burden was such that he was restricted to routine paper work, and was therefore unable to scrutinize the work of his subordinates, or to plan for major initiatives or for the future in general. The Commission set up by the Cinq Cents to consider this advised that a Ministry of Public Works and Estates, which would also relieve the Interior, was preferable but the whole principle was rejected by the legislature because it was too costly and not sufficiently pressing. However, the new Directory was able to last to realize its ideas of an Agence des Contributions Directes, run by the *Commissaires du Directoire* with some clerical and other assistance, in place of collection by local authorities.[42] A little later it was also able to reorganize the Comptabilité Intermédiaire and re-establish the Lottery, but this was the limit of the structural and other initiatives which it felt necessary to try after Fructidor.

One reason for this was perhaps the renewed preoccupation of the Directory with major political problems in which the bureaucracy was only partly involved. Having disposed of the threat from the right, the Directory had been able to push through some reforms held up before Fructidor as well as attacking the Church and renewing its policy of expansion abroad. In doing this it had, particularly at local level, to rely on the left. As Woloch says, once the Directory allowed free assembly, with Sotin protecting the clubs, it found matters slipping out of its hands.[43] So it hardened its attitude towards the neo-Jacobins yet again. The Directory may indeed have been sincere in its belief that there was a long-term Jacobin threat to the Republic of the Year III, but the concept of 'le royalisme à bonnet rouge' which it dreamed up was a myth designed to play on the fears of the property-owning classes. The electoral means of exploiting such fears were worked out, under the guidance of Merlin, in the Ministry of the Interior than in the hands of Letourneux, and several of its staff were employed as *agents des barrières*, under which guise they toured the country organizing the elections of the Year VI.[44]

The electoral *coup* of 22 Floréal was also preceded by something of an administrative purge, mainly on the political side as in the Nièvre but also in the Ministries of Police and war where men like Tissot and Sijas, who had been brought in after Fructidor, were removed. The *coup* actually bore more heavily on non-legislative appointees than on deputies, with 30 per cent of the former being purged as against some 25 per cent in the Councils, notably in the Cinq Cents.[45] Moreover, both the judiciary and the Councils received an influx of government officials as a result of the *coup*. The centre thus consolidated the majority denied it by the elections of 1797. It should be noted, however, that such changes involved the political side of administration rather than career civil servants, amongst whom there seems to have been little or no movement.

The 22 Floréal shattered the democratic movement, which may have been adjusting itself to constitutional action in order to acquire the extra powers about which it had apparently been thinking. So it offended many people by the pettiness and selfishness of its motives, and gained little advantage in return. It did not enjoy markedly greater security or authority, mainly because the *coup* was somewhat botched. Not all the real opponents of the Directory were ejected while many of those recruited as 'Directorials' were in fact hostile to the government. Moreover, the conservative elements who had supported the Directory against the left now turned their backs on it, preferring to ally with other opposition elements. They thereby paved the way for a further challenge to the regime in 1799.

What with this and the new economic and military difficulties associated with the war of the Second Coalition, the Directory gave little thought to the administration after Floréal. When it did address itself to the matter, its relations with the Councils were not as amicable as had been expected.[46] Thus in Fructidor VI the latter considered withholding funds from ministers who did not render accounts, and on the 19 Fructidor the 'loi Jourdan' on conscription specifically stated that civil service employment did not exempt people from their military obligations. In Pluviôse VII a motion calling for the most minute scrutiny of all government expenditure was only narrowly defeated. For once the Councils showed themselves almost more attuned to the needs of the administration than the Directory. For the latter, having solved the salary problem to its own satisfaction at least, felt that the administration could afford to make generous contributions to the subscription for the planned invasion of England, whereas the Councils, in the person of Demoor of the Cinq Cents, canvassed the idea of a definitive settlement of the salary question in Messidor VI. He pointed out that this had been implicit in the return to payment in cash, but that it had never been put in hand.

In the event, the Cinq Cents as a whole would not agree to pay an indemnity to those who had lost their jobs in the reorganization of the national debt agencies. They preferred both to continue making threatening noises about ministerial expenditure and to join the Directory in attempting to milk the civil service. This took the form of a deduction of 5 per cent on all state salaries in Nivôse VII, imposed in an effort to provide for the rising costs of the war. The Directory and the Treasury were both doubtful about this gesture, and the former partly circumvented it by continuing to grant bonuses to ministerial staffs, thereby returning somewhat to their previous stance.

The opposition in the Councils was aware of the Directory's support of the bureaucracy, and on 25 Floréal VII Sedillez voiced their growing hostility to the executive and its policies towards what he called 'tout ce qui compose les premiers rouages de la machine politique'.[47] The opposition, and probably the country at large, was also aware of the growing crisis facing the 'grande nation' with the defeat of Italy, revolt in Belgium, and the deterioration of economic conditions and public order at home. Hence, although the Ministry of the Interior under François de Neufchâteau tried again to 'make' the elections in

1799 by using the red scare, it met with little or no response. Only a third of the official candidates were returned. Consequently, with the last of the *deux tiers* of 1795 out of the way, the opposition in the Councils was able to extract its revenge for 22 Floréal when on 30 Prairial they almost gleefully removed the remaining members of the old Directorial élite from the government. The *coup* of 30 Prairial is infinitely more significant in the history of the Directory, not to mention that of its administration, than is often realized.[48]

After the fall of the old Directory the Councils were, for the first time, bereft of a clear majority, even if previous majorities had been 'manufactured' as often as they had appeared naturally. For if the opposition was agreed on its detestation of the Old Directory, it was anything but agreed on almost everything else. The Councils were thus split between the reanimated neo-Jacobins and the more conservative 'revisionists', who were themselves divided on the extent to which the constitution needed amending, so that the initiative lay largely with Sieyès. So although the neo-Jacobins had the upper hand at first, they were never able to consolidate their position and the revisionists were able to counter-attack and to launch their own assault on the now much weakened constitutional order. Inevitably, both groups were much concerned with the administration, which came under increasing pressure during their various periods of ascendancy.

The neo-Jacobins were able, during their moments of triumph, to revive their club and papers. They also pushed through the first modern conscription act and threatened the social consensus. This came about through the forced loan, the law on hostages, and the threat to declare anew 'la patrie en danger'.[49] Not surprisingly they also turned on the administration, preparing the way for a possible impeachment of the ex-Directors along with former ministers such as Scherer, putting in hand the most intensive purge of Directorial *commissaires* to take place during the existence of the constitution of 1795, and renewing traditional left-wing reproaches about bureaucracy.

All this had a very detrimental effect on the efficiency of the administration, since much of the experience and influence which had been so painfully built up was destroyed by the *coup*. Where the employees of the administration were concerned the new deputies contented themselves at first with increasing the sliding scale of emergency deductions on state salaries. These went up from a minimum of 5 per cent on salaries of up to 3,000 francs to one of 10 per cent on salaries between 600 and 2,000 francs, with corresponding increases in higher salary ranges.

Even though salaries were amongst the least of their interests, their intervention seems to have embarrassed even the sympathetic new Directory. The latter was forced to limit the deleterious effects of the deductions on a service which, whatever was said by their allies in the Councils, was still vitally necessary. In the Councils for instance, on 18 Messidor, Levallois and Briot denounced the Directory's habit of issuing *arrêtés*, which allegedly violated legislative powers over the administration, and of ignoring legislative messages in the name of 'government prerogative'. For Levallois, 'cette mot "gouvernement" était devenu une espèce de baguette magique avec laquelle on voulait concentrer tous les pouvoirs dans un seul, et tout rapporter à une autorité que n'est que sécondaire par l'ordre constitutionnel comme par la nature des ses fonctions'.[50] New ministers like Quinette promised to avoid such usages and to keep the executive within its own bounds. However, it was found impossible to agree that any connection with private business should debar people from holding public office, or that officials should make a declaration of fortune before taking up their posts, ideas which were then being canvassed by the left.

The neo-Jacobin attack on the Directors petered out in the face of the reluctance of both their former supporters and the revisionists to take such extreme and potentially embarrassing action. So their hostility was diverted to easier targets such as Lagarde and Scherer, on the one hand, and to the need to appoint politically reliable people to the administration on the other.[51] The old Directory had given little attention to the political colouring of the civil service after Fructidor, although it had called for the submission of *états des bureaux* in Brumaire VII. With the appointment of ministers such as Dubois-Crancé, this again became a vital consideration. The possession of 'republican virtues' began to assume a new importance, although these were not apparently incompatible either with service under the Ancien Régime or even with cuts made on grounds of economy. The urgent appeals of ministers for political reports on their subordinates within forty-eight hours, ran into the blank assertion by some heads of sections that all their employees were equally devoted to the constitution. The way heads of sections preferred to devote themselves to protecting rather than persecuting their subordinates probably did much, even in the Ministry of War, to alleviate the effects of ministerial purges.

So although there was talk of large-scale purges in the War Office and elsewhere, it is once more probable that the number who actually lost their jobs for political reasons was fairly small, save perhaps in the Ministries of Police and War. More changes were made for non-political reasons. None the less, a number of very well-known political names were appointed to the bureaux. They included Baudot, Chodieu, Rouz-Fazillac, Francastel, La Chevardière, Saint-Aubin, Tissot, and the ex-*cordelier* Marchand who were recruited by Bernadotte or Fouché to the Ministries of War and of Police.

The Councils also continued their attacks on the working of the administration, attacking the unsatisfactory way in which the ministries carried out their tasks, and criticizing both the use of advisory commissions and the general proliferation of bureaux and employees.[52] In particular, they denounced the establishments of secretariats-general and forced the Ministry of External Relations to abandon its own. It was Letourneux, an ex-minister, who then sat with the opposition, who went even further and launched the idea of very large-scale cuts in staffing so as to help the Treasury out of its difficulties. This idea was very popular because of the continuing belief that there was widespread pluralism, nepotism, and overstaffing throughout the administration. However, there was no major restructuring at this time, although ironically the intervention of the left seems to have been responsible for a major increase in the level of staffing within the ministries. The major effect of the neo-Jacobin *poussée* was to undermine the economic position of the civil service once more by diverting funds notably to the war effort. The decline of the position of the left in the face of the revisionist counter-offensive, and notably the defeat of the motion to declare the country 'in danger', the closure of the Manège, and, most important for the administration, the dismissal of Bernadotte and the subsequent departure of many of his appointees, made more far-reaching changes impossible.

Moreover, the ruthless pruning of the ministries by the revisionists in the anxious autumn of 1799 undid many of the changes made by the left. The continuing popular appeal of Bernadotte and other leaders of the left and the uneasy manœuvres amongst the generals and the revisionists made it impossible for the latter to do anything more constructive in their turn. None the less, the neo-Jacobin *poussée* as a whole, had gone far to shake the foundations of the constitutional regime of 1795, so painfully set up and nursed towards maturity by the pre-Prairial Directories. The methods of nursing may have been a bit crude and the health of the patient still somewhat suspect, but it was nevertheless living and functioning normally. Whereas after the events of Prairial VII the patient acquired a mortal illness, and the remedy which the Consulate was to offer was a very drastic one as far as constitutionalism and the administration were concerned.[53]

If the government was still in chaos in 1799–1800 and if many of the Directory's aims remained unfulfilled, as Boulay de la Meurthe amongst many others was to claim, then the conflicts of Sieyès and his associates with the neo-Jacobins were largely to blame. In any case, the Consulate was not to bring any immediate remedy. It was eighteen months before many employees received their arrears of pay. So there was no immediate chance of any general civil service reform act, given the uncertainties created both by the *coup* itself and by the establishment of new institutions.

How far then had the development of the Revolution and the policies of the Directory brought the new bureaucracy by 1799? Even by 1797 things had gone some way towards consolidation as far as salaries, size, abuses, and politicization were concerned. This was to continue even into 1799. So despite the very difficult problems of installation, which affected the ministries more than most since they had to build new foundations on the basis of very variegated legacies from the revolutionary government, the positive achievements usually ascribed to the Directory belong almost exclusively to the pre-Prairial governments. This is not to say that they were totally successful in their efforts. They could not make all their initiatives work, as, for instance, the monthly lists of personnel changes or, more importantly, the attack on *sollicitation*. Nor could they shake themselves free from all their old preconceptions about the superiority of 'little government'. Similarly, they could not resolve the financial problems which dogged both the state in general and the administration in particular, with very detrimental effects on the activity of the latter in consequence.[54]

Yet through the concentration on the somewhat banal realities which stand out in discussion of its policies, rather in contrast to the more grandiose concerns of their predecessors, the Directory, despite its own initial caution and the rigid and often doctrinaire attitudes of the Councils, found the bureaucracy to be less unsavoury and more necessary than was allowed by the conventional wisdom. Hence, it kept it going until its fall on 30 Prairial, more or less unchanged in its basic characteristics, and more or less undamaged, and sometimes even improved by government intervention. It also came to terms with the fact that to a very large extent the bureaucracy was above party politics, and preserved it from the worst of the political upheavals of the time. So the bureaucracy itself was able to resist the troubles of 1799. Similarly, it led the bureaucracy, as will be seen, towards a more centralized structure, while at the same time improving its working efficiency, and resolving a few of the problems of the economic and social status of government personnel.

As far as the structure of government was concerned the Directory attempted to bring the revived ministerial structure more into line with the needs of a post-revolutionary society in which the main task was social and economic reconstruction. It failed to establish ministries for economic or educational affairs, ministries which would have facilitated the solution of such problems both then and in the early nineteenth century, as well as making for a more rational division of responsibilities amongst the ministries. Yet there were certain advantages in their failure.[55] Had radically new departments been carved out of the six re-established ministries—neither the Secretariat-General nor the Ministry of Police really coming into this category—this would have meant yet further upheaval for them to cope with. This might have resulted in a lessening of emphasis on their executory role. It may therefore have been that the failure to establish more new departments was a stabilizing factor for the ministries, making it easier for them to play an active part in the

Directory's reform programme as well as preparing them to reassert their old influence. In some cases also the ministries were enabled to develop the stability that was to be needed in the time of later revolutionary upheavals. Similarly, the introduction of new local and field services was not without success, and there was something of a revival in fields such as the Ponts et Chaussées and maritime administration.[56]

The relative lack of structural change also made possible a considerable decrease in the numbers of staff employed in the ministerial bureaucracy. The decrease may not have been large enough for the Councils. Given the fact that the opposition in 1799 at first actually increased the size of the bureaucracy, whereas the Directory had not merely to provide for the reformist activities of 1797–9 but also to cope with the pressures of the new pool of would-be employees created by the winding-up of revolutionary and Thermidorian institutions, it was a considerable achievement. The Directory inherited upwards of 4,000 men, partly in the slimmed-down executive commissions and partly from other revolutionary agencies which were often tacked on to the ministries in the early days. In late 1796 the ministerial bureaux proper made up only 42 per cent of the staff classed as ministerial.[57] These inflated figures were reduced in three stages. In nearly every ministry the first months of the regime saw very large numbers of men being laid off, notably in the Ministry of War where 800 went in the first eighteen months of the Directory's existence. Thereafter a further slimming-down took place in 1797, partly in the spring, and partly in the summer as a result of the introduction of new ministers just before the *coup*.

So the numbers involved fell, from a little over 3,000 late in the Year IV to 2,000 midway through the Year V and again to 1,750 early in the Year VI. From then on the pressures of the *coups* of 18 Fructidor and 30 Prairial, reform, and war combined to increase the numbers employed to about 2,600 by the late summer of the Year VII. This was cut back by something under a 1,000 in the next two months, something like 160 coming from the War Office alone. This was the one positive contribution of the post-Prairial regime. Perhaps the reduction may have gone a little too far, though not in the Ministry of Police as Figure II shows. Probably, since there was not a great deal of change up

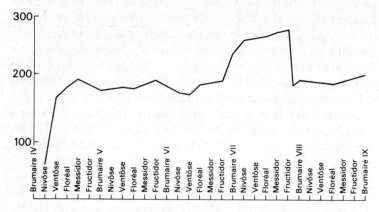

II   The Expansion of the Ministry of Police, 1796–1800

to the 1870s, the levels of 1799 as well as being a great deal lower than those at the outset, were in line both with the aims of the Directory and with the needs of the early nineteenth century. At the same time the Directory also presided over a reduction in the numbers employed in other central agencies like the Treasury, in field services like the Customs, and, after a great deal of pressure, in local government.[58]

The way in which the Directory and its ministers reduced the size of the central civil service testifies to the extent of the control over the administration which the regime enjoyed. This was another contrast with earlier periods as well as a major source of organizational consolidation. The clearer chain of command provided by the constitution, the co-ordination provided by the Secretariat-General, and the informal influence over bodies such as the Treasury served to keep lines of communication open, so that pressure could be brought to bear. The ministries themselves served as mechanisms of control for the network of dependent administrations which had detailed oversight of the field of operations entrusted to the ministries.[59]

In addition, the Directory also had at its disposition a negative form of administrative law, which at least gave the government some theoretical support for its control of the administration, even if very little stress was then placed on the principles involved in its control of *le contentieux administratif*.[60] The Directory was less concerned with the 'strategic' responsiveness of administration to government, which had preoccupied the Thermidorians with their fear of wholesale ideological incompatibility between the two, and much interested in its 'tactical' responsiveness. The Directory could, or did, assume that it would not be betrayed to Louis XVIII by the bureaucracy, whereas it could not be certain that the bureaucracy could live up to the government's standards of honesty, efficiency, and reliability. Most of its efforts were directed towards the latter.

These banal but nevertheless important ends stand out in Directorial policy towards the bureaucracy. For the first time in the revolution there was a sensible ideal of 'good governance', the precursor of the moderate use of authority which Legendre sees as one of the main safeguards against excessive administrative power in France.[61] Whereas the first generation of revolutionaries had demolished the old order, the Jacobins had oscillated between overstrengthening the bureaucracy and wishing it not there, and the Thermidorians had been naïvely inexpert, inconsistent, and ineffective, the Directory was more able to come to terms with administrative realities. To do so went initially rather against the grain, but it learnt the hard way that a common-sense and practical approach was the best way to control the civil service. It ceased to believe that there were easy answers and faced up to the need to accept that the service had legitimate interests which had to be met if the potential of the administration was to be realized.

It was able to do this in part because the time at which it was operating was slightly less frenetic than under the Thermidorians, and there was therefore less temptation to rely on penal pronouncements, investigations, and disciplinary measures for controlling the administration.[62] Through the powers given to it by the constitution it was able to exercise its control through administrative *arrêtés* on specifice subjects, just as through its role as titular head of the administration it was able to insist on the adoption of regular and proper procedures. Both approaches could be co-ordinated, as will be seen, by the Secretariat-General, so that it had some chance of monitoring both the needs and the output of the civil service. Obviously this policy of administrative management on the basis of 'softly, softly, catchee monkee' is very appealing to the English love of gradualism and empiricism. It has to be admitted that neither the mechanisms nor the effects were wholly successful. None the less they did exist and they did work up to a point.

Another reason why the Directory was able to understand the administration better than its predecessors was that it was a much less ideologically orientated regime.[63] It was therefore less drawn to sweeping and punitive procedures to ensure the acceptance of a particular political line, and more concerned with providing a uniform hierarchy in which everyone knew his place and prospects and within which the new men of the Revolution could be integrated with those who had worked in the Administrations Centrales under the monarchy. Uniformity was also forced on the bureaucracy by subjection to the revised ministerial framework, and, even more emphatically, by exposure to the same economic stresses. It was the latter which probably led to the largest number of changes inside the administration.[64]

For though there were many complaints of, and indeed some cases of, political dismissals, the majority of those dismissed from the service were the victims of a readjustment to a consti-tutional and inflationary situation. It is sheer nonsense to attribute the consolidation of the bureaucracy to reactionary political aspirations as did Deville, when he argued that:

Le formalisme administratif, qu'il ne faut pas confondre avec la correction—on en eut la preuve dès la debut—et la puissance des bureaux commencèrent à se déveloper dans cette période; ce fut l'œuvre, en grade partie, des réactionnaires à qui on les livra et qui s'y fortifièrent. On y entra grâce au favouritisme, on y resta grâce à la servilité envers les chefs directs.

The independence which the bureaucracy gained was the result, not of ideology or of any desire to thwart the government, but of what Pleville-le-Peley in the Admiralty called 'l'espèce de confraternité, which reigned in the bureaux.[65] An *esprit de corps* in other words, which was the product of training, shared experiences and general acceptance of the revolutionary state, if not of the rule of particular factions. Recognition of this led the Directory for example to drop its concern for open access to the bureaux in favour of a stress on confidentiality, more in tone with the way executive privilege had replaced democratic fears. Despite many critics then, the bureaucracy was neither hopelessly corrupt, nor politically autonomous.[66] It was in co-operation with the executive and not in conflict with government that it had become established in France under the Directory.

The dynamic behind this transformation seems to lie largely in the skilful use made by the Directory of the advantages which its position in the revolutionary process and circumstances in general conferred upon it. It used all the avenues open to it within the constitution, and some which were not, to follow up the logic of the faltering reforms begun in the Thermidorian phase of normalization. It was also able to extract positive advantage from the unpropitious financial and institutional circumstances in which it found itself, for example the weakness of the *fonctionnaire* element in government.

If the growth of the bureaucracy was due to external factors, its continuity and character were the product of Directorial policy, and to a much lesser extent, its own internal dynamic, making a nice blend of nature and nurture. The Napoleonic bureaucracy was, as Brinton has said, in place before Brumaire, and the Directory's role was much greater than has often been allowed.[67] It functioned, however, as a multiplicator and refiner rather than as a creator. The Directory added to the new bureaucracy, which was already fairly formal, a new dimension of hierarchy and specialization, new ideas and rules of operation, and, above all, a career pattern leading to pensions, consistency, and permanence. If its size had been reduced it was still substantial and its power was growing. It was therefore closer to the Weberian pattern in 1799 than it had been in 1794–5, even though it still was not identical with the ideal type.

If the Directory had such success with the bureaucracy, one is tempted to ask why it was not more successful overall.[68] The Directory's administrative work has always been reckoned more efficacious than its politics. It was able to solve a number of minor problems but could not get to grips with some major ones. It also added to its difficulties by its own fears and prejudices notably where religion was concerned. This alienated the broad masses of the population for whom administrative techniques had no appeal. Hence what was really at question was power and authority. Once the inspiration behind the constitution of 1795 was destroyed by the decrees of the two-thirds the new regime never had an adequate social basis on which to rely. It could therefore devise but rarely implement with anything like the same conviction.[69] Because of this it had to resort in politics to what has been called a policy of 'timid audacity' which intensified its malaise by further alienating opinion without any compensating increase in authority. It managed to get the worst of both worlds in its treatment of the almost sacrosanct constitution. Many things, and particularly the all important local and international spheres, were therefore unresponsive to the regime's control.[70] The administration, because of its lack of constitutional and public regard and because of the Directory's own need for an appreciation of it, was much easier to manage than the nation at large.

So far the discussion of both the nature of this management, and indeed of the character of the new bureaucracy, has been rather general. A closer examination of the structures, personnel, and socio-political situation of the bureaucracy in the late nineties will show more of the nature of the bureaucracy as it moved towards consolidation under the cautious and painstaking tutelage of the Directory.

CHAPTER V: THE STRUCTURE AND FUNCTIONING OF GOVERNMENT UNDER THE DIRECTORY

Amazingly little is known of the wider framework of government within which the ministries worked. The Directory itself was certainly not consonant with all the kinds and conditions of men and institutions who then represented public authority and activity. Even today very little is known about exactly who served the eighteenth- and nineteenth-century state or how they went about it.[1] Much has been written on the constitutional structures of government and on the *grands corps* but the functioning of many other central organs and virtually all the field services still remains largely unexplored. So although the general framework of government is an important consideration both for the organization of the bureaucracy as a whole, and particularly for an understanding of the role of the ministries, it is impossible to do more than provide a brief introductory survey of the main lines of government structures, together with some indication of how a representative group of central organs, and notably the Directory's own Secrétariat Général, were organized and worked.

Organizational structures are perforce rather dull things, and often do little to explain exactly how government does work.[2] Unfortunately, the historian is bereft of the kind of information which would enable him to bring the informal organization of government to life. None the less, the attempt to etch out the broad outlines of government activity is worth making, for without it discussion of government policy and civil service reactions to it is harder to appreciate. Moreover, discussion of internal ministerial structures shows how the Directory helped some ministries to achieve stability in terms of internal organization, not merely then but, with the exception of the Ministry of the Interior, for much of the nineteenth century.[3]

Internal structures have to be considered, however, in terms of their relationship to the values of their inhabitants, to other administrations, and, above all, to the external environment. Structures and functions are held to be a reflection of an administration's external situation.[4] Hence it should not be assumed that a discussion of structures and functions by themselves fully explains how a bureaucracy works.

Two other methodological problems are those of timing and definition. The picture that is given here is a composite one, representative of the Directorial period as a whole, rather than of any one particular moment. The sources do not permit such specific descriptions, and in any case, to do so would be to miss the element of change. Change was produced by circumstances, by Directorial policy, and, to a lesser extent, by internal forces. Administrations have a habit of indulging in frequent changes in their internal structure without really altering the way it works.[5] The picture is also one of the machinery of the executive arm of the state as a whole, and not of the whole political system of which the state, as a nexus of formal institutions, was a part, even though the term 'Government' is often used to describe the latter as well. And it obviously deals only with formal organizations, there being no real means of finding out much about informal organization.[6]

Obviously the nature and operation of the machinery of state was much affected by the political system. The constitution with its complicated checks and balances assumed a more peaceful and harmonious situation than was actually the case. The continuance of war, the pressure of social and economic deprivation, and the perseverance of political animosities of all kinds meant that the kind of support of, and participation in, government which had been posited by the constitution was not forthcoming. The regime had therefore to seek new supports and methods. The administration was there and was able both to buttress the regime and to provide it with ways of assuring a measure of obedience that other channels could or would not.

From an analytical standpoint there were seven areas of the state machine which the Directory could utilize to sustain and execute its policies. The first element was the Directory itself, its Secretariat, and attached political agencies like the Councils, which enjoyed direct jurisdiction over such bodies as the

Treasury and perhaps even the Directory's *commissaires*. It was through the Directory and the Councils that basic policy was evolved and through the former and its *commissaires* that some check was kept both on the implementation of policy and on the provision of necessary resources. This could not be done by the Directors themselves, and so they came to depend on the services provided by their Secrétariat Général. At first this was a duplicate government modelled on the Comité de Salut Public but later, as will be seen, it came to play a more restricted but equally significant part as the goad and co-ordinator of government. However, even with this, and other such bodies as the Cabinet Historique et Topographique Militaire, the Directory could not hope to see the implementation of its policy throughout the country.

There was thus a large role of overseeing the implementation of policy and in some cases of actually executing decisions for the second element of the state machine, the ministries. They used their central role much more positively than is sometimes realized for co-ordination, control, information, and even the evolution of policy. In addition, they very often used the third element of government, the many agencies which were attached to them for the performance of basic and executory tasks. Obviously, the Administrations Centrales were absolutely essential to the proper functioning of the machine and need to be examined in depth, but the range of dependent bodies attached to them was quite extensive and has very rarely been studied or even appreciated.

Three Ministries, those for the Navy, the Police, and for External Relations had few substantial agencies in their charge, but the Ministry of Justice was closely linked with the Imprimerie Nationale and the Agence des Lois which were responsible for the printing and the dispatch of the flood of laws, decrees, and other administrative acts which gave impulsion to the whole state machine. Moreover, the other three Ministries had a large number and variety of dependent administrations. The Interior controlled literally dozens in Paris alone in 1796 with a total staff of at least 2,000.[7] These included various national manufactures, architectural and building services, schools, and agencies for winding up the affairs of now defunct revolutionary bodies. The Ministry of Finance was also well provided with such liquidation agencies, especially where food supplies were concerned. In addition it also maintained a variety of state warehouses and looked after state property in the capital, tasks involving at least 1,630 employees in late 1796. The Ministry of War has some 950 dependent employees engaged in servicing specialist committees and schools and in maintaining the logistical supplies and services which the army needed.

In addition to all these dependent central agencies there was a fourth element in the Parisian areas of state administration. These were the other central organs, largely financial. One example as the 1,250 strong Treasury, the Mint, and the various *commissions de comptabilité*. For political reasons these were outside the executive arm proper, although performing vital administrative tasks.

Outside Paris, the business of the state was carried on by three further groups of people. These were, firstly, the elected representatives and officials in the departments, cantons, and communes, together with their dependent clerical services. Secondly, came the field services, that is the employees of technical corps, usually under the ultimate authority of a ministry, but providing services throughout the country on lines laid down by their own partly autonomous headquarters. Finally, there were those services provided simply by the paid or nominated servants of local government authorities. It is the first of these which has attracted most attention from historians. Of course in addition to the activities of elective *fonctionnaires*, the departmental administrations and others did maintain a body of clerks who applied and monitored central and local policy in many fields, as well as exercising a certain *tutelle* over those authorities subordinate to them, and over the services which they themselves provided.

Large towns were often administered as cantons in their own right and, especially in the case of large centres like Lyon where a *bureau central* was necessary to co-ordinate the activities of the several cantons into which they were divided, and could be the seat of a fairly complex set of services. For the most part, however, local government, especially at the lowest level of the commune, was mainly in the hands of elected *fonctionnaires* who had little clerical help and offered even less in the way of directly undertaken services. A small and somewhat sparsely populated department like the Haute-Marne had in 1799 a central clerical staff of 33, with about 65 secretaries shared between the seventy or so cantons, along with a dozen or so messengers and as many *concierges*.[8] Its local services extended to the maintenance of about 100 schoolteachers, 400 *gardes champêtres* and *forestières* and the 140 *Juges de Paix* and their *greffiers*. It was with such locally maintained personnel, along with those of nationalized field services such as the *gendarmerie* and all the tax collection agencies, that the local population would have had most to do. Yet very little is known about them. In larger centres there would have been more service employees of this type looking after such prisons, hospitals, and other establishments as there then were. More of them would have been full-time appointments.

The majority of public services, however, were directed from the centre and formed part of national corps, ultimately attached to the ministries, though usually working closely with other parts of local government, from whom it is often hard to separate them in practice. All the ministries were responsible for some such services. The Ministry of External Relations controlled the consular and diplomatic corps outside France, the Ministry of the Navy looked after the dockyards and associated logistical installations and their personnel in the ports and elsewhere, while the Ministry of Justice serviced the courts and the Ministry of Police the rudimentary urban police personnel. The bulk of the field services like the *gendarmerie nationale*, which though it worked for local authorities and sometimes for the Ministry of Police, was the responsibility of the Ministry of War, were subject to the various ministries.[9] The Ministry of War was also responsible for its very complex transport and food supplies services, half provided by Régies by 1799 and half provided by private contractors. In addition, the Ministry also had its own system of administrative regions, its own corps of *Commissaires des Guerres* for overseeing the pay and supplies of military units, and a number of medical and other inspection services.

The Ministry of Finance had its own network of *percepteurs, receveurs,* and *payeurs,* for raising and processing government revenues, a task in which they were aided after 1798 by the Agence des Contributions Directes. In the Haute-Marne the latter counted some 26 employees in the last year of the Directory's existence and also supervised a large number of important

Régies. These included the postal services, the Régie Nationale de l'Enregistrement et des Domaines, which administered national properties and various dues partly connected with land-ownership, the Régie des Douanes, and the Régie des Poudres et Saltpetres, along with the lottery, the mortgage service, and the forest administration. The Interior had fewer *régies* but more technical services such as the Cadastre, the Inspections des Bâtiments, and de Santé, the Administration des Mines, the supervision of canals, prisons, and hospitals, and, above all, the Ponts et Chaussés and all the services still used to ensure the national food supply.

Taken altogether, these seven areas formed for the times an immense and extraordinarily complicated web of services and institutions. On the macro-level they were mainly structured on the functional principle.[10] That is they were divided into separate agencies according to the services they were to provide rather than on the client principle by which divisions depend on the nature of the recipients of the services. Only perhaps in the area of local services was this not wholly true. These various functional services also employed staff estimated at the time as at least 50,000 and possibly involving anything between 130,000 and 250,000.[11] No government could have been expected to utilize or control such a structure unaided, so in beginning a more detailed discussion of the seven areas, it is important in looking at the Directory and those bodies associated with it to pay particular attention to the former's Secretariat since this played a very vital role. The Secrétariat Général du Directoire Exécutif was primarily responsible for co-ordinating the activities of the ministries and other Parisian elements of the state machine. Through its liaisons with departmental administrations it was also not wholly without influence on the other services of the state. In liaison with the ministries then, whose role has too often been undervalued at this time, the Secretariat helped to hold together the interdependent and interlinked elements of government and monitored something of their output. Moreover, a close examination of the former provides an interesting contrast with the ministries, as well as offering a little-known exemplar of how government worked and developed under the Directory.

The Secrétariat Général was an anticipation both of the

Napoleonic *Secrétairie d'État* and of the later Secrétariat Général du Gouvernement first set up in 1917 and much expanded by the Fifth Republic. It was also the development of an idea first launched by the Polysynodie and later applied more emphatically by the reformed Conseil d'État of 1791 and its successors.[12] The reformed Conseil d'État was required to have a secretary to take its minutes, but in the event the holders of the post began to play a much larger role, to judge from contemporary complaints. This was especially the case after 10 August when the holder was elected from amongst the least successful candidates for the ministerial posts of the Conseil Exécutif Provisoire as it was then called. The post was written into the proposed Girondin constitution and, as has been seen, it received an implicit boost from the emergence of Saint-Cyr Nugues as the *Directeur Général des bureaux* of the Comité de Salut Public. It was obviously under the latter that the infrastructure of the new institution developed. By the end of its life the staff of the committee were divided into 8 divisions, one of which was a secretariat some 33 strong and divided into 3 bureaux: the Secretariat proper under Aubusson and Pierre, the two senior career officials, the Dispatches section, and a Library-cum-Dépôt des Archives. This and the way in which the other divisions of the committee's organization paralleled the organization of government in general was to be a precedent from which the Directorial Secretariat was to find it rather hard to escape.

The constitution of 1795 called for a Secretary-General, chosen from outside the Directors, to countersign their acts and to keep their minutes.[13] From the beginning, however, the Secretary-General had to do more than this, and therefore became a figure of some more general importance. As a result his bureaux, which were inevitably moulded on those of the Comité de Salut Public, developed to accommodate this enlarged role. The post of Secretary-General was first entrusted to La Revellière's protégé, Trouvé, the editor of the *Moniteur*, but he was forced to resign when Carnot joined the Directory. He was replaced by Joseph-Jean Lagarde, allegedly a former Secretary of the Department of the Nord, who was probably pushed by Carnot. None the less, he soon became a fixture, an 'eternel' according to the hostile Barras. Through his ability and by his skill in avoiding compromising himself by too close links with any individual or group, he laid the foundations both for the *Secrétaire d'État* and for the reputation of being one of the best cabinet secretaries in recent times, although both of these claims have not passed uncontested.[14]

Lagarde found the kind of Secretariat bequeathed to him by his predecessor and employers far too cumbrous and costly, as Figure III suggests. He set about making it more effective and more economical, although this was to take a long time. Not till Pluviôse VI was he really satisfied with its organization. On his appointment he found a staff of 87, two-thirds of which had come from Salut Public, and including both clients of Barras and people whose dismissal had been recommended by the Commission des Dix-Sept. They were organized into 10 bureaux and wee overwhelmed by the joint tasks of transferring all the old committees' papers to the Luxembourg and of providing all the information and resources which Lagarde felt he needed.[15] To cope with these problems of installation a further 50 employees had to be engaged, although many of these were to prove transitory.

Not until Nivôse was Lagarde able to turn from problems of installation to other matters, and at first he had to work through his heads of section who enjoyed a certain autonomy since they had been in place before him. Only by an *arrêté* of 22 Floréal IV was Lagarde's complete control over the appointment and the dismissal of staff recognized. This enabled him to check both their political credentials, and in some cases, their statutory right to be in the bureaux at all. He held the size of his staff down to 130, while at the same time increasing the proportion in the Secretariat proper rather than in the 9 specialist bureaux which were the main legacy from Salut Public: Internal and Police Affairs, Judicial Affairs, Finance, Navy, External Relations, Press Analysis, War, Artillery, and the Cabinet.

In Frimaire V further changes were made owing to the continuing need for economy and also to Lagarde's own feelings that the persistence of a large staff to scrutinize the work of the executive led to triplication in which the Secretariat proper, the specialist bureaux, and the ministries all processed the same papers, thereby helping to reduce the latter to 'des chefs d'administration at non des ministres tels qu'on les conçoit'.[16] Lagarde wanted the Secrétariat Général to remain within its

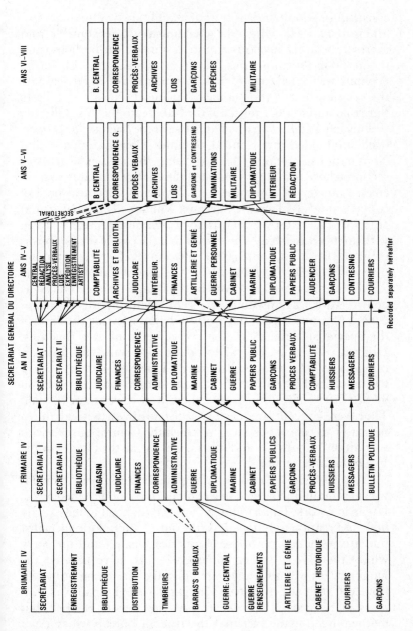

III   The Structures of the Directorial Secretariat-General

constitutionally defined role and, in addition deal with nominations to offices for which the government was responsible, and
thereafter confine itself to acting as a simple clearing-house and
monitor for the ministries. However, it was quite obviously
economy which led then to make dismissals, and in Nivôse V to
the winding-up of the Judicial, Financial, Naval, and Press
bureaux, and to the transfer of the Cabinet to the War Office.

This left a staff of 80 divided between the Secretariat proper,
itself subdivided into Central, Minutes, Correspondence, and
Nominations bureaux (the last being the erstwhile artillery
section whose head had suggested the change probably so as to
ensure himself of continuing employment), a central pool of
copyists, and 3 specialist bureaux: Military, Diplomatic, and
Interior. The latter was in turn to disappear in Floréal V. Even
with an increase in pay, this meant that the cost of the establishment was reduced from 360,000 *francs* to 186,000 *francs*, though
this was still 36,000 *francs* above the amount allowed by the
legislature. Lagarde, however, having shaped the secrétariat as
he wanted it was unwilling to accept any further dismissals or
cuts in pay, and solved the problem by transferring the costs of
the specialist bureaux to the respective ministries' budgets.
Later in the year, for partly political reasons, the Military
bureau was halved and in Brumaire VI the Nominations bureau
was abolished as redundant, as was the Diplomatic bureau a
month later.[17] By Pluviôse VI there were fewer than 70 staff.
They were concentrated, as Lagarde had always wished, into a
basically secretarial service, in which the Central bureau with
its staff of 23, copyists and others, was by far the biggest of the
five remaining sections.

From then till the end of the regime the Secrétariat Général
was to remain unchanged in essentials, proof of the efficiency of
Lagarde's work. Unfortunately, it is very difficult to tell exactly
how his creation functioned. At the outset some of the specialist
bureaux—though not those of Finance, Justice, and the Navy
where there were strong ministers—must have advised the
Directory, as well as analysing, filing, and discussing proposals
from the relevant ministry. The Diplomatic bureau was thus
fairly active, possibly because of its closeness to Reubell, but
neither this nor the fact that the Interior bureau which dealt
simply with police and administrative matters and was staffed

by Barras's clients enabled the bureau to resist Lagarde. Military affairs on the other hand were so important that three bureaux were originally felt necessary, and one of them, the Bureau Militaire was the only specialist bureau to preserve even a vestigial existence throughout the regime.[18]

Originally the military services of the Directory resembled those of Salut Public, but Carnot consolidated them into one section which dealt with everything except artillery and strategy. Having all the information accumulated by their predecessors they were able to advise reliably on the loyalties and the capabilities of the army and no decisions on promotions or legislation were taken without their being consulted. They were therefore able to survive the fall of Carnot, unlike the strategy centre, the Cabinet, which was transferred, or the Artillery bureau which, despite Chabeuf's ingenuity in finding new work for it, was finally made redundant because the ministries were increasingly making their own suggestions for official appointments. By Nivôse VII indeed, the strength of the military section had been run down so far that it was necessary to appoint Milet-Mureau and other senior officers to act as an advisory committee on military matters. In this context one should perhaps also note the Bureau de l'Examen des Papiers which was a specialized bureau even if it was officially part of the secretarial division.[19] This employed journalists and others to place articles, analyse the press, and aid Lagarde in his own public relations duties.

A good deal of Lagarde's time was, however, occupied with more clerical and supervisory tasks. These were executed by the Secretariat proper and notably by the Bureau Central, where minutes and Directorial acts were processed, and the Enregistrement et Analyse section where all incoming correspondence was scrutinized, assessed, and filed, along with the papers of earlier regimes. The Archives bureau thus played an important part in the institutionalization of continuity and consistency across the revolutionary era. The secretarial division also had its own warehouses for supplies, a post room, messengers, and one or two other specialized personnel. Lagarde spent even more time of course on the more creative side of his role, dealing with petitions and complaints about administrative abuses which always came to him, transmitting information and instructions to the ministers, and ensuring that the latter responded quickly and in the proper forms. The department thus gave some kind of impulsion to government as well as co-ordinating and controlling its output.

It was this role which explains why the Councils and the Directory made such use of Lagarde's services. It also explains why one recent authority has said that the Imperial Secrétairie 'était la continuation directe du service que Lagarde, Secrétaire du Directoire, avait constitué et parfaitement organisé, et que les consuls, aprés le coup d'état du dix-huit brumaire, gardèrent et utilisèrent dans les mêmes conditions. Les employés euxmêmes furent peu affectés par les événements politiques, et la plupart restèrent en fonctions sous le nouveau gouvernement'.[20] In other words the Directory's progress towards bureaucratization was visible within its own private domain, achieving 'perfection' according to Fain, even if it was the result of a rather personal effort.

None of the ministers whose departments make up the next section of the state to be investigated here enjoyed anything like the same length of tenure as Lagarde. Yet the normal assumption that they were merely the Directory's clerks devoid of any powers of their own is not borne out by the facts.[21] It was their activity and efficiency after all which enabled Lagarde to drop his own specialized bureau in the way he did. In the circumstances this represents quite an achievement for the ministries, given the problems of renewing their links with the traditions of the past inherent in the resuscitation of the old ministerial framework. The role of the Directory here was important, but less so than the nature of the tasks handled by the ministries. Sensitive areas like War, Police, and the Interior were too important for the government to resist over-intervention, while the changing nature of the tasks they handled, such as the extension of territory to be policed in 1798, also made for instability. As a result the Directory did not always get the simplicity and smallness it desired. Able ministers were denied the formal freedom of action which might have boosted efficiency and long-term stability such as was found in the other department. Informally they were freer and more active than is often supposed, as a brief examination of their internal structures shows.

The Ministry of War for instance had already gone through a long series of upheavals internally and these were to be continued under the Directory, although they are hardly worth detailing here.[22] None the less, the pictorial representation indicated in Figure IV gives a general idea of ministerial structures and the changes through which they then went. Its duties were basically the raising and maintaining of the armies of the Republic and their ancillary services, which involved a vast range of tasks basically connected with equipment, transport, personnel, welfare, artillery, funds, and general administration. In addition there was the Bureau du Mouvement and the partly autonomous Cabinet Historique et Topographique which were responsible for such strategic planning as could be mustered.[23] The whole organization of staff work both then and later was disorganized and amateurish in comparison with Prussia.

There was a bewildering series of changes in the way these basic tasks were structured. The first minister, Albert-Dubayet, believed that they fell into five natural divisions: funds, equipment, personnel, artillery, and welfare, together with a secretariat. This number was increased to nine by Scherer at the time of Fructidor, by when some 900 clerks had been combed out, leaving about 450. Further structural changes followed in 1798–9 due to the problems of paying off old accounts and the ministerial instability of the Year VII. Dubois-Crancé, for example, reverted to the much earlier pattern of three large directions for Personnel, Material, and Secretarial matters, while at the same time expelling a further 160 clerks. Although this restructuring was subsequently reversed, Scherer's complaint about the disorder that prevailed throughout his department remained largely unremedied.

The Ministry of the Interior found itself with an even larger task of consolidation of revolutionary services, and it was not helped in dealing with this by the new tasks imposed upon it by the Directory.[24] Once the Ministry of Police had been established and Benezech and François de Neufchâteau were left in charge for a reasonable period, coherence and stability began to develop. None the less, the Ministry still had a bewildering range of functions, local government and elections, prisons, social welfare, culture, economic management, population policy, statistics, and industrial development among them. Initially

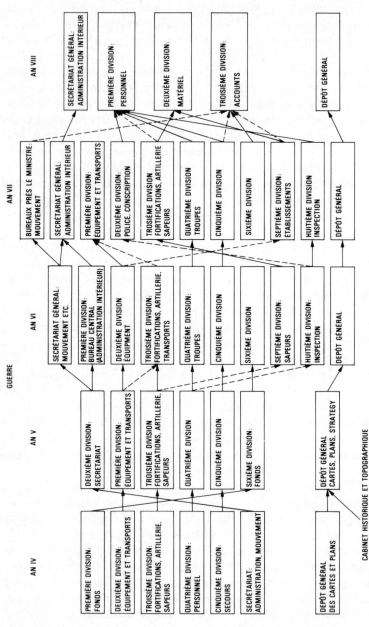

IV The Structures of the Directorial Ministry of War

these tasks were entrusted to a secretariat, a first division responsible for elections, local authorities, and administration, a second for public assistance, a third for public works, a fourth for agriculture, industry, and commerce, a fifth for education, and a sixth for the still pressing question of food supplies. About a quarter of the staff were shaken out in the early days of the regime, but the only structural change was the winding-up of the sixth division late in 1796 when its duties were transferred first to the first division and ultimately to the fourth. By then the original staff of 900 had been further whittled down to about 270.

Thereafter numbers began to grow again through the expansion of the Minister's private bureau within the Secretariat (no doubt because of Fructidor), the education division, and the creation of advisory councils of experts, and the formation of a new sixth division, responsible for canals and, ultimately, for ministerial funds. This expansion alarmed François de Neufchâteau during his second period in the Ministry and the numbers of staff were brought back to their previous level, though the Councils desired further cuts in 1799. However, the relative stability thus achieved was to be short-lived, since the basic problem of the overloading of the Ministry could not be solved by the creation of new departments. Nevertheless, the effort deserves more consideration than it was accorded by Pouthas, who seems unaware how closely the ideals of Guizot resemble those of earlier periods.[25]

The establishment of the Ministry of Police and the extension of its remit throughout the country was resisted by the Councils, and though it never had full control of the National Guard or or the *gendarmerie*, and though its duties included questions of public health, roads, entertainments, and welfare, it was so fought over by factions that organizationally it was a house built upon sand.[26] Its founding father was Merlin de Douai who took on staff somewhat indiscriminately so that it outgrew its first premises and had thus to face its own problems of establishment. Basically its work fell into seven main categories: the pure administration of the Secretariat, the *haute* police work performed by the Bureau Particulier, commerce, surveillance and security, *émigré* affairs, laws, and public opinion. At first these duties were split among an infinity of little bureaux, but gradually four main divisions emerged, for Commerce, Observation, Opinion, and Dispatches, which employed a total of 190 staff. Before Fructidor new divisions for accounts and laws were created, and the *bureau particulier* also grew with the preparation of the *coup*. The latter shrivelled away but the annexation of the Rhineland and the troubles of 1799 were the cause of further growth. Yet although politics prevented it from putting down real structural roots, its potential was already apparent.

The four remaining ministries all enjoyed a greater degree of stability both under the Directory, and perhaps as a result, during the nineteenth century and even after. The Ministry of Justice perhaps fared best of all, though even this most stable of ministries underwent some upheaval in the early days with the coming and going of Merlin and the appointment of some eighty archivists to deal with the papers of the previous regime and its courts.[27] But by the time Merlin returned to the Ministry in Germinal IV it was on the point of settling down into the shape it was to maintain for generations. Its constitutional duties embraced both the dispatch of laws and the supervising of the courts and other legal services of the Republic, but only the second was done in the Ministry, the former being hived off to a hundred-strong Agence des Lois and the Imprimerie de la République. The Ministry proper had 13 bureaux organized on fairly functional lines—a secretariat, registration, civil courts, criminal courts, legal opinions, the appeal court, judicial orgniz-ation and personnel, legal decisions, archives, accounts, laws, dispatches, and the minister's own bureau. At first these were all independent, but this meant so much double checking that the staff rose from 90 to 134. Hence in Ventôse V they were brigaded into five divisions: the Secretariat, Civil Affairs, Criminal Affairs, Accounts, and Dispatches. Thereafter the numbers fill, but the structure remained unchanged in essence though some Directorial bureaux were eventually upgraded.

The Ministry of Finance had had a much more disorganized past, so the new dispensation meant a return to simplicity, especially as Faipoult, the first active Minister, set out to choose the more sensible form of internal organization.[28] He established six divisions: Direct taxes (organized into regional bureaux), Indirect taxation, National property, Alienated and *émigré* lands, Posts, coinage and other government enterprises, and a

Secretariat. This enabled him to cut his staff by 160 from an initial strength of over 500. Thereafter both he and Ramel left the complement of staff alone, although the latter upgraded bureaux for Funds, Liquidation, and Alienation into three new divisions. After Fructidor these nine were again consolidated, this time into an enlarged Secretariat and four divisions for Direct Taxes, Indirect Taxes, Properties and Enterprises, and Funds. The extra staff taken on to help the secretariat in its new task of clearing up old accounts made the Ministry a special target for criticism in the summer of 1799, and about 50 clerks had to be dispensed with. The real trouble was that although the general structure was sound, too many little bureaux continued to exist within it, which called for divisional co-ordination sections, thereby making for additional complexity.

The Ministry of External Relations also underwent much travail before returning to relative stability, although this was not because of, as Masson claims, any simple return to the Ancien Régime.[29] The revolutionary Ministry carried within itself the seeds of its own regeneration as is seen in the low level of recruitment during the Directory. Initially, although the constitution gave it responsibility for dealing with all French envoys and consuls abroad and all diplomats stationed in France, and the upholding of treaties, the Directory was so active that it was somewhat underemployed. Its tasks were shared between a private secretariat where dispatches were decoded, a general secretariat, four political bureaux, and several more specialized services, for consular affairs, legal problems, archives, and boundaries, the whole employing 112 people. Relations between the two Secretariats were to be acrimonious and complicated, so the private Secretariat eventually vanished, while the political bureaux took over consular correspondence, as the over-all staff was gradually cut back to 74. Eventually, after Tallyrand had let numbers creep up again with the creation of a new Consular bureau, Reinhard abolished the secretariat altogether and consolidated the political bureaux into two, and sacked 20 employees leaving a structure of 5 bureaux and the Cabinet du Ministre.

There was much less initial upheaval in the Admiralty, but it was still very slow to settle down.[30] Its constitutional tasks included the recruiting and maintaining of sailors, the development of ports, arsenals and magazines, the building and deployment of ships, and the maintenance of shore and colonial establishments and their laws. These tasks were shared among 13 sections, including the Dépôt des Chartes et des Archives and the Dépôt Général des Cartes et Plans, while agencies for organizing naval supplies and transport were also closely attached to the Ministry. The staff of 330 grew gently until Germinal V when some 63 were dismissed and the rest consolidated into 6 divisions: Ports, Supplies, Seamen and Navigation, Accounts and Welfare, Colonies, and Personnel. Despite this and further change by Pleville-le-Peley, the problem of winding up old accounts again caused the staff to increase, to about 360. The Directory ordered that this should be cut to 160, but in fact 240 were kept on though the attached services were run down and the 6 divisions were further consolidated into 4. However,the cuts proved too drastic and in order to keep the department going many of the dismissed staff had to be re-engaged in 1799.

The remainder of the central nexus of government was made up of financial organs such as the Treasury which were almost of ministerial status. The Treasury employed a vast staff headed by a number of professional agents and divided into five main sections and some attached services, the largest of the former being the Caisse des Acquits which was engaged in auditing recent revolutionary accounts.[31] Once the bulk of this was done the treasury halved its size down to 600. The task of liquidating offices, lands, and other pre-revolutionary debts continued under the auspices of another sizeable organization, the Direction Générale de la Liquidation. The accounts of all financial organisms were vetted by the 200 and more staff of the Commission de la Comptabilité Nationale, the ancestor of the Cour des Comptes, while from 1798 accounts from the earlier phases of the Revolution were made the responsibility of the Commission de la Comptabilité Intermédiaire which itself had a sizeable staff divided into 5 divisions.

Alongside this were the headquarters of some of the major field services such as the Régie d'Enregistrement, the Régie des Douanes, and variety of others. These did not form one coherent version of 'Whitehall', either functionally or geographically. The various organs of government in Paris tended to work somewhat in isolation, which is why the Secrétariat Général du

Directoire and its co-ordinating role were so important.
Geographically speaking they were no longer centralized as
they had been at Versailles. They were divided into two main
complexes, one on the right bank around the old Contrôle
Général offices and off the Place de la Concorde, and the other
on the left bank, mostly in the rue de Grenelle and the rue de
Varenne.[32]

It is probably easier to discuss the location of the ministries
and the other Paris-based organs of government than to explain
exactly how they functioned. Very little research has ever been
done on the way in which government actually did work, and to
establish this demands a rather different approach from that
necessary for the rest of this study. One cannot for instance
deduce the methods of operation of an institution simply from a
description of its structures. As has been shown, the structures
of the ministries under the Directory were fairly closely tied to
areas of public life for which constitutional law made the department in question responsible, so to that extent they were more
rational than those of the pre-1792 vintage.

In this respect the ministries were based on the functional
principle of macro-structure. Where the micro-, or internal,
structure was concerned they were still at a mechanistic stage,
despite the frequency of change inside their organization.[33]
They were all normally divided into a formal hierarchy of
divisions and bureaux. More precisely they all seem to have
fallen into the category of what modern administrative scientists
call 'vertical' organization, in which the institution is divided
into sections according to the various spheres in which it
operated. Thus the Ministry of the Interior was divided into
divisions which each handled one aspect of the Ministry's brief:
local administration, welfare, public works, agriculture and
industry, and education etc., rather than being divided
'horizontally' as is sometimes now the case, according to the
functions which a department has to exercise. For example, the
Directions of Health, Social Action, and Pharmaceutics make
up the vertical directions of the modern Ministry of Health in
France, and these are supplemented by Directions for Administration, Planning, and International Relations which act in all
three of the vertical areas. Such a 'horizontal' structure tells one
quite a considerable amount about the relationships between

the various sub-units of the Ministry and the way in which they work, but a 'vertical' structure is less eloquent. Hence one knows little either about the informal organization of the Ministry or indeed about the way in which authority ran throughout the vertical divisions.

In the majority of cases it is probable that all the divisions were of equal importance and that they had direct access to the Minister himself and did not have to use the channel of the Secretary-General where there was one, though obviously the Secretariat-General of a ministry must have exercised some degree of internal co-ordination. It was in the Ministries of Justice, the Interior, Police, and External Relations, where there was often a Bureau Particulier or Cabinet, that the coordinating role was at its least and the Minister's own liaisons at their greatest. Only the Secrétariat Général du Directoire seems to have been based on the internal Secretariat as a *tronc commun*. The most obvious moves towards a horizontal organization and a client principle at the micro-level came with the concentration of the Ministries of Police and of War into two or three very large Directions at the end of the Directory. Perhaps too much should not be made of this since the bureau was the most common and essential cell of ministerial organization and functioning. There do not seem to have been great differences between ministries in organizational structure and they seem to have had a common, if at times slightly limited, view of their tasks.

If the internal organization of the ministries became somewhat more rational as the years went on, it was also probable that they became more efficient as a result, although this is less easily proved. In theory they existed not to devise policy but simply to execute laws. Roederer in 1791 had argued that they should be called 'Ministère des Lois de. . .' as a result.[34] At most theory could also act as control mechanisms, research centres, and agencies for formal registration of administrative acts in addition to this basic role. In reality while the other central organs were simply supervisory and executory, the ministries could be more positive. Although they often seemed to depend on the inflow of paper for their momentum, there was in fact some room for the exercise of initiative and for influencing policy-making.[35] François de Neufchâteau seems to have expected that 'vertical' organization meant not just watching and recording what was happening in the field of activity in question, but doing something practical about it. He urged his staff to be active in planning useful public works, or in getting rid of the obstacles to starting teaching again in the schools. The only reservations he expressed was lest they should overload the Directory with their ideas. He seems to have accepted the principles of civil service initiative and of delegated legislation. One commentator in fact believed that the staff of the ministries were so active that the ministers were reduced to merely correcting the work sent up by their subordinates.

Exactly how this could happen comes from a rare insight which the Daru papers offer into how a ministry could actually work.[36] Daru, the future Napoleonic minister, was under the Directory a Commissaire-Ordonnateur des Guerres serving as head of the second division of the War Office with responsibility for secretarial affairs, the movement and transport of troops, and the military police. He urged his minister and patron, Petiet, to enhance his reputation by some imposing act, such as a Code of Military Practice—for which the bureaux had all the relevant materials to hand—or a new system of military administration. For Daru such a thing was then totally lacking and he suggested the establishment of two councils, for administration and accounts on the one hand and military organization on the other, so as to systematize and record the working of the ministry and reduce the cost and influence of the bureau. 'Je ne puis pas vous exprimer combien de changement produiront d'heureux effets. D'abord plus d'infidélités et d'inadvertances à craindre, les bureaux chercheraient eux-mêmes à réduire leur travail au lieu de multiplier les minutes; les grandes affaires termineraient et quant au public il ne pourrait pas voir sans reconnaissance le dévouement d'un ministre qui donnerait tous les ordres sans intermédiaires.' In the event Daru felt that, when asked, he could not divest himself of many of his staff despite his criticism. Public opinion was less generous than he had hoped over the vast report to the Directory showing how the armies had been concentrated, reformed, and made less costly and unnecessarily aggressive, and over his work on *vivres* and *fourrages*.

While Daru himself was also responsible for drafting ministerial speeches and for briefing the ministers on questions raised in the Councils, an analysis of the ministry as a whole shows that many members of the staff had specialist knowledge and the ability to take decisions, rather than just the task of circulating papers as is often alleged.[37] In Daru's own division the likelihood is that much of the specialist information which he used came from his subordinates and that employees even in secretarial sections could be sufficiently briefed on technical matters to offer advice. In other ministries clerks actually claimed to have initiated technical legislation in the Councils or to have prepared reports which showed their technical expertise and value to their department. The Ministry of Finance confirms this since matters such as accounting, estates, alienation, and the legal and other problems arising from taxation could not be dealt with without some technical knowledge. Ramel's report on the working of the Ministry in the Year V and the problems then encountered because of inflation, the low recovery of taxes, and the problems of controlling *ordonnateurs* and field services makes this very plain.[38] Indeed, the very limitations placed by constitutional and popular suspicion on the administration's overt role in policy-making forced them to concentrate on technical details, through the mastery of which they came to exercise influence of a different but far from negligible kind.

Even so, the ministries were still quite dependent on the impetus of incoming paper for their activity.[39] When letters or other documents arrived they were centrally numbered, analysed, and registered in alphabetical order or according to date of arrival, subject-matter, or sender for instance. Most of the letters would be seen by the Secretary-General who would abstract the most difficult or confidential for himself or the minister to deal with. The rest would go to the appropriate divisions whose *chefs* would again abstract the unusual and then pass them on to the bureaux whose heads would likewise sort through them. Before passing papers on to the *rédacteurs*, the course of action would be tersely indicated in the margin in general terms: to acknowledge, answer, discuss with one of his superiors, draft a report or just ignore.

Once written by the *rédacteur*, who was in many ways the key figure, the draft report or reply was then checked by the *sous-chef* and the *chef de bureau* before usually being prepared for dispatch. In this case a junior clerk would analyse and file the reply and an *expéditionnaire* prepare a fair copy for checking by the *rédacteur* and his superiors. Less frequently papers were referred back up the hierarchy sometimes even to the minister or to the government. Similarly, important papers retained by section heads for their own consideration would form the basis for a report or a discussion paper for the minister or a gathering of heads of division and others. So the elements of the modern system of circulating minutes did exist, though they tended to be based on external stimuli and to be somewhat obscured by the proliferation of registers of correspondence and other such sources. All this took place during a day which could start between 7 a.m. and 9 a.m., depending on the time of year and on the department in question, and go on till lunch-time, only to resume between 3 p.m. and 5 p.m. for three or four hours, and sometimes longer if there was a crisis which necessitated an evening session.

Once a letter or report was approved—signified by the draft being marked 'Vu' or 'à expédier' or just initialled—and copied out, whether in a central bureau or by a *bureau des expéditions*, it could also give rise to a second copy or an entry in a register so that there should be some record of it. In many departments like the Secrétariat Général du Directoire an entry could be made in the same register in which the arrival of the piece had been noted, so as to ensure that matters were resolved and to note how long it took to do this. The Directory had 'Feuilles d'exécution' on which its decisions were noted, together with the ministry to which they were sent, and these had to be returned to show what action had been taken and when.[40] Other bodies had printed note paper with *enregistrement* and *départ* numbers, draft minute and letter sheets, and lists of affairs to be dealt with. In addition to this there were the beginnings of filing-systems and card indexes in which factual material, on laws, administrative acts, personnel, and other useful topics were filed. All this involved a great deal of circulation of paper within the ministry involved, especially if it occupied more than one building. The actual movement of papers usually developed on the *garçons de bureau*, although there were post-rooms and employees for dealing with general mail. The former also trimmed pens, fed and cleaned fires, trimmed lamps and candles, received callers, and ran errands.

All this reinforces the impression of bureaucracy, if not of bureaupathology, under the Directory. It shows that it would not really have been sufficient for a clerk merely to be able to read, as the Goncourts claim. They spoke of thousands of clerks 'chapeau rond sur l'oreille, le pantalon en croupe, la houppelande en sautoir, cadenettes retroussés, gambadant et se donnant des chiquenaudes; la plupart ne sont que des desœuvrés qui arrivent midi sonné, et leur toilette faite et parfaite, sans le moindre hâte'.[41] Other periods and other countries have similar complaints about the wearing of old clothes in the office to protect good ones, the problems with the public, and the use of office time for private ventures, so the Directory was far from unique.[42] In any case this hardly proves that the clerks had no technical expertise or were present in unnecessarily large numbers. The Directory, in fact, only spent 1 per cent of its 6,000,000 franc budget on the central administration, which is hardly excessive.[43]

Yet no matter how cheap or how active the various elements of central government were they would have been helpless without arms such as the field services. Despite the importance of these and the other non-Parisian elements of government, virtually nothing has been written about them.[44] It seems as if there were slightly fewer services then than now: no Direction départementale du travail et de la main d'œuvre for example. They were much less organized than today, but essentially their structure was not all that different. Then as now there were services dealing with the estates, taxes, customs and excise pertaining to the state, along with the Ponts et Chaussées for roads and other public works and forest services. Some of these had been inherited from the Ancien Régime but had been greatly reformed and expanded by the revolutionary government. Hence they too had problematic relations with the other elements of local government, for whom they were supposed to work under the direction of the minister and of their own superiors. In fact they often came into conflict with them, as over tax roles and police affairs.[45]

Although they were not properly an administrative service, one should remember that the *juges de paix* and even the government *commissaires* and *accusateurs publics* in the courts could play an administrative role. This was very necessary, given the paucity of police services at the time.[46] Apart from towns of over 5,000 people in which there was a commissioner of police, policing depended on the *gendarmerie*, the courts, the National Guard, and the army. Given the smallness of the former and the fact that the National Guard was often only a paper institution, it is obvious that field services were not always very developed.

This was also true of some of the field services under the aegis of the Ministry of the Interior and especially of the Ministry of Finance. The former was responsible for a number of public service schools which trained cadres for the field services, and in some cases provided a service like the Bureau de Cadastre or the École des Mines.[47] Much more important than these was the Conseil des Ponts et Chaussées which responsible not merely for roads and bridges, but for canals, inland navigation, surveying buildings, collecting road taxes, maintaining workshops and engineers, and financing roads and other public works. The financial services were even more numerous: these included the Treasury's *Payeurs* in each department and army, the regional mints, and later the Lottery and the new Administration des Contributions Directes. The Régies d'enregistrement and des Douanes had larger duties and structures than is often realized, with regional and departmental outposts as well as local stations. So too did the forest administration, the postal services, and the many other revenue collectors and inspectors whom Ramel found so costly and so trying.

The field services accounted for the majority of the non-Parisian elements in government, at least in terms of numbers. In the Haute-Marne in 1799 they provided 500 out of the 1,150 officials in the department, compared with 310 elective functionaries and their subalterns and 270 locally appointed schoolteachers and field guards etc.[48] Altogether this meant about one official per two hundred of the population which does not suggest a very intensive administration at local level, even though the three elements were usually very much intermingled. Local government acted as agents for the central authorities and the field services worked in with locally appointed personnel, as in taxation, education, and forest administration.[49]

This interaction made it more than ever necessary not merely for the elected Administrations Centrales of the departments to build up their own clerical staff, but also for the *commissaires* to do so. This undermined the Directory's design of centralizing all communications through the Administrations and also of reducing the, to them, inflated staffs employed locally. This is a rather different picture from that found in most textbooks which usually refer simply to changes in the political elements of local government and never ask how the elective officials actually got their tasks done.[50] However, the attacks on the size of local clerical and other establishments during the Thermidorian period implies that such people were by then already well entrenched.

Like most historians, the Directory was also more interested in the general and elective structure of local government, the five-man Administrations Centrales at the departmental level, the four and a half thousand cantons with their President, *commissaire*, and assembly of communal agents, and the communes themselves. The latter had very limited responsibilities for the *état civil*, public order and other tasks devolved upon them, whereas the cantons were much more influential. Hence it was in the cantons that many of the field and local services interacted.[51] They were responsible for the execution of laws, for a variety of military tasks, for welfare and food supplies, and for religious affairs. Increasingly historians seem to be accepting that they were not quite so inept at dealing with them as used to be said. Their problem was less one of structure and area and more one of time and money. They were supposed to be financed out of *sous additionnels* on taxes but it took so long to levy such monies that they and their staff were often bereft of resources.[52] Similarly, the central administrations and *commissaires* who had much wider powers still, including the *tutelle* of the lower authorities, have also been neglected and underestimated.[53]

Nowhere was the *commissaire* more active than in Paris. Paris, or the Department of the Seine as it was then known, which otherwise constitutes something of an exception. It's Administration Centrale had some 115 clerical *chefs* and employees, together with 80 archivists, auctioneers, and other expert personnel, though Tulard believes that the financial and other trials endured by the bureaucracy had reduced its efficiency and standing. It was also subject to particular government controls because the capital was so politically sensitive. It was because of this that the Bureau Central came to play such a large part in the Directory's policing of working-class activity which ensured the continuing quiescence of the capital. In this the Directory set a precedent for the next regime which Bonaparte was not slow to follow.

All these elective officials and political institutions generally needed clerical support, but neither Paris nor most historians were willing to recognize the fact that departmental clerks and municipal secretaries were, in Reinhard's phrase 'la cheville ouvrière de toute administration'.[54] Despite the efforts of the Ministry of the Interior, local clerks felt themselves to be the most neglected and worst rewarded of all state employees, and some made sure that they were paid by taking their salaries directly from cantonal tax receipts in coin. However, some departments like the Mont Terrible and the Haute-Marne had as many as 60 clerks at the beginning of the Directory. While this was cut to an average of about 25 to 35, some departments like the Allier and the Haute-Vienne always managed on 17 or 18. Most departments divided their staff into the same kind of structure, with bureaux for secretarial affairs, taxation, military business, domains, public works, and education, etc. Their methods of work were very much the same as those prevalent in Paris, with the slight difference that in the departmental administrations it is evident that all communications between the political direction and the clerks went through the Secretary-General, save where individual members of the Administration Centrale had responsibilities for specific areas of activity. The Secretary-General was thus a very important figure, so that some were politically very sensitive and others were quasi-perpetual administrators.[55]

It was through the clerical staff that much of the elective local government's dealings with field and local services were routed. Amongst the latter, which is an area of investigation even less frequented than the other elements of government, must be counted things like schools, hostels, *bureaux de bienfaisance, dépôts de mendicité,* and *monts de piété,* and officials such as the *inspecteurs des barrières* of the municipal *octroi,* the *sages-femmes,* the *gardes champêtres,* and the *officiers de santé.*[56] This kind of list would probably have been typical of many rural departments. More urbanized ones and particularly large cities, would no doubt have had rather more municipal employees than this, looking for secondary schools, prisons, and other institutions which, although they were subject to ministerial control, were mainly established at the discretion of the local authorities. This is the main reason for making what was in practice a somewhat unreal distinction between them and other field employees, such as the inspectors for collecting road-upkeep levies, the *gendarmerie*, and the employees of the forest and public works administrations.

It is to be regretted that more is not known of such employees for it was with them that the administrative 'buck' finally stopped. If the majority of the population came into contact with the state, more often than not it would have been through them. Hence they played an absolutely crucial role in providing the rudiments of public services which were necessary to conse-crate the return to normality signified by the constitution of 1795. They also enabled the Directory to achieve those improve-ments in the material conditions of life on which it had set so much stress in its first proclamation to the nation. The role of clerical, field, and locally employed personnel was thus just as vital to the Directory as was elective local government, and indeed, almost as important as central government itself. For if the Directory was ultimately dependent politically on elective local government, so it was also dependent administratively on the ensemble of local services of the state.[57] Had they not been there, then there would have been nothing for the ministries to supervise and no means of implementing policy changes and initiatives.

Similarly, it needed the ensemble of local forces in order to provide not merely services to the public but also the statistical and general information without which it could not function, and to co-ordinate the attempt to fulfil the aims set by the central government. Obviously, these aims were only very partially fulfilled. Officials were often ineffective or ill-disposed, money was short, corruption not uncommon, and facilities were often very sparse. As the administration of the Corrèze com-plained to Paris in 1797:

Nos maisons de détention de toute espèce ne sont nî sûres ni réparées, aujourd'hui même un prêtre s'est évadé de la maison de reclusion. Les concierges, sans paymens, depuis trois mois vont déserter leur poste, et nous mêmes allons voir nos bureaux abandonné, parce que sans autre resource que leur travail, nos employés dont le salaire depuis une année est réduit à moins de moitié, ont usé toute leur patience et toutes leurs resources, qu'ils n'ont rien perçu de ce trimestre et ne voyant point le moment out il leur sera soldé.[58]

Even so, without even this partial aid the Directory's broad aims and the functioning of the state as a whole would have been quite impossible to realize. Far more radical changes in the organization of the state would have been required after 1799 than was actually to be the case.

Not a great deal of this, of course, had initially been in the minds of the men of 1795. They had continued to assume that the circulation of information would enable the citizen to implement and to obey the law, leaving only residual functions to the executive. In fact rules and written communications alone cannot make government work, and an establishment of men and resources was necessary. Moreover, the men in question had to exercise a certain amount of initiative. So in the gaps left by the constitution, a complex machine of employees and semi-technical specialists developed, which the elective and *fonctionnaire* elements of government were increasingly called upon to control.

In theory the machine was only expected to perform regulatory functions and indeed it did certainly monitor policy and much beside.[59] Moreover, it also developed a creative and adaptive role, albeit often as part of the informal organization or so the brief glimpses of this suggest. Had its structure been less functional and less vertical it might have developed this further. However, the structures which it adopted did allow it to begin some kind of management role. Its very existence was, in any case, a source of support for the regime. Had it enjoyed greater status this support might have been greater. As things were it could not respond fully to external needs, these being but imperfectly mediated by a still somewhat suspicious government. It relied partly on its own limited dynamic and interrelationships to define its organization and its role.[60]

The interlocking structure which resulted was, as far as one can tell, not merely very different from the 'little' government expected a few years earlier, but was also much more akin to the classic nineteenth-century state than has often been realized. This discussion has shown that there was little of the omnipotent about the Directorial state, while even the judicial and fiscal drives were somewhat blunted. None the less, one can see the beginnings of the classic *réglementation* and *tutelle* of later eras, as well as the attempts at intervention and provision of the services necessary in a civilized community. What was lacking were the resources and the political will to make a reality of the potential inherent in the slowly emerging structure which has been so briefly studied here. Similarly one can see the beginnings of a new relationship amongst the various personnels of the new machine of the state, and also new relationships between them and their society. This aspect of government organization, however, like many others such as the effect on personnel and policy of the new structure, still remains unexplored.

Structures alone cannot tell one how government worked, or how far bureaucratization had set in. One can see the latter in the institutionalization of information storage, the growing functional specialization and division of labour, and the clearer-cut hierarchies and aims of the administration. The picture, however, is still incomplete. A discussion of the personnel of the new bureaucracy, and thereafter of their place in society and politics, is necessary to complete the appraisal of the increasingly bureaucratic nature of the Directorial administration.

CHAPTER VI: THE PERSONNEL OF CENTRAL GOVERNMENT UNDER THE DIRECTORY

If the role and growing unity of the administration is partly visible in its structures, it is shown even more clearly by a consideration of the personnel of government.[1] Their legal situation and the realities of their origins, their administrative formation, and their career patterns show something more of the way in which the Directory helped to reform and consolidate the top-heavy staffs of the revolutionary era, producing a much more obviously bureaucratic corps of administrators than before.[2] The political authorities had always wanted to treat the administration as a group of differing services subject to varying juridical and constitutional restraints but the evidence of the personnel files is that there was a great deal more unity and interrelationship amongst the various elements of the state machine than was often palatable.[3] Similarly, the realities of individuals' interests and careers often counted for more than the texts of multifarious but totally uncodified legislation on the statutory position of employees and *fonctionnaires.*

The Directors came to appreciate this much more than had previous regimes. So although they and their predecessors never lost sight of the social and political dimensions of administrative life, they did evolve a kind of 'personnel management', the legal and practical bases of which need consideration first. For it was questions of personnel, of social and economic need, of career aspirations and mobility, as well as the growing governmental role of the administration that came to the fore. This was a concomitant of the way the administration became increasingly professional and how governments like the Directory gradually took cognizance of the fact.

In trying to study the nature and situation of ministerial personnel under the Directory one comes up against a number of problems of method. Thus, although there are a good number of studies of modern government personnel they tend to be concerned with the *grands corps* and other élites, and such 'aristocratic' studies, as Jean Rivero call them, are not a very useful guide.[4] Similarly, one cannot hope to cover all the aspects of administrative life and careers, which are implied either by the Weberian model of bureaucratization or by the present-day *Statut Général des Fonctionnaires*. Hierarchical structures, qualifications and nominations, selection procedures, *congés, détachement*, and medical rights were either very different under the Directory or had not then been thought of. Moreover, the administration under the Directory had not achieved full bureaucratization in every dimension. So some Weberian categories are inapplicable for this reason. A further problem is that although the situation of staff was becoming more precise and more formal, the evolving legislation which surrounded it was full of confusion and omissions. It did not therefore always connect with the realities of the administrative career dynamic which stand out from the sources.

These present a third problem, for even when an aspect of an official's career was enshrined in legislation which ties up with modern thinking, it may be only partially or often very differently recorded in the sources.[5] At this stage there were no proper personnel dossiers in central government, and indeed there was never a proper enumeration of the number of clerks in the Directorial ministries. The remarks which follow are based on an analysis of 4,350 of the 5,500 employees who can be presumed to have served in the 8 departments in question throughout the Directory's existence. These are people on whom there is some minimal and reasonably convincing evidence of their existence. It was all too easy for someone to pass through the administration without leaving any trace or leaving evidence which it is impossible to relate to any particular clerk, especially when common names are concerned. Even so, of the four thousand and more some 34 per cent are simply names, and 38 per cent are only partly documented. Anmongst the remaining 28 per cent the majority of the documentation tends to come from those who served a fairly longtime in the service and who reached reasonably senior positions. This bias, along with the fact that the information is often so fragmentary, as well as being unreliable and imprecise, means that the following analysis is best regarded as a gauge of the nature of the civil service rather than as a scientific sample.

This is particularly so given the fact that the aim has been not to produce a photograph of the ministerial staffs at one exact moment in time, but rather to give an impression of the staffs throughout the Directory's existence. One can thus take account not merely the slimmed-down service of 1798–9, but also the rather different service of 1795–6. This has meant using fairly wide categories of analysis—doubly necessary given the unclear and contradictory habits of description in the sources—and also taking median points for things like age and level of employment. These would make the utilization of the more sophisticated computer-based analyses used elsewhere somewhat gratuitous. What can be done is to offer a generalized statistical survey of the often very disparate information provided by the personnel files. Such as they are these are still the most reliable source, especially when supplemented, not with exhaustive searches in genealogical sources, but with the evidence of other official documents and dictionaries of biographies, where relevant. This covers motives for and methods of entry into the administration, conditions of employment and promotion, length and date of service, and the general origins of the most striking of Directorial bureaucrats, their traditions of administrative service, and their search for a secure career.

Obviously this needs to be supplemented by consideration of their social and political origins and characteristics. None the less it does provide both an interesting parallel to the legislation on the status of civil servants, and a counter to many previous accounts of the post-revolutionary administration which usually ignore this aspect of its personnel.[6] Unfortunately, it remains true that 'Certes on peut suivre une carrière, calculer un traitement, parcourir un rapport; mais l'homme nous échappe. Nous restent inconnus ses origines et ses idées, son genre de vie et son mentalité.'[7] None the less, despite all these problems, some knowledge of the theoretical and real position of the employee within the reformed ministries is an indispensable adjunct to an appreciation of their new character.

The first question which has to be asked is what caused people to embark on an administrative career, since the unstable

conditions of the times and the constant attacks on the administration would not lead one to expect the way in which people
almost fell over themselves to gain and, where necessary, to
retain administrative posts. There seem to have been two reasons
for this. Firstly, many of those involved had administrative
experience which meant that they had a trained incapacity for
any other kind of work. Since, as one *Sous-Chef* in Relations
Extérieures explained, they were only fit for bureau work, they
naturally sought jobs where they could use such talents as they
had. The second fact is that, for all its faults, administrative
employment did offer some shelter and advantage in time of
crisis, whereas some other businesses and professions offered
none. Many of those without previous administrative experience
entered the civil service because their wealth had evaporated or
because their post or profession had ceased to exist.

The dislocation caused by the Revolution thus helped to
swell the pool of administrative talent already in existence.[8]
One in three entered because of their antecedents and one in ten
because of their lack of prospects elsewhere, far more than the
one in ten who, reflecting also the psychological crisis of the
times, entered because of a sense of duty, enthusiasm, or civic
ambition. Even fewer entered for purely political reasons, indeed
fewer than those who entered after military service or because of
their being requisitioned on account of their expertise. So that
even when deputies applied to Reubell and others for administrative jobs, they usually placed a heavy emphasis on the
economic and administrative motives which led them to do so.
This fits in with recent thinking on the importance of security in
leading people to join a bureaucracy. It differs somewhat from
the situation under the Ancien Régime when the hope of welfare
or privilege was a much more common imperative than the
sheer necessity found in the 1790s.[9]

If there were only a few motives for entry to the administration, there were a variety of ways in which entry could be
obtained. The question was debated throughout the eighteenth
and nineteenth centuries, but despite the many experiments
with training schools and programmes, nothing definitive was
ever created.[10] The old patterns of entry through relatives,
patronage, and family tradition continued until shattered by
the Revolution. Yet, despite their punitive legislation, the revolu-

tionaries never succeeded it setting up a properly defined system of requirements or procedures for entry into the civil service. They ruled out entry through birth, purchase, and inheritance as well as excluding non-residents, priests, *émigrés*, and conscripts. Save for the law of 8–20 March 1791 giving priority to former employees of field services and save for the experiments with examinations in the naval administration and elsewhere, they never sent further.[11] They left entry to *la libre choix du ministre* and to a vision of what the ideal employee should be like: utterly honest, virtuous, and public spirited, a good father and citizen, intelligent, zealous, well-informed and experienced, and of course a patriot and republican. In reality politics, patronage, nepotism, requisition, and personal initiative all played a part in securing jobs.

Ultimately some people did take a rough and ready kind of examination, as was the case in the War Office during the Late Empire, but the only other major means of training was the habit of taking young men on as *surnuméraires, extraordinaires* or *auxiliaires* either to satisfy patrons or to give young men experience of administrative life, though not all departments believed in such practices. In the Ministry of Justice *surnuméraires* were only appointed on the understanding that they could claim no seniority when applying for a vacancy. This and other forms of refusal to grant security of tenure meant that ministries could sometimes be bombarded for years by would-be or one-time clerks who felt that they had a claim to office. This suggests that there was less of a legislatively imposed pattern of entry and more of the free play of governmental needs in conjunction with the economic and administrative dynamics already mentioned. No doubt the Directory would have liked to have tidied up the situation but in fact it was not till the Empire and after that any major initiatives were taken. Even these were more often honoured in the breach than in the observance.[12] In practice, however, given the predominance of those with a history of prior administrative service one can say that people were more or less qualified for office, even if they were often nominated in irregular ways.

Once in the administration, the civil servant, although not in the *situation statutaire et réglementaire* established in 1946, was not short of regulations governing his standing and activities. However, many were never enforced, some had fallen into desuetude, and until 1794–5 none were of general applicability. None the less, few of them had been repealed and in theory at least they greatly circumscribed the activity of the civil servant, while leaving little room for the rights and privileges since negotiated by trade unions. The burden of revolutionary and Directorial legislation was on the obligations of the official, since state service was considered to be a duty for all citizens.[13] He was 'responsible', subject to an oath of loyalty, and required, among other things, to reside in the district where he worked, to stay at his post in time of crisis, to supply his own equipment, and above all to conform to the prevailing norms of political and social behaviour. He enjoyed few rights and privileges, though at times theoretical freedom from arrest and harassment in certain specific circumstances was conceded. Here again, the relevant texts were rarely evoked. Where his work was concerned there was usually some precision, as the many tables of duties and functions left in the archives testify.

There was equally little certainty about an official's tenure of office. There were few guide-lines on ineligibility and incompatibility, while rules on the appropriate age to commence office-holding were but spasmodically and eccentrically enforced until the Empire, when administrative service was only counted from an employee's sixteenth birthday.[14] Although expressions such as *titulaire* and *en pied* were often used to describe clerks who had passed through the period of apprenticeship often demanded, these gave no security of tenure. Not only were contracts unknown but very often there was no written proof of employment. Lagarde had to decree that only entry in the *états des appointments* constituted prima-facie evidence of employment in his department. There was no procedure for appeals agianst the dismissals which economy, political change, and ministerial whim so frequently produced. Against such dismissals the clerk's only defence was his indispensability, his contacts within the bureaux, the cyclical nature of reforms, and above all his own persistence in demanding his reinstatement in what all Directorial employees considered their rightful post.[15]

One can find clerks pleading for the restoration of but briefly held rights, years after they had lost the place in question. The politician Riou recommended one clerk, who had been dismissed for reasons of economy from the Admiralty, not to claim compensation there and then, but to wait until things calmed down. Persistence and the swing of the pendulum could often secure reinstatement. This was never definitive and there are plenty of cases of people who were fired and then rehired five or six times in a career of twenty years. The lucky ones would be taken on as *titulaires*, the less fortunate as *auxiliaires* or more commonly rewarded with grudgingly given compensation of a few weeks salary. The fact that years of devoted, and often unpaid, service could be repaid with a curt dismissal without having a greater effect on civil service morale, is proof of the fact that conditions outside could be even worse.

For those who managed to preserve their positions there was little guarantee of adequate reward or advancement. There were no formal criteria for promotion, and though salaries were obligatory after the abolition of venality, the economic situation was such that they could not always be paid in full. Sometimes they were never paid at all. Hence people often had to stay in one grade for many years, while the majority of legislation in this area dealt not with rewards but with disciplinary offences. As well as the often draconic penalties for non-compliance with political norms—such as the two years in irons threatened for those who failed to apply the post-Fructidor legislation—there was also a series of penalties for minor administrative offences. These could range from deductions from salary for lateness to dismissal for corruption and other major offences. Here again there was no machinery for the application of such penalties, let alone for appealing against them.

On the other hand, the Directorial civil servant was somewhat more secure in the location of his employment since he was forbidden to work for a foreign government or in an occupied area, while obligatory transfers from one service to another were rare.[16] Hardly 3 per cent of the total Directorial central civil service moved from one ministry to another, and one in three of these did so because they were made redundant. The rest moved because there was a particular need for their specialisms in another department, or because their bureau was moved from one ministry to another. Similarly, as well as working long hours, normally employees had to work on *fêtes* and on religious holidays and found it almost impossible to take leave or holidays.

Again, such welfare provision as there was—subsidized food, lodgings, and clothing—was provided grudgingly as a favour, not as a right. Pensions, as will be seen, rarely stood up to inflation or to the shortcomings in the way they were paid. All this compares unfavourably with expectations both under the Ancien Régime and with those of comparable English employees, and explains in part why the search for a *Statut Général* embodying improved conditions was so actively pursued throughout the nineteenth century.[17]

All this assumes that the administration was not merely one recognizable body, but also a homogeneous one. In fact, there were many measures dealing with specific categories of civil servants which have not been discussed here, while even the main body of the central administration was much divided by department or grade. The evolution of grading-systems is one of a number of areas related to the standing of personnel where increasing bureaucratization is revealed by closer consideration. Similarly the Directory's personnel management, which so far has been most noticeable by its absence, stands out more through an examination of practice than of theoretical enactment. Thus though the civil servant may have been uncertain of his tenure of office, he was usually sure of his position within the hierarchy.[18] By the end of the eighteenth century attempts had been made to introduce more differentiation amongst ministerial clerks than had originally been the case. However, grades such as those introduced in the Admiralty in 1785 contained very wide ranges of salary and very little indication of the function undertaken by those who held such positions. However, allowance was made for progress to the top salary of the grade inside three years, and for extra allowances for long service and for good conduct.

With the coming of the Revolution and the replacement of the old *Premiers Commis* by large numbers of employees from the old field services the need for further refinements and grades became apparent. Many new titles and functions were added to those inherited from the old order, but this was done unsystematically and spasmodically. Moreover, the general confusion of the times and the suspicion with which the administration was regarded made it difficult to introduce fixed grades involving appointments to well-paid and responsible senior posts. As a result there was a decline in the number of senior and technical posts and a growth in the number and variety of titles used. One observer in the War Office commented that: 'la confusion règne dans les dénominations des chefs de service. On voit en même temps à la tête des bureaux . . . des seconds adjoints, des premiers commis, des chefs, des sous chefs suppléant le chef, des Commis Directeurs, des Commis principaux et même des principaux commis.'[19] Hence if the executive commissions seem to have had relatively few grades, the Comité de Salut Public had at least twenty-four, some of them highly specific and technical. The legislation of 1795 intensified the confusion by classifying people according to salary or residence.

The arrival of the Directory on the scene led to a partial clarification of the situation through the continuing use of salary classes, whether those inherited from the Thermidorians or those derived from their own *arrêtés* of 7 and 17 Frimaire IV. The latter went a step further by assimilating varying grades to the salary classes.[20] Even so there were still many different titles which often carried differing salaries and which could be divided into anything up to ten sub-grades. This confusion was partly a product of the fact that nobody was certain whether they were classifying positions in a hierarchy or distinguishing between various types of specialized function. Thus the Ministry of Marine in 1796 had seven grades—each of which was subdivided into a number of classes according to salary—in which posts were ranked according to the seniority of the functions they covered. The Ministry of Police, on the other hand, had a much larger range of grades but many of them carried the same salary and only gradually did they come to be at least partly subdivided into salary classes. When the regime's initial problems were past, legislation began to have more effect so that hierarchies became slightly less complex and salaries rather more uniform, paving the way for the stricter hierarchies which were to be normal in the following century.

Yet even with this consolidation it is possible to find at least a hundred separate titles and grades, many of which were sub-divided internally, and in which similar titles could cover differing roles and salaries.[21] The Admiralty in Floréal V compared grades in the various ministries and found that a *Chef de Bureau* and a *Rédacteur* in the Interior were what it called *Chefs sous-Divisionnaire* and *Commis Principal*, whereas a naval *Rédacteur* was the equivalent of a *commis d'ordre* in the Interior. This lack of consistency makes it impossible to use contemporary categories for analysis. Instead all the grades have been assimilated to one composite, ten-point scale which seems to represent a reasonable compromise between the varying hierarchies as well as enabling one to make a more informed comparison between the proliferation of grades at the time and the broad general classifications into which today's even more variegated functions are divided. Obviously it is impossible to allocate clerks with complete certainty, but on the basis of their salary, title, functions, and apparent standing they can usually be placed with some accuracy. Table I has already provided a concordance between the contemporary titles and the composite scheme adopted here, explaining something of the various tasks covered.

The table shows that the average ratio of senior to junior staff throughout the ministries was 1:3.5 so that there were more senior staff than there had been in 1793. This reinforces the view that not merely did the ministries play a more positive role than has often been allowed—and for which senior staff would be necessary—but that opinion was slightly more willing to tolerate the exercise of responsibility than had previously been the case. The only noteworthy divergences from this norm were in the Ministry of Marine, the division of which into a few large divisions each with only a small number of bureaux meant that few senior staff were required. In the Ministries of Justice and of Finance the presence of a number of leading jurists and the proliferation of small bureaux respectively produce the reverse situation. Their ratios were 1:2.5 and 1:2.1 whereas that in the Admiralty was 1:6.

Despite such divergences and the continuing differences in the way grades were interpreted, the general impression is an accurate one. Not merely does it tie in with the social cleavages which can be seen inside the ministries, it also shows how the gradual development, if not of an incremental scale or of a system of 'notation', at least of salary points within the major grades, both reinforced the process of bureaucratization and did something to offer more of a career pattern. This did something to offset the general insecurity of tenure and the barriers which prevented promotion between grades.[22]

In theory the Revolution brought the career open to talents.

TABLE II: THE MINISTERIAL HIERARCHY

	Sec. Gen.	%	Finance	%	Justice	%	Ext. Rel.	%	Marine	%	War	%	Interior	%	Police	%	Total	%
I Chefs de Division	4	1.6	18	4.3	14	3.5	10	3.6	34	6.1	35	4.2	34	3.4	33	5.4	182	4.2
II Chefs de Bureau	27	10.7	27	5.2	39	9.7	13	4.8	11	2.0	68	8.0	86	8.8	64	10.5	335	7.7
III Sous-Chefs	20	8.0	75	18.0	74	18.6	35	12.8	32	5.7	63	7.4	116	11.8	54	8.7	469	10.8
IV Senior Clerks	20	8.0	39	9.5	29	7.2	32	11.7	97	17.6	200	23.6	126	12.9	101	16.5	644	14.8
V Technicians	15	6.0	—	—	24	5.8	17	6.2	41	7.4	28	3.3	23	2.3	10	1.6	158	3.6
VI Junior Clerks	39	15.5	100	24.5	78	19.2	69	25.2	174	31.6	249	28.4	206	21.1	148	24.2	1063	24.6
VII Expéditionnaires	50	20.6	100	24.5	61	15.0	42	15.3	40	7.2	140	16.6	201	20.6	144	23.5	778	18.0
VIII Surnuméraires	4	1.6	4	1.0	6	3.8	23	8.4	32	5.8	22	2.6	18	1.8	3	0.5	122	2.8
IX Garçons	58	23.2	38	9.1	29	7.2	16	5.8	46	8.4	37	4.5	111	11.6	40	6.6	375	8.6
X Domestics	12	4.8	16	3.9	41	10.0	17	6.2	45	8.2	12	1.4	56	5.7	15	2.5	214	4.9
Total	249		417		405		274		552		854		977		612		4340	

Inside the administration the reality was slightly different. To begin with there was almost as much chance of demotion in the troubled times of the revolution, as the absence of security of tenure suggests. For every three people promoted, one seems to have been demoted, although the vagaries of grading make it difficult to be sure of this. In comparison with the eighteenth-century Ministry of War there seems to have been equally as little promotion and much more demotion. In all the careers of Directorial civil servants only 247 cases of significant promotion have come to light. Less than one in twenty of all those employed under the Directory thus seem to have gained greatly from careers which could often, despite insecurity of tenure, last up to forty years. For those who were lucky enough to rise, promotion could be anything but a smooth process. There are plenty of cases of employees taking one step forward and then one, if not two, back because of ministerial whims or because of reorganization.

Of the 247 known cases, 28.4 per cent reached the top grade, 37.6 per cent the second, and 23.6 the third. The remaining 10.4 per cent had to content themselves with an even more modest degree of success. Only a handful of those who reached Grade I posts were able to go beyond this and establish themselves as *haut fonctionnaires* or political officials with a status and authority beyond that of the employee in a ministry. This category, which excludes those who were political figures etc. before entering the administration and who later returned to their old rank, includes such people as Marc Antoine Bourdon, who became Minister of Marine and later a *Préfet*, Agathon Fain, who was to be private secretary to both Napoleon and Louis Philippe and who was to end up as a baron having once been a clerk under Lagarde, and Tabarié, a Restoration *Sous-Secrétaire d'État pour la Guerre*. In additon there were a number of officials who were made Napoleonic *Conseillers d'État* while retaining their foothold in their ministry of origin, such as La Besnardière, Laforest, and Lecamus. There were also a number of officials, like Legraverend of the Ministry of Justice, who became *sous-préfets* or deputies. In the case of the latter this often happened under the Directory.

However, it is hard to say whether such cases of promotion

were the result of administrative talent or were made for more personal and political reasons. Certainly the largest number of promotions to political roles came in the War Office, partly no doubt because many employees, like Daru for instance, had impressive careers behind them before they were attached to the War Office. Similarly, war also increased mobility in the army and its attached services and provided more visible opportunities for successful service than did a career passed wholly in Ministerial bureaux. The Directory also made use of former civil servants as ministers, with Bourgnuignon and Dondeau of the Ministry of Police, along with Reinhard in External Relations and Faipoult in the Ministry of Finance being selected at least in part because of their administrative background. Benezech, Milet-Mureau, and Gaudin had also held posts only slightly above those covered by Grade I before becoming ministers, Petiet and Reinhard were willing to accept comparable posts after having been Directorial ministers.

For the vast majority, however, control of a bureau or division, or at most Secretary-Generalship, was all that they could expect. On the other hand if promotion was achieved, there was a good chance that it would lead to the top of the internal hierarchy. Thus some 33.6 per cent of those involved began their careers in Grade VI posts, as against 22 per cent from posts in Grade IV. Conversely, only 17.6 per cent rose greatly from Grade VII posts and only 16 per cent from those in Grade VIII. The remainder rose either from very near the top, 7.2 per cent, or from very near the bottom, 3.2 per cent. There was a vicious barrier between domestic and clerical posts for the most part. One domestic servant in the Admiralty managed to finish as a senior clerk while another, Durand of the Ministry of Justice, along with four *garçons de bureau*, managed to establish themselves as junior clerks. Two other *garçons* achieved posts in Grades VII and VIII. Hardly anybody rose from technical posts to high administrative ones.

All this suggests that the higher one started, the easier it was to rise. If one started out as a *rédacteur*, rather than as a mere copyist or auxiliary, one had a better chance of becoming a *chef*. Those who managed to create the appearance of 'rising men' were likely to rise even higher, a fact which reinforces the impression of the importance of prior social and administrative standing even during the Revolution. The latter, in the long run, did not undo all social bonds.

This also throws into relief the lack of attention paid to recruitment and training. Given the haphazard promotion policy, entry to the administration was probably the most important and decisive step in a civil service career. Failure to obtain a satisfactory post then could dog a man for years. Yet the Directory, like its predecessors, not merely failed to take sufficient interest in recruitment to the administration, but also gave no thought at all to the need to train those who had just been admitted, especially if they had not been recruited as supernumeraries. Promotion thus rested less on experience and ability than on longevity. The longer a career lasted, and particularly if it continued into the Empire, the greater did chances of promotion become. Promotion thus demanded either a good start—at which point politics and patronage were probably at their most influental—or a good deal of persistence.

There were no formal procedures for promotion, and though attempts were made by conscientious ministers and *chefs* to institute a system of reports and to take account of merit, this happened fairly infrequently.[23] Even where it did take place it was rarely done for very long because of changes in minister and structure. The bulk of the Directory's senior staff in fact were recruited at a fairly high level, because of their ability or experience, or because of their status and connections. They then either rose imperceptibly to the top of the hierarchy or left the ministry altogether. They were much less likely to drop back down the hierarchy than were those recruited at lower levels. If a man joined the administration as an *expéditionnaire* hoping to rise to the highest positions in the state he was likely to be brutally disillusioned. *Expéditionnaires'* desks did not contain a *brévêt* of appointment as a minister. There were fairly obvious limits to the social and administrative democratization achieved by the Revolution, and to the degree of bureaucratization then achieved. It may well have been the case that the Directory was actually marginally more favourable to the career open to talents than the highly suspicious and politicized phases of the revolution which had preceded it.

There was a similar chance of disillusionment over the provision of pensions and, as has been seen, over salaries. The problem of salaries, in so far as the *statut des fonctionnaires* was concerned, lay not in any judicial or legislative bar to their payment, but in the problematic situation of the revolutionary era and the vicissitudes of government policy. The receipt of a salary was thus obligatory, but the state was not always able to pay salaries on time or in full. Hence in a period of rapid inflation, even though salaries were raised to thirty times their 1790 value, they were still valueless.[24] The obligation to receive a salary thus created an obligation to accept penury. This was the problem that most affected Directorial civil servants, many of whom had of course entered the service for economic motives. The question of pensions was often a less pressing matter, and one in which the Directory's responsibility was much less since only a small proportion of its civil servants retired before 1799. None the less, the provision of a pension is part of both the Weberian definition of the bureaucratic condition and of the general expectations of the civil service at the time and it therefore needs consideration.

Under the Ancien Régime pensions had been freely and generously conceded, as a form of fringe benefit, long before pensionable age was reached.[25] They were more a supplement to low basic salaries than anything else. Yet they were partly reversible to families and were paid after official service was ended as well as before. The alleged scandals of the *Livre Rouge* led to the disappearance of this system. In its place was the law of 3–22 August 1790 which conceded that 'tout citoyen qui a servi, défendu, illustré, éclairé sa patrie ou qui a donné grande exemple de dévouement' had a right to a pension.[26] Unfortunately this rather generous dispensation was interpreted very narrowly. No cumulation of salaries or pensions was allowed at first and no *gratifications* could be accepted. Moreover, service had to be of sufficient duration, importance, and public benefit for a pension to be payable. Thus thirty years' service would yield a basic pension of a quarter of the terminal salary, together with a further 5 per cent for every subsequent year's service, up to a maximum of 10,000 *livres*. Proportionately less was to be paid for shorter terms of service or where payment was made to a widow. All existing pensions paid by agencies which no longer existed had to be assimilated to the new norms.

This ruling deluged the administration with work, and before it was finished further legislation was passed, adding further complications. Thus the law of 24 July 1793 reduced the qualifying period to twenty years but made it dependent on good conduct and efficiency. The real problem, however, was less the increasingly restrictive nature of the legislation, since almost all those who were compulsorily retired at the beginning of the Revolution were in fact given pensions, than the lack of funds. Hence many employees of the War Office, having once retired, were forced to return to work because their pension had totally failed to keep up with inflation. This situation made civil servants one of the groups to suffer most from the financial crises of 1790–7. Relief payments to pensioners had to be made as early as 1791. A further problem was that very often it took so long to settle and begin paying a pension that the eventualy recipient could be reduced to penury in the interim. There may have been a political motive in this since leading officials of the old Ministry of Foreign Affairs like Henin and Rayneval did not get their cases resolved until the Directory, while less prominent people had got pensions long before this, even though they had had close relations with the old court. Whether it was any use when it was paid was another matter.

The situation hardly improved under the Thermidorians for in Fructidor III they further limited pensions to 50 per cent of a man's final salary with a maximum of 3,000 *livres* per annum. Thus someone like J. L. Moreau, a War Office clerk from 1774 to 1792 who had taken his pension of 5,138 *livres* in Germinal III after extra service in India, and who was then farming near Chartres, found that something like 40 per cent of his allowance was deducted.[27] When the Directory took up office it tried to bring some kind of order into the situation. It first transferred control of pensions to the Direction Générale de la Liquidation, over which it watched carefully. Then by the law of 28 Pluviôse IV, to try and keep pace with inflation, pensioners were allowed 1,000 *livres* in paper for the first 100 *livres* of nominal pension plus a decreasing proportion for each succeeding 100.[28] On 17 Germinal IV this was replaced by payment in *mandats* and, finally, *arrêtes* of 22 and 27 Vendémiaire V allowed pensions and related payments to be paid in cash.

Here again this was not always possible. The Directory and

the ministries remained in control of pensions policy providing, for instance, special application forms on which one's services and certificates of birth, residence, health, and good conduct could be entered, until the summer of 1797. The pressure of the legislature on pensions was maintained even after the *coup*, although increasingly ministers were allowed a freer hand. Under the Consulate pensions were made payable again after thirty years' service and subject to stringent limitations, though for once all administrative service could be counted towards a pension even though the bulk of it was outside the department which actully paid the pension. Similarly, efforts were made to settle the many remaining Ancien Régime claims.

One reason why it took so long to resolve the problem was that pensions were non-contributory. This was in line with the spirit of revolutionary legislation in which pensions were treated as a right. In practice employees were made wholly dependent on the government, which had no reserves with which to meet pension claims. Moreover, without any money of their own tied up in pensions the clerks had only a moral claim on the government. Hence employees, like Vauchelle, who had seen some of their salary cut as a result of revolutionary legislation, could not get a pension even under the Consulate with Carnot's recommendation.

As far as the very scattered documentation allows one to judge, the Directory was less generous in its application of revolutionary legislation than in its reaction to inflation. People like Deleforge, the eighty-year-old librarian of both the Comité de Salut Public and the Directory, Lafond, a *garçon* in Foreign Affairs from 1750 to 1796, and Firmin Cocquet, the *doyen* of the Admiralty's clerks seem to have got no pension.[29] Other well-established clerks who died during the Directory seem not to have moved the Directory into giving death grants to their families, while Michel François Dimanche, a clerk in the Invalides bureau of the Admiralty, who had been born in 1748 and had served for sixteen years in the army, eight in the Fermes, and five in the ministry, was refused a pension in 1797 on the grounds that he was too young. He was forced to continue working as a supernumerary until 1803, whereas L. A. Huet of External Relations was retired in 1796 when he was 76 on the grounds of his advanced years, and given relief payments until his pension was settled. This was rarely done with people who were forcibly retired, as the cases of Mottet and Baud show. The Directory's goodwill towards pensions was somewhat limited and showed itself more in the formalization of application procedures than in anything else.

None the less, the Directory seems to have realized that the best guarantee of pensions was for the employees to invest their own money in them. The precedents of the Fermes Générales and the Caisse des Invalides de la Marine was followed first by the Comité des Finances which set aside 1 per cent of the down payments on national lands to form a pension fund for the Régie de l'Enregistrement whose employees were required to pay a tenth of their own salary into the fund.[30] The laws of 28 Vendémiaire VII then set aside certain *sous additionnels* towards the payment of some administrative pensions. It was under the Consulate and the Empire that deductions were regularly made in most of the ministries, beginning with the War Office in 1801, and then the Interior in 1806, the Ministry of Police in 1809, and many local authorities in 1811.[31]

The employees of the Ministry of Police for instance were required to pay 2.5 per cent of their salary and the resulting monies were then invested in shares, something which would have been impossible in the more disturbed financial conditions of the Directory. By the late Empire there was therefore virtual certainty of the payment of a pension provided the service was sufficiently long enough and regarded as justified by the Cour des Comptes. Thus one War Office clerk who was dismissed in 1806 after twenty-nine years service was only allowed to stay on and complete the requisite thirtieth year because of his son's military service.[32] So even the solution of the legal problem did not make government any less small-minded about the granting of pensions.

The average civil servant of the Directorial period was thus in a very partially and very confusingly regulated judicial position. Many of his duties were enforced by law but his right to security was conceded neither in theory nor in practice. If the state of a civil servant was so hedged about with obligations and so little provided with rewards or preparation, one still has to ask why so many people were willing to embark on a *cursus honorum* which could take them not on the neat path suggested by Woronoff, but on a virtually unpredictable pilgrimage in and out of the new state mechanism. Again the answer is economic security. The fact was, as a deputy once pointed out, that ministers did have *some* funds available for their staff.[33] In the disturbed conditions of the Revolution the proverbial half loaf was definitely better than no bread.

What this *cursus* meant in practice can of course only be explained by reference to the personnel files. Happily, with all their faults these provide much more information than the still fragmentary legislation on *la fonction publique*: as Table III shows, for instance, for the majority of clerks this *cursus* could be a short one as 60 per cent served for under five years in the ministries and a third of this group for only a few months.[35] The average length of service was between six and seven years, since the short-term appointments were balanced by the substantial number who served for over fifteen years. The reason for this distribution with its very low median length of service of about three years is that the Directory at the outset rid itself of a large number of by then redundant revolutionary clerks, and thereafter set about reducing the civil service to a hard core of long-service employees, on whom it could depend to help in its work of consolidation. Hence there is actually an increase in the length of service in the over-twenty-years range. Antoine Nicolas Rosman indeed only ended in 1843 as a *Chef de Division* and *Maître des Requêtes* a career which had begun as an *expéditionnaire* in the Travaux Publics of the Interior nearly forty-nine years before.

If one looks at service in the administration as a whole rather than just at that in the individual ministry, a somewhat different pattern emerges. For if service of less than a year was only fractionally less common overall than in the ministries, and if there was only a slight increase in the number serving for medium terms of from five to twenty years, there was a marked fall in the number who spent up to five years in the bureaux. More significantly, however, there was a very substantial increase in the number who served for more than twenty years where the figures are 12.1 per cent for the ministries but 22.1 per cent for administrative service in general. So if the median of five years service was low, the average length of service was at least ten years. In fact, there is a very high probability that these low

TABLE III: LENGTH OF MINISTERIAL SERVICE

	Less than 1 year	%	1–5 years	%	5–10 years	%	10–15 years	%	15–20 years	%	Over 20 years	%
Sec. Gen.	91	36.6	108	43.3	9	3.6	9	3.6	20	8.0	12	4.9
Finances	96	23.0	205	49.2	66	15.8	23	5.5	8	1.9	19	4.6
Justice	110	27.2	166	41.0	47	11.6	15	3.7	19	4.6	48	11.9
Ext. Rel.	59	21.6	129	47.0	29	10.5	12	4.5	10	3.6	35	12.8
Marine	103	18.7	217	39.3	58	10.6	34	6.2	28	5.1	112	20.1
Police	196	32.0	330	54.0	24	3.9	13	2.1	29	4.7	20	3.3
War	79	9.3	336	39.4	120	14.0	39	4.6	83	9.7	197	23.0
Interior	201	20.6	547	56.0	59	6.0	52	5.3	37	3.8	81	8.3
Total	935	21.6	2034	46.9	412	9.5	197	4.5	234	5.4	524	12.1

figures are as much the product of deficiencies in the documentation as of the presence of fly-by-nighters. Very often the presence of clerks in a service can only be explained on the basis of prior service elsewhere. Rarely can this be proved. All these statistics, unreliable as they are, can be not fairly regarded as minima.

Hence if one went further with the analysis of long administrative careers than has been done here, one would find two significant things. Firstly, there is not a steady pattern of numbers decreasing as service gets longer. There are a number of irregularities which suggest that if a clerk served more than a minimum period he was likely to go on for a very long time. In other words, numbers actually rise as the term of years creeps up into the thirty- and forty-year marks. Secondly, long-term careers are most common in services like the Admiralty where there was a well-established interconnection between field and central employment. This again suggests the existence of a long-term career dynamic. In a handful of cases this went on for over fifty-five years. The longest serving official of all, against whom Rosman's career—which itself was extended by a few years in the office of a Receiver of Taxes in Lunéville—almost pales into insignificance was François Julien Deshayes. He was an Ingénieur-Mécanicien in the Admiralty who entered naval service in 1759, became an engineer in 1787 and served till 1825,

TABLE IV: LENGTH OF ALL ADMINISTRATIVE SERVICE

	Less than 1 year	%	1–5 years	%	5–10 years	%	10–15 years	%	15–20 years	%	Over 20 years	%
Sec. Gen.	76	30.3	78	31.4	33	13.3	8	3.2	22	8.9	32	12.9
Finances	89	21.3	129	31.0	75	18.0	38	9.1	20	4.8	66	15.8
Justice	100	24.8	159	39.2	53	13.1	17	4.2	23	5.7	53	14.0
Ext. Rel.	57	20.8	104	38.0	25	9.1	14	5.1	18	6.6	56	20.4
Marine	98	17.7	165	30.0	57	10.3	21	3.8	28	5.1	183	33.1
Police	190	31.0	248	40.5	67	11.0	14	2.3	21	3.4	72	11.8
War	67	7.7	216	25.2	120	14.0	50	6.8	77	9.0	324	37.3
Interior	190	19.4	491	50.4	58	6.0	35	3.6	30	3.0	173	17.7
Total	867	20.0	1590	36.6	488	11.3	197	4.5	239	5.5	959	22.1

a total of sixty-six years, unequalled even by any of his many long-serving relatives.

Probably the average length of service was greater than that which a similar analysis for 1793 would produce. Certainly the figures for service in all forms of administration—which does not include the army, the courts, and education—do show how the Directory recruited the already trained. This is not to underestimate the size of the apparent fly-by-night contingent. In fact, however, it was predominantly for the young and low-grade employees, and particularly for those in politically sensitive ministries like that of the Police that insecurity of tenure was at its height. The service thus described could stretch from the 1750s until the 1840s. It lasted right up till 1848 in the case of B. M. Rouillard of the Interior. However, it was predominantly the revolutionary and imperial periods which counted.

The reason that service came to an end, according to the evidence of a sample drawn from the Ministry of the Interior, was usually quite orthodox. A third of those on whom information is available retired normally, and the next largest category left because of economic and organizational reforms.[36] It also seems that wherever possible they stayed in the ministries. Only about one in ten returned to professional or business life, a fact which, when considered in relation to the realization that nearly a third of the 2,500 cases on whom information is available held more than three administrative posts in their careers, reinforces the impression of a group of men resolutely wedded to administrative service whatever its drawbacks.

For a majority, as Table V shows, a ministerial career usually began quite late in the day, since nearly half joined under the Directory, compared to a fifth during the revolutionary government and as many again during the Thermidorian period. However, since so many of those who joined the Directory were taken on in its early days, Bosher's claim that the Directory was the single most important period in the peopling of the new bureaucracy is perhaps a little too strong.[37] The Directory, after an initial period of hesitation, in fact brought to an end the wave of recruitment which had begun earlier in the Revolution, and by dropping superfluous and generally unsatisfactory staff was able to make room for more mature, tested, and reliable men.

As Table VI shows, six times, as many clerks had actually entered state service in general under the Ancien Régime as had entered the ministries, and three times as many had been recruited under the Constitutional Monarchy. Only thereafter was recruitment to the ministries more or less comparable with that into state administration in general. By then the main reservoir of experience talent had been drawn into the ministries, and the latter's continuing need for men led to the direct recruitment of rather more young men than before. The fact that the ministries were obviously restored to their old position at the top of the administrative hierarchy must have added to their attractiveness.

Something like 18 per cent of those on whom information is available entered the ministries in search of their first paid employment, usually at a fairly junior level. There they mixed with the slightly smaller proportions of people who had joined the ministry because of the transfer of a bureau, as a result of patronage, or in search of advancement.[38] The role of family influence and connections was much less than in the past. Obviously the ministries were not just a young man's occupation, although the youngest employee listed, a *garçon* in the Interior called J. C. Delangle, was born only in 1788. In fact over half the sample were born between 1750 and 1770, so if the centre of gravity was near to twenty when the Revolution began, by 1800

TABLE V: DATE OF ENTRY TO MINISTERIAL SERVICE

	Before 1774	%	1774–88	%	1789	%	1790	%	1791	%	1792	%	1793	%	1794	%	1795	%	1796	%	1797	%	1798	%	1799	%
Sec. Gen.	—	0	—	0	—	0	—	0	—	0	—	0	—	0	—	0	161	64.9	62	24.9	6	2.4	13	5.0	7	2.8
Finances	7	1.7	46	11.1	2	0.5	6	1.5	19	4.9	9	2.1	29	6.9	46	11.1	110	26.3	65	15.6	23	5.5	5	1.2	50	12.0
Justice	3	0.7	14	3.4	—	0	13	3.2	28	6.9	12	3.0	17	4.2	15	3.7	111	27.4	107	26.4	40	9.9	20	5.0	25	6.2
Ext. Rel.	14	5.1	15	5.5	2	0.7	2	0.7	2	0.7	17	6.2	24	8.8	32	11.7	69	25.2	50	11.2	26	9.5	6	2.2	15	5.5
Marine	25	4.5	55	10.0	5	1.0	5	1.0	5	1.0	39	7.0	55	10.0	28	5.1	61	11.1	72	13.0	88	15.8	89	16.0	25	4.5
Police	—	0	—	0	—	0	—	0	—	0	—	0	—	0	—	0	—	0	341	55.7	71	11.6	88	14.4	112	18.3
War	26	3.0	29	3.4	7	0.8	5	0.5	26	3.0	82	2.5	159	16.2	123	14.8	180	21.1	83	9.6	47	5.5	69	8.1	38	4.4
Interior	11	1.1	25	2.6	2	0.2	7	0.7	16	1.7	30	3.2	69	7.1	297	30.2	192	19.7	128	13.2	86	8.8	63	6.4	51	5.1
Total	86	2.0	184	4.2	18	0.4	38	0.9	96	2.2	189	4.3	353	8.1	541	12.4	884	20.3	908	20.8	387	8.9	353	8.1	323	7.4

TABLE VI: DATE OF ENTRY TO ANY ADMINISTRATIVE SERVICE

	Before 1774	%	1774–88	%	1789	%	1790	%	1791	%	1792	%	1793	%	1794	%	1795	%	1796	%	1797	%	1798	%	1799	%	Total
Secretariat	8	5.4	20	13.5	10	6.7	10	6.7	9	6.1	18	12.1	27	18.1	20	13.5	13	8.6	8	5.4	3	1.9	2	1.3	1	0.7	149
Finances	22	9.2	71	29.8	15	6.6	36	15.1	19	8.0	12	5.1	25	10.5	26	10.9	5	2.2	3	1.4	4	1.8	1	0.4	0	—	239
Justice	4	1.9	25	12.0	9	4.3	30	14.3	30	14.3	21	11.1	28	13.4	28	13.4	16	7.7	10	4.8	4	1.9	1	0.5	3	1.4	209
Ext. Rel.	18	10.4	40	23.2	10	5.8	16	9.2	4	2.3	15	8.7	25	14.4	22	12.7	10	5.8	7	4.1	3	1.7	0	—	3	1.7	173
Marine	75	25.6	96	32.7	7	2.4	20	6.8	7	2.9	12	4.1	21	7.2	24	8.2	7	2.4	9	3.1	9	3.1	5	1.7	1	0.3	293
Police	10	4.1	26	10.7	19	7.9	49	20.2	13	5.4	18	7.4	29	12.0	33	13.6	12	4.9	17	7.0	3	1.3	7	2.9	6	2.5	242
War	76	10.5	187	25.7	17	2.3	48	6.5	29	4.0	61	8.4	106	14.7	118	16.5	46	6.4	9	1.2	10	1.3	16	2.2	2	0.2	725
Interior	74	14.6	101	20.0	21	4.2	27	5.4	16	3.2	40	7.9	65	12.9	84	16.6	28	5.6	16	3.1	18	3.5	8	1.6	7	1.4	505
Total	287	11.3	565	22.4	108	4.2	236	9.3	127	5.0	197	7.8	326	12.9	355	14.0	137	5.4	79	3.1	54	2.1	40	1.6	23	0.9	2535

some 54 per cent of the staff were over forty. It seems fair to say that the ministerial bureaucracy was a nice blend of youth and experience. The highest proportion of young staff seems to have been in the 'new' departments like that of the Police.[39]

Moreover, youth and experience were not always opposites, since many people gained their experience fairly early in life. As Table VIII shows, if one considers the age of entry to all forms of state employment the largest group began their careers as teenagers, compared with a third who joined when they were between thirty and fifty and about one in twenty who joined after their fiftieth birthday. Over half seem to have entered in fact before they were more than about twenty-seven, whereas, to judge from a sample from the Ministry of the Interior, the trend towards youthful entry was much less marked in the ministries. People continued to join the ministries even when they were in their seventies, whereas it was much less common to join them when they were very young. The reverse situation applied to *la fonction publique* in general. All this shows, that with the partial exception of the Ministries of War and of Justice the service was far less well provided with callow youths than people like Masson have claimed.[40]

Such accusations ignore the tremendous predominance of trained career officials in the ministries. Even if one considers their birthplace one finds that along with geographical, economic, and educational factors, the importance of easy access to administrative employment stands out in towns such as Dijon, Montauban, Paris, Toulon, and especially Versailles.[41] Similarly, the high percentage of state employees amongst those whose parentage is known points in a similar direction, while the 8 per cent of the service who had had some sort of further education may also have been the beginnings of the nineteenth-century preference for graduate entry to the administration. Again, although there were social divisions in the ministries, as will be seen, without the requisite experience even many of the more privileged would not have got admission to the ministries in the first place.

The importance of this prior experience is shown by the fact that so many people held more than one administrative post, so that the following analysis bears on the number of posts rather than on the number of individuals involved. Where pre-

TABLE VII: DATE OF BIRTH

	Before 1720	%	1720–30	%	1730–40	%	1740–50	%	1750–60	%	1760–70	%	1770–80	%	After 1780	%	Totals
Sec. Gen.	—	0	1	0.9	13	11.5	22	19.5	29	25	19	16.8	27	23.8	2	1.8	113
Finances	2	2.8	—	0	11	15.5	19	26.8	19	26.8	13	18.3	7	9.8	—	0	71
Justice	—	0	—	0	6	6.3	11	11.6	25	26.4	31	32.6	17	17.9	5	5.2	95
Ext. Rel.	2	1.3	6	4.1	11	7.4	27	18.1	47	31.6	34	22.8	19	12.9	3	2.0	149
Marine and Col.	—	0	8	2.8	27	9.6	51	18.4	77	27.8	73	26.6	29	10.5	12	4.3	277
Police	—	0	5	1.8	11	4.1	32	11.9	62	23.0	104	38.5	52	19.2	4	1.5	270
War	—	0	8	1.7	19	4.1	56	12.1	108	23.3	156	33.7	108	23.3	9	1.8	464
Interior	2	0.4	11	2.6	48	10.3	90	19.2	157	33.5	106	22.6	41	8.8	11	2.6	466
Totals	6	0.3	39	2.1	146	7.7	308	16.1	524	27.4	536	28.2	300	15.7	46	2.5	1905

TABLE VIII: AGE ON ENTRY TO ANY ADMINISTRATIVE SERVICE

	Under 20	%	20–5	%	25–30	%	30–5	%	35–40	%	40–5	%	45–50	%	50–5	%	55–60	%	Over 60	%	Total
Sec. Gen.	24	22.7	23	21.7	5	4.7	15	14.2	8	7.5	8	7.5	9	8.5	6	5.7	5	4.7	3	2.8	106
Finances	16	23.5	16	23.5	15	22.0	6	8.9	5	7.3	7	10.3	—	0	1	1.5	2	3.0	—	0	68
Justice	25	31.2	13	16.3	14	17.6	11	13.8	7	8.7	3	3.7	4	5.0	2	2.5	1	1.2	—	0	80
Ext. Rel.	29	20.2	32	22.3	18	12.5	22	15.3	15	10.4	13	9.0	6	4.1	2	1.4	3	2.0	4	2.8	144
Marine and Col.	103	39.0	51	19.4	43	16.3	25	9.4	15	5.7	13	4.9	9	3.4	2	0.8	—	0	3	1.1	264
Police	23	13.7	40	23.8	40	23.8	22	13.1	15	9.0	13	7.7	6	3.5	4	2.4	2	1.2	3	1.8	168
War	154	35.2	81	18.4	75	17.1	56	12.8	28	6.4	25	5.7	12	2.7	6	1.3	1	0.2	1	0.2	439
Interior	83	18.4	96	21.3	58	12.8	52	11.5	54	12.0	48	10.6	21	4.6	16	3.5	10	2.2	14	3.1	452
	457	26.6	352	20.6	268	15.5	209	12.2	147	8.5	130	7.5	67	3.9	39	2.2	24	1.4	28	1.6	1721

revolutionary service is concerned nearly half the occupations were in government employment of one kind or another.[42] The Ministries themselves accounted for 13.3 per cent, with the Contrôle Général being the most frequently encountered. Most of these passed directly to the corresponding ministry during the revolution, especially where the defence ministries and the Ministry of Finance were concerned.

However the field and dependent services of the monarchy provided the Directorial Ministers with nearly twice as many staff as the monarchical ministries', notably the Fermes, the Aides, and then the Vingtièmes and other lesser services. The *Receveurs*, Rentes, Monnaies, Douanes, the Chambres des Comptes, and all the other taxation services also supplied a substantial number of men, a surprising number of whom finished up in the Ministry of War. Similarly, the external services of the defence ministries also provided themselves with a good number of recruits. There were also many clerks drawn from a host of institutions that are hard to classify: the royal buildings service, the Garde Meuble, the Contrôle des Actes, and the Inspection de Commerce. Finally, about 4 per cent had been locally attached, especially in the old Intendancies, including those in Paris and Dijon, or had held minor venal office or worked for the various provincial and municipal authorities of the Ancien Régime.

This tendency to recruit from those with knowledge and experience of the administration is even more marked in the occupations held during the Revolution when 82.4 per cent of the sum of 5,438 jobs recorded can be classed as administrative.[43] Even allowing for multiple employment this still represents a very large percentage of the bureaucracy. Since the number who had been engaged in other professions was so small, the Directory had a bureaucracy the vast majority of which had some administrative experience. Revolutionary experience came in particular from the ministries, the bodies dependent on them, the legislatures, and local government. The first was the largest category with 38.3 per cent, of which nearly a quarter came not surprisingly from the War Office. The second group, the dependent and field services, provided 24.8 per cent of the posts in question, with the financial services, notably the Direction Générale de la Liquidation, the Caisse de l'Extraordinaire, the Fabrication des Assignats, the Trésorie Nationale, and the expanded judicial services of the Revolution being the most frequently encountered employments.

Another new source of recruits was the legislatures, especially the Constituent and the Convention whose committees, notably the three major committees of the Thermidorian period, provided the greater part of a quarter of the sample covered by this area. Others had worked as secretaries to *représentants en mission*, while 9.5 per cent, rather more than previously, had worked for local government bodies, above all those in Paris. Elected officials and judges went in quite substantial numbers to the Ministries of Police and of Justice where their contacts and experience could be put to good use, as could those of National Guard officers in the former apparently. Less prestigious local government employees tended to finish up in the Secrétariat Général and the Ministries of War and of the Interior. Lastly there was the 1 per cent of deputies who won high appointments through the ministries, usually for political reasons but sometimes because they were destitute.[44]

However, despite all the stress here placed on the fundamentally administrative nature of recruitment into the ministries, it must not be forgotten that there were considerable social dichotomies within this pattern. Certain jobs and departments provided a much higher percentage of senior staff than others. The Ministry of Finance, the Treasury, and elected *fonctionnaires*, like lawyers and members of the other liberal professions, all produced 40 per cent of senior posts compared to the norm of 25 per cent. Under the Ancien Régime a number of other institutions abolished at the revolution played the same role, such as the Ponts et Chaussées, the estate of the House of Orleans, and soldiers, while the Revolution added others such as the diplomatic corps, the Caisse de l'Extraordinaire, deputies and their secretaries, judges, and the *Balance du Commerce*. On the other hand, many of the larger and more impersonal organizations like the Postes, Assignats, the Imprimerie Nationale, and the local and Conventional committees tended to produce a majority of lower-grade employees. This administrative stratification was closely connected to social distinctions.

The reality of this general portrait is perhaps best appreciated by a brief consideration of the careers of some of the people who actually staffed the civil service. This may also do something to show that the civil servants of the Directory were not just faceless men.[45] At the bottom of the hierarchy could be found long-serving *garçons de bureau* like François Lafond. Born in Versailles about 1723 he had joined the ministry as a servant to Bussy and others. Sometimes he seems to have acted as a *garçon de bureau* and then from 1780 to 1794 he was *concierge* of the ministerial buildings. After this he served as a *garçon* to the Dépôt, where the departmental maps were kept, before apparently returning to his old domestic duties. A similar case was François Ployaut, a porter in the Ministry of the Interior. Son of a *maréchal ferrant* in the artillery, he was born at Barges (Haute-Saône) in 1727, and despite spending thirty years as a domestic to Maréchal de Mouchy he was able to secure a place as porter to the Agence des Mines in Thermidor II. He passed with his section to the renewed ministry in 1795 and remained there as *garçon* to the Conseil des Mines until his retirement in 1808. Unlike Lafond he did not have a son whom he could place as an *aspirant* in the ministry.

This was something which *garçons* often did, as in the case of Christophe Damian Ancemont, the son of a teacher, who had been born near Verdun in 1763 and who had entered the Naval Dépôt des Cartes et Plans as a *garçon* in January 1788. He retained his post unchanged until 1803 when some portering duties were added to it. Before he was pensioned off in 1828, he found a place for his eldest son, who was to serve both as *garçon* and clerk. Not all low-grade clerks had such traditions and connections of course. Pierre Bachelot, a *garçon* in the Secrétariat Général, had been a mirror-maker in Paris from about 1751 when as a fifteen-year-old, he had migrated to the capital. The Revolution had made him unemployed, and it was his need to support a family of four and his relative lack of political involvement that won him the vacancy caused by the dismissal of another *garçon* from what was felt to be a position of confidence in 1796. He evidently proved satisfactory as he kept the place till his death in 1813.

The same economic urges were even more noticeable amongst the highly insecure group of auxiliary personnel. Thus Pierre Blanc Lalesie, a teacher born at Oléron (Basses-Pyrénées) about 1767, drew on his educational experience and joined the

Commission de l'Instruction Publique as a *sous-chef* in Floréal II. He was transferred to the Interior only to be made redundant two months later in Nivôse IV. He was then briefly employed in the Secretariat of the Ministry of External Relations, but soon had to be content with a place as a *surnuméraire* in the Financial bureau of the Directorial Secretariat. But despite a recommendation from his *chef* he was unable to maintain his position in the face of Lagarde's reforms and disappears from view in Thermidor IV. A more fortunate case was that of Claude Étienne Formey of the Ministry of Justice. He first appears as a *supplémentaire* in the early part of Year VII but a year later he claimed to be in desperate straits since he had received neither pay nor tenure in the last six months. He was first accorded an advance of six francs per month and in Frimaire VIII he was established as *expéditionnaire*. By 1817 he was earning 2,600 francs per annum as a *Commis Principal*, and he was able to retire after twenty-seven years' service with a pension of just over 1,000 francs per annum.

Having a father in the service was no guarantee against insecurity as Charles Marie Lavriot Prevost found. He was born in Paris in 1778, and described himself as having been a student until Floréal II when he joined his father in the Commission des Armes et Poudres. He never fell into the ranks of the auxiliaries but though he was transferred to the Interior as an *expéditionnaire* in the Bureau Particulier, where his ability soon led him to rise, and despite the fact that his father had by then been transferred from the War Office to the Interior, he was twice made redundant. The first time was briefly after Pluviôse VI and then more permanently in Germinal VIII. It was only much later that he was able to gain reinstatement as an *expéditionnaire* in the Agriculture bureau, after a year's further apprenticeship in 1806–7, long after his father had moved on. He retired in the same rank, though in the Ministry of Commerce, in 1834.

J. B. N. Laigneau of the Interior had a much smoother career. Born in Saint-Germain (Loiret) in May 1768 he was a *Commis aux Aides* for three years till 1791. After a period of unemployment he became an *expéditionnaire* in the Commission de l'Agriculture et Commerce. Automatically transferred to the Interior he remained in the same position until 1823. A similar pattern emerges from the career of Nicolas Blériot, a soldier in the 1780s, who turned up in the War Office in June 1794. From there he moved to the Police Secretariat two year later, and remained with his bureau under different ministries until 1819.

As mere copyists such people found it hard to make themselves seem indispensable and therefore gain much promotion. Junior clerks with more variegated tasks had greater possibilities.[46] Louis Jean Mathias Vée, again from the Ministry of Police, who was born in 1772, proves the point. After serving, like Blériot, in the army, though in this case between 1793 and 1797, he was able to obtain, after some delay, a place as an *expéditionnaire*. Once he gained promotion to a junior clerkship he was able to rise and by 1829 he was a *Sous-Chef* in the Interior which was then in charge of Police Affairs. Moreover, because of his zeal in the *Trois Glorieuses* he was allowed to return as a *surnuméraire* in 1830 so as to finish some work he had been doing on the *colons* of Saint-Domingo, showing the value of both specialization and street-fighting. Rather less colourful was Antoine Belanger, under the Directory a poorly paid *Noticeur* in the Ministry of Justice and previously employed by the Commission des Revenus Nationaux and the committees of the Convention, after initially starting out in life as a solicitor's clerk. Having made contact with Merlin de Douai in the Convention he was made a *sous-chef* in the Ministries of Police and of Justice, only to be demoted after Merlin's departure from the latter. Thereafter he was never able to regain ministerial attention and seems to have retired in the same rank in 1815.

More fortunate was J. B. F. A. D. Rouillard, one of two sons of a *Commis d'Ordre* in the War Office who served as a *Rédacteur* there under the Directory, this being a grade rated much lower there than elsewhere. He was born in Toulouse in 1778 and claimed to have been a student and a journalist before becoming an *extraordinaire* in the ministry in May 1793, possible because he had served as a clerk in the Jacobin Club. Established in March 1794 he remained a *Rédacteur* until Ventôse X when he was called up for service in the cavalry. He soon moved sideways into the military field services and from there via a new auxiliary post in the War Office in Vendémiaire XI to a highly successful career leading to his retiring as an honorary *Chef de Division Adjoint* in 1816. His brother served even longer but could only rise to be a *sous-chef*. This was the rank obntained by another *Rédacteur* in the same department, J. B. L. H. l'Heureux, a Parisian born in 1760, who served in the Fermes for the five years until 1790. After this he reverted to teaching geography until December 1794 when he joined the Troupes à Cheval bureau of the War Office. He remained a junior clerk until 1813, was promoted further to *sous-chef*, and retired as such in 1822.

Promotion from domestic to *garçon* and from *auxiliaire* to *titulaire*, etc., suggest that all posts were strictly ranked, but this was not always the case. A ministerial *concierge* for example was obviously more important than a newly enrolled office-boy. This uncertainty is nowhere more visible than in the technical and specialist grades, which for this reason have been put into a separate category slightly apart from the rest of the hierarchy. Thus a man like Charles-François Beautemps-Beaupré, under the Directory apparently only a hydrographer in the Admiralty earning 3,800 francs per annum turns out to have been on a par with the administrative élite. Born near Saint-Ménéhould in 1766 he had joined the Dépôt as an *ingénieur* in 1785, and besides working on maps of the Baltic he had gone on several trips including one, in 1791, in search of La Pérouse, and one to Africa where he was imprisoned in 1796. On his release he was promoted and made *Sous-Conservateur* of the Dépôt. Six years later he was made a *sous-chef*, and following his appointment to the Institute in 1810 he became *Ingénieur-Hydrographe en chef* and deputy head of the Dépôt from where he retired, larded with honours, in the late 1840s.

Similarly, someone like Louis Guilliaume Bouteville, the former Constituent from the Somme who had held a multitude of departmental offices, was vastly more important than his post as legal consultant in the Ministry of Justice at 4,500 francs in Years V–VI might suggest. His subsequent career in the Anciens and the Tribunate confirms this. On the other hand, many of the translators and *Agents pour la démarcation des frontières* in the Ministry of External relations were of much lesser standing. Simon Pierre Brossier for instance, a well-educated Versaillois born in 1753, who had been a surveyor and soldier as well as working in the ministry and in the Comité de Salut Public, was dismissed in 1796 ostensibly because of his political views.

Although the ministry in fact sent him on other missions, the only promotion he could get came from the army and that after Brumaire.

The status of senior clerks was less likely to involve such variations.[47] Gilles Gabriel Chervise, for example, a principal clerk in the Vivres section of the Admiralty, who was born at Poissy (Seine-et-Oise) in 1748, had entered the Vingtièmes in 1774. From there he moved within a few months to the Intendance de Paris and ultimately to the Vivres service in January 1779, where he remained until he was made redundant as a *Sous-Directeur* in 1802. He was reintegrated soon after in his grade and reattached to the central administration in July 1807. He remained there until he retired to his estate near Versailles in 1813.

Another long-serving senior employee was G. N. F. Mongin, under the Directory an *examinateur* in the *émigrés* section of the Ministry of Police at a salary of 3,600 francs. He had joined the Fermes when he was about twenty-one, but then transferred to the Secretariat of the École de Guerre in 1769 where he was to remain until 1793. It was then that he acquired his familiarity with *émigré* affairs when he joined the Comité de Salut Public. As a result Merlin took him into the Ministry of Police where he stayed at least till 1798. A newer arrival was Nicolas Adam Mathez of the War Office. Once an *avocat au Parlement de Normandie* in his birthplace of Rouen, he seems to have been unemployed when he joined the ministry. He was soon promoted to a senior clerkship and by the Year IX he was *Chef* of the Équipages bureau in which he had started his ministerial career. A little later he resigned to serve with the army as an *Inspecteur* of Équipages, a post he held at least till 1811.

Likewise Directorial *sous-chefs* often had long careers behind them. Jean Bouret of the Ministry of Finances was originally a legal clerk and then a lawyer in Dijon before joining the staff of the Intendance there, where he met Amelot who took him to that of Caen. After a period in the Administrations des Économats, he rejoined Amelot at the Caisse de l'Extraordinaire, and later passed through the Domaines service to the Ministry where he stayed till about 1798. By then he claimed thirty-two-years' service. An even more interesting case is that of Demandre, the *sous-chef* in the Fonds bureau of the Interior who was responsible for paying out all the Directory's domestic monies. He had been born in Varennes about 1775 and, after a long period with a lawyer, he passed in 1792 to the Caisse de l'Extraordinaire, and thence, via the Commission des Revenus Nationaux, to the Comité de Sûreté Générale. This double competence in finance and police work earned him a transfer to this very delicate post. He stayed there until Messidor VIII after which he served in the offices of the Gendarmerie and the Garde Imperiale until 1812.

Aubin Chandeau, a *sous-chef* in the Remontes bureau to the War Office, was born in Paris in 1769 to a *commissaire des guerres*, started his career as a naval clerk in Le Havre in 1787, transferring a few days later to the Ministry of War where he stayed until his retirement in 1817. A younger man still was F. N. Felix Bertheley, a law student in Dijon, prior to joining the Greffe de Bourgogne in 1786. With the coming of the Revolution he moved to the bureaux of the new department of the Côte d'Or as a *sous-chef* in its police section. From there no doubt Prieur's influence brought him to the military bureau of the Sûreté Générale, and then to the Directorial and Imperial secretariats, regaining his old rank *en route*.

Bertheley was one of the many Dijonnais who achieved a certain amount of promotion through their abilities and through the patronage of local politicians and administrators like Amelot, Prieur, and Guyton de Morveau.[48] Thus Pierre Chabeuf, originally a clerk in the États de Bourgogne, joined the new department as its head of taxation. In the summer of 1793 he was sent to Paris to solicit extra aid from the revolutionary government, a mission which seems to have won him the position of Secretary of the Armes section of the Comité de Salut Public in Brumaire II. From there he passed to the Secretariat-General as head of its military bureau, and also, as a result of his own initiative, as the official responsible for handling all the Directory's nominations. As has been seen, even this failed to save him from redundancy in Vendémiaire VI, though his liaisons with Carnot may have played some part too. He eventually finished up as *Chef de la Quatrième Division* of the Seine Préfecture when he retired in 1815.

François Gattey was also born in Dijon, in 1752. His first administrative post was as a director in the Intendance de

Monsieur, frère du Roi in 1780, but within two years he had left this and took up a variety of posts in the fiscal services in Champagne. From 1792 he was responsible for the correspondence on food supplies of the Army of the Rhine. After this, he joined the Interior as head of its Bureau de Poids et Mesures, where he had much to do with launching the metric system before he retired in 1815. Rather less is known of Pierre Louis Nardin, a one-time lawyer's clerk from Dijon, who served in the Intendance there from 1784 until 1790 when Amelot called him to the Caisse de l'Extraordinaire. This proved to be the prelude to service in the Domaines, the Commission des Revenus Nationaux and ultimately the Ministry of Finance where he was one of the most senior *chefs de bureau* by 1798.

Much more is known of Secretaries-General and heads of divisions, and they therefore need less illustration. About half of those under the Directory seem to have been political appointments while the remainder seem to have been internal promotions on merit.[49] A good example of the latter is François Nicolas Bocquet, Secretary-General of the Interior from Brumaire IV to Vendémiaire VI. Born at Aumay (Mont Blanc) in 1746, it was the pre-Revolution which really launched his career, lifting him after twenty years in the tax service and the Intendance de Paris to be secretary to the Assemblée Provinciale de l'île de France. This earned him the equivalent post in the Seine-et-Oise and ultimately a transfer to the central government, first as head of the Armes et Poudres Commission and then of that of Organisation et Mouvement. He was then called to the Interior, after which he served in the military supplies administration. Finally he was called back to the ministry as head of the Expéditions et Archives section, a post he held till retiring in 1813.

A comparable case is Louis Charles Henri Bertin, a Secretary-General of the Admiralty early in the Directory's life. A colonial from Louisburg, where he was born in 1752, he served on board ship and in ports like Bordeaux as a naval clerk until made head of Fonds in the Admiralty in 1791. This was a prelude to his further promotion in the ministry. After Floréal V he went on to a distinguished career as *Commissaire de la Marine, Préfet Maritime, Conseiller d'Etat, Préfet de Martinique*, and, after a period in the wilderness, as adviser to Eugène Beaunharnais in Italy.

Cases who owed more to politics included Ignace Joseph Delecroix of the Ministry of Justice, once professor of law in Douai and Secretary of the Dyle. Made government commissioner to the courts there he was brought to Paris by Lambrechts in Prairial VI as Secretary-General. Despite his closeness to one minister he held the position until 1808, a tenure which subsequently earned him important legal posts. Finally, Alexandre Maurice Blanc d'Hauterive was one of those who obtained high office before the Revolution. From an impoverished noble family in Dauphiné, he was taken up by Choiseul when a lecturer of twenty-six, and attached to the embassy in Constantinople. On his return to Paris he was ruined financially by the Revolution and ejected from the New York consulate. Attached to the Ministry of External Relations in a consultative capacity in 1797 he was made head of the first political division by Reinhard in Vendémiaire VIII, which was to lead to a very distinguished Imperial career in which he did much to help create the new nobility of which he became a member.

These few case histories help to confirm the picture of the average Directorial bureaucrat as a native of Versailles, Paris, or some other north-eastern town, born between 1750 and 1770, and having entered state service when he was about twenty-one. He was likely to have joined a ministry a few years later, probably when the Revolution was well under way, and was likely to serve for seven years or more, albeit often with a break in his service. After this he was liable to have to pass to another department or to have to struggle on towards a pension or, in a few cases, a higher grade. Despite the failings in the legislation on the standing of officialdom there was in practice a *cursus honorum* which as the case histories show, was usually more important than things like patronage. Despite the lack of provision for their advancement and reward, people had no hesitation in following the *cursus* in so far as they were allowed to by the gradual decline in numbers under the Directory. In case of disappointment they reacted instinctively to defend the career pattern opened by the Revolution, just as in the early nineteenth century they were to seek greater security and rights. It is this career dynamic which stands out despite the gaps in the sources, visible even in the case histories, and despite the variations inside the civil service.

It is apparent that the Revolution created a golden opportunity for the legions of minor employees of the lesser administrations of the Ancien Régime, by creating new institutions and openings for a very different kind of career. By temperament and necessity they seized these opportunities, which became increasingly stable and assured under the Directory, basically through the latter's handling of salaries. As a result the *fonction publique* became much more hierarchical, much more qualified, ever more dependent on its salaries, and more impersonal then in 1793, let alone than under the Ancien Régime.[50] However, it had acquired no new status to replace that of *commensaux du roi*, and its position in society and politics remained somewhat uncertain. For, as will be seen, despite the development of this internal dynamic, the administration was not at all detached from the effects of the still disturbed post-revolutionary environment.

CHAPTER VII: THE DIRECTORIAL BUREAUCRACY IN SOCIETY AND POLITICS

Grudgingly and incompletely the Directory seems to have accepted in practice that 'the bureaucratic apparatus is drawn to continue functioning by the most powerful interests which are material and objective'.[1] However, many people both then and since have not accepted this. They have remained oblivious to the way shared economic hardships, mutual dependence on administrative work and salaries, if paid, and subjection to the same structural and legal constraints had fostered the beginnings of both unity and a professional *esprit de corps*. In the main, public opinion did not accept the idea of a professional neutrality amongst public servants. There was no concept of the British civil service tradition of non-involvement in political life. Of course this tradition both masks the fact that the civil service is intimately involved in political life, even if not in party politics, and has obscured the general authority and potential of the civil service.[2] Yet even a less exaggerated view of civil service neutrality would not have appealed to them.

They expected and assumed involvement in public life and would have agreed with Mansfield that 'under revolutionary conditions unswerving attachment to the regime may outweigh all considerations of technical competence'.[3] Their great fear was the opponents of the new regime and the products of the corrupt society that had fostered the old political order had together subverted the administrative machine. Such opponents were therefore in a position to overturn the social and political conquests of the Revolution from inside whether deliberately or as a by-product of their egoism and incompetence. Neither sophisticated distinctions on the nature of permissible political activity nor a stress on the functional and social forces which

213

motivate a bureaucracy would have convinced them that this was not true.

Saint-Just was typical of this attitude. He considered that an official was not good enough to merit the title of citizen: 'Employé de l'État, sujet à l'intrigue, aux sollicitations, à la vénalité, le fonctionnaire est suspect, puis que rien ne prouve son civisme et son dévouement et qu'il ne existe aucune garantie de son sens du devoir.'[4] This vision of a civil service with no notion of public service, peopled only by royalists and *sots*, as Mercier put it, was to prove lasting and compelling. It recurs today though it was perhaps most forcefully expressed by an Anglo-Saxon writer of the inter-war period when he spoke of a:

tremendous bureaucracy, mired in procrastination, trussed up with red tape. Some two thousand clerks at the Ministry of War; everyone looking for a government job, and places found for as many as possible—royalists often, infesting the bureaus—functionaries with nothing to do, coming in at all hours, or not at all except to receive their pay; many of them utterly incompetent, dismally uneducated, but all of them servile, and all of them possessed of an elegant handwriting; pupils of Desalle and St. Cyr, students of Rolland's 'Great Art of Penmanship', *habitués* of Leyat's window in the Palais Royal, where the finest examples of 'coulée', 'ronde', 'anglo-french' may be studied. In every bourgeois home, two sole ambitions for the boys—penmanship and a government salary.[5]

Although this is an obvious travesty, as the discussion of the previous experience of employees has shown, it does show how historians have inherited the 'Sorelian' myths of the time. Similarly, it shows how these myths centred on the question of entry to the administration and on that of the political role adopted once an individual was inside. They ignore the wider aspects of the social and political role of the bureaucracy, for example the way in which it reflected the social cleavages of the times, the problem which dominates present-day sociological thinking on the subject.

In trying to rectify this omission, it is not possible to answer all the questions which a modern analyst would pose. One can get some impression of the social forces which acted on the bureaucracy, and of their relationship to the variety of political activities in which the bureaucracy was involved. Similarly, one cannot be very sure about the way in which the administration fitted into the general patterns of social mobility nor be very assertive about the extent and importance of political action inside the civil service. What one finds is problems, of hardship, of accommodation to rapidly changing political conditions and to constant suspicions, and of the interaction of the two. Sometimes social change called the tune, at other times the political element was pre-eminent.[6] Both always came into conflict with the nascent professionalism of the new bureaucracy. In other words, as the previous chapter has intimated, neither social nor political factors are by themselves sufficient explanations of the bureaucracy's behaviour.

The assumptions traditionally made about the crucial step of entry into the administration stand out very clearly where the social origins of those who sought to enter the service are concerned. One observer commented on the shabby dress and mien of the clerks in the Directorial Secretariat, while General Herlaut attributed the pattern of recruitment to the Ministry of War under Bouchotte to the way the Revolution had destroyed the livelihoods of those who were too weak or too old to volunteer for the army: artisans in the luxury trades, financial employees, teachers, and legal clerks are cited as examples, people with no resources save a basic education.[7] Much of this is true, if interpreted in a very pejorative manner, and the crisis of the economy will be seen to have been a very influential factor.

Yet by looking also at such evidence as there is on the geographical origins, social heritage, and personal background of Directorial employees, along with their evolving economic situation, it becomes increasingly clear that the employees in the main were neither feckless nor totally unfitted for their new tasks. Their attitude to salaries and to fringe benefits was not a selfish search for extra 'perks' but a basic necessity. Even after the crisis of 1795–7, when their very existence was sometimes threatened, had given way to a more rewarding deflationary situation, this remained largely true. Again, it can be shown that the civil service was not drawn from the dregs of the middle class, but from its upper and more responsible echelons, for only about a quarter had lower-class fathers and they were usually in the lower grades.[8] Such social barriers confirm that the upper ranks of the bureaucracy formed a new élite, although less unrepresentative than some others, since very few seem to have become *propriétaires* and many seem to have been ultimately downwardly mobile. Finally, one can see that although the service was not socially united, all of its members experienced the same problems. Indeed, the way social movements caused the bureaucracy to act rather goes someway towards Suleiman's contention that precise social origins are less central in deciding bureaucratic behaviour than administrative socialization.

To some extent the place in society occupied by Directorial bureaucrats was a product of their place of birth. The birth-place of about a third of the total is known. The vast majority were native-born Frenchmen, and although most parts of the hexagon supplied some of them, the mass of departments supplied less than 2 per cent of the sample.[9] On the other hand, the old departments of the Seine and the Seine-et-Oise supplied 26.4 per cent and 13.5 per cent respectively, which is lower than generally accepted figures for the proportion of native-born Parisians and their neighbours in the population of the capital at that time. In fact 40 per cent of the departments produced some 85 per cent of the sample. This reflects social and geographical factors, since the departments were largely concentrated in the north-eastern third of France, as Figure V shows.

Ease of access explains much of this, since it was easier to get to Paris and Versailles from the north-east than say from Cahors or from Gap. Not merely was the north-east closer, but the terrain was easier and the military roads and navigable rivers ran more conveniently. But this does not explain why people equally close, but on the wrong side of the dividing-line from Mont Saint-Michel to Geneva, such as the Orléannais and the Nivernais, did not figure equally prominently. Even the Seine-et-Marne did not supply as many clerks as one might have expected. This seems to have been due to economic factors. The Loire valley for instance was good farming land which was able to support not too dense a population without great difficulty, thus minimizing the pressures towards internal migration.

Urbanization was another important factor, not merely in Paris and Versailles, but throughout the country, reflecting both the urban nature of the Revolution and the hesitations and resistances of the countryside.[10] Some 27 per cent of the sample

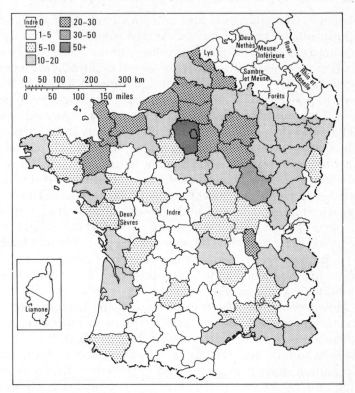

V   The Geographical Origins of Directorial Civil
      Servants, by *département*

were born in the country or in small hamlets, but in many
departments nearly all the entrants hailed from the major
towns, especially south of the line where only townspeople had
the education, inclination, or possibility of going to Paris or into
the civil service. There were apparently more and bigger towns
in the north, although this is open to question. There was also a
much higher degree of literacy and rather wider horizons in
general. Towns were to achieve a modicum of literacy much
earlier, notably in the north. Moreover, chance dictated that
many of the personal connections between *hauts fonctionnaires*
and potential employees were concentrated in the northern
zone, as in the case of Dijon.[11]

Literacy was nothern basic requirement, and the Mont Saint-

Michel–Geneva line was also an educational dividing-line.[12] Educationally France can be divided into three tiers. The northern tier north-east of the dividing-line was by far and away the best provided with towns, educational facilities, and literacy rates. In 1786–90 the average of signatures at weddings was over 40 per cent and many areas returned scores of over 70 per cent. The central tier from Brittany through the Loire valley to Belfort was the poorest of all in terms of schools and of literacy. The average literacy rate at marriage was below 20 per cent. The third tier, south of a line from the Gironde to Grenoble was nowhere near as advanced as the north-east but recorded an average of over 30 per cent of signatures at marriages. This is in line with findings that the south showed the greatest advance of all parts of France in the eighteenth century as the countryside began to catch up with the towns in the provision of schools. This pattern ties in with the distribution of civil servants. It points to the value of literacy as an aid to social and career mobility, as the figures show.

However, if the administration, with the exception of its service grades, was literate, very few of its members had any advanced secondary or tertiary education. About 8 per cent claimed to have had this, in two cases out of three before the Revolution, and significantly about 40 per cent of them achieved high rank by the time of the Directory, notably in the Ministry of Foreign Affairs. Some 125 of them claimed to have attended a University or Collège, and the remainder were educated privately in religious institutions, or less commonly in professional training-schools like the Écoles des Mines.[13] Law was the most common subject, followed by military science, theology, and the humanities. So the level of technical qualifications was low. What was at work was not the requirement for a degree-level of entry but simply the availability of legal and secondary education in the towns, especially in the north-eastern third of France as Figure VI implies. This rather fits in with Louis Chevalier's claim that:

Paris, à la fin du XVIII e siècle, et pendant une partie du XIX e siècle, est peuplé en majorité d'habitants venus des départements de l'Est et du Nord. Ce sont des gens de l'Est et du Nord qui ont fait la Révolution Française à Paris ainsi que les Révolutions de 1830 et de 1848. Ils appartenaient à des régions plus profondément urbaines que les autres régions de France et conservant des traditions de vie municipale active, tourmentée et souvent sanglante.[14]

For many, birth in a province was followed by an appointment there in the field services of the Ancien Régime. For others it was followed by a move to Paris or entry into a professional, service, or commercial occupation and sometimes the two together. Just over a quarter of the sample whose pre-revolutionary occupation is recorded were in the liberal professions, with lawyers—*avocats, procureurs*, and *notaires*—the largest single group at 7.5 per cent.[15] The 5.4 per cent of teachers fall into two groups, the lowly

VI   The Geographical Origins of Directorial Civil
     Servants, by towns

instituteurs discussed by Herlaut, and the professors in the
Sorbonne and other universities or colleges, specializing in
mathematics, languages, and *belles-lettres*.[16] These often found
their way into External Relations or the Education Division of
the Interior. They were joined in the latter by many of the fifty
former clerics found in the sample. Of the other professions
many of the soldiers, and more surprisingly, some of the writers,
architects, and doctors found their way into the Ministry of
War.

The importance of such professional experience has often
been underestimated in the past, while the role of those coming
from inferior service and commercial occupations has been
overemphasized. In any case, many of these like the lawyers'
clerks used such employment as a means of acquiring basic
skills rather than as a career, so that few went on to be managing
clerks, and when they entered the administration they tended to
occupy much lower grades than their former employers. Similar
jumping-off points were provided by clerical employment in
banks or business houses. Such employment was much more
common than that as small businessmen and street-traders. Yet
even former *limonadiers* seem to have finished in positions above
those occupied by former domestic servants, *hommes de confiance*,
and artisans, who often finished up as employees of the
Imprimerie Nationale or as domestics and *garçons* with little
chance of promotion.

Such wide social divergences were by no means new. The
ministerial staffs had never been homogeneous. Under the
Ancien Régime the *Premiers Commis* and their subordinates lived
in separate worlds. Yet the elimination of the former by the
Revolution did not lead to great opportunities for social
promotion of the latter, presumably because of the divisions
inside the bourgeoisie and because of the creation of a new élite,
the *notables*. Within the new bureaucracy this new élite was
almost totally middle class in origin, there being only 24 known
nobles in the sample, mostly minor gentry and ennobled officials.
However, they held high positions, in External Relations and
the advisory Councils of the Interior in particular. In the place
of the old élites came a new group of speculators, *négociants*,
land-owners, farmers, lawyers, politicians, and administrators

who seized the change to rise in the social scale both inside and outside the civil service.[17]

Once in a position of supremacy they showed no inclination to accept similar promotion on the part of those beneath them, especially in such cases as former domestic servants who had entered the administration in search of advancement.[18] The division between employees and functionaries was partly mirrored within the new ministerial bureaucracy, in an interesting anticipation of future patterns of *haute* and *basse* administration. As a result of these barriers 'the smaller fry', as Cobban once said, 'continued to inhabit the shallows'. The middle classes remained as divided as ever. While a *Chef de bureau* might have been a *Lieutenant de Police* or a doctor and might look forward to holding elective office, the *expéditionnaire* would probably have been a petty scribe in a legal office or a bank clerk, with little to look forward to but the statutorily ordained penury of the ministries.

This is borne out by an analysis of the jobs held during the Revolution. Administrative employment and the effects of depression are even more marked than before, as state service became manna from heaven for those who were inclined to it, although only a few seem to have entered the ministries because they were unemployed.[19] There were, however, fewer domestics and craftsmen than before which suggests that the depression affected them early. There were plenty of students, while the professions and the service trades accounted for only 11.7 per cent and 5.9 per cent respectively of revolutionary occupations. Soldiers, often former conscripts or wounded veterans taking up posts in the War Office, were equally common. The next largest professional group were teachers, though only a third of these had held chairs compared with a half before the Revolution. Amongst the clerics there were some Protestants and three constitutional bishops. Many of the artists, actors, musicians, and *hommes de lettres* found their way into the Ministries of War and of External Relations, while the latter, along with the Ministry of Police, attracted many of the journalists. Of those who had worked in service and commercial life, trade had occupied the largest group at 2.1 per cent, followed by lawyers' clerks.

So the ministries were not an amalgam of lower-class seekers of refuge, or even a shelter for an intellectual proletariat. There were such people in their ranks, but they were part of a staff drawn from a wider range of social levels and occupations. Indeed many of them had been in more than one social class since two-thirds of the 2,400 on whom information is available had had between two and five jobs in their career. A quarter had held more than five, sometimes even as many as ten. This shows the extent both of the depression of the revolutionary era and the very disturbed nature of the period. It also suggests how vital entry to the administration could be, a point that is not always conceded. Yet by the relative under-representation of artisans etc., it reinforces the impression that normally there had to be some liaison between the jobs held in civilian life and the administration for people to seek to enter the latter. Mere unemployment or hardship would not produce this.

The frequency with which clerks changed jobs is one of the reasons why it is difficult to be precise about the social status of the Directorial bureaucracy. Another is the paucity of information on the occupation of the fathers of clerks which is known in only 376 cases, over half of which are from the War Office. Only 84 of these came from the lower strata of society: coachmen, masons, wigmakers, stone-cutters, and the poor in general. Few of their sons rose very high save in cases like those of Monge, Guiraudet, and Lombard-Lachaux where politics intervened. Similarly, patronage would explain the rise of Famin from being a domestic of Marie Antoinette and other to the post of Secretary-General of the Admiralty under the Directory. The majority of cases involve fathers with good bourgeois occupations or who were themselves state employees. Family connections were still present in other words, although much less frequently than before.

It must also be remembered that although the senior posts went to people from better backgrounds, there were none the less internal forces which, by uniting the administration, tended to cut across such social divisions. Subjection to the same laws, structures, and economic problems gave the civil service as a whole a particular place in society which cannot be explained simply by reference to the social origins of its members. This is despite the fact that the operation of regulations on the service often put a premium on the possession of capital. Many of these regulations centred on the award, as it was often regarded, of a salary. The combination of inflation, excessive reglementation, and vicissitudes in the implementation of such regulations made dependence on salaries a somewhat hazardous necessity.[20]

Hence as Lameire remarks for the local level 'lorsque les registres de délibérations parlent du sécrétaire en chef, c'est toujours à propos de réclamations pour le retard dans son traitement'. At the central level the employees of the Ministry of Justice were saved from prosecution for non-payment of taxes because the Treasury was three months behind in paying their salaries. Regulations on the necessity to declare one's fortune, to refrain from speculation, and to submit to deductions to help the war effort must, in such circumstances, have been very galling. A newspaper remarked in 1798 that the Directory had asked the Treasury to release funds for the payment of salaries: 'rien de plus juste . . . quand on pense qu'il est dû à des pères de famille jusqu'à cinq mois de traitement. Mais, par malheur, les arrêtés du Directoire ne sont pas des billets de caisse. . . .'

All too often Directorial acts were aimed not at securing payment but at abolishing the irregular forms of payment, often in kind, which had grown up so as to remedy the situation. They tried to abolish all fringe benefits in Frimaire IV, but though they raised salaries at the same time, this went little way to keeping pace with inflation to judge from the stream of recriminations from the provinces.[21] Such interventions in fact made fringe benefits and special aid more rather than less necessary, as did payment in *mandats*, especially when coupled with the reduction in salary levels demanded by the Councils and the continuance of part payment in *assignats*. The Directory came to realize that their employees had lasted through the winter only as a result of 'dettes contractées ou des privations multiplées'. Eventually new levels were agreed and further aid provided, thereby paving the way for the transition to payment in cash. This, in a deflationary age, brought some relief, provided salaries were paid in full and on time. Even the clerks of the Treasury had once to threaten to walk out to get paid. Complaints came to centre on this and the costs of educating children, living in the capital, and providing things needed in government work.

The neo-Jacobin revival led to a new deterioration, with arrears of payment growing, and new deductions on salaries being imposed to finance the war. At first the latter ran at 5 per cent of the first 3,000 francs salary, and thereafter 10 per cent on each successive 1,000. This was later raised to rates of between 10 per cent on 600 francs and 25 per cent on salaries over 4,000 francs. This was bitterly resented, the employees of the Ministry of Justice even asking for their salaries to be cut so as to minimize the deductions, and though Reinhard, then Minister of External Relations, believed that 'ils perdent un état dont ils avaient prié l'habitude; aucun ne convient de son insuffisance ou de son utilité', they saw it very differently.[22] A little later they told Bonaparte that: 'Il nous est impossible de bien remplir nos devoirs, lorsque nous sommes suivis dans nos bureaux par les angoisses du besoin qui assiège nos familles; et le titre des employés de la République fait fuir devant nous ceux qui pourraient nous secourir et dont la confiance a été tant de fois trompée.' This feeling, produced by the Prairialists much more than by the Directory proper, may go some way to explaining why there was no administrative resistance to Brumaire.

Even the benefits of deflation had, in any case, been a long time coming, and the total insufficiency of salaries in the early days of the regime had made the provision of such 'fringe benefits' as fuel (coal, wood, and oil), candles, clothing, alum, cochineal and other food stuffs, and occasionally lodgings, which were absolute necessities financially impossible. One local administration, reporting that officials and employees were especially badly hit by the economic crisis, observed that 'Les employés les plus favorisés ont 450 francs par mois, qui n'en faut que 4, pas de quoi acheter leur pain . . . ils sont bien en dessous des salaires des hommes de peine.'[23] Barras remarked that the civil service depended on state warehouses for their very existence, and one newspaper was moved to claim that:

Les commis sont devenus marchands. Cette armée d'employés auxquels, on ne sait pourquoi, la république distribue de l'huile, du savon, de la cassonade, du sucre, de la chandelle, et *du drap dont nos troupes manquent*, dont nous ressentons une si affreuse pénurie, ces employés, dis-je, préferent la *bourse* à leur *bureau*, et abandonnent la besogne qui les ennui, pour l'agiotage qui les enrichit. Quelques-uns d'entre eux poussent l'impudence jusqui'à prendre des patentes.[24]

Then, as now, special cases were not always easily agreed on, and great resentment was caused by the fact that not all clerks were able to claim special allowances. Some employees in the Naval Liquidation department complained that they were particularly hard done by since despite three applications they had been unable to get the clothing from government magazines that others had done. Sometimes disappointment was due to government intervention, and at others due to the fact that the demand from the administration had been so heavy that there were no supplies left in some stores. The Service des Étoffes in fact once had to buy cloth for army uniforms at a very high price on the open market because of this.

The Directory was usually willing to tolerate grants of household goods. Perhaps surprisingly, it was very hostile to the provision of free lodgings, even though this was usually only conceded to employees whose presence on ministerial premises was considered vital.[25] Yet, while denouncing Merlin and others for doing this in the spring of 1797, they themselves were not above interfering in the housing market to prevent the eviction of officials. Similarly, they did not, for reasons of humanity and of equity, always enforce their own rules. Eventually such fringe benefits became rarer and were replaced by advances for things such as winter clothing, or by special welfare grants, such as those paid to Restif de la Bretonne, then in the Police Ministry. By 1799, however, the Directory was trying to stop even this, as well as abolishing the remaining supply of goods, but it is not apparent that they were wholly successful.

In any case the mere provision of a limited amount of household goods was no answer to the problems of the administration in 1795–7. Only the assurance of a basic ration of food at subsidized prices, or, as one head of a bureau said, 'l'espoir d'un traitement proportionné et au travail et à la cherté des subsistances', would do.[26] Perhaps today one is better able to appreciate both the concern felt by staff and the general gravity of the situation, which as well as leaving behind demographic ruin, produced violence, profiteering, and an economic crisis which added thousands to the already large number of *indigents* in Paris. For the administration the *subsistances* crisis had begun in 1792 when the depreciation of the *assignat* induced by the war was compounded by the disastrous harvest of 1792. Rationing, however, did not really come in until late in 1793 when *fonctionnaires* were allowed, in the wake of the Maximum, to buy two pounds of bread a day at a controlled price of three *sous* the *livre*. The abolition of the Maximum destroyed the fragile stability thus achieved, and even before the catastrophic harvest of 1795—which was to bring on the final paroxysm—bread prices had risen to 3,000 per cent of their 1790 levels.

The government had to accept the continuance of subsidized supplies to officials and others, but the cost of doing this on the open market in a time of rapid inflation led the Convention on 27 Vendémiaire IV to refuse to supply anybody with private means with cheap bread. The latter, whose increasing economic anxiety may well have been the cause of the rising earlier that month, were told to buy their own bread on the open market. The resultant savings were to be diverted to the poor. However, the progress of inflation meant that more and more people were soon bereft of all resources and were therefore able legitimately to claim aid. By the late spring of 1796 this was running at a daily rate of 1,300 sacks of wheat, 105 calves, 450 sheep and 6,000 pounds of rice. In this situation officials were treated as a special case, first allowed to buy at less than the market rate, and by 1795 being paid partly in grain or in its cash equivalent, the rate for the statutory pound and a half being fixed by local authorities.

Once in office, the Directory found themselves forced to try and cut out all such subsidies. Their humanitarian instincts and political needs gave way before the urgent need for retrenchment as conceived by *laissez-faire* statesmen.[27] Thus under pressure from the Councils the Directory tried to cancel all subsidies save those to the genuinely poor, and to limit the amount of food distributed to 150,000 pounds of bread and 10,000 pounds of meat, which was to be allocated by registered butchers on the basis of ration cards. *Fonctionnaires* were called upon to surrender their cards in return for a promise of higher salaries while the problems of *rentiers* were referred to the Councils. Despite Directorial protestations prices continued to rise and there was intense opposition to the new policy. This had some effect as the government, instead of making the cuts in Ventôse, actually increased the sums available for food purchase and tried to reorganize the supply services. But with bread prices doubling to one hundred *livres* on the Directory's own admission, it was not surprising that there were riots in the suburbs, trouble with the local *bienfaisance* committees who were supposed to repossess ration cards, and heavy migration from the starving countryside.

Fearful of a rising the Directory authorized the continuation of rations to civil servants and their dependants on 24 Pluviôse and then annulled the decision to end subsidies on 28 Pluviôse, just three days before these had been due to cease. Cards were still to be withdrawn from hotel- and restaurant-keepers, officials earning over 12,000 *livres* per month, and those who had been assessed at over 600 *livres* in the forced loan. Apparently this was without much effect as stern prohibitions had to be issued against providing rations for unauthorized persons. This went some way towards satisfying public opinion but the continuing collapse of the purchasing power of notes, even when the *mandat* was introduced, forced the Directory to restore the old system in its totality on 5 Germinal. Until 15 Fructidor IV subsidized food was made available to the vast majority of the population, though no other distribution of goods to civil servants was allowed.

The *arrêté* of 5 Germinal IV accepted that the provision of cheap food was a basic form of public assistance by dividing the population into four eligible categories. These were firstly, the old, the infirm, pregnant women, and those amongst the poor who were unable to work, who were all allowed to buy three-quarters of a pound of bread free. Secondly came the *indigents*, defined as those who earned less than twenty *sous* per day, who had been reduced to this state by the crisis, and who were allowed to buy the same amount at a twelfth of the market rate. Thirdly were the *mal-aisé*, those who were normally above the subsistence level, but who were not allowed a ration at a quarter of the market rate. Finally came all officials earning less than the equivalent of 3,000 *livres* per annum in coin. They were treated as the *mal-aisé* save that they could not buy subsidized bread if they became unemployed. Supplies were again provided by licensed dealers on the basis of ration cards, and at prices fixed by the Bureau Central of the Canton of Paris. The precise limits of the permissible salary were hard to evaluate and it seems as though all officials were allowed to buy cheap rations before long. From 20 Germinal they were also allowed to buy at a twelfth of the going rate rather than at a quarter, much to the fury of critics like Camus.

The returns to the Bureau Central under the new system suggest that out of a population of at least 662,000 in Paris, something like 550,000 were in receipt of subsidized food. Of these 20 per cent were *indigents*, largely in the eastern quarters of the city, 22 per cent were the now *mal-aisé* middle classes of the right bank and the west of the city, while the officials, who numbered 16,000, or 33,380 (5.2 per cent) with their dependants, were, as Figure VII shows, concentrated in the north-west of Paris close to their places of work. However, if this established the civil service as both deprived and middle class, it did not provide them with adequate food supplies. The employees of the Paris Tax service complained that their salary converted to not much more than 70 to 100 *livres* per day, whereas at a quarter of the standard rate bread alone would cost them 54 *livres* per day, leaving nothing for clothes and the things necessitated by their work.[28] One *chef de bureau* in External Relations got himself registered as a genuine *indigent* so as to get cheaper food. There were even graver problems in the provinces.

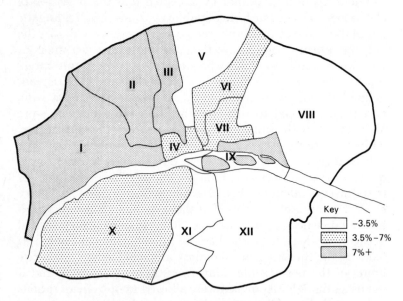

VII The Distribution of Civil Servants in Paris in 1796

The official policy kept them alive until the final cancellation of the rations on 19 Thermidor prematurely announced the return of good harvests. It did little to improve the quality of the administrative service or to solve the more basic problems of the administration. Yet the civil servants never seem to have thought of uniting with the popular *milieux* in protest against their conditions. For just as there were social barriers high up in the service, so they existed lower down, marking off the subaltern clerks from the likes of *garçons* and domestics and people of similar standing. The bureaucracy reflected the new divisions of post-revolutionary society, and, generally speaking, did not give its members the status wherewithal to surmount the divisions.[29] When a civil servant without many social advantages like the talented typographer Duboy-Laverne of the Imprimerie Nationale did penetrate the brittle world of the new social élite, the result was often a tragic frustration. Few clerks thus rose to be *propriétaires*, and Reinhard was right to say that the typical figure of Directorial society was not Barras but the petty bourgeois: 'laborieux, fidèle à sa tache, sans grandeur dans l'esprit, aimant les petits moyens, jaloux de son indépendence, hostile à l'Église et aux nobles, c'est le plus énergique soutien d'un gouvernement dont il peuple les bureaux.'[30]

Admittedly, the employee had always enjoyed a lower status than the *fonctionnaire*. Yet it is striking how few clerks, especially from poor backgrounds, were able to rise through the service to such status. Unfortunately it is not possible to go much further along this line of analysis since the after-careers of so many remain hidden, and one cannot say whether those who left were of a different social group to those who stayed. Certainly few clerks in Paris left because of the low pay. The case of an Admiralty employee dismissed in Germinal V who asked for an indemnity to help him travel the hundred leagues home as he had no hope of getting another job in the capital is more common than that of the ex-deputy Granet who later laughed off a corruption charge since his large estates in Paris and Toulon gave him no motive.[31] As in the Sarthe, upper-class *fonctionnaires* held the best jobs in Paris and the petty bourgeoisie had to content themselves with the less attractive ones. Hence the satire written by three government clerks:

Veux-tu savoir, ami, quelle est la différence,
Entre un législateur et le pauvre commis?
L'un avec sa quinzaine achète un bien immense,
Et l'autre, au bout d'un mois, va vendre ses habits.

This kind of thing undoubtedly caused resentment inside the civil service as well as between it and the *notables* entrenched in the Councils. As a political formation the Directory was more tolerant and more aware of the state's needs of such employees.

To be fair, the upper-class disdain for the administration was often shared by the popular *milieux*, and the bureaucracy enjoyed little social esteem in principle. However, people still wanted to join it and the evidence of relationships with landlords and with neighbours, such as it is, suggests that the civil servant was able to live peaceably enough amongst people who in theory detested him and his kind. Certainly the field services seem to have occasioned remarkably little criticism and, indeed, remarkably little praise. With a size of family which averages out at 2.18, excluding children over sixteen who were counted as independent, and possibly those boarded out in the country as well, the administration may not have been all that visible.[32] In Paris with their dependants they made up about 5 per cent of the population, or one official to forty-three inhabitants, and much less in the countryside. However, given that they were concentrated in the area between the *Faubourg* Saint-Denis in the east, the rue St Honoré in the south, and the rue de l'Arcade in the west, as the map showed, they must have been an appreciable element in society, especially round the ministries where the staffs of the latter were very heavily concentrated. There is virtually no evidence which allows one to explore further their relations as a group with society at large.

The glimpses one gets of individuals seem to consist almost entirely of hard luck cases, and although there is evidence that bankruptcy was common in Paris, one cannot take them all seriously.[33] People were seeking to make the strongest possible case for ministerial solicitude and they naturally exaggerated in order to do so. If the situation had been as bad as it was sometimes described the whole service would have died of malnutrition or hyperthermia long before. Moreover, since many entered the service in search of economic security or as a means of repairing a financial crisis of their own they would obviously have been resentful when the hoped-for rewards failed to materialize. None the less, it is undeniable that the civil service and the individuals who composed it did suffer extreme hardship between 1795 and 1797, even if the real personal disasters had occurred before then. Seven times as many people pleaded loss of fortune, the inability to buy bare necessities for themselves and for their families, or demanded a rise or other form of monetary aid, as admitted to any form of wealth.

Jean Lardenoire of the Secrétariat-Général claimed to have had to sell all his furniture to pay the chemist's bills occasioned by consumption, while his doctor treated him on credit. Vigneux in the same department seems to have resorted to moonlighting to make ends meet, while an employee of the Envoi des Lois service of the Ministry of Justice was dismissed in Floréal IV for making free with the section's furniture in order to keep himself warm. This was far from being the only case of corruption or theft induced by hardship. One clerk in the War Office was sacked a few years later for favouring creditors in his work. Even those who admitted to having some capital of their own were not exempt from trouble. At some point of time during the period, Tondeur of the Ministry of Justice lost 10,000 francs in a robbery and his colleagues subscribed 800 francs to help him out. Two people who were able to invest in *biens nationaux* also had problems. Lebourgeois, a *sous-chef* in the Intérieur, who had retired to live on a portion of the lands of the Abbey of Jumièges, had to return to work in Paris as he could not support himself on their yield. Sequier of the Secretariat-Général, who was given leave in the Year VI to go to Belgium to buy national lands and then asked for an extension to enable him to return to Paris to raise more money, was sacked with two months' pay as compensation since he was a worthless employee who was actually just wandering the streets of Paris.

To be fair, such things were far from unknown in other eras. For example during the Late Empire the depression, the effects of Cossack raids, the death of a general leaving a large family and a small pension, and the attractions of being an actor were all adduced as reasons for special consideration. None the less, they do show that even for the élite of the bureaucracy, assimilated to the new élite as it often was, there was no great social reward in civil service employment under the Directory, particularly in its early days. The existence of a very partial *statut des fonctionnaires* was thus as much a liability as an advantage.

None the less, even though government employment did not offer the huge rewards and opportunities for peculation sometimes claimed, the meagre and unfairly regulated security which it did offer the petty bourgeoisie was a factor which must be kept in mind, along with more purely administrative pressures in assessing the dynamic of the bureaucracy.[34] Government employment was not a sure-fire system of relief for lower-class unfortunates, since it could lead to social as well as to administrative demotion. The security it offered, especially in the early days, was meagre indeed and although the situation subsequently improved with the onset of deflation, there were still more pitfalls than guarantees. Moreover, the fact that salaries rose only 25 per cent between 1798 and 1814 meant that there was a ceiling to the gains which could be extracted from deflation.

Furthermore, even as late as the 1840s the effect of internal social barriers was to prevent an equitable division of rewards inside the service. Employment in its lower echelons could mean commitment to a narrow and not very well-esteemed or remunerated environment. The talk of the middle-class *manie de plume* is a reflection more of training and experience together with economic crisis than of greed, indolence, or upward social mobility.[35] For all its faults there was more security inside the bureaucracy than without and the petty bourgeoisie, with their roots in the geographical, educational, and professional characteristics of the Ancien Régime responded to this material urge, as did their peers at many other times. Moreover, much of the insecurity of their employment was indeed the work of those of their critics whose malevolent interventions often produced the very things they wished to avoid.

In any case one should not place too much stress on social background as the key to administrative behaviour, for as Suleiman has argued in a much more modern context, this is not the decisive factor in motivating French officials.[36] Moreover, during the Directory the service was divided by levels and departments so that no one motive or background really explains the service as a whole, even if its centre of gravity lay in the administratively inclined petty bourgeoisie. Particularly when social positions and attitudes have to be deduced rather than standing out clearly, there is great danger in generalizing. One observer during the Restoration noted, rather more intelligently than has often been the case, of the clerks of the ministries that:

Ils sont venus au ministère de toutes les sources: de Versailles, de la féderation de 1793, du directoire, du 18 Brumaire, de l'empire, de la restauration, du second empire, et enfin de Gand. Vous voyez qu'il est impossible d'assembler plus de nuances diverses sur une même étoffe. Des ministres, petits esprits, ont tenté, par des épurations, de ramener tout ce personnel à une couleur; ces grands hommes d'état ont frappés à faux; ils ont congédié ce qu'il y avait de mieux et ce qui aurait rendu les plus grands services. Rien n'est moins important que l'opinion des commis. Le meilleur système politique est, à leurs yeux, celui sous lequel les appointement sont servis avec le plus d'exactitude. L'expéditionnaire a dû dévouement pour douze cents francs, et le chef de bureau pour huit mille. Beaucoup ont à soutenir des femmes et des enfants qui ne leur laissent guère le temps de méditer les doctrines du *contrat social*; ils sont nés pour écrire sous tous les ministres, comme les violons de l'Opéra pour faire des dessus sous tous les régimes. On ne s'est point encore avisé d'exiger des Guarnerius et des Stradivarious qu'ils fussent royalistes, tout ce qu'on doit vouloir de ses instrumens, c'est qu'ils donnent du son, et d'un commis qu'il produise des circulaires.[37]

This very accurately brings out the close relationship of political and social aspects of bureaucracy.

The social problems of the civil service were very often the cause of the abuses which so much worried the politicians, just as the latter's interventions, as in 1799, could produce new economic pressures on the administration. Moreover, many of the accusations directed against the latter by the left were themselves the product of the social aspirations of the *sans-culottes* themselves. In other words, neither social nor political explanations alone are enough to clarify the actions of the civil service. Similarly, no simple social or political explanation is wholly convincing. The Directory's administrative policy cannot be ascribed to the effects of its social background, any more than a simple reference to party politics can explain the political role of the administration. One has to examine the evidence carefully and try to discriminate between the various groups and their varying roles at differing times.

At the same time such discrimination and such emphasis on the social and economic dynamic of the administration would not have been accepted. Like many recent authorities contemporaries believed in Nkrumah's dictum 'Seek ye first the political kingdom.' For them, all three aspects of the politicization of administration defined by Moulin were primordial: the appointment of people by political criteria, their activity within the administration to push the latter towards their own political ends, and the use of their position inside the administration to aid their political ends.[38] This was not because those alive at the time believed such politicization represented various interests to the general benefit or because it aided both participation and the diminution of ministerial control over the administration but because of their all-consuming conception of the loyalty demanded by the Revolution.

In their almost totalitarian concentration on the matter they failed to realize that formal politicization of the administration can also create fiefs, rancours, and double employment inside the administration as well as intensifying popular suspicions outside. The creation of formal political tensions could also unleash countervailing political forces, and could even force depolitization on the staff in order to avoid damaging commitments.[39] None the less, the view commonly held by Anglo-Saxon countries and to some extent by the Conseil d'État in France, that paid officials should be neutral and merely execute the policies of the government of the day, would have been fiercely repudiated, and not because, as Suleiman says, it is a convenient fiction or a product of a much more harmonious and unified society.[40] They would not accept any distinction between party politics and the politics of the general interest. In the eyes of the militants of the revolutionary era there was only one form of politics and that was their own version. They refused to accept the implications of their own commitment which was that there was a fierce conflict over the line which the revolutionary state would follow. Similarly, they would have regarded the modern distinction between technical administration and politics as somewhat ingenuous, although the Directory was willing to see it applied within limits when making appointments.[41] For most contemporary opinion any deviation from complete commitment to the goals of the Revolution was unacceptable.

There was no room for neutrality of any sort in their canon. And because the conflict of old and new orders was seen in such black and white terms, any deviation from orthodoxy—whatever that might be—was equivalent to treason. This stress on political conflict meant that active engagement in political duty was a civic duty for the good republican, and especially so if he held public office, as this carried even greater duties and responsibilities. As a Belgian revolutionary observed a little later: 'Servir le peuple n'est pas un moyen de parvenir; c'est uniquement un moyen de s'aquitter de son devoir de citoyen.'[42] Neutrality was a dereliction of duty and malleability, implicit in a willingness to serve several governments was equally reprehensible, if not more so.

The flaw was that in practice there was often no certainty outside the militants' mind of what constituted orthodoxy. Particularly in outlying areas it was not always as easy to be as up to date as one might wish, and militants were themselves often caught out by the abrupt changes of tone and of direction in Paris. However, even though this inevitably forced a certain caution on civil servants in so far as allegiance to any one faction was concerned, it also forced the militants to redouble their attacks on a seeming indifferentism which seemed to prove their worst fears about the administration. The power of their rhetoric was so strong that civil servants often had to adopt it themselves as a form of camouflage, a fact which makes for additional complications as far as the historian is concerned.

So, in spite of the vociferous and repeated claims of militants and historians, there was a difference between strategic political loyalty to the Revolution in general, and tactical loyalty to a particular faction or current of opinion. If some Anglo-Saxon writers have gone to excess in arguing for the complete neutrality of the civil service, it is still true that neutrality of the second kind is still extant and desirable.[43] Obviously the civil service is engaged in politics in the largest sense when it implements policies or seeks to pursue the public interest. At the same time, although it is part of the wider political process, it can and does stand aloof from party politics. The pervasiveness of party rhetoric and the failure to define what is meant by politics has often obscured this basic reality. For it was a reality during the Revolution, even if it was rarely recognized. Therefore it is essential to the following analysis.

Because the right and the need to exercise neutrality in the face of competing party claims was not recognized at the time, both left and right could attack the administration in almost identical terms because it did not measure up to their ideas of commitment. For the activist it was not enough that the civil servant should have negative virtues, that he was not involved in opposition to the Republic, or was not marked by 'aristocratic' vices such as vengeance, crass ignorance, despotism, ambition, and intolerance.[44] He was expected to have more positive characteristics. He had to have a strong love of duty, country, constitution, and Republic; which was to be demonstrated by being a father—hence with a stake in the future, by having served in the army where appropriate, and by having served on the right side at crises such as Prairial and Vendémiaire. As an official he must always put nation above faction, use republican forms of address, be at his post in times of crisis, and be of good moral character: honest, open, firm, and zealous.

It was obviously all too easy to fall short of such standards, and perhaps given the seriousness with which they were taken, the surprising thing is that there was not more ciritcism of the administration. For few could have hoped to measure up to this ideal of prophet and paragon. As it is, these was always a stream of critics convinced that people had only entered the administration because of their political leanings and solely with an eye to disrupting it, whether on behalf of Provence, Pitt, plutocracy, or personal profit.[45] Historians on the whole have been more interested in the way the left penetrated the administration than in the way the right may have done so. Sydenham claims that 'at the height of the Terror ignorance, coarseness, and brutality seemed to have become sufficient qualification for responsible office' while Woronoff ascribes entry to the fact that 'à son niveau le plus humble, la bureaucratie représentait un réfuge pour les persécutés—sans-culottes et jacobins, les déclassés, prêtres abdicataires, hommes de loi ou notaires sans clientèle'. Such claims rely too much on the rhetoric of the times. This, as is often the case with criticism of the bureaucracy, was based on considerable ignorance of administrative realities.[46] So many people had no personal contact with the bureaucracy, and those who did were often blinded by *parti pris*, to that 'everybody knew something, albeit nothing very precise about the flamboyant corruption . . .'. Yet when such charges were followed up they often turned out to involve non-existent persons and to have rested on nothing more than hearsay.

Moreover, some of the criticisms of the bureaucracy were even then recognized as being deliberate attempts to undermine the regime or to gain office by discrediting those already in positions.[47] As one police spy said, 'On crie après ceux qui occupent les places, pour les en chasser, quelques patriotes qu'ils soient, on les traite d'aristocrates ou, au moins, de modérés.' Even when such complaints were sincere there was the difficulty of defining what groups clerks actually belonged to. Scott shows that in Marseilles the term 'aristocrat' was used as a blanket term of abuse for any one who disagreed with the patriots, and the sections themselves admitted that 'il n'y a aucun caractère certain pour reconnaître le bon républicain et l'ennemi de la République'. Accusations against the bureaucracy therefore could tell one more about the accuser than the accused. However, they could lead to all kinds of unpleasantness for the staff, such as the time the dragoons were sent into the departmental offices of the Ain in Frimaire IV to arrest alleged royalists.

A further weakness is that such charges also assume that the bureaucracy played only one simple political role. This was obviously not so. Other political forces besides the actions of individuals within the administration were at work. The bureaucracy was dependent on the policies of the Directory for instance, so its role changed as did the political climate, hence when the moderate administration of the Seine-et-Oise decided to purge its bureaux in the summer of 1797 the dismissed clerks were able to appeal straight to the government which sacked the administration after the *coup*.[48] Again, the bureaucracy was also dragged into the struggles between the Directory and the Councils. It was also affected by the changing nature of the Revolution and by changes in the economic situation, all of which had political implications for the bureaucracy's political standing, as did both geography and the intervention of other institutions. Finally, in an era as turbulent and all embracing as the Revolution one must also allow for the element of change, both were individuals were concerned and where the general political role of the administrations as a whole was involved.

As a result there can be no simple explanation of the political role of the bureaucracy. Certainly it was not restricted to the sum of the activities of individuals within it, any more than it was restricted to a party role, as the somewhat derogatory use of the term 'political' in English usually implies. All questions related to the use of resources, in which even then the administration was obviously very much involved, are ultimately political in nature.[49] Even the technical aspects of advising government and executing its policy can, as Daru's example shows, be political in the general sense of the word. People were of course aware of the existence of these other forms of political activity of the administration, the way it could usurp the role of the legislature through the implementation of laws, and the way it consumed scarce resources. They placed much less stress on them than on the question of party allegiance and subversion, even though it seems to have been of much less practical importance than other forms of political influence.

The bureaucracy had a large role as 'a means to power' for example.[50] It is through the bureaucracy that all governments had to act to secure obedience, resources, and the implementation of their policies. Even at the end of the eighteenth century the translation of legislative enactment into practice was impossible without the existence of the administration. Though within the administration employees had to work for and with *fonctionnaires*, in the last resort it was the former who actually did the tasks devolved on the administration by the government. They were therefore indispensible to the exercise of power. At the same time, the bureaucracy also existed as a power in its own right. For many people bureaucracy is synonymous with rule by officials, and at times during the Revolution it had seemed as though the bureaucracy might be an autonomous force in the political process. Certainly one of the major questions of the time was how the bureaucracy might be made more responsive to the political element of government, and although it never gained full autonomy, its size made it very difficult to control.

The bureaucracy therefore had some ability to pursue its own ends, notably where conditions of service were concerned. Much more important, however, was its negative power to obstruct the execution of government policy, whether, as was often believed, through sheer incompetence, or, more consciously, through inaction, evasion, pressure on the authorities, or partial interpretation of the laws. To show how this actually happened is very difficult. There is insufficient evidence to permit a convincing demonstration of this role, although it is probable that it would have been at its height under a short-lived minister rather than when someone like François de Neufchateau was in office. Similarly, an examination of the relations between the bureaucracy and the Councils and local authorities, which were of great importance in this field, could well reveal how far the bureaucracy was held in check.

A final element in the political situation of the bureaucracy is the extent to which it was either a source of or a consumer of scarce resources. Under the Ancien Régime the central administration had been part of the courtly establishment and had provided the latter with useful patronage. When the Revolution broke out it was starved of resources until 1793–4, and thereafter, since it was regarded as too big and costly, it was often treated as the natural area for economy and sacrifice. Such attitudes persisted under the Directory, which is why the bureaucracy often became a battlefield for the contending factional forces of the time. Because of the first of its political roles, however, the Directory had to tread somewhat carefully, thereby allowing the bureaucracy more initiative than might otherwise have been the case. The Directory's growing concern for confidentiality and its caution over purges and salaries reinforce this view. Yet despite this, the bureaucracy remained, as the events of the summer of 1799 showed, somewhat vulnerable to attack because of its consumption of resources.

It might therefore be argued that, to adapt Eisenstadt's definition of the possible orientations open to bureaucracies, the French ministries had always to maintain an element of subservience in their relationship to ruling élites because of this vulnerability over resources.[51] Under the Ancien Régime the administration had been almost totally subservient to the courtly élite as a result of its search for prestige and security. With the

Revolution it developed a more rational service orientation to the state—though this was rarely recognized—as well as a heightened consciousness of its own economic interests. The latter must be borne in mind when the relationship of bureaucracy to revolution in general is considered, for the two are not synonymous, as has sometimes been suggested.[52] Although a full-scale revolutionary change in domination will obviously affect a bureaucracy drastically, the latter can also acquire a certain imperviousness to the changes in legitimacy produced by the violent aftermath implicit in the conception of revolution as a process. This admirably describes the situation of the bureaucracy under the Directory.

In other words, any assessment of the political role of the bureaucracy is conditioned not merely by the lack of evidence, but also by the complexities of real life which lay outside the contemporary obsession with royalist subversion. However, if one looks at the evidence on the latter, it becomes evident that most of it points in the other direction.[53] It very much seems as though a modicum of sympathy for the new order was necessary for the safety and well-being of the administration, whether as a body or as individuals. It was too dangerous to be an open royalist, especially when one wished to ensure both an adequate salary and a chance of promotion. Moreover, many were professionals who just wished to get on with their job. What they wanted was *a* government which would pay them and allow them to do this, but not any government in particular. The war also made it easier to identify with the Republic, while the return of the Ancien Régime would have meant new upheavals and the return of the old *Premier Commis*, which posed a double threat to their prospects. No doubt in many cases the identification with the new order was vague and inactive, but it was none the less real and conscious. Obviously this was a political stance in the wider sense of the word, but as with English officials at the same time, it was 'a kind of apolitical politics'.[54]

This was obviously not true of all Directorial officials without exception, and cases of active political party activity did exist. However, what one finds is that the Directorial civil service was very much like that of the modern United States which is divided into two distinct elements, the 'political' and the 'career', with the former containing leading and confidential posts which carry few of the guarantees accorded to career appointments.[55] The party political element under the Directory was very much restricted to this kind of area, and as in America its importance should not be exaggerated. Short-lived and inexperienced political appointees must have relied on the support of their more permanent inferiors, so that the bureaucracy was always more significant politically as a means of power and as a source of conflict than as a power in its own right. It was still vulnerable to politial pressure as the use made of the Interior in the electioneering of Year VI shows.[56] However, on the whole by 1799 the Directorial consolidation had led the bureaucracy to an enhanced sense of loyalty to the state. So instead of being denounced simply for being faction-ridden, it was increasingly also attacked by those who wished to make use of its growing strength, for being resistant to factionalism. All this is very general, however, and needs to be substantiated in more detail in the rest of this chapter, in so far as the evidence allows.

Under the Ancien Régime the administration had been closely involved in the system of honours on which the system depended, and had hence generated a certain amount of conflict.[57] At the same time it accounted for a relatively small proportion of government expenditure, given the drain of servicing the debt, the court, and the army. Remembering the fact that the employees' self-interest was bound up in the system of honours, it was also fairly well kept in hand by the *fonctionnaires*. Its primary role was therefore as a support to the existing power structure. With the Revolution this was partly called into question by the sweeping institutional changes and financial pressures which resulted, but reinforced by the development of the concept that 'servir l'état est un devoir que tout citoyen est tenu remplir'.[58] So even though it played no larger a role as a consumer of resources, it remained vitally necessary as a means of achieving the new order's political and social goals, so much so that Daunou once accused the Constituents of relying on the administration to such an extent that they thereby strengthened its power and its autonomy.

This was perhaps an exaggeration, especially when from 1792 on there came the draconian new controls and purges, the largest wave of political appointments seen during the revolutionary era, and especially the gathering wave of criticism.

Indeed Gros goes as far as to suggest that the Terror was aimed primarily against officials.[59] Late in September 1793, for instance, the Section d'Arcis for whom, like many others, such attacks were a legitimate part of party politics, formulated a complex programme of recruiting only fathers for the administration and subjecting the latter's political orthodoxy to the permanent scrutiny of sectional committees, which would control dismissals and appointments. Certainly such pressures must at the very least have cancelled out the right-wing subversion of which they were so afraid, so that on at least one occasion Robespierre took up the defence of the administration and its employees while Saint-Just made large enough use of 'Jacobin' officials despite his superficial hostility to them. Hence, although superficially the administration became something of a plaything in factional struggles, it was actually developing its autonomy, as the wastage patterns suggest, through its part in the war effort and by the manner in which the Comité de Salut Public began to protect it by excluding all other forces from interfering in its activities. At the same time it became the major consumer of resources and this on a grand scale. So despite the disgust of the *sans-culottes*, the ever more efficient prosecution of its supporting and resource roles made it increasingly autonomous.

This was anything but favourably received, so that the Thermidorians continued to subject the administration to a great deal of regimentation and, once their fears that it harboured Robespierrists were past, to an attack on the challenge which its costs, complexity, and power offered to their emerging *laissez-faire* ideals.[60] Attacks on its expensiveness, arrogance, and incompetence, which involved all three of its real political roles, led to the creation of a series of committees of enquiry into its structure and functioning. The failure of these committees to produce any appreciable change and the rise of the White Terror led to a revival of the old fears of royalist infiltration. These reached a peak with the rising of 13 Vendémiaire.

This revived the obsessive fears of the bureaucracy as a hostile political force in its own right.[61] Clerks were accused of marching with the rebels, communicating secret information to the latter, and freeing rebels once they had been arrested. These charges led to the establishment of a new committee of investigation with the task of dismissing all those who had been absent from their posts during the rising and who could not prove that they had been fighting with the Convention. These terms of reference were later extended to embrace those who had spoken against the Republic, not taken action against the royalists, or who did not fulfil the legal requirements on conscription or relationship to *émigrés*.

The Commission proved lamentably ignorant of the organization of the administration, so that it had to repeat the work of earlier bodies before it could really get down to its task. When it did so it found the civil service very reluctant to play the informer, while the very size of the latter made it impossible to examine it all. They probably considered 1,000 cases and made at least 877 recommendations, including 470 dismissals, 232 cases of unproven suspicion, and 85 suggested new appointments. Where they gave reasons for their decisions to dismiss people, 44 per cent were for simple absence during the rising, 29 per cent for actual complicity, 14 per cent for general political unreliability, 8 per cent for not having done military service, 3 per cent for incompetence, and 2 per cent for non-cooperation. Extrapolating from this it seems as if the Commission accused something like 4.1 per cent of the entire Parisian administration of absence, 3.4 per cent of general political unreliability, and 1.1 per cent of other offences.

This figure of 9 per cent in all is an upper limit. It conceals the fact that only 21 people were actually accused of being royalists, compared with 23 who claimed to have fought for the Convention. Many of the other charges were so flimsy and unjust that the Directory took very little notice of their recommendations, with the result that very few people were in the end dismissed for political motives. The Commission laboured under the handicap of contradictory legislation, an idealistic view of what could be expected of a clerk, too many prejudices about the meaning of royalism, and most importantly, from a lack of a counter-bureaucracy to carry out a real investigation.[62] The belief in party politicization was thus shown to be a myth. Even though participation in Vendémiaire always remained a mortal sin for the bureaucracy, it actually gave rise to nothing like the charges sometimes suggested. At that time public opinion only accepted large-scale changes as constituting a real purge, whereas today a few dismissals of prefects would be considered a major upheaval.

The Directory inherited many of the Thermidorians' attitudes to the administration, but it was much less frenetic and much more down-to-earth in the way it implemented them. As a result it was able to keep the administration within acceptable bounds, largely by the use of mundane administrative methods. The Directory became more concerned with the tactical responsiveness of the bureaucracy on matters of detailed policy than with the latter's more general attitude to the regime. Its style of administrative control evolved away from the simply punitive methods preferred by someone like Saint-Just.

As a result it was willing to see the development of depoliticization in the narrow sense amongst the lower echelons of the service, although still using the upper echelons for strictly political purposes. The use it made of this prerogative was, however, much less than might have been expected from a political formation struggling for its existence. It was the fact that its commitment was to power rather than to ideology which led to this situation. Moreover, the Directory did also have a commitment to good governance and to the performance of the bureaucracy's primary political role. Its view of the bureaucracy was that of a means to an end, rather than as a force in its own right.

Since, however, the Directory was never the complete master of events, the bureaucracy also figured in the political arena as a consumer of resources. Given the fiscal stringency inherited from the Thermidorian era, the Directory and especially the Councils had to maintain the tradition of austerity. This and political suspicion lay behind the way the administration became a bone of contention in the summer of 1797. Similarly, the growing service orientation and the consequent lack of sympathy for factions worried the neo-Jacobins two years later. Yet even they were really only able to affect the senior and more sensitive levels of the service.

If all three political roles can be seen in the changing position of the bureaucracy, with the exception of material on abuses which has an obvious bearing on the bureaucracy as a servant of power, the evidence tends to concentrate on the role of the bureaucracy as a power in its own right and particularly on the question of internal subversion. The Directory still reacted mechanically to such charges and they do occur in the personnel files, although usually they date from before 1795 and often they are trivial, such as the arrest of Villet of the War Office for allegedly laughing at a republican song in the Théatre Louvois.[63] They also seem to concern appointments rather more than dismissals, perhaps confirming the conservative effect of tenure on erstwhile militants. Clients of the Directors, former Girondins, and terrorists, depending on the swing of the pendulum, all sought posts.

Amongst those who held ministerial places there were many who claimed to have had *certificats de civisme*, or to have served in the National Guard, voted for the new constitution, served at the front or during some of the revolutionary *journées*, as the good citizen should have done. There are also traces of sectional and *Hébertiste* activity, but an equal number seem to have been arrested during the Revolution, particularly in Year II, for offences connected with federalism, Rolandism, or other such movements. Others claimed to have been involved in such movements without getting punished, only one in three who made such a claim admitting that he had been caught out. Like claims of royalism, these have to be treated with great caution. There are obvious cases of left-wing political appointments in 1795, involving Babeuvists in the Secretariat, War Office, and Ministry of Police, as well as in the later years of the regime, but they are not sufficient in number or duration to prevent one agreeing with one recent authority who said that 'ce pacte colonial n'intéresse qu'un petit nombre de hauts fonctionnaires et n'élève pas sensiblement le niveau de la participation politique'.[64]

This picture is borne out by a brief examination of external intervention in the life of the bureaucracy. After the storms of Vendémiaire there was not a great deal of political activity although a number of militants were appointed, notably Merlin de Douai, but only to disappear with first the major economies and then the Babeuvist scare.[65] The events of Fructidor brought a new flurry of activity and a small influx of political appointees, but the results of the Directorial *enquête* neither revealed much factional activity nor did they produce any drastic action. As a result the Directory was able to use the administration for its own purposes in the elections of the Year VI and then remove some of the new men brought in after Fructidor when the *coup* of 22 Floréal again made them a liability.

Surprisingly the Directory tried a similar experiment with the road-fund agents the next year, in the Var, with the same lack of success.[66] It may have been the way in which the Directory was able to disregard the idea of royalist infiltration of the civil service, and use it unchecked for its own purposes, that made the *coup* of 29–30 Prairial the prelude to such an intense attack on the bureaucracy. Not merely did the neo-Jacobins try and reduce the salaries and authority of the administration, but they also produced the largest number of political appointments since 1794, involving several forgotten ex-*Conventionnels* and Simon Duplay, the son of Robespierre's landlord.[67] Even this was not enough for Tissot and others in the Manège who wanted a full-scale republican purge.

In the event, the reforms carried out by Reinhard and Fouché were based more on economic and administrative criteria, and an attempt by Barbier-Neuville, the new left-wing secretary of the Interior, to draw up full dossiers on his staff failed. Significantly it was Dubois-Crancé, one of the least conservative ministers of the time, who actually came round, as has been seen, to defending his clerks against such attacks even if they had served the monarchy. The civil service was, as one *commissaire* to the Seine observed, really rather malleable. So despite the neo-Jacobin bluster the service was able to ride out the worst of the storm and convince its new masters that it was too valuable to be rudely overturned. However, the effects of the neo-Jacobin campaign on the economic position of the administration probably did nothing to endear the Jacobins to the average clerk.

The crisis of 1799 again focused attention on the independence and utility of the bureaucracy, factors which were able to survive the continued creation of a political element within the broad career pattern.[68] People at the top who worked closely with the ministers, especially with Merlin, Benezech, François de Neufchâteau, Ramel, Pleville, and Reinhard, all of whom exercised a great deal of influence, were involved in political activity of all kinds, rather in the way of a modern ministerial *cabinet*. Interestingly enough seven Directorial ministers had in fact occupied civil service posts before becoming ministers: Gaudin, Reinhard, Faipoult, Bourgnignon, Bourdon, Benezech, and Dondeau. Others within the administrative élite may also have been in line for similar promotion, while quite a number, like Veilh de Boisjolin, were involved in literary and journalistic ventures such as *La Décade*, or were to go on to hold prefectoral posts.[69]

The fact that the top echelons of the service were a social and political élite does not, of course, mean that they were all of one mind. At least half of them in any case were internal promotions of career personnel, about whose opinions little is known. There was a great variety of opinions amongst the political appointees too, ranging from Lebrun Tossa's idealistic republicanism to Vincent Lombard's social conservatism. Moreover, many of the political appointees in the long run became career officials, just as they did lower down the scale. So people who had been local servants of the Empire were attacked in 1815 as terrorists sometimes by the people who had appointed them.[70]

Sometimes even former deputies settled down to become career officials, neutral as far as allegiance to a particular party was concerned, as did the former Constituent Dupré in the Ministry of Finances and the ex-*conventionnel* Guffroy in that of Justice. This, however, was a rare occurrence. There was normally a constant coming-and-going between the executive and the legislature, with the former serving as a refuge or as a means of leverage depending on the circumstances. Yet this seems to have done nothing to ease the tense relationship between the two. Thus although a charge that the Interior paid a clerk to spy on the Councils was disproved, the very fact that it could be made is significant.[71] Two reasons for this may have been that the phenomenon of the *deputé–fonctionnaire* was impossible at that time, and also the fact that since deputies usually came in high up the hierarchy they therefore had little contact with and understanding of the realities of administrative life.

It was the élite posts which served as resting-places before re-election for such as Paganel, Secretary-General of External Relations, who was in fact excluded from the Councils after Floréal. Very few employees rose as high as this, and those who did, like Tissot and Sijas, usually did so because they were out-and-out party men irrespective of their grades. Fayau, who resigned from the post of *Chef de Bureau* in the Ministry of Justice in 1796 on the grounds that he was not competent enough, shows the problems inherent in the situation. The majority of deputies were appointed to the service in 1796 or 1799 having made their names first, and very few were able to use the service as a spring-board to a political career. Although Clément de Doubs and Jacquemont of the Interior are cases of this, even then there were outside factors working in their favour.

If the élite tended to have made their names outside the service and merely continued their participation in faction politics while they were attached to it, the great majority of the service were limited to its own frontiers for their activity. So that they were often more involved in patronage and corruption, though again this should not be over-stressed. The role played by patronage, in securing entry to the administration rather than anything else, was a product of the nature of French society combined with the economic and administrative necessity for obtaining employment. It may also have been affected by the gradual decline in the number of places inside the ministries, which by making each one that little bit more valuable, reinforced the tendency for employees of all kinds to concentrate their attentions on maintaining their career prospects.[72]

Clientage and patronage were also means of self-defence against deficiencies in conditions of service, as well as a tradition inherited from the monarchy. Family connections were still quite common, with some 360 relationships involving 200 people, mainly in low grades and especially in the Admiralty, having come to light. Under the Ancien Régime patronage was exercised by courtly and official personages, but with the Revolution the role of the *hauts fonctionnaires* inside the administration seems to have increased. It was supplemented by new-style politicians, inside and outside the service. The Directory was always pressed both by those seeking favours and by would-be patrons. At times there were internecine quarrels over patronage.[73]

This suggests that patronage was an uniquely successful means of entry to the service. In fact it was not. The ex-*conventionnel* Guffroy wrote to Reubell in Year VI that 'je compte sur toi, mon cher ancien collègue' for the preferment as a judge, *commissaire*, or head of a state enterprise which he wanted. Like many others he had to stay where he was. Many of the recommendations given were in any case very stereotyped. L. A. Detorcy, a deputy from the Marne, wrote of one unsuccessful candidate, whom he and the rest of the deputation had supported for a place in the Police department, that he had known him for years and believed him capable of filling the post with zeal, fidelity, exactitude, and patriotism. There was not a word as to what he was actually like.

Very great reliance was placed on the recommendations of deputies by those seeking to get into the service, although one sample of applications suggests that only 23 per cent cited a referee. However, amongst successful candidates and inside the service they were far less effective than ministers, high officials, and Directors. The most frequent referee was Merlin de Douai because of his very varied administrative role. The second largest volume of recommendations, after those from the minister in the department concerned, came from other ministers. Deputies came third, and then they were only marginally ahead of heads of divisions and other politicians. Directors, mainly Barras and Reubell, were even less regular referees, as were friends and local notables.

Patronage is often assumed to have been factional in origin and such cases obviously do exist.[74] However, things like family connections—which were in any case more common than patronage—and friendship or enmity were equally if not more important. This fits in with Lucas's finding that 'the Terror appears in many ways as a system of acquaintanceship and friendships at local level. The Terrorists were men who did not merely rely on their political affinities with other terrorists, but also had a claim on their affections at difficult moments.' Similarly, patronage was also useful to ministers, then as now, as a way of attracting people who might not otherwise be brought to serve in the bureau. So there were a variety of motives for patronage and a variety of outcomes. It was dependent on circumstances and on personality and carried no guarantees of success. Indeed, if the wrong patron was used it could well be counter-productive.

Corruption was never regarded as an advantage, and the left often treated it as evidence of political subversion, but again it had more mundane origins.[75] The majority of people who pestered the bureaux: 'une nuée de solliciteurs, et plus encore de solliciteuses assiégent avec persévérance les cinq rois, leur ministres, les bureaux, pour nouer des affaires de compte-à-demi' were after personal, and usually financial, advantage. They wanted confidential information—for which they were willing to pay—of decisions, of contracts, and of the progress of dossiers. The difficulties clerks encountered over taxes, rent, food, and especially over their own pay explains why such approaches were apparently received so receptively.

Exemptions from military service, court verdicts, leave permits, residence rights in Paris, and even some nominations to public posts were thus sold off.[76] Evading conscription was another abuse with unpatriotic overtones, and many draft-dodgers were said to be in the bureaux, though this was partly an exaggeration and partly the result of the failure to clarify the situation after the first *levée en masse*. Similarly the ease with which the *solliciteurs* were able to gain entry to the bureaux does not equate with the accusations of stand-offishness and addiction to revolutionary jargon that one also encounters. This is not to say that rascality and incompetence were absent, but merely that it was less common than is claimed. The desire to keep one's place must have militated against it. Similarly, its motives were not the product of party allegiance but of the failure of the state to live up to its obligations. The *manie de plume* thus contained its own safeguards as well as its own dangers.

The evidence, such as it is, suggests that above all the administration was an associational interest group whenever it acted as a force in its own right within the political arena, rather than the tool of any faction.[77] None the less, its primary role was to serve the state and its government. As a result of the Directorial consolidation, this is what it was doing by 1799. It would also go through the motions of giving support to those in power in an impersonal way in normal times, providing its basic needs were met. Times of crisis were somewhat different, and theories of revolution and bureaucracy are often too blunt to explain this. The *politique de bascule* practised by the Directory, and the somewhat desiccating effects of the desire of security of tenure, both militated against any greater commitment, even in times of crisis. So although there were obviously cases of factional sympathy and action inside the administration, there was never any of the tight interrelationship of party and state bureaucracy found for instance in Nazi Germany.[78]

The reality was closer to Edward's dictum that 'the great body of civil servants are dull, unenergetic persons, dreadfully afraid of losing their jobs and their pensions and inordinately attached to petty distinctions of official rank'. Perhaps this is an exaggeration since no revolution can be endured without the expenditure of energy, but both alleged conservatives like Cottrau and left wingers like Duplay showed a sufficient predeliction for office to cast doubts on their loyalty to any one regime.[79] If there were real influxes of militants they came before, and long after, the Directory. As Poterlet, a *Chef de Division* in the Ponts et Chaussées said many years later when reproached for having been too active in the Revolution: 'qu'il n'avait jamais été Jacobin, mais qu'il n'était point royaliste, ni le serait jamais, et quelque chose qui lui dut à rire [*sic*]'. In fact, given the ferocity of attacks on the bureaucracy, most governments implicitly accepted this by what was, in fact, the relative moderation of their purges.

Their behaviour, if not their ideas, were in line with recent suggestions that brutal purges are always hasty, incomplete, and unjust because of their retrospective nature. This injustice causes demands for revision and therefore prevents them from leading to real stability. Parodi has, in fact, argued that they are only used when more normal forms of adjustment to changed circumstances, such as self-purging and failure to promote, do not achieve a sufficient degree of turnover.[80] Historically the Administrations Centrales have escaped the worst of recent purges, and the evidence suggests that the Directory may have helped to establish this trend by allowing internal self-adjustment to work for it rather than resorting to the brutal purges desired by factional leaders.

Even faction pressures, of course, were rarely static or simple, as has sometimes been implied. They changed with circumstances and in reaction to other forces acting on the administration, so that the reasons why the latter was often a battlefield changed regularly. But in any case, concentration on this aspect usually diverted attention away from the more important aspects of the political role of the administration. For, although the administration developed a certain amount of strength, as its ability to absorb political pressures shows, this never went far enough for it to gain the ends that really mattered to it, the solution of its socio-economic and statutory problems.

The Directory helped with this, but the service was never cohesive enough to take the matter further towards a full and lasting solution. As Bertaud puts it: 'Fonctionnaires, besogneux, attachés, quels que soient, les gouvernements, à l'État républicain, ils ont acquis dans les administrations révolutionnaires l'expérience indispensable et, desormais, reconnue comme telle.'[81] In one way it had become something of a representative bureaucracy, even if it only represented the interest of the state as its clientele. So the real political role of the bureaucracy under the Directory was not as a power in its own right, but as a means to power for the state. This reflected the fact that the Directory did not rely on patriotism, surveillance, and legislative enactment for its means of control, but evolved a more sympathetic style which accepted the need for a bureaucracy and all that this entailed. Even its role as a consumer of resources was much less marked under the Directory.

The bureaucracy both made the Revolution possible by providing a channel for national efforts in 1793–4 and thereafter, and also was made by the Revolution since the latter opened up a whole new career and status for the employees. This situation is much more complex and much more related to the social and administrative character of the French administration than has often been allowed. The bureaucracy despite its growing professionalism was vulnerable both to inflation and to political attack. It was hard hit by the social crisis and by resentment over the *attentisme* forced on its by the militants. So having moved from a position of reflecting the society of the mid-eighteenth century, in which the employees had no esteem or power, it moved to a new situation in which the employees had power but no status. In turning itself from a patrimonial administration into a bureaucracy the French civil service may have done much for the state, but for itself it only exchanged one set of problems for another. So despite the important new internal dynamic released by the Revolution and maintained by the Directory, there was continuity in the way the administration was subject to external pressures. Hence the problems faced by the bureaucracy remained unsolved, and, as with the Revolution as a whole, a question mark hung over its future.

CHAPTER VIII: THE BUREAUCRACY AND BONAPARTE, 1799–1814

The end of the Revolution had often been announced prematurely, but Bonaparte's claim to have ended it in 1799 was slightly more convincing. However, the end of the Revolution obviously posed grave problems for the new ministerial bureaucracy to which it had given birth. For if the latter had been continued and consolidated by the Directory, its process of bureaucratization was still incomplete, and there was still an important role for other regimes to play in its development. In theory the ending of the Revolution might have meant the end of the bureaucracy, but in fact there was a limit to the changes which any regime could make. The bureaucracy had acquired sufficient strength and utility, not to mention its Weberian characteristics, to make its abolition was virtually impossible. Despite the many changes which it was to undergo during the first half of the nineteenth century it was never to evaporate or even to slip back into its pre-revolutionary form. Its development after 1799 was never free from complexity or from problems over its role and its status, so far as the still surprisingly scanty historiography of its evolution allows one to say.[1] So, despite the primordial contribution of the Revolution to the creation of the bureaucracy, the end of the Revolution was by no means the end of its evolution.

One reason for the uneven development of the administration lies in the rapid constitutional and political changes which France experienced in the next half-century. These caused first a rather special, and perhaps excessive use, of the bureaucracy by Bonaparte, and then a somewhat querulous, but often undervalued, relationship with the parliamentary regimes which were to follow the Empire. The two were, of course, partly interrelated since the changes made in the ministerial bureaucracy as a result of Bonaparte's use of it were to colour both the way the Bourbons treated it and the nature of the problems it encountered. Moreover, the whole period was marked by a recrudescence of the social and political subordination to a *fonctionnaire* élite which had hindered bureaucratic development before the Revolution. Whereas the Revolution had never produced a stable administrative élite, later regimes had one, and this changed the standing of the ministerial bureaucracy. This meant a subtle and changing relationship with Bonaparte, and not merely subordination to an all-powerful will. The position of the employees was bound up with the evolution of postrevolutionary society. To some extent this called into question the premisses on which the new bureaucracy was based because of its social conservatism.[2] So it would not be right to regard Bonaparte's rule as an unique and unparalleled formative period in French administrative history.

To say this is to fly in the face of much received opinion. For many the *coup* of 18 Brumaire put an end to the weak government of the Revolution and led to the erection of a new bureaucratic totalitarianism throughout Europe. As Furet and Richet put it 'l'armature de L'Etat moderne a été l'œuvre non des agents du Comité de Salut Public, mais des préfets de Bonaparte. Il a fallu Brumaire.'[3] Such judgements involve not merely a failure to define what is meant by 'bureaucracy' but also a number of misapprehensions about the realities of French administrative history. Strictly speaking Bonaparte had no need to be an innovator. The machinery of government was already there in 1799, as has often been realized, and needed only reorganization and proper direction.[4] Similarly, such assertions fail to recognize how much Bonaparte's activities were the logical development of revolutionary practice, and how much they owed to social forces, even if the machine of state was not the simple tool of the bourgeoisie claimed by Marx. Finally, there has been a tendency to over-estimate the strength and efficiency of the Napoleonic regime, which in the eyes of some later administrators was notable for poor work, caused by the effects of excessive war.[5]

For Bonaparte, the bureaucracy was a convenient tool which made possible both his seizure of power and the extraction of the resources needed to support the expansion of the Empire. So its role as a consumer of resources continued in an increased and altered form while its main role as a means to power was intensified to a point where the old suspicions of its power were no longer heard.[6] This was not because it no longer enjoyed authority, for the Empire was posited on the growth of state authority within the political system, but because it was subjected to a new form of domination. This had a marked effect on it. The administration was subjected not only to Bonaparte's personal *diktats* but also to the influence of greatly expanded and strengthened corps of *fonctionnaires* selected for their personal loyalty to the Emperor. The employee element in government thus lost much of its relative autonomy and influence, as well as its remaining hopes of improving its social status. Patronage of a new kind was brought in as well, so that although the authority exercised by the bureaucracy over the public at large was increased, its status and legal standing tended to decline.

Bonaparte once remarked that 'Je ne veux point de buro-cratie,' presumably because he regarded it as incompatible with secrecy, and his preference was always for the latter.[7] He occasionally denounced even his chosen *fonctionnaires* and expressed a desire to rule through his private secretaries alone so as to avoid sharing power and information. He also made no distinction between his own monies and interests and those of the state. As Balzac saw, subjection to this kind of authoritarianism tended to retard bureaucratization. However, he did very significantly change the environment in which the bureaucracy, with its continuing career and economic interests, had to work and this left its mark.

Basically, one can say that the Empire not merely gave the bureaucracy a new political master, better equipped to make full use of it, but also imposed both a new judicial basis and, more importantly, a new centralized structure. The latter not only drew the bureaucracy towards the Emperor but also into a new and subordinate relationship to the new *préfets* and other functionaries. However, at the same time it acquired through this subordination a new authority and freedom from public control or interference. The bureaucracy thus became a stable but subordinate part of a whole new streamlined structure of government, within which a clear-cut chain of command meant that it could be manipulated more easily and effectively than ever before. In the hands of Bonaparte this often worked to the benefit of society, but time was to show that, in the absence of strong leadership, it could often work against society. As far as the personnel of the bureaucracy was concerned, these gains were purchases at a price. It was to be many years before the bureaucracy was able to change this situation and reassert its own position within the post-Napoleonic structure of government.

All this tends to suggest that Bonaparte existed in some kind of vacuum. In reality his freedom of action was to some extent circumscribed by the situation in which he found himself and this, like the general structure of government, needs to be taken into consideration before any real estimate of the nature and the significance of the bureaucracy under the Empire can be made. What one finds is that although the latter depended ultimately on personality and force, the bureaucracy did have some effect on Bonaparte, whereas his treatment of the bureaucracy did not always produce the results he expected. It did not become a personal tool bereft of all power of its own, but became increasingly depoliticized and orientated towards effective state service, even if that service was not always wholly bureaucratic in nature.

For although the Napoleonic regime has usually been regarded as one of the most authoritarian and authoritative in recent French history, in reality it was always marked by the fact that it was both a child of the Revolution in general, and of one of a long series of *coups d'états* in particular. Hence if Napoleon is often described as having restored the monarchy, he was always very conscious of how different his situation was from that of the Bourbons. As he told Chaptal, he differed from them in that he could only maintain himself in power by force.[8] When the Ancien Régime went to war it was to gain provinces. When he went to war it was the existence of his regime which was really at stake. He had therefore to repress any challenges from outside and to keep his distance from those who, like the generals, had risen in the same way as himself and felt they had a similar claim to power.

Partly because of this his regime was not a simple military dictatorship despite the role played by Napoleon's generals. It rested on force in a more negative way.[9] His regime was not only prone to coercion but one which in the last resort could only appeal to force and not to inbuilt support or traditional constitutional niceties. When it failed on the battlefield or did not resort to coercion as in 1814 it fell. To try and minimize this fact Bonaparte liked to talk of himself as the 'Great Tribune', and in 1814 he told the Corps Législatif that they were not representative, for, 'the true representative of France is myself. France has more need of me than I have of France.' But he had, as Stendhal pointed out, to stifle political life at home in order to establish his regime and its claim to be the emanation of popular sovereignty.

On a more positive level he also had to appeal to the self-interest of those with influence in the community in order to ensure that his will was obeyed. Hence although evidence is incomplete it does seem as though he was aiming, through the *Auditeurs au Conseil d'Etat*, the new nobility, and other such bodies, to create a hereditary body of dependent state notables through whom he could unite and rule the nations of the Empire in a Gallicized social and administrative framework.[10] Hence Tulard takes François de Nantes as the symbol both of 'la despotisme civile soutenu par un corps de fonctionnaires', as Latreille defines the regime, and of the evolution of a new social élite—'les notables'—from amongst the victors in revolutionary administration, politics, speculation, business, and land sales. 'Une bourgeoisie nantie et une aristocratie rallié' were the basis of the new social system in which *fonctionnaires* had a large part. In the Mont Blanc for example they made up 14 per cent of the list of notables. The administration may even have had a double role, as a dynastic base and as a means of reconciliation if it is true that 'le but de la politique sociale de Napoléon était de réconcilier ces élites naguère antagonistes, maintenant complémentaires, et, par l'intermédiaire de l'administration les tourner en une force sociale et politique unique à la service du régime'. The enthusiasm with which a staunch republican responded to the lure of being a new-style *missi dominici* shows that the creation of such a class was far from impossible.[11]

Obviously his military upbringing impelled him towards a strong, centralized, and hierarchical state, just as did his early insecurity, but he was never quite willing to follow this social policy through to its logical conclusions.[12] It was only in the early days that he was responsive to the advice of the new class, because of his lack of familiarity with the day-to-day business of government. Later he was to dominate them and became a trifle thoughtless about their selection, so that the structure that gave his regime its vitality and its ability to impose the Revolution from above, which the Bourbons had been unable to effect, began to ossify.[13] Access to the élite was decided upon according to rigid social criteria, such as the insistence on financial qualifications—thereby excluding many competent people and halting social mobility through the administration—yet it was often done carelessly, in terms of the personalities taken on.

A further constraint was posed by the changing political and economic circumstances of the times.[14] For if the basic strategic situation of the regime *vis-à-vis* its society did not change, the tactical situation changed frequently. The uncertainty of the first days of the Consulate soon gave way to the great period of reforms, but once the war was renewed new problems always threatened and eventually developed in Spain and elsewhere. The demand for men, money, and munitions therefore grew, and conscription and social unease became intertwined with the depression that set in after 1810. Nemesis came rapidly and in 1814–15 very few social groups were willing to support the Emperor actively.

Even the notables in whose interests the regime was supposed to be and for whom the administration provided new openings, as the 2,000 applications for the 80 places in the Cour des Comptes and the *manie de plume* at lower levels shows, refused to support Bonaparte.[15] The creation of the new *noblesse* and the increasing evidence of Caesarism, as in the dynastically motivated Spanish venture, offended the bourgeoisie in general and the Brumairians in particular. So they gradually withdrew their support from the regime. This then became less something based on collaboration with a class and more an individual's caprice.[16] Each phase of the Empire thus affected the relations between Bonaparte, his administration, and his society.

The final confining condition was the nature of the *coup* of 18 *Brumaire* and its immediate aftermath. Even though it was speedy and peaceful it did not bring immediate ease to the administration and to the country. The problems of the Interior and of the War Office seem if anything to have increased, mainly because of the continuing difficulties over the payment of salaries. Changes in government attitudes towards *émigrés* also meant that the Ministry of Police was overwhelmed with enquiries, while new institutions like the prefectures were sometimes insubordinate. So new approaches to government had to be devised.[17] This situation, although not exempt from difficulties for the bureaucracy, continued to make the latter indispensable. Sweeping changes were not possible then, and once they were not made a further hostage to fortune had been given.

Chaptal may have thought that the fact that 'les chefs du parti populaire dominaient dans les administrations' was one of the main faults of government, but the total lack of opposition to the *coup* inside the administration helped to ensure that there was no real purge. In the *Préfecture de Police* the bureaux were left largely untouched and only the field services were purged, and then without real public awareness of what was going on. Indeed, not merely in the recruitment of the first prefects but as late as the establishment of the Cour des Comptes, a large proportion of the officials of the new order were drawn from those who had served under the Directory.[18] As early as a Nivôse VIII Bonaparte was also publicly recognizing the need to satisfy career desires by establishing a proper procedure for promotion in the army and in the judiciary. So the bringing in of new men, in line with his declaration that 'des places seront ouvertes aux Français de toutes les opinions, pourvu qu'ils aient des lumières, de la capacité et des vertus' did not mean a total upheaval in the Administrative system.

Such statements suggest that Bonaparte had a very definite administrative strategy. He certainly talked about it more than his predecessors, and had some grasp of administrative realities. In the last resort it was political concerns which counted. In his early days he was not very well-versed in many aspects of administration, hence his remark that 'en fait d'administration l'expérience est tout' and the relative lack of emphasis on administering as opposed to governing, revealed in his letters to Eugène de Beaunharnais.[19] After he had acquired some experience he became less of a lawmaker and less subject to ministerial advice and began to make himself felt throughout the country.

To do this of course he needed 'des bras' and he does seem to have had some feelings for the problems of and the utility of the field services. On the whole, however, he was hard and cynical about employees and more concerned with getting things done through the new *fonctionnaires*. This does not mean he could ever dispense with the former. In his case personal leadership in a post-revolutionary situation did not really oust bureaucracy in favour of 'a fluid, non-structured accumulation of power' in the ruler's hands.[20] He did, however, have to be censured by Talleyrand for his lack of appreciation of the need to allow promotion and *esprit de corps* inside ministerial services. The crisis atmosphere and the continuing lack of group consciousness probably inhibited employee protests at the way they were abused by both Emperor and élite Imperial *fonctionnaires*.

The concern for the execution of decisions was crucial and probably outweighed the distinctions he drew between the various functions of government and between administrative and other acts. The preamble to the *loi 28 Pluvôse VIII,* after distinguishing between communication, direct action, and procuring action, spends most time on the ways in which action can be procured. It stresses action by responsible individuals rather than techniques. 'Administrer doit être le fait d'un seul homme.' In making decisions it must have been impossible to observe the distinction he drew between a political or judicial act, which would deprive a Frenchman of his life or property, and an administrative act which, he believed, did not have such powers.[21] As Fain said of him, 'il cherchait dans les diverses questions qui lui étaient soumises, l'occasion d'appliquer ses règles d'administration et de gouvernement: il s'abandonnait même volontiers à leur développement; il voulait qu'aucun effort ne se perdît hors du mouvement qu'il faillait fournir en commun. La force de son gouvernement devait être dans l'unité du système dont il était l'âme, le plus important de des soins était de maintenir cette unité entre lui et ses ministres.'

Once Bonaparte had the experience and security he felt necessary, his talent for penetrating the realities of the problems facing France made itself manifest. His phenomenal activity, energy, insight, and memory enabled him to make a vast array of decisions on matters of all kinds. As Mollien said, 'in the midst of his camp and during military operations he wished not only to govern, but also to administer France by himself, and he succeeded'. He was a supreme decision-maker placed in a uniquely advantageous position as sole ruler of a powerful and centralized state machine. The key to his administrative strategy was the absolute unity of power and decision-making, backed up by fear and the supervision of what Mollien called 'cette inquiète vigilance dont il était agité'. His Conseils d'Adminis- tration thus became classes in which the ministers were taught how to govern in his image. The exhausting correspondence and other demands Napoleon required of them made them as punctilious about their responsibilities and subordinates as he thought himself to be.

Given his view of himself as the real representative of the national will he often wished to do without any intermediaries between himself and those who carried out his decisions at the grass-roots level.[22] His ideal would have been for his decisions to be translated directly into action after a communication from his private secretaries or the *Secrétaire d'État*, but he realized that the *brouillons* he threw off were not a whole answer to the complex problems of government. The advice of experts was needed, though he was aware of the difficulty of finding really capable agents and insisted on limiting their role.[23] If they showed independence, failed to act according to his methods, or were disobedient, then he was inflexible, even where his brother Lucien was concerned. Employees were not allowed to get in his way. To ensure that they did not, he delighted in playing off one service against another as he did the Conseil d'État and the ministries.

He rarely praised the administration and was often concerned about controlling it, as the *loi 28 Pluviôse* and the later idea of a special court for officials shows. It was also to exercise this control and to prevent the crudities of military or bureaucratic administration that the prefects and other *fonctionnaires* were established. This was in addition to their providing a new class who would make his regime compact, energetic, and full 'patriots for me', as Franz Josef was later to say. They would be nominated, probably allowed to hold more than one post, and possibly would be provided with free training and special stipends—over and above their salaries—drawn from the estates of the *Légion d'Honneur*. Their political role would be to provide him with a body of able men, bound to him by oath, who could be used anywhere to control the field services and tie the most ambitious elements of society to him. Damien has described the role of the *Légion* as the formation of a government party in the modern sense.

He once said that 'the French are unable to desire anything seriously except, perhaps, equality. Even so they would gladly renounce it if everyone could entertain the hope of rising to the top. Equality in the sense that everyone will be master—there you have the secret of all your vanities. What must be done therefore is to give everyone the hope of being able to rise.'[24] Hence by playing on the career open to talents he hoped to establish his regime socially and administratively, preventing the bureaucracy from becoming a power in its own right, and enabling him personally to conserve both his soverign authority and his ability to minister in detail. In the even, of course, his social conservatism tended to limit his openness to mere ability.

All this meant a very powerful and efficient state system, if not the omniscient one sometimes assumed. Yet it was not necessarily a bureaucratic one, whether in the sense of decisions being taken by clerks or in the sense of government being carried out by men who were strictly career bureaucrats. It meant a return to the Ancien Régime system of government by an administrative class, with the difference that there were fewer complications and judicial embellishments at the centre, where decisions were more a matter of will. His strategy however was, as has been suggested, never carried fully into effect. Neither the time nor the circumstances were quite suitable, while his ideals failed to allow either for unfettered promotion by merit or for the amount of routine and technical expertise even then inherent in administration. However, where control of the police machinery in Paris was concerned he did revert from the revolutionary and Directorial pattern of municipal control to that of the Ancien Régime.

To devise and carry out his decisions he needed more institutional channels than the might have hoped. Some of these were provided by constitutional structures, others through the gradual development of administrative law, and others through a variety of other bodies from the Conseil d'État down to, as will be seen, the continuing bureaucracy at the centre and periphery. Under the terms of the constitutions of the Year VIII and after, the power of the executive was vastly increased to include all appointments, all financial and military matters, and even, through the Conseil d'État, a large share in legislation as well.[25] The latter was also responsible for resolving any administrative difficulties which might arise, while the ministers were responsible for the execution of both laws and administrative acts. The powers originally offered to the legislature, the lists of notables and other bodies, were also whittled away at the same time as those of the *Premier Consul* and the government were increased.

One of the keys to the latter, along with the Conseil d'État, lay in the often overlooked Secrétariat d'État.[26] The latter was a continuation of Lagarde's creation, and though Lagarde stayed with the Secrétariat Général des Consuls for only a few years, both continued to operate along the lines he had laid down, so that the Secrétariat d'État when it absorbed the other body became, rather as Lagarde had been under the Directory, 'le ministre des ministres, donnant vie à toute les actions inter-médiaires'. Maret as *Secrétaire d'État* sorted out papers between ministries, registered decisions taken in private after Bonaparte had heard ministers or councillors, played a large role in appointments, and orchestrated the press for the benefit of the regime. A few of the old staff were dismissed at Brumaire and a further forty left as an economy measure in early Pluviôse, but the remaining twenty or so continued to run the clerical side under Lagarde and later Maret and his successors, under whom its numbers rose again to sixty and more in 1814. Since a third of these had been inherited from the Directory, some of the latter's structures and practices were passed on to the new order.

The Conseil d'État had been transformed from the initial conception of Sieyès into a body which helped to put flesh on Bonaparte's ideas and to insert them into the basic fabric of government and social life. It also provided him with the most able and reliable pool of *missi dominici,* while some of its members were also given specific responsibilities for certain field services, notably Police regions and Ponts et Chaussées. It also provided a useful sounding-board for the new administrative élite, as officials from within the ministries, like Hauterive, Miot, Laforest, and Labesnardière, were appointed to it and thereby given enhanced status. Though it did not then enjoy the administrative jurisdiction it was later to acquire, it was from the beginning regarded as a useful check on the civil service. Hence the scrutiny exercised by heads of section like Defermon over relevant ministries, and the way in which it was allowed to authorize the prosecution of officials, whose High Court its Commission des Affaires Contentieuses became in 1806. The latter also dealt with matters devolved on it by article 52 of the constitution, including arbitration over conflicts of jurisdiction and matters involving state contracts.[27] Another important step in this context was the creation of the Conseils de Préfecture, which derived their significance from the need to ensure that people did not find themselves judged either by individuals or 'après les rapports et des avis de bureaux'. In practice this was less successful since Bonaparte was still complaining in 1811 that intrigues in the bureaux could still compromise liberty and property. Both these institutions more or less fitted into Bonaparte's ideal of administration, but in fact they both also assumed the existence of subalterns who would actually do the work involved.

The whole machinery of administrative law and control is in fact silent testimony to the impossibility of the Emperor's hopes. There was no proper legislative control, but the executive had other means of action, including the machinery of fiscal control and *la tutelle administrative*. Certainly this was a major element in the prefectoral system. Damien claims that the Ministry of the Interior went so far as to use spies to check on the suitability of those nominated for office. And in fact no formal personnel policy or code was ever evolved, thereby hindering attempts at administrative control.[28] The Conseils d'Administration as well as aiding in policy-making also helped to provide a form of control, for although no decisions were taken in these gatherings of finance ministers, *conseillers d'état*, technical experts, ministers, and sometimes heads of bureaux and services, they did allow Bonaparte to keep in touch and co-ordinate the central administration's action.

He was even more specific about the role of financial control since he said that 'Le Trésor est la base de tout' and claimed to be able to govern anywhere in Europe provided Maret and the Treasury were at his disposal.[29] He paid scrupulous attention to financial details himself and insisted on strict obedience to all Treasury rulings, and supplemented the latter on occasion by the use of special inspectors. However, local control was normally exercised by the *préfets*, while more generally one should not overlook the use made of *grands dignitaires*, the police, and the Emperor's own cabinet, especially under Bourrienne, as a means of controlling administration.[30] All this happened outside the formal structures of government. So despite the apparent simplicity of both Bonaparte's aims and his structures of government, there were complications. Not only did the machine depend ultimately on its 'bras' but institutions also played more than one role so as to provide Bonaparte with the means of activating and disciplining the administration. Thus the Conseil dÉtat shared in the direction of field services in which Bonaparte took a keen interest, as well as playing the judicial and political roles already described.

The role which the ministries played in the over-all Napoleonic system of government has been much debated.[31] From Chaptal onwards, it has been argued that the ministers were reduced to the rank of simple heads of bureaux or clerks to the Emperor, an ironic complaint given the denuniciation of ministerial despotism current in the eighteenth century. This, may well have been an exaggeration due to the fact that many observers concentrate on the Conseil d'État. Bourdon points out that when Bonaparte said he could govern through Maret and a few others, he was overlooking the fact that projects presented to him or the Conseil had normally been prepared by the competent minister or on his orders. Although they did not meet as the cabinet, the close relations engendered by their individual sessions with Napoleon and the special honours with which they were endowed under the Empire, such as the elevation of the Minister of Justice to the rank of *Le Grand Juge*, gave them a special standing in the public eye. Similarly, although the Conseil d'État did disdain ministers and interfere in their affairs, they did have access to it, while the growing extent of specialization and the relatively minor importance of Ministers of State meant that the departmental ministers preserved some autonomy and standing, as well as a *de facto* share in government.

One can therefore agree with Sautel that the Napoleonic ministries prefigure the partly political, partly administrative, ministers of the later nineteenth century, so that if they were *commis* they were at least *grands commis*. Bonaparte himself often laid great stress on their innovative and regulatory role in the state, as when he said:

Les ministres parlent en mon nom; personne n'a le droit à paralyser, d'arrêter l'exécution des ordres qu'ils transmettent . . . tout ce qui existe dans l'Empire est sous la surveillance de mes ministres . . . Le Ministre n'est que l'expression directe de mon autorité . . . tour vont chez lui, lorsqu'ils ont besoin de son intervention auprès de moi; il ne va chez personne. C'est la marche de l'administration.[32]

The importance of the ministers is also suggested by the way in which significant areas of state activity were promoted to ministerial status, as happened with the Secrétaire d'État, the Trésor in 1801, the Administration de la Guerre, hived off from the War Office in 1802, the administration of Cultes in 1804, the Université in 1808, which enjoyed quasi-ministerial status although in theory it was dependent on the Public Instruction division of the Ministry of the Interior, and the department of Manufactures et de Commerce in 1811.[33]

Against this one must set the fact that the Ministry of Police was abolished between 1802 and 1804 when its staff and its duties were transferred to the Ministry of Justice. So the number of ministries oscillated between eleven and twelve. The Ministry of Police was, moreover, always paralleled by the *Préfecture de Police,* although the latter despite its successes in the fields of economics and of health up to 1810 never claimed ministerial status.[34] So here again, despite Bonaparte's self-confessed preference for government by *grands fonctionnaires* he never did very much to undermine the key establishments of central government and their heads. What he did do in the case of the administration of Paris, was to allow a new degree of arbitrariness to his agents.

The Ministry of Police was one of the key ministries of the regime due to Bonaparte's suspicions of those around him as well as to the ability and influence of Fouché. The latter was assisted by a secretariat, under the long-serving Saulnier, the *Conseillers d'État* and *Auditeurs* responsible for the three or four regions into which the Empire was divided for police matters, and bureaux reserved for affairs, security and secret police affairs (under Demarest), the press, *émigré* affairs, accounts, archives, and at times the theatre. These were all staffed very largely by men drawn from the Directorial ministry. Some 160 of them served in the first phase of the Ministry's existence and about 120 thereafter. In addition, mention must also be made of the Cabinet Noir and the *mouchards* who played a large part in police work. With all these services Fouché, and later Savary, provided a vast amount of information on the Empire and its daily life, as well as doing much to prevent and punish crime and political disaffection. When Fouché's fall from favour led to the suppression of the Ministry, responsibility for police affairs was attached to the Ministry of Justice where it formed a Direction de Sécurité. Deprived of Fouché's skill it was never able to offer the same service, as Napolean was later to find when Savary was in charge of the restored Ministry.

The Ministry of Justice itself remained a fairly small body, while some of its powers were exercised by Cambacères as *Archichancelier*.[35] It never had a staff of more than 150, but they were increasingly separated as the services of the Ministry became more established. It thus acquired a Secrétariat-Général, a Direction du Personnel—a strengthened version of the old *bureau de l'organisation judiciaire*—a Direction des Affaires Criminelles, and bureaux for civil and financial affairs. If the Minister's own bureau counted for less, he gained increased influence through the drafting of the *Codes* and the fact that he sometimes chaired the Tribunal de Cassation.

The Ministry of the Interior underwent a considerable amount of change during the period, first with the creation of specialized Directions Générales for Ponts et Chaussées, Cultes, education, and Droits Réunis over which the Minister exercised much less control than in the past, and then with the creation of the three new departments which were carved out of its still encyclopaedic duties.[36] Yet despite these transfers and the savage reductions in staffing by Lucien Bonaparte and Chaptal, which at one time reduced the Ministry to a mere staff of 85, the numbers continued to grow, reaching well over 180 by the late Empire and at one time well over 220. For much of the Empire the Ministry consisted of a large *secrétariat-général*, a division for local administration, (including its personnel and finances), one for agriculture and food supplies, and one for science and welfare, together with bureaux for ministerial accounts and archives. At the end of the Empire there were also several Directions Générales loosely attached to the Ministry, dealing with public works, mines, roads and bridges, censorship, local finances, museums, the postal services, and imperial archives. These Directions Générales and their heads, it should be said, were not really similar to their modern synonyms.

The Ministry of Finance also retained much of its structure from Directorial days, with the Secretariat (responsible for winding up old accounts), and divisions for Direct and Indirect taxation, national estates, and ministerial accounts, not to mention its own Directions Générales, although these were more like field services than those of the Interior.[37] The Treasury also maintained a large and complicated staff to deal with the acute problems of the state's cash flow situation. The Ministry of Foreign Relations, because of the long and capable tenure of Talleyrand, maintained its old influence and became smaller and more centralized with only two political divisions, staffed in part by former Ancien Régime *premiers commis*.[38] The Ministry of the Navy changed very little, retaining its secretariat, and its old divisions, later raised to the status of Directions Générales which the colonies service already enjoyed, and employing over 220 staff. Of the other ministries very little is known.[39] The Ministry of Trade, under Collin de Sussy, 'le douanier par excellence', was created to apply the continental system and had four divisions with ten bureaux between them. The former dealt with trade, manufactures and food supplies, customs, and licences, together with a number of consultative councils.

The Ministre de Cultes was originally a Direction Générale, and after its upgrading in July 1804 it maintained its original small staff, while both Ministers made great use of their relatives as their chief advisers.[40] The 4 and later 8 bureaux of the Ministry had only 113 employees throughout the Napoleonic era, a stability that owed little to the sophisticated grading-schemes discerned by Tulard. There were no salary scales, and no increments, only a pensions fund. However, salaries did rise during the period, so that 40 per cent of the staff served for the whole fourteen years of the administration's existence, despite their complaints. The 4 main bureaux were a secretariat, a Catholic nominations section, a Protestant affairs bureaux, and a financial service.

The Université was also likely to have had a small and simple organization. In all it seems likely that the staff of the ministries, including those for military affairs, rose from 1,650 at the end of the Directory to over 2,100 under the Consulate. By the late Empire there were anything between 3,600 and 4,000 staff. Of this latter figure some 1,500 were employed by the two Ministries of War.

This suggests that it was the pressure of war rather than any desire to limit the power of the Minister which led to the creation of the new department in 1802.[41] The Ministry of War proper retained responsibility for general army affairs and fighting units, while Dejean's new department for *l'Administration de la Guerre* dealt with equipment, administration, and non-combatant services. Prior to the division there had been nearly 500 employees in the War Office divided into some 8 divisions largely inherited from the Directory. Paradoxically, despite the intention of the reform, which was to reduce the staff, numbers in the two departments soared, particularly in the Late Empire. Hence, although examinations were brought in for supernumerary employees at one stage, they were soon forgotten as the administrative implications of the efforts necessary to defend the Grand Empire led to the import of vast numbers of temporary and auxiliary staff. Often these were drawn from former soldiers or employees in the field services in order to deal with such problems as prisoners of war and the provision of death certificates. This allowed generals to exercise patronage but did not offer the new men much in the way of prospects of security of tenure.

So the Ministry of War alone saw its staff rise from 526 in 1811 to 727 by March 1814, an expansion which forced it to abandon its old premises to the new Ministry and move to the rue St Dominique, although its internal structures remained fairly constant. Apart from the Secretariat, which at times was responsible for certain military operations, pay, and accounts, there were normally divisions for personnel, operations, organization, the artillery, engineering, military justice, conscription, and *rétraites*. In addition, the administration of gunpowder and the *Invalides* was attached to the Ministry. The new Ministry at first had 3 divisions, and a secretariat, with some 200 staff, but by 1813 this had risen to 439, divided between the Secretariat and divisions for food supplies and barracks, military hospitals, civilian personnel, accounts, and uniforms. Thus the vast majority of the staff in both departments actually dealt with routine administrative problems, and save for the Dépot Général, the *bureau d'opérations*—which often accompanied Berthier on campaigns, and the military geographers there was no real general staff, a sign perhaps of the Emperor's desire to limit ministerial initiative.

In addition to the ministries there were other central organs whether inherited from the Revolution like the Direction Générale de la Liquidation, or largely new like the Cour des Comptes, or promoted to a new rank such as the Directions Générales attached to the various ministries.[42] Most of these were subject to co-ordination by Maret, although they often overlapped with other field services. Those which, like the tax and customs services, were in fact field services seem to have expanded because of the demands of war. On occasions they were also more efficient, but attacks by the Emperor and others on the honesty and inefficiency of the customs and forest services for instance suggest that this was not always the case.[43] Thus the *cadastre* on which so much of the regime's hopes for fiscal reforms rested, was never completed.

However, the extension of pensions to local employees and the general subordination of local and field services to the *préfet* meant that the technical and employee element in government was more united, more recognized, and possibly more bureaucratized as a result of the Empire. Bonaparte was not happy about this, since he felt that the government was still not in sufficient control of the wider reaches of the administrative machine on which, despite his desires and in spite of the installation of prefects and mayors, the regime increasingly depended for the resources called for by war.[44] In fact, despite the enconiums heaped on the new system of local government, Van Berkel has shown that the new system actually increased the power of the bureaux. For neither the prefect nor his subordinates had the time to take decisions on all the matters which they were responsible.

This suggests that the Napoleonic machine, for all that it bequeathed a rigid strait-jacket to latter-day France, was neither so completely in line with the Emperor's intentions nor so efficient as is sometimes suggested.[45] Even Fouché has not escaped from criticisms of late, although it has to be recognized that very few administrations would have been able to stand up to the excessive demands placed on it by the Emperor and his wars. Without any parliamentary recess there was a continuous stream of demands for reports, information, or action, often called for in so brief a time that clerks were forced to sleep in their bureaux in order to satisfy 'l'œil vigilant et . . . l'esprit méfiant de l'empereur'. It was not merely a question of exhausting the administration by asking too much of it, or of blunting its efficiency by punitive surveillance. A considerable expansion of staff was called for, and even the central administration of the Ponts et Chaussées trebled under the Empire.[46] The larger the administration, the slower the correspondence and the greater the autonomy of the officials involved tended to be. So the demands which Napoleon made on the administration could sometimes be self-defeating. The extreme case came with the destruction of the Bureau Topographique of the Grand Army in Russia which placed an intolerable strain on the staff work of the remaining military administrations, since in line with his *a priori* dislike of bureaucracy Bonaparte never increased its budget after the disaster.

Moreover, the procedures used by the administration in more normal times were not without their weaknesses.[47] Over-centralization in Paris, continuing incoherence in the division of functions, and reliance on the register rather than the file, and this despite the growing use of the 'minute', told against efficiency, at least after 1810, when in Paris at least a new era of crises began.[48] However, such problems should be set against use of statistics, the development of reports, and the adoption of double entry book-keeping. This is not to mention the work of the Conseils d'Administration and of able ministers like Cretet and Montalivet in the Interior who saw the need for better staffing and working procedures to avoid continuing abuses. So, even if other administrations might not have stood up to the pressures as well as that of France, the latter was never free from the conflicts of administration, changes of decision, and unnecessarily repeated paperwork. The example of the statistical services of the Interior, which after 1804 ceased to produce either the quantity or the quality of reports on the provinces provided by their predecessors, partly because of the Emperor's control and partly because of internal rivalries, is instructive.[49] It differs significantly from the administrative nirvana some- times conjured up by the Emperor's less critical admirers. For if Napoleon had firm ideas about administration, and if he gave it a forceful and streamlined structure within which to develop, he was in the end just as dependent on his employees as his predecessors had been. Hence there were just as many ambi- guities in his practices as at any other time during the Revolution. The difference was that his will and *persona* prevented the ambiguities from interfering with the running of the machine, and from serving as the basis for a campaign by the employees.

This is not to say that the employee element in government was wholly repressed under the Empire. They did in fact gain from increased public authority acquired by the ministries and by the administration in general as a result of their contact with the Emperor. Because of the censorship and the effective policing of the country they were spared much of the carping criticism that had been visible before. Similarly, it was rarely fought over by competing factions. These gains, however, were purchased at a price. The employees may have continued to play a part in policy-making as under the Directory but they lost any chance of autonomy and self-expression. More importantly, despite the fact that Bonaparte needed them more than he cared to admit, they lost much of their self-respect and standing in society because of the rise of the new class of *fonctionnaires*. A few were admitted to Conseils d'Administration and other such insti- tutions, but these were a lucky élite. Very few subordinate employees are to found amongst the 5 per cent of civilians who were awarded the *Légion d'Honneur* by 1814, nor were salaries or chances of promotion to the *fonctionnaire* levels much larger than before.[50] Indeed, rather than this having been a silver age as Balzac suggests, the increase in the number of posts and the employment of ex-servicement would seem to have tarnished their prospects somewhat.

Certainly, the average clerk could expect to find his promotion blocked by this and by the creation of the new *fonctionnaires*, and it would seem that the latter were resented, to judge from the poetic response of the Director of the Ponts et Chaussées to the appointment of an *Auditeur au Conseil* to his department:

Gens de bureau, je vous donne
Pour cadeau du jour de l'An
Un auditeur en personne,
Qui marche, parle, raisonne,
Qui punit, gronde, pardonne,
Qui dans son petit bureau,
Au coin de son petit âtre,
Représente un petit pâtre
Comptant son petit troupeau . .

Je prétends en toute affaire,
S'il n'y reste rien à faire,
Que jamais il ne diffère
A donner son coup de main
Bien qu'il soit ici sans doute,
Moins pour s'occuper de route
Que pour faire son chemin.[51]

Moreover, the restoration of a kind of monarchy inevitably meant a return to patrimonialism of some kind, especially when the ruler enjoyed such control of official nominations. Hence if some of the older abuses were less marked, patronage was very active, beginning with the promotion of 'les Égyptiens' and going on to the acceptance of the protégés of generals.[52] On occasion, of course, the Emperor would refuse lists of nominations submitted by the ministries in order to ensure that the bureaux did not get control of such a vital area of political life. However, an examination of a sample of clerks who entered the War Ministries in his reign suggests that few entered for purely political reasons, but that many were placed by heads of sections, ministers, or court personalities, far more than were ever dismissed for political reasons too. As under previous regimes the tendency was to steer clear of political involvement and to be susceptible to dismissal in the face of economic stringency.

Moreover, many more clerks seem to have entered the ministries after sitting an exam or doing a preparatory *stage* as a supernumerary, in line with what many authorities have seen as Bonaparte's very forward-looking stress on talent, training, and testing amongst officials.[53] Some progress was made towards a *statut des fonctionnaires*, in an empirical way. French nationality was insisted on throughout the Grand Empire for officials, while pensions based on employees' contributions made their appearance in a variety of services, and deductions from salaries were gradually phased out. Moreover, within new corps like the *Auditeurs* and the *Ingénieurs Géographes* more rigid systems of grading and promotion were introduced.[54] The same thing can be seen inside the ministries. The Justice department thus moved away from a system involving some thirty grades to one similar to that found in most other ministries with fewer grades, each with a number of sub-divisions. One of the earliest examples of this was in the War Office which in Thermidor IX divided its staff into *Chefs de Division, Chefs de Bureau, Sous-Chefs, Commis Garçons*, and *Surnuméraires*, with anything up to five salary points within each grade. The largest range was obviously amongst the *Commis* whose pay could range from 1,800 to 3,600 francs per annum. This was not wholly new, but it was more complicated, and was to prove more lasting than previous schemes.

The implications of such structures were most fully spelt out in the Ministry of the Interior where a fixed system of advancement was introduced which involved seven or eight overlapping grades each containing three or four formally numbered classes, so that different tasks could be rewarded as well as different points in the hierarchy. Promotion depended on seniority and merit while there was also provision for bringing people in from outside. Such schemes were not always fully applied, and even that for the *Auditeurs* was successfully resisted by the Ministry of Foreign Affairs which preferred to train its own cadres. Similarly, both the needs of war and the Emperor's prerogative could and did cut right across neatly organized schemes, as when he was informed that the Ministry of Foreign Affairs could not supply him with information because d'Hauterive, its much-respected archivist, was ill. His response was: 'Eh bien, foutre! Quand les commis sont malades, on les envoi à l'hôpital et on en prend d'autres.'[55]

None the less, following the timid experiments of the *agrégation* in 1766 and in some state departments during the Revolution, some progress was made towards repairing the damage done by the collapse of education with the introduction of exams for entry to the administration. The *baccalauréat* of the Year XIV paved the way for the demand that would-be *Auditeurs* should have a degree as well as sitting an oral examination before a jury of three. Some ministries introduced rather more basic qualifying examinations which took the form of a trial dictation and dispatch administered to those who had some education and a reasonable hand. Such progress was still somewhat superficial.[56] Changes were made department by department, and not for the administration as a whole, whether at *fonctionnaire* or *employé* levels. Where the latter were concerned new barriers were created by the emergence of new élites and new avenues of patronage, so that one future *préfet* remarked that he had refused a salary when attached to the Interior in a supernumerary capacity because he wanted to 'suivre la carrière administrative et non celle des bureaux'.

It is no wonder that ordinary clerks detested such people, especially when their own situation could remain impoverished and governmental initiatives, such as Conseil d'État's suggestion in 1811, that there should be one uniform 2 per cent *retenue* for pensions, or the creation of the Écoles de Droit, never came to anything. In any case the Emperor's own will, often exercised arbitrarily or for political reasons, could cut right across established practices at all levels of the administration. So the steps taken towards integrating the new bureaucracy into the new society were not only superficial but insecure. None the less, some steps were taken, and the ground was prepared for a fuller realization of the problems involved under a less authoritarian regime.

Some idea of the actual results of the combination of formalism and personalism can be seen in a brief consideration of some of the entrants to the War Ministries during the period.[57] For although the numbers involved were small and their service restricted to one area of the administration, the critical importance of that area to the Empire and the relative abundance of the information available makes an examination useful, not only in itself but also as a comparison to the analyses of the ministries at other periods. At least two-thirds of the sample were townsmen, again largely from the north-east of the country, but with Versailles, and to a lesser extent Paris, supplying rather fewer clerks than before. Dijon and Rouen were the other major centres to provide staff, due in the first case no doubt to the continuing connection between Carnot and others and the town. The sample were, as is to be expected, distinctly younger than in earlier analyses, for over 60 per cent were born after 1770 and were therefore between eighteen and forty-five when the Empire fell.[58] This is significant when one considers that only a few entered the War Ministries in the first years of Napoleon's reign, compared with a third of the sample who entered between 1805 and 1810, and the half who were called in after 1811. This pattern reflects the need to get all the clerks possible, of whatever age, during the critical years of the Late Empire.

However, as Panagiatopoulos has shown, there is no simple preference for youth amongst the Imperial élites, save perhaps amongst those generals who made their name during the Revolution.[59] One finds that while young men were still being attracted directly into state service, there were not enough of them available because of conscription. So far more rather older men were able to enter the ministries without having first to prove themselves in a less prestigious branch of the administration. Nearly three times as many men joined the ministries when they were between thirty and thirty-five as had joined the civil service in general at that age. Some of these had been soldiers, others came from the Court, and a surprising number came from the professions, although, as always, the largest proportion were from the field services.

If this suggests that the field services were still well integrated into the bureaucracy as a whole, the rest of the evidence shows that like its revolutionary predecessor the Imperial government was forced to take men where it could find them. The emerging pyramidal structure leading from a whole range of government services to the ministries, which had been the norm in the 1790s and was in fact called very much into question. Transfers involving the field services were common, as was 'requisitioning' or appointment as a reward for military service, but for an increasing number of people state employment started in the Ministry of War during the Late Empire.[60] Such employment was usually at a very low level, as a junior clerk, or in over half the cases as an *auxiliaire* or trainee at a wage little better than that of a *garçon de bureau*. However, more use was made of examinations for such people, not because of growing professionalism it would seem, but because many of those who presented themselves were not up to even the simple tasks then required of them.

Not surprisingly, this hand-to-mouth form of recruitment did not produce people from elevated social backgrounds.[61] There were a number of journalists and self-employed artisans amongst the fathers of clerks whose occupations are recorded, along with lawyers, army officers, and even one or two nobles. Very little is known about the education of the clerks themselves. Under 2 per cent are known to have had a university law training, but there does seem to have been a marginal increase in the numbers who had received some kind of advanced secondary or tertiary education. Yet it was still only a minority that was involved.

The evidence on wealth and income also points to a very modest status. A fifth of the sample claimed to have no resources or to be in debt, and nearly as many were totally dependent on the salaries, leaving only one in twenty to admit to possession of some capital.[62] This is about the same proportion as under Ancien Régime, although the fact that many were able to support relatives suggests that they may not have been as badly off as they claimed. However, there were more people in economic straits than before the Revolution and there were fewer means of redressing the balance since the only fringe benefit available seems to have been the *Légion d'Honneur*. Perhaps as a result, there was still a high degree of job mobility, three times as many of the sample having had over five jobs in their lives as was the case before the Revolution, and nearly twice as many serving in between two and five jobs. On the other hand, there was only about half the level of family relations amongst the new entrants as after 1770, only one in ten having a father or some other relative in the ministry.

The situation thus revealed is one in which the exigencies of the Empire seem to have been the most influential factor in recruitment. It was not that society changed drastically, simply that the war machine took people at a low level, because it needed them urgently. Many and various were the reasons that led people to accept such employment which seems to have offered virtually no chance of promotion to *fonctionnaire* levels, although there was apparently more chance of reaching the middle of the hierarchy.[63] Some 40 per cent of the sample were promoted between one and three grades, although as was to be expected with so many emergency staff being involved, a high percentage remained static. If these are discounted, however, the chances of modest promotion for Imperial entrants seem to have been good. Hence although a quarter of the sample finished with a salary of between 750 and 1,500 francs per annum, nearly a third finished with between 2,500 and 10,000 francs. Such salaries would seem to have been more secure than during the Revolution, as was also the case with pensions, which were drawn by at least 40 per cent of the sample, the majority receiving between 1,000 and 5,000 francs per annum. Again, making allowance for the emergency employees, this seems to be a fairly high proportion.

The division between the former and the longer-term staff is partly visible in a consideration of length of service. There is a reasonable spread of people who served anything between one and fifteen years, but thereafter very few served from fifteen to twenty years, whereas a third served for over twenty years, sometimes with other government service on top of this since nearly two-thirds of the sample served over fifteen years in all forms of state service. Some of this took place after leaving the War Ministries since, whereas a third retired on leaving the Ministry, some 7 per cent went into other central administration, and about 9 per cent into the field services. Security of employment seems to have been even greater in other forms of state service and political involvement even less common, to judge from the figures for service in other forms of administration than the ministries and the high proportion of those who left it on death or retirement.

For the most part it seems that people entered the Napoleonic War Offices because the jobs were there and because they carried a certain security, although this had to be purchased at the cost of surrendering any hopes of the huge gains made by some of the new élite.[64] There was all the difference in the world between the clerks called into the Ministry in the Late Empire and the new élite with their titles, places in the Imperial household, councils, and orders, and their emphatic prefectoral or military authority. The fact that Bonaparte never went through with his ideas of extending the new élite, as for example through the idea of bursaries for members of the Légion d'Honneur and students at the École Polytechnique, or by making it formally hereditary, was small consolation for the average *commis*. For him it was, as Van Berkel has said, 'une nouvelle aristocratie administrative selon le modèle de l'Ancien Régime'.[65] As such it stood between him and further advancement and status.

Yet despite the honours heaped on the new class and the stress the Emperor placed on their being tied to him by moral obligation and vested interest, the new class grew away from him. Perhaps something of the continuing bureaucratization of the lower echelons of the administration did rub off on them, although it was to be many years before they really began to move along the same road. However, in the final resort some were willing to forsake the Emperor in order to preserve their own positions or because they felt he had broken faith with their needs and their aspirations.[66] Their concept of their superior duty to the state may also have played a part, so that one contemporary verdict on the employees of the Ministry of Finance after 1815 partly goes for their superiors as well:

Jamais administration n'a été moins occupée des opinions politiques. L'argent, ce grand mobile des girouettes, s'est tellement identifié avec les buralistes de ce ministère, qu'ils ont constamment été du côté d'où l'argent venait. Aussi, parcourez les *Almanachs* républicains, consulaires, impériaux, royaux, vous y verrez presque toujours les noms de mêmes individus en possession des mêmes places; de temps immémorial, on a rencontré là des frères Bricogne, MM. Raison, Petit, Piscatory, Bonnier, LeCamus, Corsut, Fain etcetera, etcetera. L'Empereur donna cependent à MM. Legrand, Hennet etc., la croix de la légion d'honneur. Ils n'ont pas moins travaillé pour le roi en 1814; *retravaillé* pour le l'Empereur en 1815 et *retravaillent* de nouveau pour le roi.[67]

Yet despite this evidence of administrative continuity amongst the employees, and to a lesser extent amongst the new *fonction-naires*, many historians have considered this period of the Late Empire as one in which the administration, and in particular the new socio-administrative élite, gave striking proof of incompetence.[68] As time went by, Napoleon himself grew more cynical and more brutal, less willing to accept any dilution of his personal authority particularly by the sometimes untrustworthy élite he had inherited from the Ancien Régime, and even by the Conseil d'État. Hence the latter was domesticated and became more of a court than a policy-making body. Even then its freedom of action was severely restrained, while the creation of the Domaine Extraordinaire and the increasing censorship and repression accentuated the personal and authoritarian nature of the regime. The development of the Grand Empire brought not merely increased social conservatism but also new administrative efforts. This meant finding personnel for 130 departments, the creation of new Directions Générales for technical tasks, the imposition of the Continental System, and ultimately, in 1813–14 the use of *conseillers d'état en mission extraordinaire* to raise desperately needed new troops. The ministers were thus sometimes bypassed by new officials and the *grands commis* gave way to lesser men. At the local level it has been argued that some of the new noble prefects were less energetic than their predecessors and left too much to their subordinates so that in the final crisis when Paris was unable to give direction there was virtual chaos in the countryside.[69]

This has recently been denied by Whitcomb, who argues that there was neither a purge nor an aristocratic reaction, let alone a degeneration. The *Préfets* appointed between 1810 and 1814 were in fact younger, more trained and tried than their predecessors, so that far from deteriorating, 'the corps becomes more stable, more professional and more experienced. It became subjet to fairly regular evaluation, with the advancement of careers based on promotion through the ranks and a formal system of training.' It may well be that the extent of administrative decline at the prefectoral level has been somewhat exaggerated. Although it does not of course follow that improved training and inspection schemes mean improved administration in the field.

None the less, generally speaking it does seem as if the Imperial machinery operated less positively in the Late Empire than before, although it was always able to keep things going and to enable Napoleon to raise the bulk of the men and resources he so desperately needed at that time. Thus the creation of new services meant that administrative unity was more difficult to attain and the constituent services, perhaps like the prefects, found themselves with more autonomy than they wanted, so that the burden of the final crisis was again largely carried by the bureaucracy. So while the Emperor was able to prevent the Corps Législatif from playing an independent role, he was too dependent on the administration during his last campaigns to be able to discipline it.

Wellington and others believed that in 1814–15 it was only officialdom which continued to sustain and to support Bonaparte, although the administration seems to have accepted the new regime with little demur, even though its budgetary cuts hit it hard.[70] Certainly Bonaparte himself returned from Elba highly critical of the state and opinions of the administration, convinced of the need to replace the royalists in the bureaux with 'des hommes surs'. This ironic repetition of 1793 shows that he too could mistake inertia for malevolence. Carnot when serving as Minister of the Interior in 1815 went beyond these denunciations and attacked the appointments made in 1812 and 1813.[71] These, he believed, had infected the administration with gangrene. Hence 1815 was to see a new wave of purges.

In reality, the bureaucracy remained the servant of power, and its service orientation may well have increased as a result of its relationship with the Emperor. The employee element in government was confirmed in its Weberian characteristics. It gained in continuity, permanence, and consistency because of improvements in career patterns and salaries. It became more impersonal, partly because of the introduction of the new class of *fonctionnaires* which prevented the exercise of initiative, and also because of the excessive centralization, paperwork, size, and authority necessitated by the Grand Empire. At the same time it became more specialized, more hierarchical, more regimented, and a little more qualified. In some ways it became more objective in its aims, but strategically speaking, its subordination to an authoritarian ruler blunted its objectivity and its rationality. This crucial dichotomy was due not only to the arbitrariness of Bonaparte's rule and its tendency towards social conservatism and patrimonialism, but also to the re-emergence of the new *fonctionnaires*. For although the favours bestowed on the latter failed to achieve their full effect, their very existence depressed the standing of the bureaucracy.

These changes were obviously produced by external forces. The internal dynamic which had emerged under the Directory had not come to an end. It had, so to speak, gone underground during the Empire, when it was too risky for it to show itself openly. The dynamic of change sprang from the nature of Bonaparte's domination combined with the needs of continuing warfare. Together these forces multiplied the inheritance from the past, for though Bonaparte changed many things, the continuity with the revolutionary bureaucracy is even more marked. With the exception of the mirroring of the monarchy's creation of administrative élites, his penchant for the Ancien Régime was perhaps less marked than elsewhere.

However, although the bureaucracy was larger than under the Directory, there was probably less spare flesh on it than had previously been the case. This enlarged yet refined bureaucracy he entrusted to the leadership of the new *fonctionnaires*, who at the same time also began to take their first very faltering steps down the long road to bureaucratization. This was despite his thoughts of making them into an hereditary caste and despite his final lukewarmness to unrestricted recruitment by merit. The two together he bound into a highly centralized institutional structure which has been his real legacy to France, perhaps even his *damnosa hereditas*. For although this administrative structure was to be a permanency, it is not wholly correct to see his reign as 'a golden age of bureaucracy' as Tulard does.[72] Things were more complicated than this suggests. There were tensions between the various layers of the administration. Similarly, while the new bourgeoisie needed a stronger state to protect its gains against 'demos', the caesarism of the new structure offended their constitutionalist aspirations.

With his dynamism he was able to ultilize the reforged machine so as to demonstrate the still latent power of administration in a way which had not been done before. Public opinion then and since was highly ambivalent about this. This demonstration was probably most impressive at the level of the largely ignored but increasingly vital and integrated field services. In doing this he posed new questions for administrative law to solve, questions not of how to make the bureaucracy responsive to government as in the time of the Directory but of how to protect the citizen against the new power in the land.

All this was rarely done straightforwardly, for Bonaparte was a complex and not always consistent man. He was also more interested in governing than in administering. For the former he needed 'des bras', and provided the latter obeyed him and got things done he was content. In his relationships with the bureaucracy, which was ultimately a dialogue and not the monologue sometimes suggested, he was really following out the logic of both the revolutionary creation and the Directorial consolidation. The end result was to remove any doubts about the bureaucracy's value and power, while at the same time sowing new myths about its origins and its rationality, as he himself came to realize on Saint-Helena.[73] It might well have have been him who said that 'the Bourbons ascended the throne of Bonaparte' for he was certainly, if sadly, aware that for all his aims, ambition, and authority, it was Bonaparte who passed on and the bureaucracy which remained.

CHAPTER IX: THE AFTERMATH
OF REVOLUTION, 1814–1848

Having reached stability and maturity under the Directory, the new ministerial bureaucracy was, under Bonaparte, endowed with new authority. It was also subjected anew to the leadership of an institutionalized élite of *fonctionnaires* whose general influence and administrative authority was heavily reinforced by the centralized institutional carapace Bonaparte bestowed on France. With his fall three problems faced the bureaucracy. The first was the basic question of whether or not it would be allowed to survive in a post-revolutionary world. Secondly, since, as it rapidly became clear, the chaotic transition from Bonaparte to Bourbon made the bureaucracy indispensable, how would it cope with a new socio-economic environment. And, thirdly, how would the employees react to their subordination to the *fonctionnaires* once the end of the Imperial autocracy permitted a freer debate on their predicament. The answer to these three questions slowly became plain over the next forty years so that by 1848 the ministerial bureaucracy had completed its metamorphosis by establishing itself as a recognized participant in the political process, thereby ending the phase of its development which had begun with the Revolution.

There seems to have been no real thought in 1814 or 1815 of dispensing with the civil service, even though leading Ultras like Castelbajac were always to complain that there were too many clerks about. Obviously, however, the Restoration regime did take a rather different view of the bureaucracy from that of the Empire. For while historians may appreciate the differences between the Imperial episode and the Revolution proper, the Bourbons did not. For them the Revolution had not ended with Brumaire, nor with the later Imperial consolidation of France. It was still going on. And for some of them the bureaucracy was something of a revolutionary Trojan horse, particularly after the emphatic way in which Bonaparte had used it. So while the new centralized structure was too attractive not to use there were always doubts about it. To some extent they were right to be suspicious since the effects of the revolutionary upheaval lasted much longer than the conventional historical dividing-line of 1815 leads one to imagine. So although the bureaucracy found itself entrusted to a regime which had little of the revolutionary in its make-up, the bureaucracy was still affected by the aftermath of revolution in a variety of ways. So when the Bourbons, by utilizing the bureaucracy, 're-ascended the throne of Bonaparte'—in matters administrative just as they did in many other respects—and assured 'la véritable pérennité' of the administration they also ensured that it would continue to be affected by its revolutionary origins.[1] Under the July Monarchy this was perhaps even more marked, despite the fact that the regime was farther removed in time from the original revolutionary experience.

The fact that the bureaucracy was allowed to survive did not, however, determine the conditions of its survival. This depended largely on the changing nature of the environment in which it had to operate. On the one hand French society was moving slowly and hestitantly towards economic growth and ultimately industrialization. In the long run this was bound to affect both the liberal conception of the state and the functioning of the civil service.[2] More immediately, the Restoration changed the social and political complexion of France. The fall of Napoleon allowed a resumption of normal political life and expression. This meant that previously suppressed hostility to the administration could make itself felt. At the same time the new regime, like that which followed it, was a parliamentary one. So the administration found itself caught up in the political battlefield, an experience till then largely unknown to it. The battlefield was for some time contested by the new notables and the old aristocracy. Other social elements began to make themselves felt under the July Monarchy. Both groups sought to use the state machine for their own purposes in these struggles, although it would be wrong to consider the state simply as a class instrument.[3] It did none the less mean a subtle change to the administrative structure of France, notably through the politicization of

fonctionnaires like the prefects.[4] This was also forced on the
Bourbons by their insecure position in a country from which
they had been so long absent. Inevitably this reacted on the
employees, accentuating their differences with the *fonctionnaires*,
and giving the former in turn a new political role. So one of the
prices of their survival was adaption to a rapidly changing
environment and to venomous political struggles.

Usually in these struggles the employees seem to have lost
out, and the passage of time saw their position deteriorate
further.[5] They therefore became even more subject to the *fonctionnaires* than they had been under the Empire. At the same time
the *fonctionnaires* were drawn more and more into politics.
Because of the attitudes of the nw regime and the attractions of
both office and parliamentary life they 'invaded politics', as
Pouthas puts it.[6] With the possible exception of the sub-prefects
they did not embark on anything like the process of bureaucratization which their inferiors had already completed, but
revelled in the return of patronage, politics, and patrimonialism.
This often brought the administration as a whole into increased
disrepute. It also depressed the standing of ordinary employees.
Resentment of the way this increasing subordination made
them the scapegoats of their superiors, while actually depressing
their standard of living and thwarting their hopes of getting a
just settlement of their grievances, was to prove a powerful
motivating force.

As one *chef de division* put it rather bitterly in 1828:

Les employés du gouvernment peuvent être rangés en deux classes
principales; l'une se compose des fonctionnaires; l'autre, des employés
proprement dits. Les premiers reçoivent le mouvement et le communi-
quent à leur tour; ils sont énvironné de considération, ils participent,
d'une manière active à la gestion des affaires de l'État: ils parlent et
écrivent en leur nom, et comme ils subissent la responsabilité des
actes de leur administration ils en retirent également l'honneur. Les
autres, au contraire, ne jouent qu'un rôle passif. Espèce de rouages
inaperçus qui font mouvir la machine administrative, leur existence
ne se révèle jamais.[7]

Although this could not have been said openly under the
Empire, the existence of a very active debate on the rights and
wrongs of the position of *la fonction publique* did not satisfy the
employees. The mere recognition of the fact that the employees

were a separate social category with their own interests and
needs was not enough. The employees had both to carry the
fight to their opponents and to develop their functional efficiency. But just as the political legacy of the Revolution took
some time to work itself out, so did its administrative legacy.
The gradual development of professionalization, the search for
effective systems of control—in which administrative law began
to play a role, and the development of relations with other corps
of officials can be seen throughout the period of the constitutional monarchies.[8] It was particularly bound up with the
search for a *statut des fonctionnaires* which would embrace the
whole civil service, and though this failed the latter came to play
an increasingly positive role in the political arena.

So despite continuing attacks on it from politicians and *fonctionnaires*, and despite the changing environment, the bureaucracy
remained fairly stable. The three problems with which it was
presented in 1814 were faced, if not resolved. Though the new
powers it enjoyed as a result of the Empire led to increasing
demands for it to be reduced in size and effectively disciplined,
it was able to resist its critics and force them to take it more
seriously than ever before. The upheavals of the time may
indeed have helped this by producing regimes which had no
alternative other than to rely on the administration. However,
the positive role of the constitutional monarchies was greater
than is often realized, especially where the July Monarchy is
concerned. Unfortunately their contribution has all too often
been overshadowed by Bonaparte's prodigious achievements.
In fact, although it was subject to unprecedented attacks, the
bureaucracy gained much from its association with the two
regimes which followed his. Its evolution was closely related to
the vicissitudes through which they both went.

The restoration thus opened up an important phase in the
existence of the mature bureaucracy. Between 1814 and 1848
the revolutionary impetus was completed by public recognition
of its power and its needs. For while before 1814 governments
had come, somewhat grudgingly, to understand their own need
of the bureaucracy and even something of its own needs, this
had been done on an *ad hoc* and slightly covert basis. By the
1840s this had changed. The bureaucracy's demand for stable
and systematic terms and conditions of employment became a

major issue in the political process. The fact that efforts to obtain a regularization of its position were to continue until 1946 is relatively unimportant. What matters is that by the 1840s government, parliament, and public opinion had been forced to face up openly to the problems arising from the creation of a new ministerial bureaucracy in 1793–4. Moreover, by the revolution of 1848 people were made equally aware of the bureaucracy's power by the way in which the employees helped to reject the first École Nationale d'Administration—which might have completed their exclusion by the *fonctionnaire* élite from any *droits de la cité*—and by the way in which during the Revolution they emerged as an active and organized political force.[9] For the first time the bureaucracy emerged from its relative seclusion to play an open part in the political arena. This meant the end of an era. For by 1848 the adolescent civil service had finally come of age.[10]

If the period from 1814 to 1848 is a unity for both the bureaucracy and for France as a whole, the contribution of the two constitutional monarchies to this process was somewhat unequal.[11] Whereas the July Monarchy was to face the problems clearly and openly, the Restoration did not have such a well-developed administrative strategy. This was partly because of the doubts about the bureaucracy which have already been mentioned, and partly because other questions seemed more central to it than administrative reform. Hence the civil service had a slightly painful evolution. For although ideas of changing the ministerial structure and of devolving power to the local level came to very little, and while attempts at administrative control were never well developed, the effects of financial crisis and parliamentary wrangling were such as to undermine something of the bureaucracy's position. However, there was no formal discussion about ways of remedying this until the time of Louis Philippe.

All this became apparent immediately after the fall of the Empire. In 1814 and 1815 the civil service had to bear a series of trials and tribulations. Thus the Ministry of War in 1814 had to evacuate its premises in the Rue de Bourbon as these were handed back to the Duc de Havré. More significantly the two Imperial ministries were reunited and their staff subjected to close military surveillance. The budgetary exigencies of the

First Restoration imposed cuts in staffing, every whit as important as those brought about by a political purge, and the appointment of royalist 'reliables'.[12] In fact, because of the contraction of the area previously administered by France and because of budgetary reductions the monarchy found itself faced with tremendous pressure for jobs. In the Eure for instance there were 387 applications for places in a fiscal establishment of 290 from which only 12 people were actually dismissed. This, the lack of time, and the impossibility of printing a list of all office-holders meant that the official purge did not go as far as had been intended. There was, however, a certain amount of unofficial purging as part of the White Terror.

During the Hundred Days Napoleon showed a renewed interest in the civil service which he invited to wear the tricolour and accept the *légion d'honneur*. He also made his own structural changes in the War Office and embarked on a counter-purge. This affected *fonctionnaires* for the most part and failed, partly because of lack of time. The return of the Bourbons in 1815 brought yet another purge in June and July 1815 which bore most heavily on the prefects. The White Terror also again bore heavily on office-holders, of whom between a quarter and a third were dismissed before Decazes intervened to stop it. Thereafter, although the question of whether state agents had taken an oath to the 'Corsican usurper' remained a touchstone for the Chambre Introuvable and rehabilitation of royalist sympathizers continued, it was the political whirligig of the Restoration parliament and especially budgetary considerations which led to most cost in staffing in the early years of the Second Restoration. This was despite the way political purges once again dominated public concern as they had in the revolutionary and Directorial eras.

The Restoration also had some influence on the structures of government although the Charter as such was largely silent on the civil service. However, the departmental ministers were able to fight off the attempt to go back to the conciliar system of the Ancien Régime. As a result they emerged as the centre of government particularly as they now had access to the Chambers.[13] This also preserved the somewhat unpopular Conseil d'État from premature dissolution. The number of ministerial departments soon fell with the disappearance of such Imperial innovations as the second War Ministry, the Ministry of Commerce, and the Secrétariat d'État, but from the early twenties the number began to rise from six.[14] From 1820–7 there was a second attempt to create a Ministry for the Royal Household, after an initial experiment during the First Restoration, while in 1824 a Ministry for Church Affairs and Education was established. Between 1828 and 1830 the two halves of the Ministry were given their autonomy for a brief period before they were abolished by Polignac along with the revived Ministry of Commerce and Industry. The latter was replaced by a Ministry of Public Works.

At the same the ministers were also joined by *Sous-Secrétaires d'État*, introduced during the Hundred Days, and thereafter used to carry out the growing political duties of the ministers. The Ministers of State also helped in the defence of the cabinet before the Chambers, although the departmental ministries were freed from the rivalry of the Directors-General, few of whom remained of any importance except perhaps 'Security' which replaced the Ministry of Police after 1819. Because so many of these changes involved the Ministry of the Interior, the internal structure changed much more than departments like Justice, Foreign Affairs, and the Navy.[15] Even the Ministry of War became smaller, its staff being cut from 850 in 1816 to 200 by 1822 as the country returned to a peacetime footing. Many politicians were unsatisfied by this and one leading official actually suggested the establishment of a more permanent *Sous-Secrétaire* with mainly administrative functions in 1823 in order to stop self-defeating intervention in internal organization, since each incoming minister felt called upon to stage what Dennié call a 'désorganisation' in order to make his presence felt in the bureaux.[16] The Restoration's attempt to reverse Napoleonic policy on the creation of departments failed and the process of expansion of the eighteenth-century core departments was renewed. This was hesitatingly done because of complications of political intervention, symbolized by the formal establishment of ministerial cabinets, and the further development of Directors-General, though not always under this name.

The tendency to excessive intervention was traditional but it was given a new twist by the way the ministers had now to respond to parliamentary pressure, even if in the last resort the

Chambers had little real control over them. Neither this nor the changes in structure were very conducive to the efficient working of government.[17] Similarly, the growth of party influence inside the ministries, as seen in the beginnings of ministerial 'families' and cabinets had a detrimental effect, particularly on the normal security and promotion prospects of employees. They found themselves with precious little protection against either economic reform or internal reorganization designed to impress suspicious back-benchers. There was therefore little incentive to improve the administration's techniques, but a very strong incentive to hang on to places which became ever more valuable since economy cuts led to their being in increasingly short supply.[18] This would have no doubt posed problems for any consistent strategy of administrative development and control had there been one.

As has already become obvious, financial control did exist and was backed up by the growing *technicité* of the budgetary process and the increasing influence of the Cour des Comptes, but, as Malouet once observed, 'toutes les fois que l'abonnement éprouve une réduction, il faut que les employés la supportent; de là naît l'instabilité des bureaux, le défaut de zèle, l'absence de talent et souvent le découragement de ceux qui les habitent'. Such financial control was thus a very negative thing. It never linked up with the attempt to establish a formal science of administration by Cormenin, Macarel, and Gerando, presumably because the regime had grave doubts about the wisdom of such an approach.

However, *la tutelle administrative* was strengthened by the establishment of the Direction de l'Administration Départmentale et Communale in the Ministry of the Interior, and more importantly by the growing role of the Comité Contentieux of the Conseil d'État.[19] Debarred from a political role by its Napoleonic antecedents the Conseil had to broaden its judicial role, going beyond simply hearing individuals' complaints against the state to arbitrate in conflicts between administrative bodies and ruling on the legality of administrative practices. Much of its work was concerned with local government and the field services, amongst whom the judicial role of the Conseils de Préfecture were eclipsed by the new electoral role of the prefect. This left the prefectoral bureaux to carry the burden of ordinary administration.[20] Despite this, prefectoral employees saw their numbers, salaries, and standing continually decline since the regime hardly recognized their existence, let alone their importance.

They had even less defence than Parisian employees against the stream of attacks directed against the new bureaucracy. Fievée thus claimed that 'la bureaumanie est devenue comme un religion', imposing a double despotism of excessive pensions and costs on the one hand and of abusive power on the other on the long-suffering landed interest.[21] The employees tried to defend themselves by a string of pamphlets and petitions, praising their talents and lamenting their woes.[22] They found these things doubly galling since, in their opinion, it was not they but the *fonctionnaires* and the field services who were responsible for the evils for which they were punished by the withholding of their rights.

Perhaps some of their complaints need to be taken with the proverbial pinch of salt. It is none the less true that a recent analysis of their economic situation shows that two-thirds of them earned less than 2,000 francs per annum in Paris and only 11.6 per cent of them had wealth of over 10,000 francs at their death. *Fonctionnaires*, conversely, were not merely much better paid, but were possessed, in half the cases at least, of over 100,000 francs in private means.[23] Such social barriers were reinforced by the way the nobility not merely sometimes sought posts inside the administration, but also introduced new networks of patronage to which the average employee had little access. Yet the latter had to bear the burden of extra work arising from elections and parliamentary affairs in general while letting their politically appointed superiors take the credit for it. Employees began to increase in number as the Crown took on new duties. They came to form a growing body on the fringes of the bourgeoisie, often themselves dependent on local patronage for their chance of a post.[24] Such posts often paid very poorly and offered a standard of living which hardly compared with that of the *fonctionnaires* to whose standing they had very little chance of aspiring. The employees in their complaints about this stressed not only unfairness and poverty, but also the insecurity of their position. They lamented over deductions from salaries, the lack of compensation for dismissal, and they saw it, on leaving secondary education for administrative employment they had entered a kind of contract with the state. They accepted unpaid work as *surnuméraires*, a hierarchical structure, and hard work, in return for security of salary and the promise of a pension. In reality this contract was not honoured by the state. They were therefore denied a fair wage and proper promotion, and were forced to 'moonlight' or resort to bribery.

For this reason one must be cautious about Sautel's claim that the Restoration saw progress towards a proper *statut des fonctionnaires*, for instance in the way the development of educational qualifications and training schools limited political interference.[25] In some areas there was a trend towards examinations rather than to education, and also towards a graduate entry, drawing on the reformed *baccalauréat*.[26] Initially there was also a trend towards teaching public law and administration, but this was brutally interrupted by Ultras in the mid-twenties. On the other hand, examinations for the Auditoriat of the Conseil d'État were allowed to lapse from 1814–44 and family and political relationships became, in Kessler's view, the major course of appointments and promotions. Moreover, such experiments were very hesitant and very scattered. They were most common in technical domains like the Forestry service, though the Ministries of Finance and of the Interior, along with the Prefecture of the Seine, did set examinations for applicants to their bureaux, although these required no prior training.

For, although people were still recruited who had Napoleonic administrative experience, there was a great deal of patronage at work as well, often from generals and cardinals. Family connection and wealth were also influential, although there was also a tendency to recruit more people with formal educational qualifications. The over-all picture that emerges is partly similar to that found under the Empire, although not so well documented. Recruits seem to have come in much more often at the top of the scale than they had previously. There was also a strange gap in the middle of the administrative hierarchy with very few senior clerkships being made available. The entrants were also increasingly urban, with a slight increase in the representation of towns in the south-west of the country. Well over half the sample were born before 1799, so that very few were over sixty by the time the Bourbon monarchy fell.

The significance of this becomes clearer if the date of entry is considered.[28] Nearly a third joined the ministry in the critical years of 1814–15, after which the pace of entry slackened off until the late twenties. Many of the initial recruits were in fact joining state service for the first time, with patronage and politics playing a large role. However, a third of the entrants still had long administrative experience behind them before entering the ministry.[29] There were fewer very young and very old entrants than under the Empire. So while the Restoration ministry still recruited people who had served an apprenticeship in the field services they were increasingly mixed in with people with no experience who had joined the ministry for political or similar reasons—a fifth entering through family influence and none after an exam—or because of the collapse of Imperial institutions. There were thus more former soldiers and students than under the Empire. The tension between the patrimonialism of the regime and the career dynamic of previous entrants is quite clear and helps to explain why many of the latter felt betrayed by government.

The result of this entry pattern was that average salaries tended to be rather higher than previously and promotion prospects rather poorer.[30] Particularly at the bottom end of the scale salaries tended to rise. This was a form of compensation which did not seem to work since fewer people cared to stay for long periods of over twenty years. Short—and medium—term service was more common both in the ministry and in state service in general. Most people left the administration by 1848, usually through retirement or death. This was also no doubt a reflection of frequent economy campaigns and internal reorganization. Half of those who left still got no pension, and generally treatment on leaving the service was less generous than under the Empire, despite the greater prominence of family contacts. Many of those who left went into business and the professions, as well as into the field services.

Information on social origins is still hard to come by, but there were an increasing number of sons of landowners and businessmen, and no lawyers' sons. More of them had received advanced education, whether from tutors, *grandes écoles* or universities, though the *lycées* not surprisingly provided fewer recruits. Private means were more frequent as were family connections inside the ministry, so that people were less dependent on their salary than at other times. Yet they were no more successful in gaining sinecures and grants, despite their greater involvement in patronage and corruption. In other words the Bourbons were somewhat amateurish in favouring their own, so that the undermining of the professional dynamic did not go very far. The employees remained distinct from the *fonctionnaires* in most respects.

The Restoration then did not fundamentally question the existence of the bureaucracy. Rather it exposed the bureaucracy to new political currents which, although they allowed the bureaucracy to express its interests publicly again, also made it hard for the French to decide what to do about their new administrative corps. This paradox was typical of the regime as a whole. The bureaucracy had therefore to adapt to the extension of patrimonialism, now reinforced by court, parliament, and the new structure of government and all used by the regime in a somewhat partisan way. Inevitably this led to clashes between the two and to what seems to have been a decline in the prospects of the bureaucracy, despite the contrary impression given by its many critics. The result of such tensions between the career and administrative dynamic of the bureaucracy and the new political forces was that the former made little progress save in specialization, rules, and education.

It was therefore a period of continuity for the bureaucracy, since the regime's political conditioning was largely cancelled out by the former's *esprit de corps,* leaving it largely unchanged. This is very significant since the nature and the timing of the Restoration made it the regime most likely to overturn the revolutionary state. Its failure or its unwillingness to do so ensured that the bureaucracy would, despite all the opposition it faced, survive all challenges from the right. However, the Restoration left future regimes to grapple both with the bureaucracy's need for internal change, and with the question of how it could best respond to changing social needs.

The July Monarchy to some extent took up both these questions. Thus, far from challenging the administration after the July Days save perhaps for the Conseil d'État, it developed very close links with the administration. This began almost with the revolution of 1830 itself, since, as Pinkney has shown, this was as much Bonapartist as anything else, both in the nature of those who fought for it at the barricades, and because of those dispossessed Napoleonic officials, who along with the leaders of the parliamentary opposition, were the major beneficiaries through their restoration to office.[31] Thereafter as part of the general fusion of élites that marked the period there was an interrelationship between the new political élite and the administration. This operated through the phenomenon of the *deputé-fonctionnaire* and the general parliamentary interest in the administration.

The purges which followed 1830, in which, for example, 95 per cent of the prefects were dismissed in what Tulard calls the greatest purge of the century, obviously unsettled the administration.[32] It was a repressive purge which fell on some employees as well as on *fonctionnaires*, and continued into the thirties in fields such as education. And although much of the pressure put on officials was subtle and indirect, abolishing categories of posts rather than dismissing persons for instance, there were also major legislative *textes* for the first time. Yet at the same time the July Revolution also led to a new wave of rehabilitation of former office-holders and it is possible that it was the pressure for places which actually had the most effect. Lafayette alone is reputed to have signed 70,000 recommendations for office, although here again the evidence suggests that there was a small élite of mobile political prefects and others and a great mass of locally connected sub-prefects who had virtually no chance of rising higher.[33]

Accountability and control of the executive arm had been one of the things promised by the revolutionaries late in July 1830. There were in fact a stream of measures on economy, integrity, efficiency, and political reliability in the public services, but to judge by the continuing investigations and complaints, such regulations were once again of very temporary and limited efficacity.[34] The services were denounced as being unfitted to their time because they were too big, too cumbrous, and disordered, too lacking in uniformity, order, and regularity, fearful of innovation and honesty, weak where they should be strong, and arrogantly intervening in matters which did not concern them. The reorganizations which took place were nowhere near as profound as Pouthas suggested, and indeed were later attacked as bizarre and conducive to instability rather than to the stability claimed by Pouthas.[35] None the less, the regime did lead the bureaucracy further along the road of modernization, although always within a framework of continuity. In the forties as the regime took some note of rapidly changing social problems, it did permit the kind of professionalization also being engineered in England at about the same time, despite the limits which it placed on social and on general innovations.

Its relations with the administration were very largely handled with the parliamentary arena, for the regime was very much a parliamentary one in which the 'bon plaisir du deputé' tended to replace the 'bon plaisir du ministre' of the Restoration. Most posts could be held in conjunction with a seat in the Chamber, and often nearly half the latter held administrative posts of one kind or another.[36] By 1847 there were 193 such people in the Chamber, mostly sitting with the government, 70 per cent of whose parliamentary strength came from them. To some extent these posts attracted *notables* since only they were unconcerned by the relatively low salaries they paid. This and the expansion of posts of Directors-General in new ministries like Commerce and Justice increased the politicization of the administration. The government sought to control politicians by giving them office, while *fonctionnaires* sought election as an unparalleled means of advancement. At times, as in the Ministry of Foreign Affairs, such posts could lead to dismissals, which presumably had some effect on the bulk of the service.

It may also have been because of this new relationship that people came increasingly to emphasize the power of the administration during the July Monarchy. By 1845 it accounted for 20 per cent of the royal budget, thanks to rising salaries, and its numbers were estimated at anything between 90,000 and 670,000, of whom two to three thousand were in the central administrations.[37] It may also have been more specialized and more honest as well. Laferrière notes that 'il y a aussi les petits commis qui restent dans l'ombre parce qu'il ont le sens de leur devoir, cette vocation de la fonction publique que ne se dévél-oppera que plus tard en France, ou bien parce que, ne pouvant compter sur aucun appui, ils se résignent à être exclus du système. Ces sont deux catégories de fonctionnaires qui assurent la marche des bureaux et un minimum d'administration au pays.'[38]

The structure within which these two categories of government servant worked remained much as it had been under the Empire and during the Restoration. From the ministries in Paris, originally nine in number, lines of responsibility ran out to the departments where prefectoral authority and control over local government and field services tended to become less effective in reality, due to the introduction of a limited amount of election into municipal and departmental councils, and the growing number of services needing co-ordination as the regime became more active in fields such as public works and education.[39] The Prefect was for a while deprived of the assistance of a Secretary-General but his bureaux seem to have played a growing role, and therefore tended to become larger and more complex in organization. The ministries changed almost as rapidly as they had in the last years of the Restoration, with a great deal of uncertainty as to whether certain services previously under the control of the Intérieur should be given their autonomy. Eventually in 1839 Travaux Publics did emerge as a single separate ministry, leaving a joint Ministry of Trade and Agriculture behind it. Similarly, after an uneasy tripartite existence, a separate ministry of Instruction Publique emerged, to which responsibility for religious affairs was attached, in 1832 along with that for the arts. This brought the structure back to what it had been in 1830, although with rather more stability.

This was partly because the structure was to last rather longer, and partly because it represented a reorientation of the Administrations Centrales towards the needs of the day. The burden of work that this imposed meant first that the *Sous-Secrétaire d'État* continued to exist, so as to free the minister for parliamentary duties which were no longer shared by the Ministers of State. Secondly, it meant that the staff of central government also had to grow. The War Office seems to have expanded its numbers from 400 to 700 and the *Préfecture de Police* seems to have grown almost as spectacularly, to 1,400 of whom 300 were clerical staff.[40]

As well as this growing division of labour and specialization, the administration also came in for increasing scientific study and control. This was due to its growing influence, and also to the way it continued to provide spoils for the victors, sometimes even at employee level, as with the participants in the *trois glorieuses* who were found niches in the War Office. The control was exercised through the Conseil d'État and the right to prosecute officials, although only 0.09 per cent of those protected by the Constitution of the Year VIII were actually condemned, out of 0.4 per cent of cases where prosecution was permitted.[41] In the War Office a committee hearing became necessary from the late thirties before any dismissal could take place, a provision copied from the way army officers were treated. Control was also exercised through the development of scientific study and jurisprudence and the development of new inspection agencies.

The fact, however, that the play of patronage and politics continued combined with the rapid changes in ministerial structures in the early thirties to perpetuate the problems of the bureaucracy, although in a slightly altered form. The regime needed the administration to help it face the threats that plagued its early years, to cope with the pressure groups linked to modernization, and to help it manage the elections.[42] The administration was also affected by the way the July Days encouraged the middle classes to seek places in state employment, and, once having done that, to consolidate their corporate place both in society and inside the administration. To achieve these ends they used every available means—political support, family connection, or the support of other employees. The upper-middle-class *fonctionnaire* élite thus came to exercise a virtual dictatorship over their subalterns, a relationship already consecrated by differential styles of furnishings. At the same time the regime's reductions in salaries limited access to top jobs to those who were already rich, thereby bringing the *haut administration* into ever closer contact with politics. All this made the question of the treatment of the administration more than usually highly charged and forced the regime to give way to the former more often than it might have wished.[43]

As the employees themselves saw the situation, their basic problem was that though on the surface they were powerful, well established, and secure, in reality they were none of these things. This was basically because of the continuing informality of their conditions of service.[44] They still felt that they were not properly rewarded for a job which was more technical and demanding than was often conceded. At the same time they were not permitted to exercise their talents because of the

old-fashioned structures and vested interests inside the ministries. They thus had no secure rights to promotion, pensions, or
proper recruitment policies.

Informal appointment procedures allowed in-groups to
appoint their 'own', while the lack of uniformity amongst the
services, along with the general lack of stability caused by the
failure to legislate and the tendency to over-reorganize internal
structures, discouraged the good candidates. Only the Ministry
of Public Works for instance had proper entry exams. It turned
down the idea of an interviewing panel in the War Office as an
affront to ministerial authority and patronage.[45] The same
Ministry required prior service as a *surnuméraire* for promotion
while the Admiralty did away with *surnuméraires* altogether.
Promotion in any case often depended on passing through all
the relevant grades, so that would-be 'high flyers' might have to
spend years as mere scribes. Most hard to bear of all, their
salaries were low and often reduced, so that despite their dependence on 'gratifications' their lot remained 'misère en habit
noir'. The rising prices of the July Monarchy probably intensified
their plight. Many clerks therefore called for proper examinations, officially decided 'establishments' for each department
of state, and priority to graduates, this latter pending the introduction of formal training in administrative science. Otherwise
they felt that their already deteriorating position would get even
worse.

Proposals and complaints of this kind were partly responsible
for attempts to restore the more regulated and guaranteed
position of officials enjoyed under the Empire.[46] For although
old-established ministries had personnel regulations, many new
did not, and the former still left a great deal of discretion to
ministers in any case. The way that this discretion could involve
deputies annoyed liberals like de Tocqueville and added a
political dimension to the civil servants' own concerns. The
matter was greatly debated from the late thirties onwards, with
the reformers seeing the only solution in *droit administratif* and
the provision of legislative and ministerial guarantees on matters
such as recruitment, promotion, and discipline. They believed
that the reign of *bon plaisir* in the Administrations Centrales in
matters of appointment should be replaced by parliamentary
insistence on the reward of capacity, as was already the case in

some field services. They believed that ministerial reorganization could assure this, but excluded officials themselves from the process of reform.

As a result of rival pressures the budgetary law of 24 July 1843 required ministers to publish formal statements on their establishments, structures, and personnel policies. Such statements were extracted from the various departments in late 1844 but they were to prove short-lived and ineffective. Similarly, attempts to go beyond this, to a general statement on the form careers should take also failed. A bill tabled by Saint-Marc Girardin which aimed to regularize and finalize existing practices in an attempt to make the administration more acceptable to the people was defeated on 6 February 1845. The bill failed to carry with it both those who wished to limit government powers over the administration even more stringently and also those who felt, as did the cabinet, that successful government demanded a free hand. So while the various articles in the bill were passed, the bill as a whole was turned down. A similar effort in 1846 motivated by the growing awareness of the failure of the post-1843 ministerial ordonnances to regularize personnel practices, also failed. So the idea of a legislative solution took a heavy knock and the continuing disparities of treatment between ministries continued to give rise to complaint.

These defeats, together with the anomalies produced by lack of funds and the hostility of many of those in authority inside the administration, meant that the unease in administration also continued. Moreover, towards the end of the decade annual report forms did make their appearance in the War Office, the Ministry of Commerce, and some prefectures, while in 1838 Salvandy, then Minister of Education, had begun his abortive enquiries into whether it was advisable to introduce German methods of administrative education in France, and if so, whether the Faculties would give it a home.[47] This caused much debate even though little was achieved. Perhaps as a result of the same initiative, examinations were introduced for *surnuméraires* in the War Office, alongside the reformed entry pattern for the fiscal services after 1839—notably for the Inspection des Finances in 1842, and the Ministry of Justice started to set aside a proportion of posts in each grade for clerks in the category below.[48]

A further sample of the entrants to the War Office at this stage gives a fair idea of how far things had progressed.[49] The July Monarchy turns out to have been markedly different from its predecessor. To begin with it is rather better documented, suggesting improving administrative efficiency. The entrants suggest a more balanced hierarchy. They were also more likely to come from the countryside, and from and increasingly wide area of France than before, presumably reflecting improvements in transport. Where town-dwellers were concerned the dominance of Paris grew, while Versailles faded. Obviously they were born later than their predecessors, only one in fifty before 1779 compared with over a quarter of the Restoration entrants.[50] Two-thirds of them were in fact born during the Restoration, so it is hardly surprising that more entered in the years of political stability and administrative expansion in the forties.[51] Because of the improvement in·entry procedures that began in the thirties, the numbers who had joined the administration before entering the ministry declined to a mere tenth, so that the revolutionary amalgam began to die away. This is borne out by the age of entry since sub-teenage entrants were by then unheard of and mature entrants were only half as common as previously. In contrast more men of twenty to twenty-five entered the ministry than entered administration in general, a phenomenon only found at higher levels previously. Significantly the number who had been students previously rocketed, while there were no soldiers or court employees and very few field service employees.[52]

On the other hand, an increasing number of army officers and court officials seem to have felt the War Office to be a suitable career for their sons, as did many professional men and other officials. The decline in businessmen's children among the entrants is presumably a reflection of the economic expansion of the times. As one might have expected, the number of university graduates trebled and the number of those with private tutors or diplomas from the Grandes Écoles doubled.[53] Over a third gained their position by examination, although court, family, and unpaid service were still useful means of access. Hence the number entering because it was their first job or because it played a logical part in a career rose sharply, while there were far fewer who were forced into administration because

of need. Many more started as *surnuméraires* than previously and
only a handful came in at the top, compared to a tenth under the
Restoration. Starting salaries were thus lower on average. This
reflected a general fall in salary and an attempt to create two
separate categories of *rédacteurs* and *expéditionnaires,* to avoid
qualified appointees spending years as mere copyists.

That employment in the ministries became more of a career
is borne out by the fact that the number who had only one post
in their careers rose markedly, and over three-quarters held
only three jobs. Family relationships inside the bureaux fell to
only a fraction over the Imperial levels and there was also a fall
in the number of very wealthy entrants. On the other hand, the
number who were comfortably off rose, as did the percentages
who obtained either the *Légion d'Honneur* or some other grant, or
significant promotion. Terminal salaries were thus markedly
higher than before. Similarly, the average length of service was
markedly longer than under the Restoration with less than a
tenth serving for less than three years, compared with a fifth
previously. Their service lasted right up till the end of the
century in some cases, even though a number resigned quietly
during the troubles of 1848. Resignation became a more common reason for departure even though pension prospects were
quantitatively and qualitatively better than before. Against this
must be set some falling-off in other dimensions of bureaucracy,
but generally the impression is of a reassertion of professionalism
under the July Monarchy, even though the play of politics and
élitism still continued to make itself felt within key ministries.
The kind of professionalism that emerged, moreover, was of a
somewhat different nature to that of the revolutionary era. That
had been the result of crisis recruitment. By the forties the
classic modern pattern of entry after educational preparation
had asserted itself.

So the ministries seem to have become merely one of the
senior administrative bodies in the state rather than the pinnacle
of the field services as in the past. Within them the career
pattern was becoming increasingly formal, but it was not always
well provided. Duval reckoned that many clerks married in
Paris when they were about thirty, usually to 'heiresses' who
added 700 francs per annum to a salary of some 1,800 francs,
thus permitting the establishment of a home in the far Marais or

Belleville. As a result there was more evidence of patronage and *grâces* than before, but significantly, though the latter were necessary, they were not popular with the clerks. They were too much of a reminder of the fact that they had not obtained a *statut* and were therefore still dependent on charity.

There were thus quite obvious limits to the development of professionalization, continuity, permanence, and consistency prior to 1848. There were also, however, fewer clashes with *fonctionnaires*, because the employees were now less anonymous and more hopeful of promotion. So whereas the Restoration had merely posed the problems of the administration, the July Monarchy did begin the process of seeking solutions. This is not to say that the regime always played a fully active and conscious part in the development of the civil service, as has been claimed, for much of the impetus came from the service itself and from administrative experts.[54] None the less, the new domination resulting from 1830 provided just enough room for the career dynamic, refuelled by new social inputs and new needs, to express itself. Similarly, while the Restoration had shown the way by accepting the bureaucracy, its hesitating approach allowed the dominance of the *fonctionnaires* to increase. The July Monarchy was forced to go beyond this. So although insubordination continued because of the more febrile party politics of the time, the *basse administration* did experiment with new roles and saw its status and its organization publicly debated.

When in 1848 the civil service went beyond debate to action, a phase in its development ended and another began. Its post-Directorial adolescence ended with the open recognition of its adult status. The aftermath of revolution as far as administration was concerned ended with the right of the bureaucracy to exist being publicly established. Its ability to exist very effectively was then demonstrated in 1848 when the general aftermath of the great Revolution caught up with France. The logical consequences arising from the bureaucracy's creation had been fully explored by then, although the problems resulting from them were very far from solution. That was to be the task of the next hundred years, a period in which the bureaucracy continued to grow and continued to battle with its opponents.[55]

Although this process is outside the scope of this study, the events of 1848 were symptomatic of the changing circumstances and deserve some attention. 1848 brought some of the ideas of the forties to fruition, with the establishment of new administrative courts, the reform of the Conseil d'État, the restoration of the Prefectoral Secretaries-General, and the discussion of changes in field services such as the Ponts et Chaussées.[56] Unfortunately, the major desire of the employees, the enactment of a *statut general,* got no further forward, and there were continuing complaints about the unsatisfactory situation in which they found themselves, notably at departmental level.[57] This lack of progress helps to explain why the corporate action of the employees—rejected by the reformers of the mid-forties—began to escalate. This began with the publication of *La Tribune administrative* in 1840—a journal to which the *fonctionnaires* often took exception—and during 1848 led to the establishment of a number of employees' clubs, a foretaste of the syndicalist explosion at the end of the century.[58] They produced little more than ideas but again they were a sign of the times. Their failure to develop possibly explains why the political Left did not take their case to heart and why employees ended up as bitter critics of the administration because it sided with the establishment.[59] However, the employees did help to achieve the defeat of the republican École Nationale d'administration, thereby demonstrating their power and preventing the creation of an institution which, whatever the aims of its founders, would have further repressed the employees and significantly increased the undemocratic nature of French *haute administration*.[60] This 'contestation' may not have been successful, but it was far from insignificant. What was important was not that it failed, but that it was able to take place at all. Eighty years before it would have been unthinkable. Fifty years before it would have been impossible. The tragedy for the employees was that, although it was not possible, it was to be so long before their 'contestation' was to achieve its modest aims. The emancipation of the bureaucracy did not, unfortunately, mean the end of *fonctionnaire* dominance. Thus the new generations of civil servants were to end their careers without achieving all the responsibility and all the recognition they sought, just as the generations who had served in the revolutionary era had done in the decades up to the 1840s.

CHAPTER X: PERSPECTIVES ON BUREAUCRATIZATION IN FRANCE

The July Monarchy both rounded off the process of administrative change which had begun in 1793–4 and saw the emergence of new processes which were to endure well into the present century. Much more than the Restoration the regime had seen the normal play of parliamentary and party politics affecting the civil service rather than the old-fashioned patrimonialism of the Bourbon era. The personnel of the civil service created by the Revolution had come to the end of their natural span of service and they bequeathed their desires and fears to a new generation of more highly educated recruits. In the years to come their qualifications were to make them even more resentful of *fonctionnaire* dominance, and the lack of statutory security. For a long while their resentment of the second, however, was to be little more successful in remedying their grievances than had been that of their predecessors. And by the time they began to achieve some measure of success the nature of their relationships with the *fonctionnaires* had begun to change, since the latter had begun to undergo something not far removed from the process of bureaucratization that the employees had been subjected to in the revolutionary era.

In any case, the fact that the ministerial staffs and kindred civil servants still faced problems after 1848 should not obscure the fact that their position had already changed considerably, and often for the better, from what it had been before the Revolution. Moreover, their position was to improve in later years as well, even though the improvements did not always satisfy a more educated and therefore more demanding service. One area where there had been a distinct change from the Ancien Régime was in the structure of government. By the middle of the nineteenth century France may still have been in a state of uncertainty about her political organization, but her administrative and institutional arrangements were remarkably stable, as befits what Hayward calls the 'state–nation'.[1] Whereas in the mid-eighteenth century French institutions were a complex mixture of the dignified and of the efficient, by a century later the former had gone. Government was a matter of straightforward rationality with power flowing from the centre through ministries—whose structure was gradually altering so as to enable the state to cope with the problems of an industrializing and a participatory society—to the prefects, the subprefects, the mayors, and the field services. All this was done according to very clearly defined constitutional and juridical rules, and was subject to minute examination by administrative lawyers at a variety of levels. This was the situation on paper. In practice things were very different since informal norms thrown up by 'traditional localism' and other factors often produced a situation Wright calls closer to Wonderland than Descartes. However, the informal organization did not in the nineteenth century also enjoy its own formal organizational structures as had happened before the Revolution. In legal and functional terms then, despite their defeats in 1845–6, the ministerial staffs had a far clearer idea of where they stood than they had under Louis XV. Their salaries may have been unsatisfactory but their regularity and the terms of payment were such as to link them firmly to their posts. Even Louis Napoléon found it hard to dispense with them altogether.[2]

Under Louis XV the position of the ministries had been complicated by the continuing existence of the conciliar screen for government. Similarly the standing and operation of their staffs had been affected by the social pre-eminence of venal officers and the lack of development of both administrative law and personnel management. As the War Office shows, prebendial payment systems had their unrewarding side. In functional terms their duties were not very rationally allocated, and their implementation was again complicated by the mosaic of local and regional bodies which interacted with the Intendants and the sovereign courts between the king and his subjects. So although the field services did grow under Louis XV they and all the other efficient elements in government were still *de jure* in a very ambiguous position, even though *de facto* there were plenty of institutional similarities with the organization of the post-revolutionary state.

To some extent this clarification of the position of the bureaucracy was to continue after 1848, even if the Second Empire was not the simple reign of the bureaucracy which Marx liked to suggest.[3] Under the Third Republic, whose role in promoting the expansion of bureaucracy has been much neglected, the state machine began to expand on a large scale in response to industrialization.[4] And as the Republic purged the old *notables* from the political realm the petty bourgeoisie began to flock into the lower civil service from all parts of the country, although the élite still remained in the hands of *notables*. Although the Administrations Centrales began to decline both as a percentage of the total machine and as a guiding element in the more technical civil service demanded by the État Gendarme their position began to improve in at least two ways. This was despite the problems arising from ministerial instability.[5] Firstly their status began to improve as new less prestigious elements were added to the administration. This was part of the move to what Wright calls the post-Napoleonic administrative tradition in which technical growth broke down the unity and subservience of the civil service, creating 'féodalités administratives'. Secondly, their position was increasingly secured and clarified by the Conseil d'État in one of its golden ages at the turn of the last century.

None the less, both the ministerial staffs and the new men in government in general wanted even more uniformity and certainty in their conditions of service. Hence from the 1850s onwards there was a long series of draft bills on a *statut général des fonctionnaires*.[6] Despite the fact that the later projects were accompanied by a wave of syndicalist action the campaign was unsuccessful till the 1930s, and even then its conclusion was delayed by the war. And although the solution to the problems of the civil service was ultimately found in legislation, the role of staff associations in overcoming resistance to it was significant. The law of 1946 thus crowned the piecemeal development of a well-regulated career pattern, in which purges played a part. In the interim, however, the *fonction publique* had also to endure continuing problems over salaries, pensions, and adjustment to technical innovations such as the typewriter.

During the First World War the relatively slow pace of

structural adoption to modern society became abundantly clear, and the state machine expanded rapidly in order to cope with the crisis of trench warfare.[7] Thereafter, although the return of peace and economic stringency caused something of a decline in the size of the administration, its involvement in modern society continued to increase, through what has been called the État Propulsif of the inter-war years to the État Providence of today, for which the Vichy experiment ironically partly prepared the way along with the long-drawn-out reform campaign.[8] By the time of the Fifth Republic the state had taken over a variety of new roles and structures, and peopled them with a variety of new groups of public servants, in which it is often a little difficult to recognize the ministerial staffs of the pre-1848 era since they since they have to some extent now become enmeshed with the *fonctionnaires* as a result of the 1946 reform.[9]

In other words the stage reached by the ministerial bureaucracy in the mid-nineteenth century was far from being the end of its evolution. Where administration is concerned bureaucratization was obviously not a once and for all process. Nor was its evolution as simple and direct as much of the criticism of bureaucracy tends to suggest. Both in its evolution up till 1848 as afterwards, the history of administration in France has been a very fluctuating one. Even under the Ancien Régime the shifting relationships between the venal officers who emerged in the later Middle Ages and later generations of civil servants was less clear-cut than Mousnier implies when he says that 'one of the great facts of our history is the progressive movement from the fourteenth to the eighteenth century from administration based on the judicial process to administration by professional bureaucracy'.[10] The judicial element for instance was still very evident on the eve of the Revolution, and the professionalism of the administrators of the time was a very patrimonial thing. Ironically too, the emergence of the ministerial staffs from under the wing of the Secretaries of State was neither the work of bureaucrats themselves, nor something which its progenitors really wanted. Given this, and more particularly the way the growing administration maintained its links with the honorific society of its times, it could not really expect to become fully bureaucratic in the modern sense. However its methods, structures, and legal procedures did point in this direction.

Not till the experience of total war combined with the rise to power of a group of ruthless realists, who put the Revolution ahead of the ideals of constitutional government and administration by *citoyen–fonctionnaires* which had dominated the early stages of the Revolution, did the transformation take place.[11] So even though they did not appreciate the employee element in government themselves, they first pulled all the acceptable elements of administration from the Ancien Régime into one new monolithic service and then gave it most of the Weberian characteristics of a bureaucracy. This decision has yet to be reversed. In fact, having once refined it under the Thermidorians and especially under the Directory, the revolutionaries then made it possible for new bureaucratic careers and roles to develop, with the increasing emphasis on direct entry to the Administration Centrales and other major bodies of state. Once more refined under Bonaparte, who gave it enhanced authority and a structure that largely completed the reunion with the traditions of the Ancien Régime, the bureaucracy was available to serve any and all rulers.[12]

In the early nineteenth century government was usually, as under the Restoration, still reluctant to accept the need for the bureaucracy, but gradually it reasserted itself and re-established some of the ground momentarily lost to the revived patrimonialism of the Bourbons. And whereas previously only the Directory had really evolved a *de facto* means of dealing with the needs of the bureaucracy, the July Monarchy was to do this quite openly. Moreover, public awareness of the power and predicament of the new bureaucracy was ensured by the way in which the employees of the late 1840s broke away from the relative caution of the previous generation, inhibited by their service during the Ancien Régime and by the turmoils of the Revolution. The new generation completed the process begun in the 1790s by making the conditions of employment of civil servants in general part of national political debate.

This convoluted and conflict-ridden story is rather different from the simple story of administrative continuity and conquest which is so often told. De Tocqueville's thesis should in fact be simply a starting-point, mainly because he ignored the crucial employee–functionary divide. One reason for this discrepancy is that each age likes to think that it has discovered the secret of all its problems in the shortcomings of its administration. Therefore it goes through a similar ritual of denuniciation. One of the strongest elements of continuity in the history of French administration has been the continuing criticism with which it has been faced, criticism that rarely takes account of historical precedent or of political environment. The development of the ministerial bureaucracy has been closely related to the nature of the regime which it served, and to the problems encountered by the latter, as Weber's arguments would lead one to expect. In other words changes of domination have been the major influence on bureaucratic change. It has been through the political system that the impact of social and other changes have been transmitted to the administration. Many attacks on bureaucracy thus actually say more about reactions to the problems of the times than of the realities of administration. Similarly, because the French experience of the Ancien Régime and of the Revolution has been very different from that of other countries, the French administrative experience is probably less of an example than is sometimes claimed.[13] In fact bureaucracy often developed earlier and more forcefully elsewhere, as in Prussia, while its social bases and structures were often very different from that in countries such as Scandinavia or Britain.

Nor were the relations between bureaucracy and revolution in France identical with those in other countries. In France at the turn of the nineteenth century there was a double relationship between the French Revolution and the French bureaucracy. For not only was the character of the ministerial bureaucracy contingent on the events of the Revolution—and notably on the Jacobin decision to resist the pressures of the rest of Europe—but the revolutionary process also provided hitherto impossible opportunities for lesser administrative cadres within the new bureaucracy. The Revolution provided thus the need and the means for the first self-conscious bureaucracy in France. Ironically, however, this was something the revolutionaries would rather have avoided, and it was some time before the bureaucracy's self-consciousness was matched by public and politicians. In other words the relationship between the Revolution and the bureaucracy was not an immediate and once and for all thing. It was as much a process as the Revolution itself, and changed with the phases of the Revolution.

Moreover, the real question at issue—whatever the revolutionaries liked to think—was not the political complexion of the civil service but the more general problem of how to use and control the administration on which they had to rely. Even in a revolution in which administration changes drastically, material interests and sheer common sense will lead civil servants to accept the new order, provided it caters for their needs. Moreover, the experiences of the bureaucracy after 1799 also show that even in a revolutionary age complete and lasting bureaucratization is not always possible, since countervailing pressures come into play. There is no finality to the process. Debureaucratization can set in if the circumstances are right and the internal dynamic of administration weak. Indeed it sometimes seems as though administration and bureaucracy are permanently changing places, as if motivated by the desire that makes all comedians want to play Hamlet. Revolutionary bureaucratization does not necessarily lead directly to bureaucratic totalitarianism.[14]

If the results of the Revolution are not immutable, it is still true, as Girard says, that:

les fonctionnaires . . . deviennent par leur nombre même une classe sociale, non pas, mais néanmoins un milieu professionnel considérable, dont par exemple le parlementaire est obligé de tenir compte, on peut se demander si le fonctionnaire ne devient pas, non seulement par ses fonctions, mais par son existence même, par ses intérêts professionnels, l'une des forces sociales essentielles d'une Nation.[15]

None the less, to be an essential social force is not the same as being the dominant element in society. The change from administration into bureaucracy over the revolutionary era shows that Wright is correct to say that the concept of the administrative state is probably an exaggerated one, because of the continuing problems of administration, notably its internecine conflicts.[16] Unfortunately, the conflict between employees and *fonctionnaires* has rarely been seen to have been a matter of great significance to the history of administration. The French often minimize this because they tend to dismiss *basse administration* as a mere executant of the decisions of the *haute administration,* whereas some foreign observers seem to overlook the former altogether. Thus Armstrong can appropriate a quotation from

Senac de Meilhan which deals explicitly with ministerial staffs to describe the Intendants, even though this makes nonsense of the passage in question.[17] In fact, the interrelationships between the two kinds of official do much to explain how administration evolved over the revolutionary era, and why people found such difficulty in comprehending its nature and its necessity.

Unfortunately, so little work has been done on the subject that it is difficult if not impossible to go much further down the road to a proper political history of bureaucracy at the present. It is to be hoped that the need for such a history will justify this hesitant prologomena.[18] No doubt it will not satisfy all those French critics who see administration as a matter either of class struggles or of juridical development. The reality of the matter is that the sources are so full of variations and lacunae that no one strategy will really provide a coherent account such as those who look at the history of the administration from the outside demand.[19] Certainly one needs a certain perspective of time and institution if one is to offer anything which carries conviction outside the boundaries of one phase in the life of one administrative entity. This does not mean that a separate discipline of 'administrative history' needs to be invented, merely that because of the lack of study and the limitations of the sources, the relevance of much of the sociology of bureaucracy to the study of past bureaucracies is a necessary part of orthodox historical investigation.

For the historian of bureaucracy the study of the French case reinforces the need to delimit the use and the meaning of bureaucracy. There is little to be gained by not treating bureaucracy, and even administration, as something specific rather than by confusing it with the state, or just deploring its existence.[20] Bureaucracy is one form of the machinery always needed in advanced political communities to translate decisions into reality, a process which needs variegated personnel, institutions, and practices and not just the occasional *citoyen–fonctionnaire* as the French still like to think. So as Ridley and Blondel say, 'although the French have a reputation for logic and order, homogeneity of structure has never been a characteristic of their central administration'. Even in bureaucracy there is no absolute rationality. Nor does administration have to be bureaucratic, indeed the French experience sometimes suggests that there is a kind of dialectic with employees seeking to become *fonctionnaires* and to move from the efficient to the decorative sphere of government. If so, this again suggests that some of the apparent continuity in French administration may, as well as being enhanced by a lack of rigour in conceptual definition, be cyclical or repetitive.[21]

The relevance of theoretical work to the study of bureaucracy in the past was one of the questions raised at the outset of this study. If it is possible to give a fairly positive reply does this follow for the other points? Where the evolution of other parts of the administration is concerned, it is probably unwise to place too much evidence on the example of the Administrations Centrales and their staff, since their history was often very different from that of both *fonctionnaires* and other employee agencies. Similarly, as has already been suggested, the inter-action of bureaucracy and revolution in France was no simple affair. It was also a unique relationship where administration was concerned, and a relationship which was much less dam-aging and politicized than some of the myths of administrative history in which France abounds suggest. If the bureaucracy is seen in context it appears not as an aberration but as a function of France's general development. Looking at administration in structural or legal terms alone merely serves to perpetuate myths.

That myths emerged and proved so powerful in the years of revolution and after is certainly one reason for the love–hate relationship which the French enjoy with their administration. The attitudes passed on from the Enlightenment were in quite flagrant contradiction with the realities of administrative life in the revolutionary era. This gave a boost to the demonology of bureaucracy that springs from a perverse and quasi-mythological view of the importance of the state to the French nation.[22] The protests the French make about the nature of their bureaucracy thus need to be taken with more than the proverbial pinch of salt. For, as was pointed out at the outset of this study, the French need and accept the bureaucracy even when they denounce and resist it. As Simone Weil once said, 'la haine de l'État, qui existe d'une manière latente, sourde et très profonde depuis Charles VI, empêche que des paroles émanant directe-ment d'un gouvernement puissent étre accueilliés par chaque

Français comme la voix d'un ami'.[23] This reserve is transferred from the state to its employees, and no doubt helps to produce the very resistances it seeks to demolish. Hence administration appears to outlast its critics and the strength of feeling that this generates in turn prevents the French from controlling red tape effectively.

So while, as Fourcroy once observed, 'les lois d'administration publique ne pouvaient être apprises nulle part; elles étaient en quelque sorte ensevelies ou concentrées dans les archives des bureaux et dans la correspondence des administrations; ce n'était qu'en administrant immédiatement qu'on pouvait se former à leur connaissance et à leur applications',[24] it is doubtful whether this attempt to reveal the problems of real administration will have any effect on the myths that have built up round the French bureaucracy. The myths may be false but this no doubt will merely add strength to them, just as loose usages of the concept of bureaucracy will continue. The dialogue here engaged with historians and contempories will leave most myths undisturbed. Opposition to red tape is always a unifying rallying-cry, even though many of the most vociferous opponents are at the same time calling for measures—and hence bureaucracy and red tape—against things of which they disapprove. So despite new research Balzac's ironic assessment of the new guardians of revolutionary red tape will no doubt continue to carry general acceptance. Balzac's verdict was that, 'Certes, la bureaucratie a des tortes: je le trouve et lente et insolente, elle enserre un peu trop l'action ministérielle, elle étouffe bien des projets, elle arrête le progrès, mais l'administration française est admirablement utile.'[25]

NOTES TO CHAPTER I

[1] Cited by Goronwy Rees in *Encounter* (132), xxiii (1964), 29.

[2] Few people would accept C. W. Casinelli's belief that some twentieth-century revolutions have negated bureaucracy by personalized rule, *Total Revolution* (Santa Barbara, Cal., 1976), 234–5.

[3] A. Sauvy, *Bureaux et bureaucratie*, 2nd ed. (Paris, 1967), 102. Henceforward, unless otherwise stated, the place of publication of French books is Paris and that of English books, London.

[4] P. M. Williams, *Crisis and Compromise. Politics in the Fourth Republic* (1964), 336. Cf. also A. de Tocqueville, *L'Ancien Régime et la Révolution*, ed. G. W. Headlam, new impression, (Oxford, 1965), 41–79, and G. Sautel, *Histoire des institutions publiques depuis la Révolution française* (1970), who exemplifies recent beliefs in the continuity of administration in France. For a more guarded view see J. Hayward, *The One and Indivisible French Republic* (1973), 11.

[5] For examples of modern attacks on the way the administration tends not merely to continue in being but also to capture power for itself—a charge Marx levelled against it during the Second Empire—see C. Debbasch, *L'Administration au pouvoir* (1969), and J. Billy, *Les Technocrates* (1975).

[6] De Montremy, cited by A. Diamant in W. J. Siffen (ed.), *Towards the Comparative Study of Public Administration* (Bloomington, Ind., 1957), 193.

[7] On the lack of study of French bureaucracy P. Legendre, *Histoire de l'administration de 1750 à nos jours* (1967), 3, 17, 42–3, and 68, and P. Sheriff, 'Sociology of Public Bureaucracies, 1945–1975. A trend report', *Current Sociology*, xxiv/2 (1976), 1–10. The quotation is from a review in the *Bulletin critique du livre français*, xxiii/4 (1968), no. 73228, 343.

[8] E. N. Suleiman, *Politics, Power and Bureaucracy in France* (Princeton, NJ, 1974), 14–15.

[9] The summa of the new school is G. Vedel *et al.*, *Traité de science administrative* (1966), while the historical problems are examined in B. Chenot *et al.*, *Histoire de l'administration française depuis 1800. Problèmes et méthodes* (Geneva, 1975).

[10] C. J. Friedrich, *Man and his Government* (NY, 1963), 467.

[11] J. Armstrong, *The European Administrative Élite* (Princeton, NJ, 1973), 33–4.

[12] Gortner, *Administration in the Public Sector,* 268.

[13] The major manuscript sources are to be found in the chaotic but bountiful personnel dossiers of the Ministries of the Interior, Justice, and Police which, with those of the Directorial Secretariat-General, are held in the Archives Nationales, and those of the Ministries of War, the Navy, and Foreign Affairs which are all held in separate, departmental archives. Fuller details of these almost wholly unused sources are given in the bibliography. On the possible dangers of stressing the personnel angle, see Sheriff, op. cit., 106.

[14] The Directory was defined as a bureaucratic regime by contemporaries such as L. S. Mercier, *Le Nouveau Paris* (1862), vi, 261, and the claim has been maintained by historians such as F. A. Aulard, *Histoire politique de la Révolution français* (1921), 581, and D. Woronoff, *La République bourgeoise* (1973), 51. For the myths of Directorial historiography see Church, 'In Search of the Directory', in J. F. Bosher (ed.), *French Government and Society, 1500–1850* (1973), 261–94, while the lack of study of the ministries was noted by J. Godechot, *Les Institutions de la France sous la Révolution et l'Empire* (1951), 395.

[15] For a discussion of the statistical problems and the methods adopted see Chapter II, note 29 and Chapter VI, note 4.

[16] M. C. Dareste de Chavanne, *Histoire de l'administration en France* (1848), ii, 353–7.

[17] De Tocqueville, op. cit., 65–74, 173, and 267–8. On the need to modify his thesis see H. T. Parker, 'Two Administrative Bureaux under the Directory and Napoleon', *FHS*, iv (1965), 150–1; N. Richardson, *The French Prefectoral Corps 1814–1830* (1966), i, and D. Richet, *La France moderne: L'Esprit des institutions* (1973), 79.

[18] J. R. Suratteau, 'Fonctionnaires et employés', *AHRF*, xix (1958), 71–2, and G. Lefebvre, *Le Directoire* (1958), 144–5, are convenient modern analyses of the difference, while contemporary views are well illustrated by the following speech by Isnard in the Tribunate in 1800 when he said that: 'J'entends par office public une délégation de fonction ou de pouvoirs relatif à l'action, à la direction, la décision ou à la consulation, sous la responsabilité directe envers la nation. Tout office publique est une délégation de la nation et non une délégation du Gouvernement . . . Les officiers publics seront donc distingués des commis, préposés ou subalternes, en ce que les uns auront, avec direction, décision ou consultation, une responsabilté directe envers la nation et que les autres, indépendamment de ce qu'ils n'auront aucune faculté de décider, n'auront de responsabilité directe qu'envers l'officier public qui les aura institutées . . . La distinction de fonctionnaire public et de préposé ou subalterne, est utile pour une multitude

de motifs moraux et politiques. Le concours de la loi dans la création des offices publics leur donnera toujours une stabilité qui n'est propre qu'à attacher les fonctionnaires publics à leur état; et l'on distinguera toujours dans l'opinion publique l'officier établi légalement, et le fonctionnaire établi par commission du gouvernement ou de ses agens' (from *Motion d'ordre sur la création et la suppression des offices publics*, 16 Prairial VIII (*AN*, AD 31)). For contemporary attitudes to payment see the remarks of Thibault in the *Cinq Cents* on 30 Messidor IV in *Moniteur* 304 (4 Thermidor IV) 1215, and Balzac, 'Les Employés', *Œuvres complètes* (1912), xvii, esp. 307–9. The quotation comes from an anonymous pamphlet, *Le Cri employés du gouvernement* (1828), 6. The conception is partly appreciated by some recent commentators, e.g. P. Lindgreen in C. Tilly (ed.), *The Formation of Nation States in Western Europe* (Princeton, NJ, 1975), 508–9, and E. Jaques, *A General Theory of Bureaucracy* (1976), 48–54.

[19] S. Charbonneau, 'Mutations des structures ministérielles et théories modernes des organisations bureaucratiques', *Esprit*, xxxviii/1 (1970), 121–32, argues the case for the continuing applicability of Weber's idea to France. More general discussions of his work can be found in N. Mouzelis, *Organisation and Bureaucracy* (1967), 55–64; M. Albrow, *Bureaucracy* (1970), 37–60, and Sheriff, op. cit., 11–14.

[20] Weber's major writings are to be found in J. Henderson and T. Parsons (eds.), *The Theory of Social and Economic Organization* (New York, 1946), and C. Wright Mills and H. Gerth, *From Max Weber, Essays in Sociology* (1957). The adoption of them here follows the lines suggested by R. H. Hall, 'The Concept of Bureaucracy: An Empirical Assessment', *American Journal of Sociology*, lxix/1 (1963), 32–40.

[21] Weber's definition is available in many places so that the following précis will suffice here. Bureaucracy means a formal body subject to external political and other controls and working in the interest of its state and society. It must be permanent, and is characterized by its continuity and self-perpetuation. It must have fixed and official areas of competence and jurisdiction, together with great differentiation of functions. Within spheres of competence duties must be continually and methodically fulfilled, according to stable norms and rules based largely on written communication. It must also be ordered on strictly hierarchical lines, so that lower ranks are supervised by those above them. And although posts would carry certain rights and powers these would not attach to the individual holding the post. Similarly, incumbents cannot own either the means of production or the means of administration. The staff of a bureaucracy must be 'personally free and subject to authority with respect to their impersonal official obligations'. They must by highly qualified and normally freely selected on the basis of achievement or examin-

ation performance. Their relationship to the bureaucracy must be contractual and impersonal. They must be appointed, salaried, and full-time. As a result bureaucratic office must confer security of tenure and a recognized and often very rigid career pattern leading to pensioned retirement. Moving along this pattern must depend on achievement, seniority, and other universalistic criteria.

[22] D. Warwick, *Bureaucracy* (1974), 2–6.

[23] For the view that bureaucracy in general goes back into the mists of time see J. Hurstfield in *Past and Present*, 32 (1965), 9. To give some idea of the variety of ideas as to when the French bureaucracy emerged, S. N. Eisenstadt, *The Political Systems of Empires* (New York, 1963), 283, places this in the late sixteenth century: O. Ranum, *Richelieu and the Councillors of Louis XIII* (Oxford, 1963) 29, in the mid-seventeenth century; H. Methivier, *La France de Louis XIV* (1962), in the late seventeenth; J. Samoyault, *Les Bureaux des Affaires Étrangères* (1972), 263–5, under Louis XV; G. Thuillier (ed.), *Témoins de l'administration* (1967), 24–5, during the Revolution; and W. R. Sharp, *The French Civil Service* (New York, 1934), 3, and 10–12, under the Empire and later periods.

[24] H. Koenigsberger, 'Revolutionary Conclusions', *History* (191), lvii, (1972), 375.

[25] Lingreen in Tilly, op. cit., 560, and Jacques, op. cit., 17–18, explain the process rather more satisfactorily than H. Jakoby, *The Bureaucratization of the World* (Berkeley, Cal., 1973), 9.

[26] The best guides to the semantic origins of the term are F. Morstein Marx, *The Administrative State* (Chicago, 1957), 16–17, and Albrow, op. cit., 17–18, and 127. By convention the invention of the term is ascribed to Gournai, on the basis of Grimm, but the reference is vague and second-hand. It may be that Gournai was actually talking about over-regulation of the economy when he used the terms 'bureaumanie' and 'bureaucratie'. The term does not appear in the official fifth edition of the *Dictionnaire de l'Académie Française* (Smits, 1798), 180–1, though it can be found in a semi-official edition published in 1802 by Moutardier and Le Clère, 213. There are examples of the term being used in the revolutionary era and by 1835 it was officially canonized by the Académie. Significantly, the semantic evidence suggests that what annoyed contemporaries was not the existence of state intervention as much as the usurpation of the power of the state and its legitimate functionaries by mere employees.

[27] J. Blondel in D. G. Charlton (ed.), *France: A Companion to French Studies* (1972), 591.

[28] Sheriff, op. cit., 39.

[29] A. S. Cohan, *Theories of Revolution* (1975), 216–17, and J. Rule

and C. Tilly, 'Political Process in Revolutionary France, 1830–32', in J. M. Merriman (ed.), *1830 in France* (NY, 1975), 41–86.

[30] Cited in R. K. Merton *et al.* (eds.), *Reader in Bureaucracy* (Glencoe, Ill., 1952), 18 and 25. The question is explored further by Church, 'Bureaucracy, Politics and Revolution. The Evidence of the Commission de Dix Sept', *FHS*, vi/4 (1970), 514–16. It should be noted that much also depends on the nature of the technology available to the revolution. In the present century revolutions have acquired far greater powers of action and coercion than was available at the end of the eighteenth century, as Richard Cobb has noted. See pp. 74–6 for a further discussion of this and related points.

[31] The quotation is from Cohan, loc. cit. See also F. Bon and M. A. Burnier, *Classe ouvrière et Révolution* (1971), 84, and T. H. Greene, *Comparative Revolutionary Movements* (Englewood Cliffs., NJ, 1974), 68.

[32] This was of course Weber's view, as expressed in Merton, op. cit., 64–8 and 95–6. Cf. also Tilly, op. cit., 61–2, and Sheriff, op. cit., 12–19 and 40 for more recent support. The opposite view can be found in Richet, op. cit., 75, and more powerfully, if not altogether seriously, in C. N. Parkinson, *Parkinson's Law* (1961).

[33] P. Chaunu in F. Braudel and E. Labrousse (eds.), *Histoire économique et sociale de la France*, i/1 (1977), 47 and 181–2.

[34] R. Folz *et al.*, *De l'antiquité au monde médiéval* (1972), and J. Ellul, *Histoire des institutions* (1970), iii, 57–9.

[35] F. Lot and R. Fawtier, *Histoire des institutions françaises au Moyen Âge* (1958), ii, esp. 140–1; J. G. Lemarignier, *Le Gouvernement royal au premier temps capetiens, 987–1108* (1965), and M. Pacaut, *Louis VII et son royaume* (1964), 172–3.

[36] R. Cazalles, *La Société politique et la crise de la royauté sous Philippe de Valois* (1958), 72; R. Fawtier, *The Capetain Kings of France* (1960), 173–9, and B. Guenée, 'L'Histoire de l'état à la fin du Moyen Âge', *RH*, ccxxii (1964), 331–60.

[37] Though this is the implication of Jakoby, op. cit., 15–16.

[38] G. Poggi, *The Development of the Modern State. A Sociological Introduction* (1978), 19, and 53–4. Cf. Chaunu in Braudel and Labrousse, op. cit., 41 and 47, and J. F. Lemarignier, *La France médiévale: Institutions et société* (1970).

[39] Chaunu, loc. cit. Cf. also P. S. Lewis, *Later Mediaeval France, the Polity* (1968), 196–9, and P. Anderson, *Lineages of the Absolutist State* (1975), 85–112. The argument of J. R. Major, that this was essentially a consultative monarchy [in *Representative Institutions in Renaissance France* (Madison, Wisc. 1960), 125 et seq.] has been effectively refuted by R. Knecht, *Francis I and Absolute Monarchy* (1969), 24–9.

[40] Jakoby, op. cit., 20, argues that the absolute monarchy was the

'first bureaucratic state' as does I. Wallerstein, *The Modern World System* (1974), 136–9, but the views of Anderson, op. cit., 33, Poggi, op. cit., 70–1, and especially J. Berenger, 'Pour une enquête européenne', *AESC*, xxix/1 (1974), 174–6, are more convincing.

[41] R. Pillorget dates the use of the term to the fifteenth century in 'Un Colloque sur le développement de la puissance de l'État', *L'Information historique*, 3815 (1976), 114–15, whereas Chaunu places it in the early seventeenth century (op. cit., 16). Cf. also J. H. Shennan, *The Origins of the Modern European State 1450–1725* (1974), and J. R. Strayer, *On the Mediaeval Origins of the Modern State* (Princeton, 1970), 90–100.

[42] Richet, *La France moderne*, 81–5, and 'La Formation des grandes serviteurs de l'État', *L'Arc*, 65 (1976), 54.

[43] H. Methivier, *L'Ancien Régime* (1968), sums up this view succinctly and accurately. Cf. also P. Goubert, *L'Ancien Régime*, ii (1973), and R. Mousnier, *Les Institutions de la France sous la monarchie absolue* (1974).

[44] For views opposed to the conception of *officiers* as bureaucrats see Wallerstein, op. cit., 283–97, Anderson, op. cit., 33 ff.; Richet 'La Formation', 33, and P. Goubert, *Louis XIV et vingt millions de Français* (1966), 133, Hintze as quoted by Jakoby, op. cit., 24, misses the fact that the *commissaires* were in fact *officiers* too.

[45] M. Antoine, 'La Notion de Sub-délégation dans la monarchie de L'Ancien Régime', *Bulletin de l'École des Chartes*, cxxxii (1974), 267–87, shows that only *commissaires* were allowed to delegate their authority.

[46] Ranum, op. cit., 1–29, describes the system of government under Richelieu. Aspects of that of Louis XIV are examined in J. C. Rule (ed.), *Louis XIV and the Craft of Kingship* (Ohio, 1969), in which Rule himself on pages 9 and 29–30 claims that Louis's administration was bureaucratic in a Weberian sense. On the dynasties see H. de Luçay, *Des origines du pouvoir ministeriel en France* (1881), 53–95, and 149–50. Cf. also Poggi, op. cit., 61–2, and Anderson, op. cit., 55 and 102.

[47] M. Bordes, *L'Administration provinciale et municipale* (1972), 125–8 and 200 et seq.; R. Mousnier, *État et société sous François I et Louis XIV* (1966–7), i, 119. Cf. also P. Clement (ed.), *Instructions et mémoires de Colbert* (1867), iv, 27. On *sub-délégués* there is a series of articles by J. Ricommard, e.g. *RH*, lccv (1945), and *RHDFE*, xxvi (1948). More recently M. Antoine, 'Les Subdélégués Généraux des Intendances', *RHDFE*, liii/3 (1975), 395–435, has shown the continuing concern of government not to proliferate them and the way they only hesitantly pointed towards nineteenth-century *fucntionnaires* such as *Secrétaires Généraux*.

[48] M. Antoine, *Le Conseil du Roi sous le règne de Louis XIV* (Geneva,

1970), 47–53, and *Le Conseil Royal de Finances au XVIIIe siècle* (1973), xix–xx.

[49] P. Berger, 'French Administration and the Famine of 1697', *ESR,* vii/1 (1978), 118–20.

[50] E. G. Cruickshank, 'Factions at the Court of Louis XV and the Succession to Fleury, 1737–45', unpublished doctoral thesis of the University of London (1956), 340–2 and 349–80, is the best account of the trials of the ministries after 1715. B. Behrens, 'Government and Society', in C. H. Wilson and E. E. Rich (eds.), *Cambridge Economic History of Europe,* v (Cambridge, 1977), 567, details the hesitation of the *épée.*

[51] On government as a whole see R. Mousnier, *État et société en France au XVIIe et XVIIIe siècles* (1969), i, 121–51, and Goubert, op. cit., ii, 229–30. For criticism of ministers see D. Oster (ed.), *Montesquieu: Œuvres complètes,* (1964), 951, and on the return of the *épée,* Anderson, op. cit., 107–8.

[52] Lindgreen, op. cit., 503–7, 547–52, and 560 on the declining efficiency of government despite its technical development. On the problems of government see also R. L. Curry and L. L. Wade, *A Theory of Political Exchange* (Englewood Cliffs, NJ, 1968), 67–71, and F. Pietri, *La Réforme de l'État au XVIIIe siècle* (1935), 1–11.

[53] On the War Office see H. Michaud, 'Aux origines du Secrétariat d'État à la Guerre', *RHMC,* xix (1972), 389–413, and Anon., *Notice sur le Ministère de la guerre* (1879). For the Ministry of Marine, G. Dagnaud, 'L'Administration centrale de la Marine sous l'Ancien Régime', *Revue maritime* (1912), 326–7, and A. Duchêne, *La Politique coloniale de la France* (1928). The Foreign Ministry is described by A. Outrey, *L'Administration français des Affaires Étrangères* (1954), 18–31, and C. Piccavet, 'Les Commis des Affaires Étrangères', *Revue d'histoire moderne,* i, (1926), 103–15. The Contrôle Général is covered by H. de Jouvençal, *Le Contrôleur Général sous l'Ancien Régime* (1901). Cf. also M. Antoine, *Le Secrétariat d'État de Bertin* (1948). There is no study of the Secrétariat à la Maison du Roi *per se* but H. Tersen, *Origine et évolution du Ministère de l'Intérieur* (Montpellier, 1913), covers the ground in part. The origins of the Chancery can be followed from H. Michaud, *La Grande Chancellerie et las écritures royales au seizième siècle* (1967), 127–54, and later developments in P. Durand Barthez, *Histoire des structures du Ministère de la Justice* (1973).

[54] The views of N. Sutherland, *The French Secretaries of State in the Age of Catherine de Medici* (1962), have been critically developed by R. Kierstad, *Pomponne de Bellièvre* (Evanston, Ill., 1968), 52–5, and Chaunu, op. cit., 80–1.

[55] Sutherland, op. cit., 78.

[56] Ranum, op. cit., 45–76.

⁵⁷ Sutherland, op. cit., 47–9. Cf. also, for the later period Piccavet, op. cit., 115–20, Duchêne, op. cit., 28–39, and Tersen, op. cit., 24–7.

⁵⁸ On the question of bribes, *AHG*, A 3208 f 35, lettre circulaire à tous les colonels, 3 viii 1701, and on the problems of dismissals P. Gaxotte, *Louis XV and His Times* (1934), 292–5.

⁵⁹ Mousnier, *Les Institutions*, 177–81.

⁶⁰ M. Antoine, 'Les Comités des Ministres sous Louis XV', *RHDFE*, xxix (1951), 193–222; A. Racinet, *De la spécialisation ministérielle en France* (1910), 62–72; A. Buot de l'Épine, *Du Conseil du Roi au Conseil d'État: Le Comité contentieux des départements* (1972), 35 and 82–100; and J. Tarrade, 'L'administration à la fin de l'Ancien Régime', *RH*, ccxxix (1963), 104–7 and 110–15.

⁶¹ Bordes, op. cit., 143–7 and D. D. Bien, 'The Army in the French Enlightenment' *Past and Present* 85 (1979), 95.

⁶² In addition to ibid. the Intendants are discussed by G. R. Mead, 'The Administrative Noblesse of France during the Eighteenth Century', unpublished doctoral thesis of the University of London (1954), and V. R. Gruder, *The Royal Provincial Intendants: A Governing Élite* (Ithaca, NY, 1968). The growing role of the bureaux is documented by R. Van Berkel, 'Recherches sur le centralisme français', unpublished *thèse en droit*, Université de Lille (1974), i, 66.

⁶³ G. Dawson, *L'Évolution des structures de l'administration locale déconcentrée* (1969).

⁶⁴ Examples are G. T. Mathews, *The Royal General Farms in France* (1958), J. Petot, *Histoire de l'administration des ponts et chaussées* (1958), and for the *maréchaussée*, I. A. Cameron, 'The Police of Eighteenth Century France', *ESR*, vii/1 (1977), 47–76 and Martin *AHRF* 240.

⁶⁵ J. Rothney (ed.), *The Brittany Affair and the Crisis of the Ancien Régime* (NY, 1969).

⁶⁶ Sheriff, op. cit., 107–8.

NOTES TO CHAPTER II

¹ M. Vovelle, *La Chute de la monarchie, 1782–1792* (1972), 26–7, speaks for many in his belief in such a feudal reaction. It should be noted that W. Doyle , 'Was there an Aristocratic Reaction in Pre-Revolutionary France?', *Past and Present*, 57 (1972), takes a more sceptical view while D. D. Bien, 'La Révolution Aristocratique', *AESC*, xxix–xxx (1974–5), moves in the same direction. However, J. R. Gillis, 'Political Decay and the European Revolution, 1789–1848', *World Politics*, xxii/3 (1970), 352–60, points to the fact that, whatever the reality of the feudal reaction, the administration became more regressive and less efficient as the century went on.

[2] Mousnier, *Les Institutions*, 552-8.

[3] The quotation is from J. M. Roberts, *Revolution and Improvement* (1976), 111. He also makes the point, on pp. 73-4, that the reform policy merely aided the opposition, as does P. Miguel, *Histoire de la France* (1976), 257-8. The desire for reform is explained by Poggi, *Development of the Modern State*, 84-5, and D. Richet, 'Autout des origines idéologiques lointaines de la Révolution', *AESC*, xxiv/1 (1969), 1-23.

[4] On the crisis of 1770-2 see W. Doyle, 'The Parlements of France and the breakdown of the Old Order, 1771-1788', *FHS*, vi/4 (1970), 415-48, and J. F. Bosher, 'The French Crisis of 1770', *History* (190), lvii (1972), 17-30. Cf. also Goubert, *L'Ancien Régime*, ii, 230-3.

[5] E. Strauss, *The Ruling Servants* (1961), 184-5, and Bosher, *French Finances 1770-1795. From Business to Bureaucracy* (Cambridge, 1970), 11-21.

[6] Antoine, *Le Conseil du Roi*, 430-1.

[7] The contrary case is argued by A. Corvisier, *La France de 1492 à 1789* (1972), 292-3, but the evidence of Vovelle, op. cit., 38, Cameron, 'The Police', 70, and L. Trenard, 'Les Intendants et leurs enquêtes', *L'Information historique*, xxxviii/1 (1976), 14-15, seems more convincing.

[8] Mousnier, op. cit., 182, claims that such ennoblements constituted 'l'ébauche de cette noblesse de fonctionnaires que Napoléon Ier cherche à créer' which is an interesting judgement both on their non-bureaucratic nature and on the character of the Imperial administration. Cf. also Lindgreen in Tilly, *Formation of Nation states*, 503-7.

[9] *AHG*, Y[a] 19-20 and 195-196 are the sources of such personnel references.

[10] Bordes, *L'Administration provinciale*, 311 and 343-5.

[11] R. Marichal, in Chenot, *Problèmes et Méthodes*, 57-8, offers a not wholly convincing account of the semantic history of the term at this period, since bureaucracy then very often meant the power of the administration in society. Moreover, Marichal does not always give some of the earliest usages of some of the terms he discusses, such as employees. It has also apparently been argued that the *Cahiers* actually demanded bureaucracy, cf. Sasha Weitman, 'Bureaucracy, Democracy and the French Revolution', unpublished doctoral thesis of Washington University, St Louis, Mo., 1968, and John Markoff, 'Who wants Bureaucracy? French public opinion in 1789', unpublished doctoral thesis of John Hopkins University, Baltimore, Md., 1972, both theses cited by G. Schapiro *et al.*, 'Quantitative Studies of the French Revolution', *History and Theory*, xii (1973), 169, but this very much depends on the meaning given to the term and on

the motives of those using it.

¹² A general account of structural changes can be found in J Godechot, *Les Institutions de la France sous la Révolution et l'Empire*, 2nd ed., (1970), 15–22; while for the Council see J. Egret, *La Pré-Revolution française* (1962), 76–8 and for financial administration, Bosher, *French Finances*, 26–39 and 148–61.

¹³ P. Sandevoir, *Études sur le recours de pleine juridiction* (1964), 33–4, and J. Laferrière, 'La Raison de la Proclamation de la règle de la séparation des autorités', in *Mélanges Paul Negelesco* (Bucarest, 1935), 435–7, deal with improvements in administrative law provision at this time.

¹⁴ M. Becaud, 'Le Bureau de la Balance de Commerce', *Revue d'histoire économique et sociale*, xlii (1964), 361, and Egret, op. cit., 110–13. Cf. also J. F. Bosher, 'French Administration and Public Finance in its European Context', in A. Goodwin (ed.), 'The American and French Revolutions, 1763–93', *New Cambridge Modern History*, viii (Cambridge, 1965), 565–91.

¹⁵ A. Logette, *Le Comité contentieux des finances près le Conseil du Roi, 1777–1791* (Nancy, 1964), 57–62. Cf. also Pietri, *La Réforme de l'État*, 160–70.

¹⁶ Petot, *Histoire de l'administration des Ponts et Chaussées*, 171–82, and Mathews, *The Royal General Farms*, esp. 184–210. Cameron, op. cit., 55, notes that the need to purchase commissions in the *maréchaussée* ended in 1768.

¹⁷ Petot, op. cit., 319. Cf. also Gruder, *Royal Provincial Intendants*, 87–9, and Van Berkel, 'Recherches sur le Centralisme Français', i, 103 and 110–3 on the new services attached to the Intendants.

¹⁸ J. F. Bosher, 'Jaques Necker et la naissance de l'État moderne', *Société historique de Canada:* Rapport 1963 (Québec, 1963), 165.

¹⁹ Antoine, 'Les Comités des ministres', 226–9. The quotation is from Bosher, *French Finances*, 62.

²⁰ On the decay of the provincial responsibilities of the Secretariats the evidence of *AN*, O¹ 745 no. 125 and a variety of papers in *AHG*, A⁴ 50 and 50A, amongst other sources, is proof of how far the decline had gone by the reign of Louis XVI. Cf. also Racinet, *De la spécialisation ministérielle*, 84–92, and A. Buot de l'épine, 'Les bureaux de la Guerre à la fin de l'Ancien Régime', *RHDFE* liv/4 (1976), 533–4 and 552–4.

²¹ The approximate figures (drawn *inter al.* from *AN*, BB⁴ 7 and F¹ᵃ 565 and *AHG*, Xˢ 128) are:

	Maison	C. Gén.	Chanc.	Aff. E.	Marine	Guerre	Total
1760	22	100	6	40	83	150	401
1788	30	250	10	70	141	149	670

[22] Antoine, *Le Secrétariat d'État de Bertin,* 12–13. Cf. also Durand Barthez, *Histoire des structures du Ministère de la Justice,* 13–14.

[23] *AN,* F^{1a} 565, 'Ministres et leurs bureaux', and F^{1b1}2 (Dossier 1793) for other 'états des appointements'. Cf. also H. Tersen, *Origines et évolution du Ministère de l'Intérieur* (Montepellier, 1913), 30–1. Dagnaud, op. cit., 60–2, reports an even more notable case of prebendal reward. Accoron was a *Premier Commis* in the Marine during the sixties whose salary of 42,000 *livres* was backed by a gratification, and a pension of 24,000 *livres,* reversible to his family. He also had a grant of 120,000 *livres* to provide a dowry for his daughter on her marriage to the Comte de Grasse. The generosity of his treatment allegedly led to proceedings being instituted against the donor, the Maréchal Duc de Castries.

[24] De Jouvençal, *Le Contrôleur Général* 48–56, 62–71, and 93–5 and J. F. Bosher, 'Le Comité contentieux des finances près le Conseil du 477–84. On the suppression of the *Intendants des Finances* see A. Logette, 'Quelques Nouvelles Sources pour l'administration des finances à la fin du XVIIIe siècle,' *RHDFE,* xlviii (1969), 411–13, and J. F. Bosher, 'Le Comité Contentieux des Finances près le Conseil du Roi: A review and a document', *Annali della Fondazione Italiana per la Storia Amministrativa,* iv (1967), 598–607.

[25] F. Masson, *Le Département des Affaires Étrangères pendant la Révolution 1787–1804* (1877) 10–54, and Samoyault, *Les Bureaux des Affaires Étrangères* 88–90, 166–9, 176, 205–17, and 231–3.

[26] Duchêne, *La Politique coloniale,* 54–88, and Dagnaud, 'L'Administration Centrale de la Marine', 29–46 and 721–35.

[27] Buot de l'épine, loc. cit., complains of the limits to the documentation on the War Office. None the less, it is still somewhat richer than many other departments. Her article is devoted mainly to the duties of the various bureaux and gives only limited attention to the personnel, especially those at the lower level (538–56). This is in line with the tradition of *l'histoire du droit.* However, she does agree with the stress placed here on the special status, role, and powers of the *Premier Commis* and the generally patrimonial and honorific nature of pay and conditions in the War Office (536–7 and 557–8) though perhaps overestimating both their generosity and the rationality and efficiency of the work of the department as a whole.

[28] Bosher, *French Finances,* 276.

[29] Most of the War Office *règlements* are to be found in *AHG,* X^s 128 which also contains details of staff numbers as does Y^a 24 and 25. X^s 115 contains an 'Aperçu sommaire de la composition du Ministère de la Guerre'. A fuller discussion of the Ministry of War at this period will be found in Church, 'Words, theories and realities in eighteenth

century French administration' forthcoming in *Annali della Fondazione Italiana per la Storica Amministrativa.*

[30] Saint-Germain is cited at length by P. Legendre, *L'Administration du XVIIIe siècle à nos jours* (1969), 157–8, while *AHG*, Mémoires 1790, 'Papiers Guibert', and 1791 no. 15: 'Projet du Traivail rélatif aux vues de M. le Comte de St. Germain' contain Guibert's views.

[31] *Notice sur le Ministère de la Guerre*, loc. cit. Cf. also *AHG*, X^s 128 in general.

[32] *AHG*, Y^a 24 (Dossier 1789: Bureau des Fonds). There are other versions of the same document in Y^a 24 (dossier 1790) and Y^a 25 (Dossier 1788).

[33] The information for the following analysis is drawn from the 'dossiers individuels' of the old War Office staff, *AHG*, located in Y^a 26–31, and was analysed by a MCV 2 Data analysis program in the University of Lancaster Computer Laboratory, under the supervision of Brian Dalby. Further information on the sources and modes of analysis will be found in Church, loc. cit. and also 'The Personnel of French Central Government under the Directory', *Past and Present*, 36 (1967), 59–71. For later comparisons using the same program see chapters VIII and IX. There is a fuller analysis of a slightly different kind of sample, where the program was neither available nor appropriate, in chapters VI and VII. In all cases the same list of ranks, as shown in Table I, have been used to structure the analyses.

[34] A. Daumard, 'Une référence pour l'étude des sociétés urbaines en France. Projet de code socio-professionel', *RHMC*, x (1963), 185–210, which is followed by a critique by J. F. Tirat, 'Problèmes de méthode en histoire sociale' on pp. 211 et seq. On the marriage patterns etc. of *Premiers Commis* compare Samoyault, op. cit., 204–6 and 211.

[35] Samoyault, op. cit., 180–9 and 201.

[36] Ibid., 195. Cf. also Mathews, op. cit., 208.

[37] Bosher, 'The Premiers Commis', 486–94 puts the opposite case.

[38] The examples come from *AHG*, Y^a 193–5.

[39] E. N. Williams, *The Ancien Régime in Europe* (1970), 22. Cf. also G. J. Cavanaugh, 'The Present State of Revolutionary Historiography', *FHS*, vii (1972), 598–600.

[40] *AHG*, Y^a 24 (Dossier 1763), note of 12 February, which shows that suppression of interpreterships could only be carried out by compensating the holders from another royal fund. X^s 128, 'Projet d'un traitement général', shows that some of Saint-Florentin's clerks in the *Maison du Roi* department were paid as agents of various provinces and towns.

[41] M. Reinhard, 'Élite et noblesse à la fin de l'Ancien Régime', *RHMC*, iii (1956), 1–37. The quotation is from Bosher, *French Finances,*

277.

[42] M. Waline, *Droit administratif*, 9th ed., (1963), 22–5

[43] J. G. Ymbert, *La Bureaucratie* (1825), 3.

[44] Bosher, op. cit., 133–6 and 277. For the opposing view see G. Schapiro, *et al.*, op. cit., 189–90. The quotation is from 'Avis important sur le Ministère et sur l'assemblée prochaine des États Généraux' (1788) *BL*, R 143/7.

[45] Quoted in G. Thuillier, 'Comment les Français voyaient l'administration', *RA*, xv (1962), 379. Cf. also the very title of an anonymous pamphlet 'Bureaucratie du despotisme ministeriel de la Guerre' (25 Février 1788), *BL*, F 564.

[46] H. Carre, P. Sagnac, and E. Lavisse, 'Le Règne de Louis XV', *Histoire de la France,* ed. E. Lavisse (1910), ix (1), 89–90.

[47] This is still argued by J. Armstrong, 'Old Regime Governors', *CSSH*, (1972), 11–15, whereas Gruder, op. cit., 184–9, and Bluche, 'L'Origine social du personnel ministériel', loc. cit., more convincingly argue for a somewhat wider recruitment. Cf. also D. Richet 'Le Catchécisme révolutionnaire', *AESC*, xxvi (1971), 271, and C. Lucas, 'Nobles, Bourgeois and the Origins of the French Revolution', *Past and Present*, 60 (1973), 84–126.

[48] Bosher, op. cit., 178–80, and 191.

[49] It has recently been argued by P. Mathias and P. O'Brien, 'Taxation in Britain and France, 1715–1810', *Journal of European Economic History*, v/3 (1976), that the rich in France were already taxed more heavily than their English counterparts (629) even though England was generally subject to a heavier burden of tax overall. It was the failure of the State to increase its share of GNP which precipitated the crisis, a failure due to the greater visibility of the incompetence and inequality of taxes in France.

[50] J. Egret, op. cit., 80–93 and 103 et seq. Cf. also P. Gousset, 'Évolution historique de l'Administration Centrale du Commerce et de l'Industrie', *RA*, xiv (1961), 133.

[51] Egret, op. cit., 76–8.

[52] Legendre, *Histoire de l'administratiòn*, 498. Cf. also F. Furet and D. Richet, *La Révolution française* (1966), i, 55.

[53] Antoine, *Le Conseil du Roi*, 634, who is supported by Schapiro, Markoff, and Weitman, loc. cit., although Chaunu, *Histoire économique*, i/1, 199, believes venality was already dead by 1789.

[54] De Tocqueville, *D'Ancien Régime et la Révolution*, 198 and 208. Schweitzer is quoted by A. B. C. Cobban, *A History of Modern France*, 2nd ed. (Harmondsworth, 1965), i, 112.

[55] For an appreciation of the Ancien Régime administration see W. Doyle, *The Old European Order* (Oxford, 1978), 248–64.

[56] For the background to the events of 1789 see, *inter al.*

J. Godechot, *La Prise de la Bastille* (1965).

[57] J. Dunn, *Modern Revolutions* (1972), 18, and B. Hoselitz, in J. La Palombara (ed.), *Bureaucracy and Political Development* (Princeton, NJ, 1963), 195–6. Cf. also J. Baecheler, *Les Phénomènes révolutionnaries* (1970), 150, 156, 193, and 249.

[58] Peuchet is here quoted in G. Thuillier, *Témoins de l'administration* 21–2. Cf. also F. Braesch, *1789: L'Année cruciale* (1941), 38–45.

[59] F. Heady, *Public Administration: a comparative perspective* (Englewood Cliffs, 1966), 37. Cf. also Sautel, *Histoire des institutions publiques*, 54–5, and Van Berkel, op. cit., ii, 176.

[60] M. Brugière, 'Histoire Financière et Histoire Administrative', in *Problèmes et méthodes,* esp. p. 38. Cf, also C. Tourdes, 'Une Étude de sociologie historique: Administration et décisions sous le Convention et le Directoire', unpublished thesis for a *Diplôma des études supérieures,* Université de Paris II (1973), 61, which notes the fallibility of strategies for implementing policy decisions. The quotation comes from A. Soboul, 'Anarchsis Cloots', *AHRF,* lii/1 (1980), 51.

[61] A. F. Bertrand de Moleville, *Mémoires sécrètes pour servir à l'histoire de la dernière année du règne de Louis XVI* (London, 1797), i, 13. Cf. also Van Berkel, op. cit., ii, 269–70.

[62] *BL,* FR 97/13.

[63] L. Dupriez, *Les Ministres dans les principaux pays d'Europe et d'Amérique* (1893), i, 253–65. Cf. also E. A. Thompson, *Popular Sovereignty and the French Constituent Assembly 1789–1791* (Manchester, 1952), for the way French political thought turned against the English ministerial system at this time, and J. Godechot, *Les Institutions de la France,* 1st ed., 136, on Rey's initiative.

[64] 'Opinion de M. Lamy sur l'importance de décréter la responsabilité des chefs du bureau', *BL,* FR 96/8. Cf. also ibid. R 143/7 'Avix Important sur le ministère' of 1788. Lamarque is quoted in the *Moniteur* 175 (22 June 1792), 1. All references to the *Moniteur* are to the original edition.

[65] 'Idées d'un patriote au sujet du remplacement des ci-devant ministres' (s.d.), *BL,* FR 97/20. Cf. also N. Hampson, *The Life and Opinions of Maximilian Robespierre* (1974), 165.

[66] Quoted in Thuillier, op. cit., 39–40. On *cartes de civisme* see the decrees of 2 September 1792 and 5 February and 6 April 1793, details of which can be found along with all other legislation discussed here, in Duvergier, *Collection complète des lois* etc.

[67] Thuillier, Tulard, and others in *Les Épurations administratives* (Geneva, 1977), 60 and 120 etc.

[68] *AN,* Marine BB[8] 110. Personnel 'État'.

[69] For early experiments with examinations see *AD,* Loir-et-Cher, L 276: 'Règlement de police à observer dans les bureaux' and M. Sibert,

Le Concours comme mode juridique de recrutement de la fonction publique (1912), 23–4.

70 Bosher, op. cit. 270–3.

71 The quotation is from *AN*, AD^1 31, 'Lettres Patente du Roi, 29 Novembre 1789'. Cf. also the law of 22 December 1789–January, 21 June 1790–21 February 1791, and 3–22 August 1790.

72 Bosher, *French Finances*, 233.

73 J. Chevallier, *L'Élaboration historique du principe de séparation de la juridiction administrative et de l'administration active* (1970), 61–80, and F. P. Bénoit. *Le Droit administratif français* (1968), 275–9. Cf. also Sandevoir, op. cit., 46–55, 66–7, 89 and 97–100 on the relative lack of interest in questions of administrative law at that time, contrary to the impression given by Buot de L'épine, op. cit., 234–7. For an almost unique local example see *AD*, Seine-et-Marne, L 15 on the *Conseil de Jurisprudence* established in January 1792.

74 Durand Barthez, op. cit., 8–9, discusses one of the exceptions, though reference should also be made to *AN*, D vi 12 (Dossier 127), nos. 22–3 of 25 May 1791.

75 On ministerial responsibility, see Thompson, op. cit., and *inter al.*, Sautel, op. cit., 49–53. The most important laws were those of 13 July 1789–23 February 1791 and 26 August–3 November 1791. The constitution is conveniently printed in J. Godechot (ed.) *Les Constitutions de la France 1789*, 2nd ed. (1970), 33–67.

76 H. Olive, *L'Action exécutif exercé par les comités des assemblées révolutionnaires* (Marseilles, 1908), 36–9 and 53–73. On the new Council of State, created by a merger of the old Conseils d'en haut, des Dépêches, and des Finances et Commerce etc. under the terms of a decree of 9 August 1789, see J. Godechot, 'Mémoires de De Joly', *AHRF*, xviii (1946), 189–382. The position of the ministers is also usefully illustrated by E. Bernardin, *Jean Marie Roland et Le Ministère de l'Intérieur* (1964), 23–62.

77 H. Buisson, *La Police, son histoire* (1958), 131–52, and Gen. Berthaut, *Les Ingénieurs-Géographes militaires 1624–1831* (1902), i, 123–4.

78 The decrees of 5 June 1790–25 March 1791; 13–17 June 1790; 5 July 1790; 6–11 February 1791; and 13 May 1791 relate, along with many others, to the ministries, while those of 18–22 December 1790; 2–17 March 1791; 10–20 March 1791; 9 April–12 September 1791, 20 May–11 June 1791; 25 September –6 October 1791; 29 September–2 October 1791; 9–12 November 1791 and 13–17 December 1791 are amongst the many acts that dealt with *fonctionnaires* in general. There were also a number of regulations on the working of various bureaux. In June 1790 the salaries of the minister were made subject to a normal limit of 100,000 *livres*.

[79] *AHG*, Pensions civiles: J. P. Davrange shows the financial complications of the move from Versailles at the personal level and F. Masson, *Le Départment des Affaires Étrangères*, 68–9, reinforces this impression and shows some of the implications for one department seen as a whole.

[80] 'Rapport sur les employés supprimés' *BL*, R 569/27, and for a local example, C. Gabolde, 'De la juridication de l'Intendant au Conseil de Préfecture', *Bulletin de la Société des Antiquaires de Normandie*, liii (1955–6), 329–30.

[81] J. Godechot, 'L'Origine des institutions de l'époque révolutionnaire', *Revue internationale d'histoire politique et constitutionelle*, i (1951), 92 et seq. On the inheritance from the Ancien Régime in general, see Goubert, op. cit., ii, 243–7, and more specifically J. F. Bosher, *The Single Duty Project in France* (1964), and Buot de l'épine, *Du Conseil du Roi au Conseil d'État*.

[82] *AN*, AD I 31, 'Addresse à l'Assemblée Nationale' from employees of the Department of Paris who wished to see an end to venality in the municipal tolls service and the creation of special personnel relations committee to look after their affairs.

[83] On changes of title see the laws and decrees of 7 August 1790–25 March 1791, 5 June 1790, and 27 April–25 May 1791. On provinicial responsibilities see *AN*, F^{1a} 22 (Dossier 1789–92), 'Ministre de la Guerre aux Départements, 3 Avril 1791', and for the problems of the Interior, Demeunier's 'Rapport sur l'organisation du Ministère', *BL*, FR 97/21.

[84] *AN*, AD^1 and F^{1a} 565 for details on the Administration des Finances in 1790.

[85] The details on Petigny de Saint-Romain's division come from *AN*, F^{1b1} 2 (Dossier 1793), 'État Nominatif'.

[86] Masson, op. cit., 73 and 85.

[87] *AN*, BB^4 7 and AD, I 76–8.

[88] *AN*, F^{1a} 22 (Dossier 1789–92), 'Ministère de la Guerre aux Départements, 3 Avril 1791'.

[89] Dagnaud, op. cit., 734–6; Bosher, op. cit., 300; and Tersen, *Origine et évolution du Ministère de l'Intérieur*, 37–55. On Delessart himself see *AN*, F^{1a} 1 (2), 'Ministre au Roi, 26 Octobre 1791'.

[90] *AN*, D^{VI} 12 (Dossier 127), nos. 22/3.

[91] *AHG*, X^s 128 Brahaut 'Chronologie historique'.

[92] *AN*, F^{1b1} 266^2 for Fleurigeon; F^{1b1} 3^1 for Sausseret and AD, I 78 for Laprime.

[93] *AHG*, X^s 212. Other cases are Lelu (X^s 115), Sevin (Y^a 197), Louis (X^s 115), and Hervet (Y^a 195).

[94] F^{101} 11–14. Dossier: Du hautoire.

95 *AN,* AF II 21 (168)f 9, Rapport par le Bureau de Comptabilité.

96 *AN,* F^{1a} 4, 'Delemare à Commissaires du Trésor', 7 July 1791, and AF, II 21 (168) 9.

97 The Régie des Poudres created on 23 September 1791 with a *Caisse* for its staff pensions was an exception to this rule.

98 Good examples occur in *AD,* Loir-et-Cher, L276. Cf also *AD,* Oise, L^{1}21 f 561, and *AD,* Cher, L 1118* f 2 bis no 4, together with H. Poulet, 'L'Administration Centrale du départment de la Meurthe', *La Révolution française,* LI–LII (1909–10), 440–57, and R. Van Berkel, 'Recherches sur la centralisme français' (Lille, 1974), ii, 192–4, 280–1, and 412–14.

99 *AN,* F^{1a} 4, 'Protocols Dispositifs' etc. Cf. also F^{1a} 5 'Dufresne de St Léon au Ministre', s.d.

100 *AN,* AF II 24 (196) f 4.

101 *AN,* AD I 77, 'État des Bureaux du Département de la Justice et du Sceau de l'État', etc. January 1792.

102 *AN,* Justice BB^{30} 512^1 provides most of the personnel information.

103 *AN,* AD I 76–8, for expenses in 1791–2 and F^{1a} 565 for those of the old Conseil d'État in 1790.

104 *AN,* AF II 24 (196) f 15.

105 *AN,* AD I 76–8 again provides information on this. The probable figures were Foreign Affairs 55, Justice 70, Marine 116, War 120, Finance 145, and Interior 162 = 667. Cf. Notes 21 and 106 for estimate of 1788 and 1792 respectively.

106 These estimates like those for 1791 are based largely on the early printed *états de personnel* demanded by the revolutionary assemblies, e.g. for *Affaires Étrangères* the 'État du Février 1792' (*AN,* AD I 77/6), for Finance that of 1792 (ibid. no. 14), for War one of 1792 (ibid. no. 12), and for Justice one dated *c.*1791–2 (ibid. no. 16).

107 *AN,* F^{1b1} 2(1792), nos. 31–2 on the Fifth Division of the Interior in addition to the preceding sources.

108 *Notice sur le Ministère de la Guerre,* 45–7; Duchêne, op. cit., 121; Masson, op. cit., 111–285; Durand-Barthez, loc. cit.; and H. Fontaine de Resbecq, *L'Administration centrale de la marine et colonies* (1886), 11–12.

109 Decrees and laws of 4–11 August 1789; 28 February 1790; 8–20 March 1791; 31 July 1791; 18–22 August 1791 and 10–14 October 1792. Cf. also A. B. C. Cobban, *The Myth of the French Revolution* (1954), 16–19, and Michaels in Merton, *Reader in Bureaucracy,* 140.

110 Tilly, op. cit., 214–18.

111 Bosher, op. cit., xii and 276; Ymbert, op. cit., 3 and also Outrey, *L'Administration française des Affaires Étrangères,* 39.

112 De Tocqueville, op.cit., 44–5. Cf. Gillis, op. cit., 351, and es-

pecially J. Baecheler, *Les Phénomènes révolutionnaires* (1970), 249.

[113] Senac de Meilhan, *Du gouvernement, des mœurs et des conditions en France avant la Révolution* (London, 1795), 92–3, and also Lamy, loc. cit., on the efficacity of Ancien Régime administration, while the opposite view, that the administration was fundamentally inefficient, is urged by Lindgreen in Tilly, op cit., 560.

NOTES TO CHAPTER III

[1] R. C. Cobb, *Reactions to the French Revolution* (Oxford, 1972), 139.

[2] A good example of the relative lack of interest shown in this aspect of the Revolution is its total omission from the items discussed in the Encylopoche Larousse volume by J.-P. Bertaud *et al.*, on *La Révolution française* (1976). Cf. also A. Soboul (ed.) *Voies Nouvelles pour l'histoire de la Révolution Française* (1978).

[3] In other words where the administration is concerned there is no real case for accepting Furet and Richet's theory of the 'dérapage de la révolution'. The war brought new dimension to the Revolution, but the bureaucracy emerged only because, as a result of events and ideas earlier in the Revolution, the political nation was determined to fight and win it. Similarly the logic of the growth of the bureaucracy and the way it was treated owes much to preceeding phases.

[4] G. Ferrero, *Les Deux Révolutions françaises* (Neuchâtel, 1951), 18. On the background to the Year II see A. Soboul, *Les Sans-Culottes parisiens en l'an II* (1959), and, more generally, M. Bouloiseau, *La République jacobin* (1972).

[5] M. Pertué, 'Les Luttes de Classe', *AHRF*, xlix/3 (1977), 459 which argues the case for the revolutionary government as being from the very beginning aimed equally at *enragés* and sans-culottes as well as against 'aristocracy' at home and abroad, rather than merely being influenced by the former as is more often suggested, e.g. by Bertaud, op. cit., 35, 44–5, and 155. In this sense it may be true that direct democracy can be a check on bureaucracy, Jakoby, *Bureaucratization*, 184–5, but in fact the logic of their ideas probably pointed in the other direction.

[6] Petot, *Histoire de l'administration des Ponts et Chaussées*, 368. For the opposition to bureaucracy see Bouloiseau, op. cit., 218–20 and Hampson, *The Life and Opinions*, 168.

[7] *AN*, AF II 24 (196) f. 20 of 25 Floréal II.

[8] De Tocqueville, *Ancien Régime et Révolution*, 18–19. Cf. also M. Vovelle in G. Duby (ed.) *Histoire de la France* (1971), ii, 311.

[9] *AHG*, Pensions civiles: Pourrin père: a clerk born in 1730 who had joined the War Office in 1757 only to have his salary cut.

He returned in 1793, after a brief exclusion under Pache, to a senior position in the Veterans bureau. Slower re-establishments were those of A. N. Rochon (I,72), a former writing-master to the pages of the Comte d'Artois, who began a twenty-nine-year career in the *équipages* bureau in February 1793 and J. H. Willemenot. The latter lost his place in the Hospitals bureau in 1788 but in 1793 was taken on by the *Agence de l'habillement* in its Metz office, which was to prove a stepping-stone to eventual reinstatement in the Ministry proper. Cf. the état of Vendémiaire VI in AF III 28 (96).

[10] P. Caron (ed.), *La Commission des subsistances de l'an II: Procès-Verbaux et actes* (1924), xii.

[11] *AN*, F^{1b1} 280^3 for Treuil, and 282^1 for a similar case in Vaillant, an employee of the old Conseil du Roi who also retired as a *Chef de Bureau* in the Interior in 1815 after periods in the Ministry of Justice and in the Commission des administrations civiles as a financial controller. That clerks were not allowed to live off the fat of the land is shown by the Commission de l'instruction publique's treatment of a *Teneur des registres* called Alliot who had to choose between his own job and that of his wife so that they did not claim two ration books in the family in Nivôse III. F^{17A} 101 2 (dossier 6) s.n.

[12] Cobb, op. cit., 7 and 14. For the difference between revolutions in 'traditional' societies like eighteenth-century France and those in 'technological' societies, see K. Kumar, *Revolution. The Theory and Practice of a European Idea* (1971), 81–6. The quotation comes from J. C. Perrot, 'L'Âge d'or de la statistique régionale', *AHRF*, xlviii/2 (1976), 237. R. B. Jones, *Napoleon, Man and Myth* (1977), is even more reserved and feels that the Comité de salut public failed to produce a centralized bureaucracy, a somewhat individual judgement.

[13] Recent studies of revolution include Dunn, *Modern Revolutions*, esp. 18; J. Monnerot, *Sociologie de la Révolution* (1969), and P. Calvert, *Revolution* (1970), 18. On the relationship of revolution to bureaucratization, see *inter al.* J. Baecheler, *Les Phénomènes révolutionnaires* 173–4, and D. Waldo, 'Public Administration in an age of revolution', *Public Administration Review*, xxviii (1968), 366–7. Weber's position can be found in Merton, *Reader in Bureaucracy*, 18, and 25.

[14] E. Kamenka, in 'Revolution', ed. C. J. Friedrich, being *Nomos*, viii (New York, 1966), 130; the opposite point of view is put by Kumar, op. cit., 40–1.

[15] The relationship between the process of revolution and the process of bureaucratization in France is further examined in a paper presented to a colloquium at the University of Bamberg in June 1979 on the 'Révolution française. Evénément nécessaire ou contingent' (forthcoming).

[16] L. P. Edwards, *The Natural History of Revolution* (New York, 1927, and recently reprinted), 107.

[17] For another example of this argument see Church, 'Bureaucracy, Politics and Revolution', 514–16. Cf. also O. Kircheimer, 'Confining Conditions and revolutionary breakthroughs', *American Political Science Review*, lix (1965), 964 et seq., and D. Warnotte, 'Bureaucratie et fonctionnairisme', *Revue de l'Institut de Sociologie*, xvii (1937), 219.

[18] On the ministries in general see Racinet, *De la spécialisation ministerielle*, 102–14, and for the Ministry of Justice Durand-Barthez, *Histoire des structures*, 16–18. On the Interior compare *AN*, F^{11} 1 (2), 'Ministre au Roi, 26 Octobre 1791' with Bernardin, op. cit., 209.

[19] *BL*, R 565 has further details of ministerial staffing in 1792–3, from which this can be deduced.

[20] For a further discussion of this point see below, pp. 387–9. *AN*, F^{1b1} 2 (Dossier 6), 'Composition des bureaux' indicates that the Interior lost its élite personnel like Étienne after 10 August. Cf. also the decrees of 14–18 January 1792; 25 March 1792, 5–8 July 1792, and 23–5 July 1792.

[21] Goyard in *Les Épurations administratives*, 5–7. Cf. also Kessler 'Historique de systeme', *Revue français d'administration publique*, i/1 (1977), 11–12.

[22] P. Caron, 'Conseil exécutif provisoire et pouvoir ministériel 1792–4', *AHRF*, xiv (1937), 11.

[23] Cf. the laws and decrees of 5–7 August 1792, 10 August 1792, 15–23 August 1792, 27 August 1792, 2 September 1792, 3–14 September 1792, 26–28 September 1792, 10–14 October 1792, and 25–28 December 1792.

[24] 'Rapport sur l'inéligibilité temporaire de quelques fonctionnaires, 16 juillet 1792' in *AN*, AD^{1} 31. Cf. also A. F. Artaud de Montor, *Histoire de la vie et des travaux politiques du Comte d'Hauterive* (1839), which stresses the importance of security of tenure and career prospects as a means of motivating the administration in the thinking of a leading Napoleonic *fonctionnaire*.

[25] The constitution is printed in L. Duguit, H. Monnier, and R. Bonnard, with G. Berlia (eds.), *Les Constitutions et principales lois politiques de la France*, 7th ed. (1952), 33–61.

[26] Caron, op. cit., 6–7, and 10–14, and Olive, *L'Action exécutif*, 76–85.

[27] The laws and decrees of 5–6 and 14 February 1793; 5, 14, and 28 March 1793; 4, 14, and 29 May 1793 all dealt with ministers and officials. Cf. also Bernardin, *J. M. Roland*, 190–9.

[28] Pertué, op. cit., 458.

[29] Barère, quoted in Tersen, *Origne et évolution*, 59 et seq. and also in *BL*, FR 97/27. Cf. also Gen. Herlaut, *Le Colonel Bouchotte, ministre de la*

guerre en l'an II (1946), i, 24–44.

³⁰ A. Patrick, *The Men of the First French Republic* (Baltimore, 1972), 135, and 296–7.

³¹ The background to the enquiry is discussed by Herlaut, op. cit., i, 53–4, and Bosher, *French Finances*, 295, while the sources are the printed returns to the enquiry: *AN*, AD 1 78 (Interior); BB⁸ 273 (Navy); BB³⁰ 512¹ (Justice); F³⁰ 112 (Finance), and AD 1 77 (War). These, however, need to be supplemented by the manuscript returns of the Sixth Division of the Ministry of War (*AHG*, Xˢ 115) and more importantly for the Ministry of Foreign Affairs, where no return was apparently ever drawn up, by earlier *états* and secondary material.

³² For the Ministry of Foreign Affairs, which then had about 95 clerks, see Masson, *Le Départment des affaires étrangères*, 179–304, and for the other ministries, in addition to the *Almanachs nationaux* and the other sources already mentioned, Duchêne, *La Politique coloniale*, 112–37, for the French Admiralty, which had some 200 clerks; *AHG*, Xˢ 3 (Dossier I) for the War Office with 410 clerks; and more generally Godechot, *Les Institutions* 2nd ed., 356 et seq.

³³ On the Interior, with about 170 clerks, see the lists in *BL*, R 565 and Tersen, op. cit., 55–9; on Justice with about 145, *AN*, BB⁴ 7 and Durand-Barthez, op. cit., 18–22; and on the Finance Ministry, M. Marion, *Histoire financière de la France* (1921), ii, 123–30, and Bosher, loc. cit., for the 180 clerks in the department.

³⁴ The documentation is limited and somewhat different from that in other samples. When analysed in detail elsewhere it revealed results not very different from those provided in the major sample under the Directory. Hence few statistics have been included here. Of those, however, for whom a date of birth was given (817), 77.1 per cent were under 19; 13.2 per cent were between 25 and 29; 16.1 per cent between 30 and 34; 12.8 per cent between 35 and 39; 14.7 per cent between 40 and 44; 6.5 per cent between 45 and 49; 7.8 per cent between 50 and 54; 4.4 per cent between 55 and 59; and 3.8 per cent over 60.

³⁵ Out of a sample of 1,053 whose date of entry is known 13.14 per cent entered the ministries before 1779 (and 56 per cent of a sample of 114 from the Ministère des contributions publiques alone entered state administrative service of all kinds before then); 6.1 per cent between 1780 and 1784; 6 per cent between 1785 and 1789; 0.95 per cent in 1789; 0.86 per cent between January and June 1790; 0.77 per cent between July and December 1790; 5.24 per cent between January and June 1791; 11.9 per cent between July and December 1791; 8 per cent between January and August 1792; 23.9 per cent between August and December 1792 and 23.14 per cent between January and early August 1793. The figures for the smaller sample from Contributions

publiques show a very different pattern, with nobody joining state service as a whole for the first time after August 1792, compared with 13.46 per cent between 1789 and August 1792 and 34.6 per cent between 1780 and 1789.

[36] Out of a sample of 689 the largest concentrations were in Lepeletier (61 or 8.9 per cent), Butte des Moulins (57), Picques (54), Mont Blanc (45) Tuileries (33), Mail (31), République (28), and Halle aux Bléds (26), all near to the main administrative complexes.

[37] J. Caritey, 'Note sur le personnel des ministères en 1793' *RA*, xiii (1960), 24–7. Cf. also Herlaut, op. cit., i, 44, and Bernardin, op cit., 212–13.

[38] G. Walter, *La Conjuration du neuf Thermidor* (1974), 83–6, claims that the Comité de sûreté générale recruited wherever possible from waiters, lackeys, and journalists, so that resultant administrative chaos was used by Robespierre as an excuse for creating his own *bureau de police générale*. Carnot was accused of peopling his bureaux with royalists and 'gentlemen'. (55) A fuller exemplification of the argument advanced here is to be found in a forthcoming contribution to *AHRF* by the present author on 'Quelques aspects de la bureaucratie ministérielle et son role à travers la Révolution Française'.

[39] *AN*, F^{17} 1045, Dossier 15, 'Mathieu (RDP), Président du Commission temporaire des arts, au Commissaire, 24 Germinal II'.

[40] *AHG*, Pensions civiles i, 9: Bocher; i, 43 Hervet; and for Chovot the *état* of *an VI* in AF III 28 (196).

[41] The pressure was maintained both in the Ministry of War (Herlaut, op. cit., i, 49–53 and 79) and more generally through a number of decrees. Against this one must set the fact that the decree of 9 April 1793 allowed *représentants en mission* to appoint as many agents as they liked (cf. J. Hall Stewart, *A Documentary Survey of the French Revolution* (Cleveland, 1956), 425), while those of 9 and 11 September 1793 gave officials some freedom from arrest by the Paris police and also allowed the ministers a free hand in the choice of agents to be sent to the armies. As to action on the *enquête*, it is just possible that a committee was set up to watch the bureaux, but the evidence is thin and unconvincing. In any case, it is obvious that, if it did exist, the committee did absolutely nothing. (See note 61 below.)

[42] Quoted in W. Markov and A. Soboul (eds.), *Die Sans-Culotten von Paris* (East Berlin, 1957), 96. Cf. also ibid. 15–16, 38, 84, and 88 for further examples of *sans-culotte* feelings about the administration.

[43] Godechot, *Les Constitutions de la France*, 79–92. For an interesting prohibition of pluralism see *AD*, Seine-et-Marne, L 118, 'Lettre du Ministre de l'Intérieur, 18 juin 1793'.

[44] Soboul, op. cit., 194–201, and, on the more general development of the revolutionary government, his *Précis historique de la Révolution*

française (1962), 281 et seq.

⁴⁵ Compare the criticisms directed against *réprésentants en mission* for the waste of money and other resources caused by their proliferation of employees in *AN*, C 356 (1888), 'Mesure économique à employer dans plusieurs administrations' *c*.an III.

⁴⁶ Walter, op. cit., 32, quotes Barère, however, as admitting that most of the Committee's business involving diplomacy and the navy was prepared for it by the appropriate ministerial bureau, and that on education by the Comité de l'instruction publique, although on p. 55 he also shows that Carnot did create a shadow ministry of war. J. P. Gros, *St. Just. Sa politique et ses missions* (1976), 61–5, emphasizes the role of his subject.

⁴⁷ The basic laws of the revolutionary government can be found in Hall Stewart, op cit., 424–525. The loi 14 Frimaire an II, Section 5, article viii, refers specifically to subaltern agents of government as having 'aucun caractère public', while Billaud-Varennes's article appears in *BL*, F 1107/9. Cf. also Walter, op cit., 73.

⁴⁸ The limitations of the revolutionary government are well brought out by Cobb, op cit., 7 and 68–70, and C. Lucas, *The Structure of the Terror etc.* (Oxford, 1972), 142–4.

⁴⁰ *AN*, F^{lbl} 2 (Dossier an II) details the growth of a special auxiliary bureau to deal with the administration of welfare funds; AF, II 24 (192), Arrêté 2 Pluviôse II, gives the rights of the Commission des subsistances et des approvisionments to negotiate contracts, and F^{17A} 101/2 (Dossier an II) shows the use of ministerial clerks as secretaries to deputies. Cf. also A. Bovier La Pierre, *Les Employés de préfecture et de sous préfecture* (Nancy, 1912), 177–80.

⁵⁰ *AN*, AF II 24 (196), f 21 (pp. 21–2), together with (192) f 50; and (193) f 10 and f 11.

⁵¹ *AN*, AF II 23^a contains the lists of personnel etc. from which the following section is drawn, along with AF III 7 which has the early minutes of the committee. Cf. also Walter, op. cit., 16–21.

⁵² F. A. Aulard (ed.), *Recueil des actes du comité de salut public* (1889), i, vi, 80, 89, 375, and 589, contains decisions on the directorship while a minute, in Robespierre's hand, of late July 1793, lays down the qualities necessary in a holder of the post (*AN,* AF II 23a, (180), f. 13). Neither G. Bourgin, 'Quelques lettres de St. Cyr Nugues à Julien de Paris', *ARHF*, xv (1938), 453–8, nor G. Six, *Dictionnaire des généraux et amiraix de la Révolution et de l'Empire* (1934–5), seem to have been aware of his role, while M. Bouloiseau, *Le Comité de salut public* (1962), 38–44, has little to say of either Nugues or the bureaux in general. He is wrong to date the change of structure of the latter to the autumn of 1793 rather than to the spring of 1794. A clerk in the Instruction publique commission, one Publicola Chaussard, a 'man of letters'

born in 1766, claimed at Thermidor to have been Director General of the Committee's bureaux but this seems unlikely (*AN*, AF II 24 (197) f. 11).

[53] *AN*, AF* II 284 contains a good deal of information on the Comité de sûreté générale to supplement that in the unreliable G. Belloni, *Le Comité de sûreté générale* (1928).

[54] *AN*, D*XXV[a-c] 5 includes information on other committees, while Petot, op. cit., 362–8, provides an example of how one committee, that of Travaux publics, worked. Cf. Walter, op. cit., 16–21 and 86 on relations with other committees.

[55] A. Ording, 'Le Bureau de Police du comité de salut public' in *Skifter Ulgitt av Videnkaps Akademi i Oslo* (Oslo, 1930), Gros, op. cit., 357–61, and M. Eude, 'Le Comité de Sûreté Générale de la Convention', in J. Aubert *et al. L'État et sa police en France (1789–1914)'* (Geneva, 1979), 13–25. Cf. also Soboul, *Les Sans-Culottes*, 1031–4, for the degeneration of the popular revolutionary dynamic as a result of the 'emploeomania' denounced by Saint-Just.

[56] *AN*, AF II 24 (192), f. 11 of 2 Germinal II, on the authority and activity of agents in the field and f. 32, on the decision of 3 Prairial II to create *surveillants*, which was reversed on 2 Frucidor. Cf. also F[lbl] 2 (Dossier an II), on the complications involved in trying to reduce the size of the welfare bureau.

[57] Ording, op. cit., 10–17; Caron, 'Conseil exécutif provisoire', 14; A. Mathiez, 'Le Dictature économique du comité de salut public', *Annales révolutionnaires*, xvi (1923), 463–5, and P. Mautouchet, *Le Gouvernement révolutionnaire* (1933), 33, discuss some of the preliminaries to the creation of the Executive Commissions, the motivations for and results of which were interestingly analysed by L'Hôte, the Secretary to the District of Porrentruy, in Ventôse III; *AN*, C 356 (1888).

[58] In the spring of 1794 the ministries seem to have had nearly 3,000 staff (though L'Hôte, loc. cit., claimed only 1,100) with about 1,800 in the War Office, 300 in the naval department, 275 in that of Contributions, 250 in the Interior, 200 in Justice, and 125 in Foreign Affairs. Estimated for the commissions, both later in Year II and midway through Year III, deriving from *AN*, C 355–6, are as follows:

1.	Administrations civiles, police, et tribunaux	102	134
2.	Instruction publique	101	168
3.	Agriculture et des arts	70?	386?
4.	Commerce et approvisionnements	77	97
5.	Travaux publics	196	271
6.	Secours publics	90	150?
7.	Transports militaires, postes, et messageries etc.	90	440
8.	Revenus nationaux	300	400?

9. Organisation et mouvement des armées de terre	331	450?
10. Marine et colonies	200	300?
11. Armes, poudres, et exploitation des mines	100	500
12. Relations extérieures	93	154?
	1,750	3,500

In addition there were a large number of agencies which were very closely attached to come of the commissions, and which may by the Year II have employed a further 3,000 and more staff. Certainly by Year III they accounted for up to 7,000, including 900 in the *Agènce des loix*, 1,400 in the *Approvisionnements* services, 2,250 in the Treasury and other financial bodies, and rather more than this in the Transport and Postal services.

[59] *AN*, F^{1a} 1 f. 60 and AF II 24, (196) f. 5; (196) f. 24 and (197) ff. 4 and 8. The quotation comes from F^{1b1} 2 (Dossier, Personnel an III), memorandum of 22 Germinal from Herman.

[60] Details of the internal organization of the executive commissions etc. can often be found in the same archival locations, and also in the *Almanachs nationaux*. Some examples are given by Berthaut, *Les Ingénieurs-géographes*, i, 127–34, Herlaut, op. cit., ii, 306–9, and Berthaud, op cit., 138–9.

[61] C. Jones, 'The Welfare of the French Foot Soldier', *History*, lxv/2 (1980), 207–8 and Godechot, *Les Institutions*, 2nd ed., 353–74 provide same information on a subject often ignored and misattributed as by Blondel (in Charlton, *France*, 580).

[62] The nature of the control exercised by the Comité de Salut Public stands out very clearly from the missives filed in *AHG*, 'Organisation du Ministère', Cartons hors série, i. The administrative basis of its control is usefully discussed by A. Cochin and C. Charpentier, *Les Actes du gouvernment révolutionnaire* (1920), x, xiv, and xxvii–xxxi. The *arrêté* of 28 Prairial II, forbidding employees of one administration to correspond directly with those in another body without prior permission from their superior is in *AHG*, X^S 115 (an II).

[63] P. Bessand-Massenet, *De Robespierre à Bonaparte* (1970), 113, estimates that 30,000 new jobs were created by the Terror, while Cobb puts it as high as 150,000 in 'Social Mobility', *Past and Present*, 32 (1965), 8. The evidence of *AN*, C 355–6 suggests that there were about 11,500 posts in Paris in 1794–5, while a list in F^{1b1} 105–6 gives a figure of 9,000 for Paris in early 1796 (see note 57 to Chapter IV). Extrapolation from evidence on the Haute-Marne suggests that there could have been over 250,000 officials in the country as a whole by 1799 although the extrapolation is of doubtful logic. See a forthcoming article by the present author in *Les Cahiers Haut-Marnais* on

'L'Appareil étatique dans l'Haute Marne à la fin du Directoire'.

[64] J. and R. Lacour-Gayet, *De Platon à la terreur* (1948), 249.

[65] *AN*, AF II 24 (193), f. 15: 'Arrêté du 21 Thermidor an II'.

[66] *AN*, AF II 24 (196), f. 23. 'Commission des transports et convois militaires'. Cf. ibid., f. 21 p. 5 for similar use of the rank of *Secrétaire de Correspondance* to denote the positive role his employees played. Similarly he wished to revise salary scales so as to reward legal qualifications and expertise.

[67] *AN*, F^{1b1} 11–14 and M. J. Guilliaume (ed.), *Les Procès-verbaux du comité de l'instruction publique* (1921), esp. ii, 219–31, on Grandjean himself, while *AN*, F^{17} 1045, and F^{17A} 1012 (Dossier 4/5), provide many examples of his work. F^{17} 1032/33, Dossier 3, shows ministerial initiatives in the same field.

[68] *AN*, F^{1a} 4 'Comité de législation au Ministère, 21 Frimaire II' on the formulary and, for details of working procedures, AF II 24 (196) f. 4 and f. 15.

[69] The *Revenus Nationaux* 'Ordre du Travail' comes from *AN*, F^{1a} 1 f. 1.

[70] Further details on *surveillants* can be found in Masson, op. cit., 318–19 and 331 for those in External Relations. For decrees such as those of 23 Ventôse, 7–10 Floréal, 13 Prairial, and 3 Thermidor II see *inter al.*, *AHG*, X^s 115 (an II). The quotation is from Bessand-Massenet, loc. cit., while for attacks on the bureaucracy see H. Meister, *Souvenirs de mon dernier voyage à Paris*, ed. P. Usteri and E. Ritter, (1910), 110–12, and L. S. Mercier, *Le Nouveau Paris* (1862), vi, 261.

[71] *AN*, AF II 24 (192) f. 23–30.

[72] The usual view is that advanced by Soboul, *Précis historique*, 345, and D. Guerin, 'D'une nouvelle interpretation' *AESC*, xx (1965), 89–90, but contemporaries saw other reasons, e.g. Lacuée, quoted in Marion, *Histoire financière*, iii, 123. Cf. also W. F. Shepard, *Price Control and the Reign of Terror* (Berkely, Cal., 1953), 25–8, and R. C. Cobb, *Terreur et subsistances* (1965), 66–78, and 154–7.

[73] Quoted in the *Moniteur*, 147 (27 Pluviose II), 466–7. One possible example of political militancy is provided by the careers of Claude and Arsène Thiébault from the *Meurthe*. The former began life as a local government clerk until his radical views led to his dismissal. He than embarked on a new career as a neo-Jacobin journalist in Nancy. At one stage, in 1789, his information on events and opinions in Paris was being allegedly supplied by his son Arsène who was then supposedly employed in the War Office, according to J. Jalounieux, 'Le Journal de la Meurthe de 1798 à 1830', unpublished *thèse en droit* Université de Nancy II (1974), 22–40. Unfortunately, Thiébault *jeune* has left no trace in the files of the War Office though there was a man

of this name in the Interior from Messidor V to Messidor VII who held a very junior post in the Minister's private bureau. Cf. also J. L. Chalmel's denunciation of the *Commission de l'instruction publique* under Garat and Ginguené, included in vol. 24 of the *Rowan Tracts*, John Rylands University Library, Manchester, though this must be set against things like the example of entry by examination given by Caron, *Commission des subsistances*, xxxviii–xxxix.

[74] *AN*, AF II (197) f. 19 for the Commission des administrations civiles, Police et Tribunaux, and F^{1bl} 11–14 for that of Instruction publique.

[75] *AN*, F^{17A} 1012 (6), and AF II 24 (194) f.1 on the decree of 8 Vendémiaire III and its working. Cf. also Guilliaume, loc. cit., on Clément de Ris.

[76] Herlaut, op. cit., ii, 80–100 and 179 et seq. Cf. also Godechot, op. cit., 357, and Soboul, *Les Sans-Culottes*, 847–50. Bouchette is quoted in the *Papiers inédits trouvés chez Robespierre*, collection Berville et Barrière (1828), iii, 332–3.

[77] On Lejeune se A. Bégris (ed.), *Curiosités révolutionnaires: St. Just et les bureaux de la Police Générale au comité de salut public en 1794. Notice historique par A. Lejeune* (1896), esp., 1–4. On La Bussière see N. J. Lienart (ed.), *Charles, ou Mémoires historiques de M. de la Bussière* (1804), ii, 107–9, and W. R. H. Trowbridge, *A Whoreson, Mad Fellow* (1933), 126–63. The stories can be checked against the evidence of Ording, op. cit., Gros, loc. cit., and *AN*, AF II 23^a. A similar case is that of J. G. P. Morice discussed by H. de Broc in 'Un témoin de la Révolution à Paris', *Revue des questions historiques*, lii (1892), 454–73.

[78] Legendre, *Histoire de l'Administration*, 45–6. The figures for the Ministry of War, which are drawn from *AN*, AD 77, AF III 28, and AF III 171 etc., can be compared with those given in Mousnier, *Le Conseil du Roi*, 23, and Bosher, op. cit., 283–6 and 311. See also Chapter VII.

[79] On Thermidor see G. Walter, op. cit.; M. Lyons, 'The Ninth of Thermidor, Motives and Effects', v (1975), 123–46; K. Tonnesson, *La Défaite des sans-culottes mouvement populaire et réaction bourgeoise en l'an III* (Paris/Oslo, 1959), and, more generally, G. Lefèbvre, *Les Thermidoriens* (1951).

[80] P. Gaxotte, *Le Directoire* (1957), 23–4, claimed that Thermidor was a direct attack on 'la bureaucratie socialisante' but in fact one can find Robespierre before the *coup* saying much the same kind of thing about the administration as the Thermidorians were to do. It was the latter, moreover, who actually abolished the inspectors of the bureaux. None the less, the decrees of 9 Thermidor, 15 Thermidor, and 19 Fructidor II (*AN*, F^{1bl} 11–14 and AF II 24 (193) f. 12) did request that a picture of the organization of the executive commissions

should be prepared for the new regime. They also led to a purge in the military commissions. The general problems of government after the *coup* are explored by F. A. Aulard, 'Le Régime politique après le 9 Thermidor', *La Révolution francaise*, xix (1900), 7–21, and Church, 'Du nouveau sur les orignes de la constitution de 1795', *RHDFE*, liii (1974), 38–71. Cf. on the theoretical implications of Thermidor for bureaucracy, M. N. Hagopian, *The Phenomenon of Revolution* (New York, 1975), 229–31.

[81] The controls are exemplified in *AHG*, X^s 148 (I) by Pille's 'ampliation de l'arrêté du 9 Frimaire' and possibly by the creation of a committee of surveillance. In the index to the Convention's proceedings (G. Lefèbvre, M. Reinhard, and M. Bouloiseau *et al.* (eds.) *Procès-verbaux des séances de la Convention Nationale: Tableau analytique* (1959), i, 289, and 455) there is mention of a 'Comité de la surveillance active des bureaux' which was requested to draft a bill to ensure that 'les citoyens soient entendus dans les bureaux' but the reference is vague and contradictory. On page 455 the date of 23 Vendémiaire III is given (and the minutes of that session do, on p. 149 show that a motion to this effect was passed after a 'défenseur de la patrie' had complained of being refused a hearing) but the implication there is that this was an *ad hoc* gathering of all bodies responsible for supervising executive commissions etc., presumably under the terms of the law of 7 Fructidor II. A little lower down there is reference to a Comité des agences exécutives being entrusted with the same task on 23 Ventôse III. Although neither the date not the page reference given in the second entry yields anything in the actual minutes of the Convention, there is still the possibility that there was a committee of enquiry set up after Thermidor or, less likely but not impossible since no evidence on the actual establishment of the committee whatever it was is given, after the *enquête* of 1793.

[82] For other changes see Buisson, *La Police*, 160–1, and Berthaut, op. cit., i, 146–8. The decline of the External Relations department is documented in *AAE*, France 518, no. 91 f. 107 as well as in Masson, op. cit., 149–51.

[83] On the expansion of the government after Thermidor, see E. and J. Goncourt, *Histoire de la société française sous le Directoire* (1896), 185–6, and E. Desgranges, *La Centralisation républicaine sous le Directoire* (Poitiers, 1954), 16. G. Lefèbvre's claim, op. cit., 48, that the bureaux were now peopled with men of the right must be set against the belief of A. Danican, *Notice sur le 13 Vendémiaire ou les parisiens vengés* (1796), 84, and 101 that they were inhabited solely by terrorists. For what actually happened see Shepard, p. cit., 96–7, and Tonnesson, op. cit., 104. The *Moniteur* in question is 353 (25 Fructidor II), 1.

[84] The essential source for the history of this attack is Thibaudeau's

Mémoires (1824) but cf. also Mautouchet, op. cit., 283 et seq. and the more recent, but rather less up-to-date, study of M. Sydenham, *The First French Republic* (1974), 49–50. On local government see Lapierre, op. cit., 180–2.

⁸⁵ Church loc. cit., which is interestingly reviewed and expanded by J. R. Suratteau in *AHRF*, xlix/1 (1977) 151–3, which offers useful chronological, political, and prosopographical analyses of the movement for constitutional reform. Cf. also L. Gershoy, *Bertrand Barère, reluctant terrorist* (Princeton, NJ, 1962), 264–72, and 287–8.

⁸⁶ The decrees of 13 Brumaire III, 4 Frimaire III, 11 and 18 Nivôse III, 4 Pluviôse, and 1 and 5 Ventôse III all relate to the bureaux and those of 4 Pluviôse and 1 Ventôse, esp. *Procès-verbaux de la Convention Nationale*, liv, 57–60, and lvii, 6, were basic in establishing the right of the committees of the Convention to decide on the cost and the establishment of various public agencies, a right which it was hoped would lead to the drawing-up of a central register of employees and officials.

⁸⁷ The view of Formialhe of Cadillac (Gironde) on 20 Floréal III in *AN*, C 227 (183 bis 3/2) no. 75. Cf. also nos. 57 and 72 in ibid.; in C 228 (183 bis 4/1) no 5; (185 bis 5/1) no 6; in C 229 (193 bis 6/1) no 6; in C 231 (183 bis 11/3) no 126 and in C 232 (183 bis 13) no 7.

⁸⁸ *AN*, AF II 23ᵃ (182) f. 75; AF II 23ᵇ (185) f. 51 and (190) f. 54 detail changes inside the Comité de salut public. At the end it had eight sections (AF II 191e f. 62): Secrétariat, with 33 staff plus 37 couriers; Ier Division: War, with 110; IIe Division: Navy, with 10; IIIe Divison: Arms and Gunpowder, with 36, IVe Division: Food Supplies, with 131; Ve Division: Correspondance with administrative authorities, with 25; VIe Division: External Relations, with 55 and VIIe Division: Information, with 65. Cf. Belloni, op. cit., 114–49.

⁸⁹ This was the opinion of the writer of a memorandum of 29 Nivôse III, 'Des idées générales sur les rapports entre les comités de la Convention et les Commissions', in *AN*, C536 (1888).

⁹⁰ The law of 29 Prairial III (*Bulletin des Lois* 157, no. 922) and the Comité des Finances *arrêté* of 2 Messidor III (*AN*, AD XVIII E 231) in amplification of the law were the nearest to a *statut des fonctionnaires* so far achieved by the Revolution, although the law of 4 Pluviôse was the first really general act on the civil service. For the application of these acts at the local level see *AD*, Haute-Marne, L* 106, 30 Messidor III, and A. de Giradot, *Des administrations départmentales électives et collectives, 1790 à l'an VIII* (1857), 236–7 and 245.

⁹¹ Hostility to employees is shown both by the way those in the military construction park in Brienne were illegally refused a vote in Fructidor III (*AN*, C 229 (193 bis 7/3, no 103) and by the continuing series of penal decrees on the civil service, for instance on 7 Prairial

III, 15 Vendémaire IV, and 1 and 4 Brumaire IV. On the separation of administrative and civil jurisdication in this period see G. Deville, 'Thermidor et Directoire', *Histoire socialiste de la Révolution française* (1904), v–vi, 169, and Bénoit, *Le Droit administratif français*, 280–4.

[92] The rising of 13 Vendémaiaire and the subsequent Commission des dix-sept is also discussed below and in Church, 'Bureaucracy, Politics and Revolution', loc. cit.

[93] *AN*, C 227 (183 bis 3/3 no 117): 'Enguehard à la Commission des Onze', *c*.13 Prairial III.

[94] Edwards, op. cit., 189–94.

[95] N. Hampson, *Social History of the French Revolution* (1963), 215.

NOTES TO CHAPTER IV

[1] For the background to the Directorial era see G. Lefèbvre, *La France sous le Directoire*, new ed. by J. Suratteau (1979), and J. Godechot, *La Vie quotidienne en France sous le Directoire* (1977). Also D. Woronoff, *La République bourgeoise* who, at 8 and 52, argues a similar case to that advanced here, as does Sautel, *Histoire des institutions publiques*, 225–7, whereas Thuillier and Tulard, in *Problèmes et méthodes*, 108, take the contrary view.

[2] Godechot, op. cit., 97.

[3] P. M. Blau, in O. Grusky and G. A. Miller (eds.), *The Sociology of Organizations: Basic Studies* (New York, 1970), 176–7.

[4] Church, 'The Organisation and Personnel of French Central Government under the Directory 1795–99', unpublished doctoral thesis of the University of London (1963), 48–9 and 165. Cf. also Bosher, *French Finances*, 317, and J. C. Perrot, 'L'Âge d'or', 231.

[5] On the desire for a return to normality see Church, 'In search of the Directory', esp. 285–6. J. Tulard, *Napoléon ou le mythe du sauveur*, 2nd ed. (1977), 111–12, and also G. Homans, *Jean-François Reubell* etc., (The Hague, 1971), 113, deal with the problems of the Directory. For useful discussions of some of the problems of the aftermath of revolution, see A. Decoufle, *La Sociologie des révolutions* (1970), 108–11, and J. Rule and C. Tilly, '1830 and the Unnatural History of Revolution', *Journal of Social Issues*, xxviii (1972), 55.

[6] The historiography of the Directory is reviewed in Church, loc. cit., although this now needs to be supplemented by J. R. Suratteau, 'Le Directoire d'après des travaux récents', *AHRF*, xlviii/2 (1976), 181–214, which deals with more recent interpretations. This, together with a review in ibid., 1973, 615–19, also queries the argument advanced here, although at one point at least this is taken to be the opposite of what it actually is (201). Cf. also Soboul, *Voies Nouvelles*.

[7] Suratteau in 'Le Directoire d'après des travaux récents' has

rejected this interpretation of the Directory as a political élite, on pp. 209–14, arguing that the 'revolutionary bourgeoisie'—elsewhere confusingly described as 'la petite bourgeoisie dirigeante'—was responsible for the constitution of the Year III, a draft which reflected both the middle-class ideals of the Enlightenment and the conservative views of property, and which moreover was made in a period which saw the emergence of a new capitalist society. Even though the criticism has come more to grips with the original thesis in *AHRF*, xlix/1 (1977), 149–51, it still seems to miss much of the original point. Neither the essentially middle-class nature of the constitution nor the changes in social structure were ever in question. What was questioned was the intention behind them. Suratteau prefers to see the drafting as a reflection of a pre-existing middle-class dominance. The evidence points to an attempt by politicians, with their own interests, to buy support by offering this dominance. In the event they failed to secure it because of the clash between their politics and those of the bourgeoisie. Not to accept this makes a nonsense of the whole history of the Directory which is thus made to end with the bouregeoisie abandoning their very own regime for a Bonapartist unknown. Even when revised as by Bertaud, *La Révolution française*, 195, this fails to convince. As Edward Whitcomb, in an unpublished paper, 'Left, Right and Centre: the Politics of the Directory', points out, this view leaves unresolved the dichotomy between a regime composed apparently 'new' bourgeoisie in which the political élite was inherited from the past. In fact Whitcomb's analysis of elections shows that the belief in 'new men' cannot easily be sustained. On the other hand, the lack of fit between the political élite and the centrist middle-class constituency it sought to attract does seem to be upheld. Cf. Lefèbvre op. cit., 796 et seq. and Godechot, *AHRF* lii/2 (1980), 308.

⁸ On the Directory's lack of support see A. Ollivier, *Le Dix-huit Brumaire* (1961), 28, and Church, op. cit., 272–3 and 279–80. Cf. also J. R. Suratteau, *Les Élections de l'an VI et le coup d'état du 22 Floréal* (1971), 452; I. Woloch, *Jacobin Legacy* (Princeton, NJ, 1970), 29–30 and 188, and C. Zaghi, 'Dalla Democrazia direttoriale all'autoritarismo consolare', *Rassegna Storica del Risorgimento*, liii (1966), 6–9 and 12–14 for aspects of Directorial politics.

⁹ C. Lucas, 'The First Directory and the Rule of Law', *FHS*, x/2 (1977), 231–60, would add to these problems both the very constraints of the legalistic system of government and the need to rely at the crucial local level on the people it had to convince of its impartiality and its authority. His stress on legality as a cause of the Directory's problems is at variance with Suratteau's view, 'Le Directoire d'après des travaux récents', 183. Cf. Hunt *et al.*, *JMH* 1979/4, 734–49.

[10] A good example of this is Bertaud, op. cit., 178. Cf. Godechot, *La vie quotidienne,* 7–9.

[11] On the general denigration of the Directory see M. Reinhard, *La France du Directoire* (1956), i, 4–5, and M. Lyons, *France under the Directory* (1975), 1–2. Its reforms are conveniently discussed in G. Pariset, *L'Administration, les affaires et le pays sous le Directoire* (Strasburg, 1929), while its relative greater efficacity in administration at the expense of politics is documented by P. Clemendot, *Le Département de la Meurthe à l'époque du Directoire* (Laxou, Meurthe-et-Moselle, 1966), 502; Lyons, op. cit., 160–74; Suratteau, op. cit., 206–8, and Sydenham, *The First French Republic,* 85–92.

[12] Necker is quoted in Legendre, *Histoire de l'administration,* 499, and Pelet de la Lozère in *Moniteur,* 156 (6 Ventôse IV), 528. Cf. also F. Furet and D. Richet, *La Révolution française: de Thermidor à Brumaire* (1966), ii, 245 and 259.

[13] Printed in J. Hall Stewart, *A Documentary Survey of the French Revolution,* (Cleveland, Ohio, 1965), 655–6.

[14] Woloch, op. cit., 187–8. Cf. also C. Durand, *Les Études sur les rapports entre la loi et le règlement gouvernmental au XIXe siècle* (Aix, 1976), 14–30, on the use made by the Directory of its power to issue *arrêtés.* The Directory did not restrict its activity to subjects on which there was a specific law. Goyard, in P. Gerbod *et al., Les Épurations administratives XIX–XXe siècles* (Geneva, 1977), 5, notes that the constitution allowed the Directory to dismiss officials, provided there were reasons given for the dismissal.

[15] The text of the constitution can be found in Godechot, *Les Constitutions,* 100–41, while the reasons for its drafting are rediscussed in Church, 'Du nouveau sur la constitution de 1795'. Say is quoted in J. Kitchin, *La Décade, journal philosophique* (1966), 42–3.

[16] R. David d'Angers (ed.), *Mémoires de La Revellière-Lépaux* (1895), i, 328; G. Duruy (ed.), *Mémoires du Barras,* (1895), ii, 350, and for the state of the ministries, C. de Montigny Turpin, *Grands épisodes inédits et causes de la politique* etc. (1852), 192, on the War Office under Scherer; and P. Bonnassieux, *L'Administration d'un département sous le Directoire* (1996), 19–20, on the Interior under François de Neufchâteau.

[17] *AHG,* Mémoires 2015 no. 35, 'Dubois-Crancé à Courtin, Chef de la Cinquième Division', 4 Vendémiaire an VIII. Cf. on the political activity of the ministries, Suratteau, *Les Élections de l'an VI,* 314–19, and 438, who in fact is unaware of the ministerial employment of some of the Directory's electoral agents. See below, note 44.

[18] Homans, *Jean-François Reubell,* 132.

[19] On this classic middle-class belief in the efficacity of 'niggling economies' see D. M. Young, *The Colonial Office in the Early Nineteenth*

Century (1961), 7, and Reinhold Bendix in Merton, *Reader in Bureaucracy*, 127–8.

20 The sources for this discussion are basically, for the Directory, A. C. Debidour (ed.), *Recueil des actes du Directoire exécutif* (1910–17), e.g. i, 31, 107, 143, 209–10, 243, 309, 358, 434, 453, 494, 598, and 611, and for the Councils, the *Moniteur*, e.g. 66 (6 Frimaire IV), 264; 90 (1 Nivôse IV0, 360; 97 (7 Nivôse IV), 385; and 166 (16 Ventôse IV), 660. Cf. also *AN*, F^{1b1} 3^2 'Ministre de l'Intéreur au Commissaire de la Seine', 24 Pluviôse IV.

21 Debidour, op. cit., i, 665, and ii, 20, together with *Moniteur*, 186 (6 Germinal IV), 743.

22 The following sections draws largely on *AN*, F^{11} 1181 which contains a set of detailed statistics on the provision of subsidized food to civil servants and others in an IV, a problem further discussed in Chapter VII below. Cf. Debidour, op cit., ii, 34, 171, 268, 428, 529, 536, 613, 649, and 759.

23 Ibid., ii, 767–8, and iii, 37, 56, and 66, together with the *Moniteur* 277 (7 Messidor IV), 1104; 304 (4 Thermidor IV) 1215; 306 (6 Thermidor IV), 1222; 311 (11 Thermidor IV), 1244; 322 (22 Thermidor IV), 1287, and 326 (26 Thermidor IV), 1303.

24 Ibid. 95 (5 Nivôse V), 380, together with Debidour, op. cit. iii, 105, 278–9, and 326, and iv, 34, 93–4, 126–7, 350, 478, 551, 572, 744, and 754–5.

25 Suratteau, 'Le Directoire d'après des travaux récents', 192–6, places great stress on the return to coin as a cause ofcontinuing economic and social fragility in France, a point echoed by Godechot, op. cit., 70, 97, and 132.

26 Debidour, op. cit., 113, 325–6, and 710, and ii, 62 and 722–3, together with the *Moniteur* 97 (7 Nivôse IV) 385, and 107 (17 Nivôse IV), 426.

27 Debidour, op. cit., i, 21, 107, 217, 292–3, 311, 627, 668, and 800; iii, 544 and 555, and iv, 5–7 and 92–4. Thereafter, since Debidour is incomplete, reference has to be made to the manuscript registers of Directorial decisions, e.g. *AN*, AF* III 6 (29 Ventôse V); cf. also *AN*, AF* III 157 (27 Pluviôse V), 175 (6 Vendémiaire V), 181 (12 Nivôse V), and 202 ff. 128 and 145, together with *AHG*, X^s 148 (iii) 'Règlement du 13 Nivôse V'.

28 Debidour, op cit., i, 105, 112, 222, 500, and 835–6; ii, 367; iii, 74–5 and 248–9, and iv, 19–22, 100–2, and 433.

29 *Moniteur*, 193 (13 Germinal V), 773; 203 (22 Germinal V), 810 et seq.; 211 (1 Floréal V), pp. 845–6; 230 (20 Floréal V), 921; 270 (25 Prairial V), 1081; 282 (2 Messidor V), 1113; 301 (21 Messidor V), 1163 and 305 (25 Messidor V), 1179. Cf. also *AN*, AF* III 7 and 8 for

the sittings of 7, 15, and 17 Messidor, 15 Prairial, and 18 Thermidor V.

30 *Mémoires de la Revellière-Lépaux*, ii, 402.

31 Woloch, op. cit., 40–56, and Sydenham, op. cit., 125–7.

32 A. Soboul, *Le Directoire et le Consulat* (1967), 41.

33 *Moniteur*, 203 (22 Germinal V), 810.

34 Woloch, op. cit., 76–9, and Homans, op. cit., 117–26.

35 F. A. Aulard (ed.), *Paris sous la réaction thermidorienne et pendant le Directoire* (1901), iv, 352, and *La Clef du cabinet des souverains de l'Europe* for 9 Vendémiaire VI.

36 The returns are to found in *AN*, AF III 29 (99) and show the Interior with 262 clerks, Police with168, War with 473, Finance 251, and Justice with 197. The figures for the two remaining ministries, External Relations and the Navy, have to be deduced from other sources and would seem to have been 94 and 250 respectively. For the legislation on the enquiry *AN*, AF* III 8, 1 complémentaire V; 9 for 16, 18, and 28 Vendémiaire; 12 for 23 Fructidor VI, and 13 for 5 Vendémiaire VIII.

37 On the 'Cabinet' see the reports in *AN*, AF* III 220 (110–1) and *AHG* 'Dépôt Général IV', 30 Vendémiaire VI. Mollien's case is documented in AF* III 175, of 12 of 15 Brumaire VI and Masson, *Le Département des Affaires Étrangères*, 417, while the situation in the Interior was discussed by a 'rapport au ministre' of 23 Fructidor V in *AN*, F^{1b1} 11–14. On the Ministry of Police see F^7 12250.

38 Lucas, op. cit., 260.

39 *AHG*, X^s 148 'Rapport au Directoire', 13 Vendémiaire VI. Cf. also *AN*, AF* 11, minutes of 16 Brumaire VI and *Le Sage Observateur* for 10 Brumaire VI.

40 Church, 'Organization and Personnel', 97–8.

41 For Roux's report on the idea of a new ministry see *BL*, FR 98/47 and the *Moniteur*, 80 (20 Frimaire VI), 321–2, and 123 (3 Pluviôse VI), 495–6.

42 Marion, *Histoire financière* (1922), iv, 82–6. Cf. also Deville, *Thermidor et Directoire*, 151–69.

43 Woloch, op. cit., 83, 102–3, and 232–3 and Suratteau, *Les Élections*, 297 and 447–50.

44 Ibid., 186–7, 314–23, 438, and 450. It has proved possible by using the personnel dossiers of the Ministry of Interior to identify more of the agents used as employees of the Ministry, for instance: Antoine François Letellier, Augustin Jean Morel, Jean Baptiste Charles Lecomte, Étienne Morel, and, from other departments, possibly Philippe Louis Ortalle and Alexande Lenoir.

45 Ibid., 312, 438, 446, and 450–1, and for a critique of Suratteau's figures, Woloch, op. cit., 310, and Whitcomb, loc. cit.

⁴⁶ Cf. Cacault in *BL*, FR 98/46, and more generally the *Moniteur*, 286 (12 Messidor VI), 1128 and 153 (3 Ventôse VII), 627–8, together with the Directorial minutes in *AN*, AF* III 11, 12 Germinal VI; 12, 5 Messidor VI, 4 and 6 Thermidor VI, and 14 Fructidor VI; 13, 24, and 29 Vendémiaire VII and 2 Frimaire VII; 14, 8 Pluviôse VII and 8 Ventôse VII, and 15, 7 Germinal VII. The laws of 16 Fructidor can be found in the *Bulletin des Lois* 2e series, an VI, 197–8, and Hall Stewart, op. cit., 738, respectively.

⁴⁷ In the *Anciens* on 25 Floréal, quoted in the *Moniteur*, 240 (30 Floreal VII), 977. Cf. also Woloch, op. cit., 363–8.

⁴⁸ Church, 'In Search of the Directory', 254 and 275. Cf. also A. Meynier, *Les Coups d'état du Directoire* (1928), ii, 202–30.

⁴⁹ *Moniteur*, 303 (3 Thermidor VII), 1233–4 and 304 (4 Thermidor VII), 1238. Cf. also *AN*, AF* III 16 which shows that after 30 Prairial the Presidents of the Directory never signed its minutes while, according to a report by the Minister of War on 2 Fructidor VII, the resentment of the administration at the new deductions being imposed on this pay was deliberating slowing down its work rate, a move which succeeded in forcing the Directory to change its policy. On the *Commissaires* of the Directory, see *AN*, AF* III 168.

⁵⁰ *Moniteur*, 289 (20 Messidor VII), 1178; 290 (21 Messidor VII), 1180–1, 325 (25 Thermidor VII), 1322; and 337 (7 Fructidor VII), 1369. The quotation from Levallois is to be found in nos. 289–90 while for Quinette see *BL*, FR 551/14 and R 565/33, 112.

⁵¹ The changes which took place in the political composition of the bureaux are mentioned in Aulard, op. cit., v, 628 and 688. Cf. also *BL*, FR 553, and Woloch, op. cit., 375–6. The Directory's requests for *états* can be found in *AN*, AF* III 13, minutes for 17 Brumaire VII, while Dubois-Crancé's ideas can be found both in *AHG*, Mémoires 2015 no. 35 and in his *Analyse de la Révolution française depuis l'ouverture des États Généraux* etc. (1885), 207–21 and 263–4. In the latter he claimed that because jobs had been created for men, and not vice versa, the War Office was complex, corrupt, and uncontrollable, so that he had to purge half its staff and simplify its organization by creating three large divisions together with new Inspections and organs of control.

⁵² *AN*, AF* III 16, Directorial minutes of 12 Thermidor and 12 Fructidor VII. Cf. also *BL*, FR 551/15, 3–4; 553/22, 1–2 and 553/47, 16.

⁵³ Furet and Richet, op. cit., 302–5 and 318–21; J. Cain (ed.), *Nouvelle Histoire, de la France* (1967), xxiii, 2883–6, and Tulard op. cit., 108. Boulay de la Meurthe is quoted in P. Bessand-Massenet, *La France après la Terreur* (1946), 259.

⁵⁴ Petot, *Histoire de l'administration des Ponts et Chaussées*, 403.

⁵⁵ Aulard, op. cit., ii, 688.

[56] Duchêne, *La Politique coloniale*, 138–407, and Petot, op. cit., 385–9.

[57] Church, 'Organisation and Personnel', 116, 127–8, 135, 144–5, and 163–5. The statistics on the Ministry of Police make a very useful sample, since it was a wholly Directorial creation, and are drawn from *AN,* F^7 12249–50. On the size of the state civil service in late 1796 see *AN,* F^{1b1} 105/6 which contains an estimate which by rights would seem to belong in F^{1b1} 123 to judge from the inventories.

[58] *AN,* AF III 137 (654) for cuts in the *Direction générale de la liquidation* and J. R. Suratteau, *Le Département de Mont Terrible* (Paris–Besançon, 1965), 72–3 and 591–2 for those in local government.

[59] Homans, op. cit., 100.

[60] M. Chemillier-Gendreau in J. Sallois (ed.), *L'Administration* (1974), 182, and Sandevoir, *Études sur le recours*, 131–7 and 144–9.

[61] Legendre, *Histoire de l'administration*, 483–4.

[62] Tourdes, 'Une étude de sociologie historique', 24, sees a growing awareness of the administrative problems involved in implementing educational policy in 1798, although he attributes this to personal insight rather than to administrative continuity.

[63] Compare the attitudes of both La Revellière, op. cit., 178, and Crassous, in the *Moniteur*, 277 (1 Messidor IV), 1104–5, with those of Saint-Just or other men of the Year II whose attitudes are redolent of those which R. C. Day and R. L. Hamblin ('Some effects of close and punitive supervision', *American Journal of Sociology*, 1964, 499) call self-defeatingly punitive.

[64] Bosher, *French Finances*, 292–4. For the opposing view Deville, op. cit., 169, and, more recently, Soboul, op. cit., 24. Contemporary accounts of political motivations are conveniently to hand in Aulard, op. cit., ii, 574, 590, 593, and 647; iv, 7 and 262; and v, 628.

[65] *AN,* BB^8 (Marine) 277, 'Rapport au Directoire du 1 Brumaire III'.

[66] On corruption see Artuad de Montour, *Histoire de la vie . . . du Comte d'Hauterive*, 79–81; E. Wilson-Lyon, 'The French Directory and the United States', *American Historical Review*, xliii (1938), 529, and C. Oman, *The Lyons Mail* (1945), 3–5. The political autonomy of the bureaucracy at this stage is asserted by Strauss, *The Ruling Servants*, 188, whereas C. C. Brinton, *A Decade of Revolution 1789–99* (New York, 1934), 222, and Legendre, op. cit., 371–6, offer more balanced verdicts.

[67] A. Meininger, 'D'Hauterive et la formation des diplomates', *Revue d'histoire diplomatique*, lxxxix/1–2 (1975), 30, and Perrot, op. cit., 238–40, give two more specific examples of the consular debt to Directorial administration.

[68] Lucas, op. cit., 231–3.

[69] G. Trausch, *La Répression des soulèvements paysans de 1798 dans le département des Fôrets* (Luxembourg, 1967), 18, 31, 170, and 193, and F. Boyer, 'Le Directoire et les musées des départements réunis de la Belgique', *Revue d'histoire diplomatique*, lxxv/1 (1971), 5–16. Cf. also M. Reinhard, *Le Département de la Sarthe* (Saint-Brieuc, 1936), 637.

[70] Church, 'In search of the Directory', 284, Godechot, op. cit., 257 and J. Popkin, *The Right Wing Press in France* (Durham, NC, 1980), 173.

NOTES TO CHAPTER V

[1] A. Darbel and D. Schnapper, *Le Système administratif* (The Hague, 1972), 20, imply that the ignorance also extends to contemporary structures.

[2] H. Simon, in Merton, *Reader in Bureaucracy*, 53.

[3] This is contrary to the view expressed by C. Pouthas in 'La Réorganisation du Ministère de l'Intérieur et la reconstitution de l'administration préfectorale par Guizot en 1830', *RHMC*, ix (1962), 242–4.

[4] Darbel and Schnapper, op. cit., 54–9.

[5] Ibid., 65–7, and F. Bloch-Lainé, *Profession: Fonctionnaire* (1976), 249.

[6] R. J. S. Baker, *Administrative Theory and Public Administration* (1972), 142.

[7] Cf. *AN*, F^{1b1} 105/6 and AF III 28, (169) and (171) for details of some of the agencies in question. No complete list is available, even in the *Almanachs nationaux*.

[8] The information on the Haute-Marne is drawn from documents in the departmental archives at Choignes near Chaumont, notably L474. For a fuller discussion see below, note 48, and especially the forthcoming article in *Les Cahiers Haut-Marnais* by the present author.

[9] Cf. the unpublished *Diplôme des études supérieures, mémoire* of P. Wagret, 'Les Services auxiliaires à l'armée de Sambre et Meuse en l'an II', Université de Paris (1945). On *Régies* and private enterprise see Woronoff, *La République bourgeoise*, 18 and 79, and Dubois-Crancé, *Analyse de la Révolution français*, 199–202.

[10] Baker, op. cit., 160–2.

[11] The estimation of 50,000 *fonctionnaires* and at least 15,000 employees is that of F. d'Ivernois, *Histoire de l'administration des finances* (London, 1797), 122. See also the discussion in 'Social Mobility' in *Past and Present*, 32 (1965), 3–11.

[12] Louis IV de Phélypeaux, Marquis de la Vrillière, was the Secretary to the Regency Council according to the *Recueil général des anciennes lois françaises* (1830), xxii, 38, while the article of the loi 27 Mai 1791 (cf. *Loix et actes du Gouvernement* (1806), iii, 231) deals with

the establishment of the new government Secretariat. On the latter see also J. Godechot, 'Mémoires inédites de Dejoly', 189–382, and, for a more critical view, C. F. D. Dumouriez, *La Vie et les mémoires du Général Dumouriez* (Berville et Barrière, 1823), iii, 354–5. The only detailed survey of the Directorial Secretariat is that in Church, 'Organisation and Personnel', pp. 180 et seq., but reference can also be made to Debidour, *Recueil des actes*, i, 16–17; R. Guyot, *Le Directoire et la Paix de l'Europe* (1911), 49–51; A. Mathiez, *Le Directoire, de Brumaire an IV à Fructidor an V*, ed. J. Godechot (1934), 57–60; M. Reinhard, *Le Grand Carnot* (1952), ii, 168–71, and *La France du Directoire*, ii, 107–9, and Furet and Richet, *De Thermidor à Brumaire*, 90–1. The later history and role of such bodies is discussed in G. Belorgey, *Le Gouvernement et l'administration de la France* (1970), 109–11.

[13] Godechot, *Les Constitutions*, 101–41. The sources for the following section are to be found AF III 20[a], 20[b], 21[d], 28, and 29.

[14] *Mémoires de Barras*, ii, 8. Cf. also *Mémoires de la Revellière-Lépaux*, i, 346–7; J. P. Fabre de l'Aude, *Histoire secrète du Directoire* (1832), 95–106, and *Le Courrier universel* of 5 Messidor VII for estimates of Lagarde's standing. Account of his career can be found in A. Arnault *et al.*, *Biographie nouvelle des contemporains* (1920–5), x, 297–8; L. G. Michaud *et al.*, *Biographie universelle, Supplément* (1834–60), lxix, 428, and T. L'Huillier, *Un Préfet de Seine-et-Marne* (Melun, 1877), but not in Van Berkel, 'Recherches sur le centralisme français', despite his alleged role in the Nord.

[15] Lagarde's thinking is detailed in documents in *AN*, AF IV 1326[b]. Cf. also La Revellière, op. cit., i, 359–60, and Guyot, op. cit., 51.

[16] La Revellière, loc. cit., and for the quotation, G. Dejoint, *La Politique économique du Directoire* (1951), 58. Cf. also *AN*, AF* III 29, for 5 and 10 Floréal V; AF III 55 (213 I), 'Mémoire sur la bureau diplomatique'; and AF III 21d (75), 'Rapport sur la réorganisation des bureaux'.

[17] Barras, op. cit., ii, 479, said that in Messidor V the Directory considered the abolition of the *Secrétariat Général* as a whole, although the Directors would, had this been done, have relied even more on their private secretaries.

[18] *AN*, AF III 21[d], 'Note concernant le bureau militaire', and AF III 152[a], 'Avis du Bureau Militaire'. Cf. also Guyot, op. cit., 71–5, on the Directory's diplomatic bureau.

[19] Woloch, *Jacobin Legacy*, 289–90, and, amongst earlier writers: Aulard, *Histoire politique*, 609 et seq., L. Sciout, *Le Directoire* (1895), i, 453–4, and Mathiez, op. cit., 356–74. Cf. also *BN*, Nouvelles Acquisitions françaises 23642, f. 9, and L. Stoll, *The Bureau Politique and the management of the Popular Press* (Ann Arbor, Mich., 1975).

[20] P. du Verdier, J. Favier, and R. Mathieu (eds.), *Inventaire générale de la Série AF IV* (1968), i, and also the fleeting verdict of Fain cited in J. Massin (ed.), *Napoléon Bonaparte, l'œuvre et l'histoire* (1971), viii, 549.

[21] Dejoint, loc. cit., and for a fuller account of ministerial structures and the changes they underwent during the Directorial era, Church, op. cit., 107–65.

[22] *AHG*, X^s 148 (V), 'Observations d'un Commission du Conseil des Cinq Cents'; X^s 148 (3), 'Règlement du 13 Nivôse V', and generally X^s 115, with *AN*, AF III 144a, 'Compte Rendu du Thermidor V'; AF III 146 (689), 'Tableau de l'organisation' and AF III 202 (128, of 20 Fructidor IV.

[23] The Basic sources for this aspect of military administration are in the four 'Dépôt Général' cartons in the *AHG*, but cf. also Berthaut, *Les Ingénieurs-geographes militaires*, esp. i, 144–58, and E. Titeux, *Le Général Dupont* (1903), i, 56–7.

[24] Debidour, op. cit., i, 11, 15, 21, 26, 31, 214, 293, and 595. Cf. also *AN*, AD I 78, 'Ordre du Travail du 2 Thermidor II', and more generally, F^{1b1} 1, 3 and 3^2.

[25] Pouthas, loc. cit.

[26] Basic sources are in *AN*, F^7 12249 and 12253, but see also Buisson, *La Police*, 162–5, nd J. A. Lebrun-Tossa, *Portefeuille politique d'un ex-employé au Ministère de la Police* (1800), 68–9. On its creation see, *inter alia; Moniteur* 103 (13 Nivôse IV), 408; 104 (14 Nivôse IV), 414, and 107 (17 Nivôse IV), 426–7, together with Aulard, *Paris sous la réaction thermidorienne*, iv, 352 and 712.

[27] The main sources are *AN*, BB^4 1, and 9, and BB^{30} 512. Cf. also Debidor, op. cit., i, 31, 63, and 303; Durand-Barthez, *Histoire des structures*, 27–35, and Darbel and Schnapper, op. cit., 66–7.

[28] *AN*, AF III 29 (100), 'Compte Rendu du 23 Brumaire IV', and also AF III 28/9, (114) f. 532 and AF* III 181 f. 82.

[29] The basic sources for this are to be found in *AN*, AF III 52/55 but see also *AAE*, France 518, nos. 91 f. 107, and Masson, op. cit., 380–6, 406–8, and 431.

[30] The main sources are in *AN*, BB^8 (Marine), together with the *Comptes Rendus, ans VI–VIII* (1801–2).

[31] Bosher, *French Finances*, 248–52 and 270–2. There seem to have been no studies of the other central organs though something of their structures can be deduced from the *Almanachs nationaux*.

[32] Cf., the frontispiece to Church, op. cit., which, again drawing on the *Almanachs*, shows that the Ministry of Marine was already in the Place de la Concorde and the Ministry of Justice in the Place Vendôme. The Ministry of Finance was mainly in the Rue Neuve des Petit Champs, the Ministry of External Relations at the corner of the Rue du Bac, the Interior in the Rue de Grenelle, where the War Office was

also to be found, and finally, the Secretariat-General was in the Luxembourg, and the Police Ministry on the Quai Malaquet.

[33] Darbel and Schnapper, op. cit., 41 and 69 et. seq. Cf. also F. De Baecque, *L'Administration centrale de la France* (1973), 234–89, together with F. F. Ridley and J. Blondel, *Public Administration in France*, 2nd ed. (1967), 55–84, and Belorgey, op. cit., 91–8, on micro-structural patterns.

[34] *Moniteur*, 102 (12 April 1791), 421.

[35] *AN*, AD I 78, 'Ordre du Travail du Ministère de l'Intérieur, 2 Thermidor VI', for the formal picture and F 1017 (4): T. Mandar, 'Mémoire au Ministère de la Justice', 2 Thermidor VII, for an insight into the realities of the situation.

[36] *AN*, 138 AP 2 (Dossier de l'an V), 'Lettre au Ministre', s.d. The writer is happy to thank Mme la Comtesse Daru for kindly allowing him to consult the *Papiers Daru* in the Archives Nationales. For further information on Daru's administrative activities see H. de la Barre de Nanteuil, *Le Comte Daru ou l'administration militaire sous la Révolution et l'Empire* (1966), 61–75.

[37] *AHG*, 'Dépôt Général', i, 'Attributions du Ministère, Brumaire V'. Cf. also Robiquet (Interior, *AN*, F^{1b1} 278^3); Horville (Navy, *AHM*, C^7 I) and Maas (Secretariat, *AN*, AF III 20^a).

[38] *AN*, AF III 29 (100), 'Attributions des bureaux du Ministère des Finances, an IV' and 'Compte Rendu au Directoire par le Ministre des Finances sur l'administration de son département pendant l'an V', Thermidor VII.

[39] On the routines of the bureaux see Bernadin, *Jean-Marie Roland*, 219–38; Parker, 'Two Administrative Bureaux under the Directory and Napoleon', 153–8 and 164–7, and *AN*, F^7 3006 (Dossier an V), 'Aperçu Raisonné', and F^{18} 10^A (1) Dossier IV, ff. 12–14, 40, and 46.

[40] *AN*, F^{18} 10^A (2), F^{17} 1018 and *AHG* X^s 148 for examples of formularies. Cf. also Thuillier, *Témoins de l'administration*, 25.

[41] E. and J. Goncourt, *Histoire de la société française*, 187–8.

[42] H. Roseveare, *The Treasury, the evolution of a British Institution* (1970), 156, and J. G. Ymbert, *Mœurs administratives* (1825), i, 185–6, and ii, 193–4, offer interesting comparisons of working conditions.

[43] *AN*, AD I 78, 'Compte Rendu', cited above, note 38.

[44] On present-day services Belorgey, op. cit., 307–20. There is virtually no discussion of field services in Godechot, *Les Institutions*, even of those like the *Douanes*, which employed thousands of people. Cf. M. Marion, *Dictionnaire des institutions de la France aux XVIIe et XVIIIe siècles* (1923), 12, 183, 202, 234, 250, 380, 443, and 447 for some monarchial precedents.

[45] Ridley and Blondel, op. cit., 109–13.

[46] Reinhard, *La France du Directoire*, i, 82, and ii, 90, and for a local

example, Clemendot, *Le Département de la Meurthe*, 129–31.

⁴⁷ Woronoff, op. cit., 112–16.

⁴⁸ *AD*, Haute-Marne, L 474, 'Contribution de Retenue, an VII', and other sources show that, in addition to·1,000 *Agents Communaux* and their *Adjoints*, there were amongst paid technical personnel 308 *Gardes Forestières*, 167 *percepteurs*, 108 *gendarmes*, 101 *Gardes Champêtres*, 98 primary schoolteachers, 85 secretaries to cantons and the like, 72 *Juges de Paix*, 70 *Greffiers* to the *Juges*, 69 *Commissaires*, 33 members and clerks in the departmental administration, 27 *Agents Forestières*, 26 employees of the Agence des Contributions Directes, 22 employees in each of both the Domaines and the Droits d'enregistrement, 21 in the Civil Court, 20 *magasiniers*, 15 staff in the Criminal and Correctional Courts, 14 *préposés aux subsistances*, 14 in the Ponts et Chaussées, 12 cantonal *piétons*, 12 directors of posts, 11 roadmenders, 10 *concierges*, 10 professors in the Ecole Centrale, 9 *gardes de barrières*, 8 clerks in local Bureaux Militaire, 6 assorted fiscal employees, 5 drummers, 3 miscellaneous military officials, 1 health officer, and 100 or so unidentified personnel making a total of 2,500. This has to be set against a population of at least 226,000 which suggest one state official to every ninety inhabitants. Of these the teachers, *concierges*, and field guards etc. count as local sevice personnel. Cf. also Cobb, *Reactions to the French Revolution*, 290, and Woronoff, op. cit., 223, on the intensity of government at this time.

⁴⁹ *AD*, Haute-Marne, L 472, 'Lettre du Ministre des Finances aux Commissaires', of Frimaire VI, and *AD*, Indre-et-Loire, L 83, f. 125, of 29 Frimaire VI.

⁵⁰ On local government and technical services see Sautel, *Histoire des institutions publiques*, 276–80 et seq., and G. Dawson, *L'Évolution des structures*, 49–50.

⁵¹ The cantonal system has been favourably appraised by A. Metin, *La Révolution et l'autonomie locale* (Toulouse, 1905), 27, and J. Morange, *L'Idée de municipalité de canton de l'an III à nos jours* (1971). For local examples see Reinhard, *Le Département de la Sarthe*, 155–68, and G. Lameire, *Les Municipalités de canton sous le Directoire* (Lyon, 1941), 159–60.

⁵² The financial problem is discussed in *AN*, F ¹ᵃ 22 (Dossier de l'an IV), 'Ministre de l'Intérieur à l'Administration Centrale de l'Haute Marne'. On Paris see J. Tulard, *Paris et son administration 1800–1830* (1976), 57–68.

⁵³ Much evidence on the Directorial *commissaires* can be found in *AN*, AF* III 168, and F ¹ᵇ¹ 103 and 122. Cf. also E. Desgranges, *La Centralisation républicaine sous le Directoire* (Poitiers, 1954), 4–6.

⁵⁴ Quoted in Reinhard, op. cit., 168–9. The clerk who ensured his payment in kind was Virey in the Canton of Hortes during the Year

VI (*AD, Haute-Marne*, L* 109, 6 Thermidor VI). Details of the size of clerical establishments come from *ADs*, ibid., L 234–5, 375, L* 106, 110, and 474; Indre-et-Loire, L 83 and L^m 277; Haute-Vienne, L 236; Creuse, L* 33, and Allier, L 206, ff. 30–6. Cf. also Suratteau, *Le Mont Terrible*, 71–3, and, for the economic crisis, F. Vermale, 'La Cherté de la vie en province', *Annales révolutionnaires*, vi (1913), 375–82, and *AN*, F^1b1 82, 'Ministre de l'Intérieur au Directoire', 3 Prairial IV.

55 Examples of such 'Ordres du Travail' can be found in *AD*, Creuse, L* 33, f. 108, of 25 Brumaire IV; Indre, L 14 f. 82 of 25 Brumaire V; and Haute-Marne, L* 109, of 9 Prairial VI. On Secretaries-General see *ADs*, Nièvre, L 48–50; Allier, L 64 no. 125 f. 36 and Clemendot, op. cit., 167–8.

56 There is little discussion of this in Godechot, *Les Institutions*, 469–70, but Dawson, op. cit., 180–217, and J. Siwek-Pouydesseau in B. Gournay *et. al., L'Administration publique* (1967), 115–206, do pay some attention to it, albeit in a more modern context. The references here are to the Haute-Marne and are from *AD*, L 474, L* 111, of 25 Germinal VII; L* 109, 22 Floréal VI and 6 Prairial VI; and L* 107, 28 and 30 Nivôse IV.

57 Woloch, op. cit., 188–9. The claim that the Directory had no control over such people, which is made by Mme C. Kollefrath-Lapart, 'Les Modalités de l'organisation et de l'activité du Ministère de l'Intérieur sous le Directoire', *Mémoire:* for the *Diplôme des études supérieures*, Université de Paris II (1977), is not substantiated by the sources, primary and secondary, which the author claims to have read. As has been pointed out elsewhere, the study is not to be taken seriously.

58 *AN*, F^1CIII (Haute-Marne) 5, 'J. N. Laloy au Ministre de l'Intérieur, 8 Vendémiaire VII'. Cf. also Suratteau, op. cit., 975–84. The quotation I owe to a former student, Mr David Breckon; it comes from *AD*, Corrèze, L 126 f. 55, 'Administration Centrale au Ministre de l'Intérieur', 11 Frimaire V.

59 Baker, op. cit., 145.

60 Darbel and Schnapper, op. cit., 59.

NOTES TO CHAPTER VI

1 Sheriff, 'Public Bureaucracies', 71, discusses the value of the study of career patterns to an understanding of bureaucracy.

2 An earlier version of parts of this and the following chapter has previously appeared in print as 'The Social Basis of the French Central Bureaucracy under the Directory', *Past and Present*, 36 (1967), 59–72. For a modern comparison see J. Siwek-Poudysseau, *Les Personnels des administrations centrales* (1969).

[3] Compare the reaction of Delaquelle to administrative *esprit de corps* in 1795, cited in Church, 'Bureaucracy, Politics and Revolution', 500–1.

[4] In the preface to J. Pappalardo, *Étude sociologique d'un centre de tri* (1969), which is one of the few studies to concern itself with the lower ranks of the civil service. These are, for example, totally ignored by Armstrong, whose *European Administrative Élite* (Princeton, NJ, 1973), raises questions one cannot really hope to answer about the people who made the role of *haut fonctionnaires* possible, for instance where their ideologies are concerned.

[5] For a discussion of the sources see the bibliography. The numbers recovered for each department are: Interior: 977; Justice: 405; Finance: 417; Police: 612; External Relations: 274; War: 854; Marine: 552, and Secretariat-General 249, making 4,340 in all. It was on the basis of this enquiry that the questions later posed in the computer programme used in the Ministry of War samples were developed. Since the sources on which this present enquiry are based are different from those in the Ministry of War, and especially since the sample there was constructed on much more selective lines than the earlier enquiry, which both covered a different time-span and aimed at being as exhaustive as possible, it would be unwise to submit the original materials to computer analysis. A broadly similar decision was made in the case of the 1793 enquiry.

[6] Goncourt, *Histoire de la société française*, 185–7, and more recently Woronoff, *La République bourgeoise*, 51. The quotation is from J. Tulard, *La Préfecture de Police sous la Monarchie de Juillet* (1964), 19, while for the rewards to be obtained from genealogical research see G. Aylmer, *The King's Servants. The Civil Service of Charles I* (1961), 255.

[7] *AN*, F[11] 1182, 'lettre du P. M. L. Decaisne', and for a more vigorous defence of this position a letter from Corqueur to the Minister of Police on 1 Prairial IV in F[7] 3009 (II).

[8] Cobb, 'Quelques conséquences sociales de la Révolution' in *Terreur et subsistances*, 159–78. For the motives of deputies and others see the various series of 'Demandes des Places' in *AN*, AF III 309 (1214), F[1b1] 3[1], and F[7] 3009–10.

[9] R. K. Merton, *Social Theory and Social Structure* (Glencoe, Ill., 1957), 197 and 214; A. Diamant, in Siffin, *Towards the Comparative Study of Public Administration*, 193–4, and Crozier, *The Bureaucratic Phenomenon*, 208.

[10] C. Tranchant, *De la préparation aux services publics en France* (1878).

[11] Cf. the laws of 4–11 August 1789, 30 November 1791–26in the Ministry of Justice are documented by the *arrêté* of 5 Nivôse VI in *AN*, BB[4] 1. For a typical republican view on appointments see *Les Nouvelles Politiques* 54 (24 Brumaire IV), 215–16.

[12] A. Prost, *Histoire de l'enseignement en France, 1800–1967* (1968), 225, and A. G. Bellin, *Des avantages du concours* (1846). Compare, for the Ancien Régime, Mousnier, *Institutions*, 552–8.

[13] Cf. the laws of 13 July 1789, 3–22 August 1790, and 27 September, 16 October 1791 on the obligations of officials, to be compared with those of 19 Fructidor V, and 23 Fructidor VI on the norms to be followed, and that of 21 Ventôse IX allowing partial protection against the seizure of public salaries in case of debt.

[14] For two conflicting examples see *AHM*, C[7] Série ii, Dossiers: Dargé and Bertrand-Dupré. The former began his career at fourteen only to discover later that his first two years of service were not pensionable while the latter was ejected in 1795 because at seventeen he was deemed too young. He was soon recalled by the Directory because of abilities and his contacts. By the time of the July Monarchy only service after one's twentieth birthday was allowable.

[15] One slightly unusual case is Adrien Marie Blin Saint-Moore, the son of a well-known writer (see Darnton in *Past and Present*, 51), born in 1776 and dismissed as an economy measure in 1796 and again in 1799 for failure to do his military service. He was able, however, to obtain a new post in the Theatre bureau of the Ministry of the Interior before returning to the War Office from 1800 to 1817 (*AHG*, Pensions civiles, i, 9). For even more frequent entries and exits see ibid., i, 18, Champallier, and i, 25, Delangle. None the less, such attempts to secure employment were very different from the attitude to office enshrined in venality. Roles for Directorial clerks were neither permanent nor detachable from the place they held. See Jacques, *General Theory*, 31.

[16] Cf. the laws of 9 April–12 September 1791, 4 November 1791, and 22 Pluviôse VII, together with *AN*, BB[4] (Justice), i, 'Douet d'Arcq au Ministre', s.d.

[17] H. Parris, *Constitutional Bureaucracy* (1968), 31, and A. Lefas, *L'État et le fonctionnaire* (1913), 213 et seq.

[18] Church, 'Social Basis', 62 and 69. Cf. also Dagnaud, 'L'Administration centrale de la Marine', 44–7 for the *règlement* of 1785.

[19] *AHG*, X[s] 115, 'Aperçu Sommaire de la Composition de Ministère' (1776–1870), and Balzac, *Les Employés*, 87. For the example of the grading system developed by the Comité de Salut Public by Brumaire IV see *AN*, AF II 23b, (191E) f. 62. The loi 4 Pluviôse III divided staff into ten categories according to their monthly salaries while the *arrêtés* of Messidor classified staff according to rank and the size of the commune in which they worked.

[20] The *arrêté* of 17 Frimaire IV recognized as class one employees 12,000 francs in *assignats* per month), *Chefs de division* and Secretaries-General, as class two (7,500 francs) *Chefs de bureau*, as class three

(5,000 francs) *Sous-chefs*, and as class four (3,000 francs) all other employees, Cf. also *AN*, BB[4] (Justice), 275, F[7] 3006 and 12249.

[21] The sources for this discussion are, *inter alia, AN*, BB4 (Justice) 1; F[7] 3006 and 12249, F[1b1] 6; AF III 29 (99) 52/55, and BB[8] (Marine) 275. The nearest contemporary scheme to that adopted here is that of the Ministry of Justice in 1799–1800 (cf. AF III 39). The division according to the modern categories A, B, C, D would probably be A = I, II, III; B = III, IV, V, VI; C = VI, VII, VIII, and D = IX, X, although there was then no educational basis for entry as with the modern system. Cf. also Balzac, op. cit., 87–94, and Pappalardo, op. cit., 125–35. The comparison of naval grades with those in other ministries comes from *AN* BB[8] (Marine), 275 (Dossier de l'an IV), 'Rapport du 12 Floréal V'.

[22] The *arrêté* of 2 Thermidor IX on the Ministry of War (*AN*, AD 1 77) laid down that a Secretary-General should be paid 15,000 francs per annum, a *Chef de division* 10,000 or 12,000 francs, a *Chef de Bureau* 5,000 to 8,000 francs, *Sous-chefs* 4,000 or 4,500 francs, *Commis ordinaire* 1,800, 2,000, 2,400, 3,000 or 3,600 francs, and *Garçons de bureau* 800 or 1,000 francs.

[23] Attempts to secure promotion by merit can be found in a letter from Pleville-le-Peley, then Minister of the Navy, to one of his heads of division, Cottrau, on 21 Pluviôse VI (*AN* BB[8] (Marine), 277 (Dossier de l'an VI)) and also in one from a War Office head of division called Arcambal to his Minister on 15 Frimaire IX (*AHG*, X[s] 128).

[24] Woronoff, op. cit., 109–10. For an example of the problems this could cause see the complaints of the *Dépôt Général* Staff on 11 Vendémiaire VI in *AHG*, B[12] 12*.

[25] Bosher, French Finances, 204–6, and Marion, *Dictionnaire des institutions*, 68, for the *Caisse des Invalides de la Marine*. For examples see *AHG*, Y[a] 24 (Dossier 1768: Capet) and X[s] 128, 'Rapport sur Le Brun'.

[26] The subsequent legislation was considerable, there being three regulations in 1790, eight in 1791, one in 1793, two in an II (including that of 10 Ventôse), and three in an III, see *AHG*, X[s] 128 and 227. For an example of the difficulties which could arise see the case of J. F. Rozai *père*, in *AN*, F[2] 102 (Calvados), who lost 40 per cent of his salary as a result of the law against cumulation and who only received a pension because the authorities stretched a point. Later on, the law had to be relaxed because of the renewal of war, so that at first 1,000 francs could be claimed in addition to one's basic salary, and then up to 3,000 francs.

[27] *AHG*, Y[a] 30, Moreau. Cf. also Moniteur 339 (9 Fructidor), 1364.

[28] Debidour, *Recueil des actes*, i, 625, and iii, 172. Amongst the Directorial acts on pensions were those of 15 Brumaire, 17 Germinal, 5–8 Messidor IV, 22–28 Vendémiaire V, and the laws of 26 Germinal and 23 Prairial V. On the inability to pay pensions in cash see *AN*, AF III 114 (535), 'lettre de Pluviôse VII'. The major consular acts were the decrees of 3 Germinal and 2 Thermidor IX.

[29] Vauchelle (*AHG*, Y^a 31), Deleforge (*AG*, AF III 28), Lafond, Huet, and Baud (*AAE*, Dossiers du personnel), and Bluteau, Cocquet, Dimanche (*AHM*, C^7, ii), and for Mottet (*AN*, C^7, i, 221 Marine).

[30] *AN*, AF* III 187 (7), memo no. 2087 of 9 Floréal VI refers to the Comité des Finances *arrêtés* of 4 Brumaire IV. Cf. also Debidour, op. cit., ii, 172.

[31] The law of 2 February 1808 offered a pension based on the average salary during the last three years of service. This could be taken after thirty years' service, with varying grades being able to draw different percentages of the average salary. However, a minimum pension could also be paid after ten years' service. Service throughout state administrations was counted, which leads the historian to tackle all the ministries rather than a sample. *AN*, F^{1a} 63 (4) also details the acts of 4 July 1806 and 17 November 1811 on the deductions to be made towards the pensions of employees of the Interior and of local authorities, as well as the failure in 1824 to establish a central pension fund for the latter. The Ministry of Police scheme of 22 December 1809 is described in F^7 12253. The next major legislation on pensions came on 9 June 1853 instituting an obligatory deduction of 5 per cent towards a pension for which thirty years' service and an age of sixty were required, a system which was more widely available but often less generous than departmental schemes.

[32] *AHG*, Pensions civiles i, 77 Simonin, and for another example of rigid application of the letter of the law, ibid. i, 79, J. B. Thiébault.

[33] Johannot in Nivôse V, told the Council that the departments had no monies to pay their employees, whereas the Minister had alienable funds at his disposal, *Moniteur* 95 (5 Nivôse V), 38. Cf. also Woronoff, op. cit., 51–2, and for the way this situation continued into the next century, F. Julien LaFerrière, *Les Deputés–Fonctionnaires sous la Monarchie de Juillet* (1970), 24.

[34] Church, op. cit., 65.

[35] This may sound all too brief, even for an era of revolution, but it should be compared with the fact that even today membership of a ministerial cabinet lasts on average only three years, even where the ministers themselves do not change very often. At the lower level it may not be wholly true that, as Lautman claims, 'administrative stability comes from the memory of the bureaux more than from personal stability'. In M. Dogan (ed.), *The Mandarins of Western Europe*.

The Political Role of Top Civil Servants (New York, 1975), 11 and 201.

[36] Church, 'Organisation and Personnel', 323–5, gives precise figures on the reasons for retirement, subsequent careers, and the number of posts held during an administrative career.

[37] Bosher, *French Finances*, 293.

[38] The reasons that clerks joined their ministries appear to have been first employment 17 per cent, transfer from another post 16.2 per cent, patronage 14 per cent, career aspirations 13.9 per cent, loss of another post 11 per cent, discharge from the army 7 per cent, unemployed 6.1 per cent, and other reasons 12.5 per cent, the total sample being 3,825.

[39] The statistics are: 10 per cent were born before 1740, 43 per cent between 1740 and 1760, 28 per cent between 1760 and 1770, and 19 per cent after 1770, which is very much in line with the population at large as is shown by J. Ibanès, 'La Population de la Place de Vosges' in M. Bouloiseau *et. al.*, *Contributions à l'histoire démographique de la Révolution français* (1962), 86. Cf. also Pappalardo, op. cit., 42.

[40] Masson, *Le Département des Affaires Étrangères*, 169 and 257.

[41] Church, 'Social Basis', 65–7.

[42] The actual figures are ministries 371—13.3 per cent, Fiscal field services 351—11 per cent, other field services 245—7.7 per cent, local and judicial services 134—4.2 per cent, and others 221—6.9 per cent.

[43] For more precise details see Church, 'Organisation and Personnel', 373–7.

[44] On the deputies see ibid., 370–80. About 60 sat before entering the civil service and about 40 after, the Interior attracting most.

[45] Lafond, *AAE*, Dossiers du Personnel, and Samoyault, *Les Bureaux des Affaires Étrangères*, 34, 271, and 293; Ployaut, *AN*, F^{1b1} 270; Ancemont, *AHM*, C^7, ii,; Bachelard, *AN*, AF III 28d; Blanc Lalesie, *AN*, F^{1b1} 11–14 and AF III 28d; Formey, *AN*, BB^4 (Justice), 1 and BB^{30} 516^2; Prevost, *AN*, F^{1b1} 276^4; Laigneau, *AN*, F^{1b1} 272^1, and Bleriot, *AN*, F^7 12278.

[46] Vée, *AN*, F^{1b1} 282^2; Belanger, *AN* BB^{30} (Justice) 573; Bouillard, *AHG*, Pensions civiles, i, 73 and X^s 115; L'Heureux, *AHG*, Pensions civiles, i, 54; Beautemps Beaupré, *AHM*, C^7; Bouteville in M. Prevost *et al.*, *Dictionnaire de biographie française* (1956), vii, 49; Brossier, *AN*, AF III 52/55, and Debidour, op. cit., iii, 107 and 281.

[47] Chervise, *AHM*, C^7, ii; Mongin, *AN* F^7 12279; Mathez, *AHG*, Pensions civiles, i, 59; Bouret, *AN*, AF III 28 (94); Demandre, *AN*, F^{1b1} 5; Chandeau, *AHG*, Pensions civiles, i, 18, and Bertheley, *AN*, AF III 28d.

[48] For Chabeuf see J. Brelot, *La Vie politique en Côte d'Or sous le Directoire* (Dijon, 1932), 33–40, and *AN*, AF III 28d, while Gattey is discussed in F. Hoefer, *Nouvelle biographie générale*, new ed.

(Copenhagen, 1966), xix, 627, as well as in *AN*, F^{1b1} 267^1, and Nardin's career can be found in *AN*, AF III 28 (94).

^{49} Boucquet, *AN* F^{1b1} 262^5; Bertin, *AN*, BB^8 (Marine) 269, and *AHM*, C^7, ii; Delecroix, *AN* BB^8 (Justice), 513; and Hauterive, Masson, op. cit., 437 et seq., Rabbé *et al.*, *Biographie universelle portative des contemporains* (1834); ii, 2040–1; Meininger, *D'Hauterive et la formation*, and de Montor, *Histoire de la vie*.

^{50} Church, 'Words, Theories and Realities'; Mathews, *Royal General Farms*, 207–17, and J. Caritey, 'Note sur le personnel des ministères en 1793', 24–7.

NOTES TO CHAPTER VII

^{1} Weber, *Theory of Social and Economic Organisation*, 340–1. Cf. also Church, 'Social Basis', 70–2.

^{2} The limitations and dangers of the British view of a totally neutral or subordinate civil service are explored by B. de Gournay in 'De la politisation de l'administration', *Res Publica*, xiii (1971), 190–1, and E. N. Suleiman, *Politics, Power and Bureaucracy*, 6.

^{3} The quotation comes from a contribution to W. S. Sayre (ed.), *The Federal Government Service* (Englewood Cliffs, NJ, 1965), 123.

^{4} J. P. Gros, *St. Just*, 59 and 220–1.

^{5} M. Minnigerode, *The Magnificent Comedy* (1932), 220–1. Almost the same picture appears today in Godechot, *La Vie quotidienne*, 109–10, also drawing on Mercier, the Goncourts, and similar sources and using virtually the same words and examples although without the mention of royalism. Cf. also L. S. Mercier, *Paris pendant la Révolution* (1882), 261–3.

^{6} Sheriff, 'Public Bureaucracies', 99–100, is inclined to go further and discount the political system as the preponderant factor.

^{7} A. Babeau, *La France et Paris sous le Directoire* (1888), 268. Cf. also Guyot, *Le Directoire et la paix de l'Europe* 51; Herlaut, *Le Colonel Bouchotte*, i, 44.

^{8} The question of social allegiance and mobility is discussed by B. Chapman, *The Profession of Government* (1954), 315–16, and Legendre, *Histoire de l'administration*, 532–45. If Suleiman, op. cit., 109, has decried the influence of birth and social class on adminsitrative behaviour, Sheriff, loc. cit., while agreeing that the problem of the social origins of civil servants is given too much prominence, due to frustrated social democratic aspirations, sees the thesis as needing testing in the actual output of administrative policy.

^{9} For details on place of birth see Church, 'Organization and Personnel', 296 and 372. Cf. L. Chevalier, *La Formation de la population parisienne au XIXe siècle* (1950), 14 and 58, and, for a more modern and highly concentrated pattern, Pappalardo, *Étude sociologique*, 54 et seq.

[10] H. Mitchell, 'Resistance to the Revolution in Western France', *Past and Present*, 63 (1974), 122. Cf. also on the relations of Paris and Versailles, R. C. Cobb, *Paris and its Provinces 1792–1802* (1975), 87–140.

[11] This is perhaps a first reflection of the phenomenon revealed by A. Darbel and D. Schnapper, *Les Agents du système*, 72–87, that recruitment to the adminsitration can be a function of the number and of the visibility of officials in a particular area.

[12] The classical work on this was done by F. de Damville, 'Effectifs des collèges et scholarite aux XVIIe et XVIIIe siècles dans le Nord-Est de la France', *Population*, x (1955), 455 et seq., and M. Fleury and P. Valmery, 'Les Progrès de l'instruction élémentaire', *Population*, xii (1957), 71–92. More recently, R. Chartier, M. M. Compère, and D. Julia, *L'Éducation en France du XVIe au XVIIIe siècles* (1976), 16–26 and 87–109, and F. Furet, J. Ozouf, *et al.*, *Lire et écrire, l'alphabétisation des Français de Calvin à Jules Ferry* (1977), 56 et seq., have confirmed and refined their findings. Cf. also F. Furet and W. Sachs, 'Alphabétisation en France', *AESC*, xxix (1974), 714–37, and, for details on the education of Directorial clerks, Church, op. cit., 348.

[13] Chartier, Compère, and Julia, op. cit., 185–94 and 252–6.

[14] Chevalier, op. cit., 17.

[15] For the categories used in the social analysis of the personnel see above, note 29 to Chapter II, together with P. Thoré, 'Essai de classification des catégories sociales', *Actes du 78e Congrès des Sociétés Savantes, Toulouse 1953* (Paris, 1954), 149 et seq., and for the statistics see Church, op. cit., 374–7, which lists, amongst other, 183 clerks to notaries, 174 in commerce, 155 teachers, and 82 members of the liberal professions as the large categories in a total of 3,041 pre-revolutionary employments.

[16] Furet and Ozouf, op. cit., 83.

[17] Bertaud, *La Révolution française*, 37–44, and especially A. Soboul in E. Labrousse and F. Braudel (eds.), *Histoire économique et sociale de la France* (1976), iii/1, 56–64.

[18] This is counter to the assumptions of both Weber (Sheriff op. cit., 77–80), who assumed bureaucratization would produce social levelling, and Godechot (op. cit., 104–9), who believed that the employees integrated themselves into the new society, modelling themselves on the rising capitalist élite and presumably sharing in the high status of *fonctionnaires* (J. Blondel, *The Government of France*, 2nd ed. (1974), 178). Cf. also A. Cobban, *The Myth of the French Révolution* (1955), 12–19, and A. J. Tudesq, *Les Grands notables en France* (1964).

[19] For statistics on non-administrative occupations during the Revolution see Church, loc. cit., which shows 121 teachers, 115 in

commerce, 81 lawyers' clerks, 65 journalists, 65 liberal professions, and 55 lawyers as important categories amongst the 5,843 occupations recovered.

[20] Lameire, *Les Municipalités de canton*,65. Cf also *AN*, BB[4] (Justice) 1, 'Ministre de la Justice au Ministre des Finances', 12 Brumaire and 14 Fructidor VII; *Le Sage Observateur*, 10 Brumaire VI.

[21] *AN*, F[1a] 63 (Dossier de l'an III) contains exchanges of letters between local authorities and the then Minister of the Interior, Benezech, over staff salaries, in which the latter insisted that the laws must be obeyed and that clerks could be consoled for the material insufficiencies produced by adherence to the law, by the knowledge of the solicitude of the government. For examples of the problems caused see Marion, *Histoire financière*, iii, 339–43 and 388, and for developments after the crisis of 1796 *AN*, AF* III 159 (2), f. 479 and AF* III 218, f. 862.

[22] Church, 'Organisation and Personnel', 101–2 and 355–6, which draws, *inter alia*, on Aulard, *Paris*, iv, and *AN*, F[7] 3006 and F[1b1] 1. For Reinhard see his report to the Directory of 29 Fructidor VIII *AN*, AF III 52/55 (213/IV), and for the petition to Bonaparte, BB[4] (Justice) 1, of 27 Nivôse VIII, along with BB[8] 278 of 6 Thermidor VII.

[23] Bertaud, op. cit., 179. Cf. also Soboul, op. cit., 41–53.

[24] Barras, *Mémoires*, ii, 177, and *Les Nouvelles politiques*, 48 (18 Brumaire IV), 191. For the provision of goods in Paris see *AN*, BB[8] (Marine), 275, notes of 27 Frimaire, and 277 of 14 Vendémiaire VI, and at the local level *AD*, Haute-Marne, L* 107.

[25] *AN*, AF* III 202 f. 145 of 25 Pluviôse V and BB[4] (Justice) 1, for Merlin's defence in Messidor V. Cf. also F[7] 3688[4]: Caille, for the way the Directory relaxed the rules. Later policy is to be found in *AN*, AF III 546 (3640/6), *arrêté* 5 Vendémiaire VII and BB[4] 2, 12 Brumaire VII. For Restif de la Bretonne see Hoefer, *Biographie universelle* (1968), xliii, 30. He joined the ministry in Vendémiaire VI as a *sous-chef* in the *Bureau particulier* at 4,000 *francs* p.a.

[26] Cottrau, of the Admiralty, in a letter of 29 Pluviôse IV in *AN*, BB[8] (Marine), 275. On the subsistence crisis see R. Schnerb, 'La Dépression économique sous le Directoire', *AHRF*, xi (1933), 45–7; Reinhard, *La France du Directoire*, ii, 20–38, and Cobb, 'Disette et mortalité. La Crise de l'an III et l'an IV à Rouen' in *Terreur et subsistances*, 307–42.

[27] Debidour, op. cit., i, 527, and *AF*, F[11] 1180A, 'Departement de la Seine au Ministre de l'Interieur', while the statistics themselves are printed as an addendum to Church, op. cit.

[28] *AN*, F[11] 1182, of 12 Germinal IV for Decaisne, while for the Paris tax service see ibid., their petition of 4 Floréal IV. On local costs and problems see *AN*, C 231 (183 bis 10/2), no. 93, and *AD*, Nièvre,

L 47 , f. 145, of 23 Brumaire IV.

29 L. Bergeron, *Banquiers, négociants et manufacturiers parisiens. Du Directoire à l'Empire* (Lille, 1975), deals with economic growth and the creation of a new capitalist class in this period.

30 Reinhard, *Le Département de la Sarthe*, 634; Lebrun-Tossa, *Portefeuille politique*, 60, and A. D. P. Fabre de Narbonne *Le Directoire* (1830), i, 33. It has not proved possible to take the social analysis of the average clerk much further due to problems of identification in the main even at the local level in such a town as Dijon. Some idea of their position at other times can be gained from F. Furet and A. Daumard, *Structures et relations sociales à Paris au milieu du XVIIIe siècle* (1961), 19, and A. Daumard, *La Bourgeoisie parisienne de 1815 à 1848* (1963), 214–16.

31 *AHM*, C^7, ii, Granet and Longueve (together with *AN*, F^{1b1} 261^1). Cf. also Reinhard, op. cit., 622 and 632–5, and Tulard, *La Préfecture de Police*, 54. The poem is from *Le Courrier universel* of 17 Messidor III.

32 Bachelors, 17 per cent; married but childless, 12 per cent; married with one child, 23 per cent; with two children, 15 per cent; with three children, 6 per cent; with four, 2 per cent, and with five and more, 1 per cent is the breakdown of those whose marital position is known. On the impossibility of seeing further into employees' personal lives see Tulard, loc. cit.

33 There are some 50 claims of loss of fortune and 13 of dire need, compared with only 11 admitting to possessing some capital. The examples from the Secretariat-General originate from *AN*, AF III 21d, while the others come from the normal range of personnel dossiers, e.g.: F^{1b1} 11–14, for Lebourgeois; and BB^{30} 497/516, for Douet d'Arcq and Tondeur. For the economic background see L. Bergeron, 'Profits et risques sous le Directoire' *AHRF*, xxxviii (1966), 359–89.

34 Goncourt, *Histoire de la société française*, 185, and A. Joussain, 'Le Directoire et nous', *Les Libertés françaises*, xxi (1957), 28, reflect prevailing attitudes.

35 Bertaud, op. cit., 41.

36 Suleiman, op. cit., 112–14. Cf. the police report cited in J. Hardman (ed.) *Documents of the French Revolution* (1974), ii, 201–2, and *Les Nouvelles Politiques*, 51 (21 Brumaire IV), 204, for a contrary view.

37 The quotation is from Ymbert, *Mœurs administratives*, i, 104.

38 In 'Politisation de l'administration', 167–71, along with Dogan, *The Mandarins of Western Europe*, 12, and Gros, op. cit., 31, while for contemporary attitudes, see *AN*, AF III 309 (1214), 'Bertrand à Reubell', 2 Messidor VI, and 'Clauzel à Reubell', 22 Floréal VI.

39 Gros, op. cit. 339, shows how politization caused a cross-fire

between Carnot and Hét　t.

[40] Suleiman, op. cit., 221–2. Cf. also J. Meynaud and A. Lancelot, *La Participation des français à la politique* (1961), 54, and P. Lelong, 'Trois attitudes du fonctionnaire en face de la politique', *RA*, vii/41 (1954), 490.

[41] *AN*, AF III 175, 'Le Directoire au Ministre des Relations Extérieurs', 6 Vendémiaire V. Cf. also Cambacères, quoted in Shepard, *Price Control and the Reign of Terror*, 71, and Sheriff, op. cit. 66.

[42] L. de Potter, *De la révolution à faire* (1831), 57. Cf. also R. D. Price, 'The French Army and the Revolution of 1830', *ESR*, iii (1973), 246, and, on the hazards arising from swiftly changing political lines, W. Scott, *Terror and Repression in Revolutionary Marseilles* (1975), 219–30 and 312–14.

[43] Suleiman, op. cit., 5, 219–22, 266–7, and 296–9.

[44] François de Neuchateau, quoted by Bonnassieux, in *L'Administration d'un département*, 19–20; Pleville-le-Peley in a circular of 2 *complémentaire* V in *AN*, BB^8 (Marine), 276, and a 'Rapport au Ministre' of 23 Fructidor V in F^{1b1} 11–14.

[45] The contemporary view stands out very clearly from Aulard, *Paris*, v, 628, as well as amongst historians such as Woronoff, *La République bourgeoise*, 51–2, and Sydenham, *The First French Republic*, 21–2, note 21. Deville, *Thermidor et Directoire*, 169, is an exception to the rule in stressing the role of the right in the bureaucracy at this stage.

[46] J. Dent, *Crisis in Finance* (Newton Abbot, 1972), 10. Cf. M. Janovitz, D. Wright, and W. Delaney in A. Etzioni (ed.), *Complex Organizations, a Sociological Reader* (New York, 1964), 279, and also the *Manuel des Assemblées an IV–V* (1797), in *BL*, R 539, which reproached Dentzel for occupying too much of his time with trying to find out what went on in the bureaux.

[47] Aulard, op. cit., iv, 405 and 409, and v, 387; *Les Nouvelles Politiques*, 54 (24 Brumaire IV), 215, and *La Clef des Cabinets*, 931 (21 Thermidor VII), 7849. For the quotation see Scott, op. cit., 82, and, for the Ain, E. Dubois, *Histoire de la Révolution dans l'Ain* (Bourg, 1935), vi, 65–75.

[48] E. Tambour, *L'Administration de Seine et Oise et le Directoire* (1913), 36–43, and Cobb, 'Note sur la répression contre le personnel sansculotte', in op. cit., 198–9. One might also note the way in which even 'political appointees' can become staid members of the establishment, as shown by Molitor in 'De la politisation de l'administration', 219–20, and Downs, *Inside Bureaucracy* (Boston, 1966), 264.

[49] Chapman, op. cit., 36–7 and 273, and Dogan, op. cit., 4–5.

[50] Albrow, *Bureaucracy*, 91–105 and 110, and Sauvy, *Bureaux et Bureaucratie*, 64–8.

[51] S. N. Eisenstadt, *Essays in Comparative Institutions*, (New York, 1965), 220 et seq.

[52] P. Sorokin, *The Sociology of Revolution*, new ed. (New York, 1967), 257, and A. Dunsire, *Administration, the word and the thing* (1973), 180. Cf. also Rule and Tilly, '1830 and the Unnatural history of Revolution', loc. cit.

[53] *Le Clef des Cabinets*, 8 and 11 Nivôse VI. Cf. also A. Bardeux, *La Bourgeoisie française* (1886), 95; Chapman, op cit., 284–6, and Mosca, cited in Kumar, *Revolution*, 288–9.

[54] J. Torrance, 'Social Class and Bureaucratic Innovation: the Commissioners for Examining the Public Accounts', *Past and Present*, 78 (1978), 63.

[55] Kaufman and Mansfield, in Sayre, op. cit., 54–5 and 114–62. Sheriff, op. cit., 64–5, canvasses the idea that there are two administrative orientations, one technical and the other politically aware and many commentators feel that the French administrative élite fall into the second category and the career staff into the former.

[56] Suratteau, *Les Élections de l'an VI*, for an examination of the whole problem.

[57] *AAE*, France 2095, show three clerks being awarded portraits of Louis XVI valued at 400 *livres* each.

[58] Law of 3/22 August 1790 and Dumouriez, *Mémoires*, ii, 153–4. Daunou is cited in Legendre, *L'Administration du XVIIIe siècle*, 37.

[59] The purges in some cases like that of Melin, Saint-Paul, and Delalain of the War Office led to the guillotine. For Saint-Just's views, Gros, op. cit., 58–9 and 342. For the Arcis petition see Markov und Soboul, *Die Sans-Culotten von Paris*, 134–6, although this is only one of many attacks on the administration in the collection. For Robespierre's defence see Hardman, op. cit., 184–5.

[60] Lindet, cited in ibid., 151.

[61] Church, 'Bureaucracy, Politics and Revolution'. Cf. also A. Roserot, *Mémoires de Madame de Chastenay* (1896), i, 324.

[62] This failure is very much akin to that of bodies set up after other revolutions, in Italy for example, as can be seen from A. Sorbelli, *Libro dei compromessi politici nelle rivoluzione del 1832* (Rome, 1935), x; A. Corbelli in T. Rossi and C. P. Demagistri (eds.), *La Rivoluzione piemontese del 1821* (Turin, 1927), ii, 744, 752, and 766, and P. Pirri, *'La Società Segrete ed i moti degli anni 1820–1 e 1830–31'*, etc. (Milan, 1931), 186–7. The organization of the committees' efforts compares poorly with that of the British Commission for Examining Public Accounts *pace* Torrance, op. cit., 56–81. Cf. also V. Wright in *Les Épurations administratives, XIXe et XXe siècles* (Geneva, 1977), 70.

[63] Villet is mentioned in Aulard, op. cit., ii, 766. Cf. also *AN*, BB^{30} (Justice), J. B. Viret, 'Mémoire au Ministre' of Vendémiaire VI,

and, for the appeal of Bugniâtre and others for jobs from Reubell, *AF* III 309 (1214).

⁶⁴ Meynaud and Lancelot, op. cit., 55.

⁶⁵ Woronoff, op. cit., 65–66, 197, and 210; and Suratteau, *Mont Terrible*, 591–2. M. Lyons, *France under the Directory*, 90, shows that civil servants thereafter had to prove they sent their children to state schools.

⁶⁶ E. Poupé, 'Le Département du Var, 1790–an VIII', *Bulletin de la Société d'Études . . . de Dragnuigan*, xl/28, (1963), 467–73.

⁶⁷ Woloch, *Jacobin Legacy*, 374–6, and the *Dictionnaire des jacobins vivants* (1799) in *BL*, R 541. Cf. also *AN*, F¹ᵇ¹ 11–14 and F¹ᵈ¹ 31 for evidence on neo-Jacobin nominations.

⁶⁸ One example is the promotion of François Jean Philippe, *Sous-chef* in the War Office, to be the first government commissioner in the *Léman* in Fructidor VII (E. Chapuisat, *Le Départment du Léman* [1934], 36). Cf. also the previously mentioned case of Arsène Thiébault, discussed in Jalouneix, 'Le Journal de la Meurthe', 22 et seq., and the examples given in both the *Dictionnaire des Protées modernes* (1815) and the *Dictionnaire des girouettes* (1815).

⁶⁹ See the evidence of Kitchin, *La Décade*, which shows Lebreton, Lachabussière, Ginguené, Gerando, Amaury, Duval, Garat, and Andrieux to have been in this category as well.

⁷⁰ J. Kayser in G. Michaud (ed.), *Les Tendances politiques dans la vie française depuis 1789* (1960), 76–7, offers a later parallel to this. Cf. Lebrun-Tossa, op. cit., and Vincent Lombard, *Le Dix-Huit Brumaire* (1880).

⁷¹ *La Clef du Cabinet*, 27 Prairial VII, and, for the role of deputies and officials, see Suratteau, *Les Élections de l'an VI*, 271–9 and 401–2. Cf. also Julien-Laferrière, op. cit., 127–9.

⁷² Lucas, *The Structure of the Terror*, 256–64, 339–40, and 388.

⁷³ La Revellière, *Mémoires*, i, 339, 364–5, and 406. For Guffroy see his letter in *AN*, AF III 309 (1214) and for Detorcy one in F⁷ 3009 (II). The statistics come from the applications in F¹ᵈ¹ 31.

⁷⁴ L. Gruffy, *La Vie et l'œuvre juridique de Merlin de Douai* (Douai, 1934), 62, and for the way in which personal animosities and friendships could work see Suratteau, op. cit., 369, and Lucas, op. cit., 333.

⁷⁵ Aulard, op. cit., iv, 262, and for further evidence a note in *AN*, AF* III 137, of 18 Vendémiaire. Cf. also Vincent Lombard, *Mémoires anecdotiques* (1823), i, 346, and for the quotation, ii, 303.

⁷⁶ Saint-Just, cited in Hardman, op. cit., 155–9. For examples of corruption *AHG*, Xˢ 1, a memo of 7 Thermidor III on forging letters of credit, and Roserot, op. cit., i, 413, on offences connected with the conscription laws.

⁷⁷ G. A. Almond and G. B. Powell, *Comparative Politics. A Develop-*

mental Approach (Boston, 1966), 77–8.

[78] F. S. Burin in Merton, *Reader in Bureaucracy*, 45–6 and 111 et seq., and Edwards, *Natural History of Revolution*, 173.

[79] For Cottrau see his dossier *AHM*, C[7], ii, and a so far unpublished article by the present author, and for Duplay see L. Grasilier, *Un Secrétaire de Robespierre* (1913). The quotation comes from an anonymous denunciation of January 1816 in *AN*, F[1b1] 11–14.

[80] Thuillier and Tulard, Parodi, and Wright, in *Les Épurations administratives*, 120, 116, and 79 respectively.

[81] Bertaud, op. cit., 41, together with Sheriff, op. cit., 73–7. On problems of control compare the Directory's style with that of Saint-Just, in Gros, op. cit., 31. Cf. also H. F. Gortner, *Administration in the Public Sector* (New York, 1977), 34–5, 44–7, and 67–75.

NOTES TO CHAPTER VIII

[1] On the historiography of administration after 1799 see E. Whitcomb, 'Napoleon's Prefects', *American Historical Review*, ccxix (1974), 1089; and Tulard, *La Préfecture de Police*, 55.

[2] Soboul, in *Histoire économique et sociale*, iii/1, 125–33.

[3] Furet and Richet, *La Révolution française*, i, 298. Cf. also W. R. Sharp, *The French Civil Service*, 3; C. H. Sisson, *The Mind of British Administration and some European Comparisons* (1966), 49, and R. B. Jones, *Napoleon*, 96–9. Even Engels, on p. xxxviii of his introduction to *La Guerre civile en France*, trans. C. Longuet (1925), succumbed to this view.

[4] J. Godechot, 'Sens et importance de la transformation des institutions révolutionnaires', *AHRF*, xlii (1970), 190; H. Parker, in L. Kennet (ed.), *Consortium on Revolutionary Europe, 1972* (Gainesville, Fla., 1974), 24–5, and J. Tulard, *Paris et son administration 1800–1830* (1976), 126–39.

[5] L. Bergeron, *L'Épisode napoléonien* 1972), i, 117 and 128. Cf. *AHG*, Pensions civiles, i, 83, Virgile.

[6] Exceptions are those cited by Tulard from Pichon and Chateaubriand in *L'Anti-Napoléon* (1965), 129 and 138. Cf. also G. Ardent, 'Napoléon et le rendement des services publics', *Revue de defense nationale*, ix (1953), 169–81.

[7] Quoted by G. Thuillier, 'La Vie des bureaux sous la première empire', *RA*, xi (1958), 473. Cf. also J. Tulard (ed.), 'Écrits Personnels etc.' in J. Massin (ed.), *Napoléon Bonaparte, l'œuvre et l'histoire* (1969), i, 414 and 479; E. Driault, *Napoléon: Pensées pour l'action* (1943), 345, 48–9, and 143, and C. Durand, *Études sur les rapports entre la loi et le règlement gouvernemental* (Aix, 1978), 33–227, on his growing use of administrative decrees.

[8] Chaptal and Miot are cited by P. Vigeur and J. Revel (eds.), 'Napoléon vu et jugé par ses collaborateurs', ii (1971), Massin, op. cit., ix, 48–9 and 565. Cf. also F. M. H. Markham, *Napoleon* (New York, 1972), 98 and 209–13, Kennet, op. cit., 18, together with C. Poutier, 'L'Évolution des structures ministérielles françaises', unpublished *thèse en droit* of the Université de Paris, (1960), i, 20–5.

[9] J. Godechot in a review of Latreille, *L'Ère napoléonienne* (1974), in *AHRF*, xlix/3 (1977), 970. Latreille's own discussion, which is to be preferred to that of P. Menon, 'La fonction publique', *Bull Econ. Finances*, 72 (1975) 38, is at 101.

[10] On the *Auditeurs* see J. Regnier in G. Chaussinand-Nogaret (ed.), *Une Histoire des Élites, 1700–1848* (The Hague, 1975), 249, and, for the new group in general, J. Tulard, *Napoléon*, 241–6, and Soboul, op. cit., 131–2 whence comes the quotation. Soboul, however, sees money as the defining characteristic of the new élite (129–30) whereas Tulard (245–6) argues that 'le notable est celui qui exerce une autorité, le patron sur les ouvriers, le haut fonctionnaire sur ses commis'. In fact both criteria seem to have been essential.

[11] Thibaudeau, cited by Vigeur and Revel, in Massin, op. cit., ix, 367–71. Cf. also J. and G. Arnieye, 'Stendhal et Napoléon', *Europe*, 47 (1969), 480–1, and J. Bourdon, *Napoléon au Conseil* (1963), 62, and 259–60.

[12] Bergeron, op. cit., 7–8 and 12, and Sautel, *Histoire des institutions publiques*, 237–40.

[13] Tulard, op. cit., 254.

[14] For the political and economic background see G. Lefèbvre, *Napoléon* (1965), the special number of *RHMC* (xvii of 1970) on Napoleon and his times, and Soboul, op. cit., 69–133.

[15] M. A. Baudot, *Notes historiques sur le Convention Nationale* etc. (1893), 309. Cf. also Tulard in *RHMC*, xvii, 653, and Bergeron, op. cit., 209–10.

[16] Tulard, op. cit., 320–5 and 456–7.

[17] E. Hauterive, *Napoléon et sa police* (1943), 78–80, and Thuillier, *Témoins de l'administration*, 62–8. Chaptal is cited by Vigeur and Revel, in Massin, op. cit., ix, 44, and Napoleon in Briault, op. cit., 16 and 32.

[18] J. Thiry, *L'Aube du Consulat* (1948), 25, is the source of the quotation. Cf. also R. B. Holtman, *The Napoleonic Revolution* (Baton Rouge, La., 1967), 81–5; Jones, *Napoleon*, 98; Tulard, *Paris*, 73–4; and *Les Épurations administratives*, 50.

[19] Cited in Driault, op. cit., 39, and by Tulard, in Massin, op. cit., i, 319–35. Cf. also Poutier, op. cit., i, 241–4, and, for the law of 18 Pluviôse VIII, M. Chaulanges et al. (eds.), *Texted historiques: 1799–1815* etc. (1960), 12.

[20] Casinelli, *Total Revolution*, 10 and 234–5. Cf. also V. Crabbe,

'Entretien de Talleyrand, sur l'esprit de l'administration etc.', *Revue internationale des sciences administratives.* xxii/1 (1956), 125–39.

²¹ Bourdon, op. cit., 39 and 136. Fain is cited by Vigeur and Revel, in Massin, op. cit., viii, 521, and Mollien in ibid., 198, as well as being quoted by Markham, *Napoleon*, 136–7. Cf. also E. Whitcomb, 'The Duties and Functions of Napoleon's external agents', *History*, lvii (1972), 189.

²² M. Vox (ed.), *Correspondance de Napoléon* (1943), 112–13 and note 12, 452. Cf. also Driault, op. cit., 39, and Bourrienne, cited by Vigeur and Revel, Massin, op. cit., viii, 414.

²³ J. Arnna (ed.), *Napoléon Ier: Lettres au Compte Mollien* (1959), 197, 404–5, and 415. Cf. also L. Fougère *et al.*, *Le Conseil d'état 1799–1974* (1975), 77; Bourdon, op. cit., 113–14, 122–3, and especially 177–8; and Driault, op. cit., 39–42, 48–9, and 143, while for the problem of control, see P. Soudet, *L'Administration vu par les siens* (1974), 93–4. Also A. Damien, 'Le Personnel révolutionnaire' *Souvenir Napoléonien*, xxxiii/256 (1970), 29–30, who discusses the role of the *Légion d'honneur* and the Constituent Assembly in Napoleon's personnel policy.

²⁴ In Markham, op. cit., 95. Cf. also Massin, op. cit., ii, 325–6, and viii, 47; F. Ponteil, *Napoléon et L'organisation autoritaire de la France* (1956), 120–2, Tulard, *Napoléon*, 115 et seq., and *Paris*, 106–25.

²⁵ Godechot, *Les Constitutions*, 151–65. He also offers a commentary in *Les Institutions*, 2nd ed., 482–507. Cf. also Chevallier, *L'Élaboration historique*, 89–95 and 103–4, and Fougère, op. cit., 131–45.

²⁶ C. Durand, 'Conseils Privés, Conseils des Ministres etc.' *RHMC*, xvii (1970), 814–17, and Markham, op. cit., 82–3. Cf. also Fain *et al.*, cited by Vigeur and Revel, in Massin, op. cit., viii, 535–45 and 550–60, and ix, 137–8.

²⁷ Ponteil, op. cit., 93; Sautel, op. cit., 250–63, and Waline, *Droit administratif*, 27–9. For the decree of 11 June 1806 see J. Imbert *et al.* (eds.), *Histoire des institutions et des faits sociaux* (1963), 286.

²⁸ On personnel Damien, op. cit., 313, and Latreille, op. cit., 83–5. Problems of control appear in L. Sfez and J. Feydy, 'Napoléon, Réformateur' (1970), in Massin, op. cit., vii, 270, and A. H. Mahmoud, *Justice and Administrative Deviance* (The Hague, (1972), esp. 2, 61, and 191–2. Cf. also Durand, op. cit., 818–28.

²⁹ Arnna, op. cit., vi and xv–xvi, and Napoléon to Fouché on 18 October 1807, cited by Tulard in Massin, op. cit., ii, 367–8.

³⁰ Fain, cited by Vigeur and Revel, in Massin, op. cit., viii, 460–79, and 599–606.

³¹ Chaptal, cited in ibid., ix, 53. Cf. also Sautel, op. cit., 241–9; Racinet, *De la spécialisation ministérielle*, 121; and Tulard, *Napoléon*, 129.

³² Driault, op. cit., 38–9, and, on the role of the ministerial bureaux as organs of control, Arnna, op. cit., 353.

[33] P. Poullet, *Les Institutions françaises de 1795 à 1814 etc.* (1907), 523–4 and 643–4. Cf. also P. Gousset, 'L'Évolution historique de l'administration centrale du commerce et de l'industrie', *RA*, xiv (1961), 133, and J. Vial, 'L'Administration Centrale de l'Instruction Publique en France 1792–1855', *Paedogica Historia*, ix (1969), 122–3.

[34] *AN*, F^7 12250 contains much detail on staffing. Cf. also Hauterive, op. cit., 14–24 and 196; Buisson, *La Police*, 167–91; and Tulard, *Paris*, 73–95, 139–201, and 230–2.

[35] Durand-Barthez, *L'Évolution des structures*, 24–6.

[36] Vigeur and Ravel, in Massin, op. cit., ix, 11. Cf. also Cusson, *Origines et évolution*, 50–64; R. J. Barker, 'The "Conseil Général des Manufacturiers" under Napoleon, 1810–14', *FHS*, vi (1969), 185–213; G. Berlia, *Gérando, sa vie, son œuvre* (1942); and J. Tulard, F. de Baecque *et al.*, *Les Directeurs de ministère en France, XIX–XXᵉ siècles* (Geneva, 1976), 7–8.

[37] Bergeron, op. cit., 59 and 63; Godechot, *Les Institutions*, 547, and G. Pariset, 'Le Consulat et l'Empire' in E. Lavisse (ed.), *Histoire de la France contemporaine* (1921), iii, 26–9.

[38] Masson, *Le Département des Affaires Étrangères*, 447 et seq., and Fontaine de Resbecq, *L'Administration centrale de la marine*, 12.

[39] Barker, op. cit., 199, and Gousset, loc. cit., deal with the Ministry of Trade, but there is no study of some other departments, such as the Ministry of Religious Affairs. Estimates for staff numbers are: Secretariat—50; Police—150; Justice—150; Interior—200; Finance and Treasury—600 together; External Relations—80; Navy—220; Religious Affairs—100; University—100; Manufactures and Trade—100; War—1,500; and the various Directions about 400, making 3,650 in all.

[40] P. F. Pinaud, 'L'Administration des Cultes de 1800 à 1815', *Revue de l'Institut Napoléon*, 132 (1976), 28–36.

[41] *AHG*, X^s 116 and Fonds Préval: 'Le Ministère de la Guerre pendant le Premier Empire', a manuscript assessment of 1911 by Vidal de la Blanche, have much evidence on this period.

[42] Poutier, op. cit., i, 191–239. Cf. also Nanteuil, *Le Comte Daru*, 91; Arnna, op. cit., 421–3, and J. Vilain *Le Recouvrement des impôts sous l'Ancien Régime* (1952), 282–5.

[43] Holtman, op. cit., 102; Vox, op. cit., 110 and 549, and Bourdan, op. cit., 113–14, and 122–3.

[44] Whitcomb, 'Napoleon's Prefects', 1094–8; Godechot, op. cit., 508–20, and Sautel, op. cit., 290–7, together with the more specialized studies by M. Rebouillat, 'L'Établissement de l'administration préfectorale dans le département du Saône et Loire', *RHMC*, xvii (1970), 860–79, and R. Van Berkel, 'Produit du droit par les bureaux', *RHDFE*, lii (1974), 189–90.

[45] Thuillier, *Témoins de l'administration*, 75–6; Ymbert, *Mœurs administratives*, i, 145–8; and G. Ardant, *Histoire de l'impôt* (1972), ii, 194–5. The quotation comes from J. Debu-Bridel, 'Un Régime totalitaire', *Europe*, 47 (1969), 73.

[46] Petot, *Histoire de l'administration des Ponts et Chaussées*, 421–2; Berthaut, *Les Ingénieurs-géographes*, ii, 249–56; Anon., *Notice sur le Ministère de la Guerre*, 53–7; and Barker, op. cit., 205.

[47] Tulard, *La Préfecture de Police*, 39; Thuillier, op. cit., 74–6 and 81–8; Vigeur and Revel in Massin, op. cit., viii, 161, which can be compared with the more favourable verdicts of Fain, cited in ibid., 522–6, and Josat, *Le Ministère des Finances*, 71.

[48] Tulard, *Paris*, 336 et seq.

[49] Perrot, 'L'Âge d'or', 271–5.

[50] Bergeron, op. cit., 78–9, and J. Tulard, 'Problèmes sociaux de la France impériale', *RHMC*, xvii (1970), 651–3, but cf. Balzac, *Les Employés*, 14 and esp. 159–60.

[51] Quoted in Fougère, op. cit., 76–7.

[52] Bergeron, op. cit., 66–71, together with Fain and Chaptal, cited by Vigeur and Revel in Massin, op. cit., viii, 553 and ix, 117.

[53] Prost, *Histoire de l'enseignement en France*, 225, and Markham, op. cit., 99. Cf. Bourdon, op. cit., 259–60, and the acts of 29 Vendémiaire, 21 Ventôse, and 10 Thermidor IX, 13 Brumaire X, 4 July 1806, and 17 November 1811.

[54] Petot, op. cit., 424–35; Berthaut, op. cit., ii, 125–9, and Thuiller, op. cit., 53 and 69–71, together with *AN*, BB[30] (Justice), 513, BB[4] 7, and F[1b1] 6 for the various acts and grading systems.

[55] Cited by Vigeur and Revel in Massin, op. cit., viii, 115. Cf. also Tranchant, *De la préparation aux services publics*, and the example of Babin in *AHG*, Pensions civiles, i, 3.

[56] The quotation comes from F. Barthélemy, cited in Legendre, *L'Administration du XVIIIe siècle à nos jours*, 172–4. Cf. also J. Lamothe, 'Le Secrétaire Gaspaton, ou la vie municipale à Roquefort sous le Consulat', *Bulletin trimestriel de la Société de Borda*, lxxx (1956), 52; F. Piquemal, *Le Fonctionnaire: Droits et garanties* (1973), 317; J. Savoye, 'Quelques aspects de l'œuvre de L.-A. Macarel (1790–1851). Contributions à l'étude de la naissance des sciences politiques et administratives', unpublished *thèse en droit* of the Université de Lille II (1970), i, 109 and J. Dunne, *ESR* x/3 (1980), 389–90.

[57] The records of the War Ministries—here treated as one since all their personnel records have long since been reunified—do not permit the quick and simple photograph of the administration which was possible for the Ancien Régime, and to some extent for the administration in general in 1793. Nor do they allow the more inclusive study of the Directorial ministries, which demanded consultation of a wider

range of sources. So a sample has been taken simply from amongst the clerks who entered the two ministries in the Napoleonic era. This has the double advantage of avoiding any overlap with the Directorial study, and therefore of throwing into relief the changes which took place under the Emperor. Moreover, by utilizing the same computer program for all the samples taken from the Ministry of War it is easier to assess the rate and the nature of change within the one body. The sample was of 106 individuals taken at random from *AHG*, Pensions civiles i, cartons 1, 3, 4, 8, 12, 20, 21, 23, 27, 33, 39, 49, 58, 69, 79, and 83, a selection chosen to ensure coverage of names throughout the alphabet. The example excluded domestic staff and threw up only about one senior official in twelve, which is probably an unfair representation of their actual strength. Of the sample, there is a great deal of information on 16 per cent, an average amount on 28 per cent, and a modicum on 48 per cent. As to their origins, 22 per cent came from the Seine, 10.7 per cent from the Seine-et-Oise, 4.5 per cent from the Côte-d'Or, 3.6 per cent from the Seine-Inférieure, and 2.7 per cent each from the Marne, the Maine-et-Loire, and the Somme. Unfortunately the unpublished paper by the Conservateur en Chef of the Service historique de l'Armée, J. C. Devos, on 'Origines Professionnelles des Employés du Ministerè de la Guerre en fonction en l'an IX'—which takes a different attitude and approach to the problem, came to hand too late to be considered here.

[58] Figures for date of birth are:

1740–9	1750–9	1760–9	1770–9	1780–9	after 1790
0.9%	5.4%	10.8%	24.2%	21.6%	15.2%

while those for date of entry are:

Year	% p.a.	Year	% p.a.
1800	2.7	1807	5.3
1801	2.7	1808	4.5
1802	2.7	1809	5.3
1803	6.2	1810	13.4
1804	1.8	1811	13.4
1805	—	1812	16.9
1806	4.5	1813	15.2
		1814	1.8 (including Hundred Days).

[59] B. Panagiatopoulos, 'Les Structures d'âge du personnel de l'Empire', *RHMC*, xvii (1970), 442–6. The figures for age on entry of the War Office sample are:

Age on entry	To the Ministries	To Admin. in general
0–15	—	3.8%
15–20	12.3%	33.0%

Age on entry	To the Ministries	To Admin. in general
20–5	19.8%	21.7%
25–30	10.4%	8.5%
30–5	17.0%	6.6%
35–40	9.4%	3.8%
40–5	7.5%	4.7%
45–50	4.7%	1.9%
50+	2.8%	—

The figures for previous employment are: field services 16 per cent, professions 9.4 per cent, army 8.5 per cent, private life 7.5 per cent, other central administrations 6.6 per cent, student 5.7 per cent, notarial clerk 5.7 per cent, and court posts 3.8 per cent.

[60] The date of entry to administrative service in general was as follows: before 1780 0.9 per cent; 1780–9 8.9 per cent; 1790–9 22.9 per cent, with the bulk entering under the Directory; 1800–5 5.3 per cent, 1806–10 27.7 per cent, and 1811–15 25 per cent, few of them after 1813. As to the reasons and means of entry into the ministries, 31.1 per cent took an examination, compared to 7.5 per cent who entered through court contacts or other forms of patronage or probationary service. Again, 16 per cent were transferred to the ministries from other services, 14.2 per cent joined because of economic need, 12.3 per cent respectively in search of their first job or on leaving the army, and 8.7 per cent joined as a step in their careers.

[61] The percentages for the various categories of paternal employment and education are too small to be really worth quoting individually, whereas 20.8 per cent claimed to be in debt, 18.9 per cent to be dependent on their salary, and only 4.7 per cent admitted to having any capital, although one in ten were able to support a relative.

[62] Soboul, op. cit., 83–6, shows that real wages rose by almost a quarter during the Empire, so that dependence on a salary should not have precluded a rising standard of living. It may be that the increase was not enough to cancel out losses sustained earlier, or that the inability to secure a salaried post was at fault.

[63] A third of the sample remained static in the same grade, whereas 21 per cent were promoted by one grade, 17 per cent by two, 10 per cent by three grades, and 0.9 per cent managed to reach *fonctionnaire* levels. As a result only 9.5 per cent finished with a salary of over 4,500 francs, which was roughly the same percentage as those who ended with salaries of between 2,500 and 3,500, and 3,500 and 4,500, while 17 per cent finished with between 1,500 and 2,500. The figures for political involvement etc. are hardly worth quoting individually, while those for the reasons for leaving both the ministry and the civil service as a whole are too straightforward to be worth printing. However, the figures for length of service are interesting:

Years of service	Ministries	Admin. in general
0–1	8.5%	3.8%
1–3	12.3%	1.9%
3–5	9.4%	2.8%
5–10	13.2%	5.7%
10–15	15.1%	4.7%
15–20	6.6%	10.4%
20–30	12.3%	20.8%
30–40	15.1%	22.6%
40+	4.7%	11.3%

[64] *AHG,* Pensions civiles, i, 4, Barabet; i, 49, Leboeuf, and ii, 29, Georget-Laschesnais. Cf. Bergeron, op. cit., 47–8, 68, 73, and 149–51.

[65] Ibid., 146–51; together with Palmer in Kennet, op. cit., 35–6, and Tulard, op. cit., 653. The quotation comes from Van Berkel, 'Recherches sur le centralisme français', iii, 364.

[66] Meininger, 'd'Hauterive', 31–51.

[67] *Dictionnaire des girouettes,* 180–1.

[68] T. Sauvel, 'L'Empereur et le Conseil d'État statuant sur le contentieux, 1806–15', *Revue du droit public,* lxxxix (1973), 1402–3; Parker, in Kennet, op. cit., 49–50; Cobban, *History of Modern France,* ii, 26, and Lefèbvre, op. cit., 393–6, and Tulard, *Paris,* 336.

[69] Whitcomb, 'Napoleon's Prefects', 1110 and 1116–18, and J. Tulard *et al., Les Préfets en France, 1800–1940* (Geneva, 1978), in general.

[70] Cited by Markham, op. cit., 210. Cf. also *AHG.,* X^s 116 (Dossier 114), Dennié on 13 April 1814, and *AN,* F^7 3009 (II), 'Carlier à Fouché', on 8 April 1815, and, to Louis XVIII, on 9 July 1815.

[71] In *Les Épurations administratives.*

[72] Tulard, *Napoléon,* 125–9 and 320. Cf. also Poggi, *The Development of the Modern State,* 84–5.

[73] Driault, op. cit., 178.

NOTES TO CHAPTER IX

[1] Van Berkel, 'Recherches sur le centralisme français', iii, 403 et seq.

[2] A. Daumard in *Histoire économique et sociale,* iii/1, 139–43, is a good introduction to both phenomena.

[3] Poggi, *The Development of the Modern State,* 95–119. Cf. K. Marx *The Eighteenth Brumaire of Louis Bonaparte* (1939), 70.

[4] N. Richardson, *The French Prefectoral Corps 1814–1830* (1966), 16, A.B. Spitzer 'The Bureaucrat as Proconsul', *CSSH,* vii (1965), 372–4, and more generally, *Les Préfets en France.*

[5] Tudesq quoted in Chaussinand-Nogaret, *Une histoire des élites,*

360–1.

⁶ Pouthas in ibid., 292. Cf. Poutier, 'L'Évolution des structures ministérielles', iv, 15, 117–18, and 214–17.

⁷ Anon., *Le Cri des employés du gouvernement* (1828), 5–6. Cf. also J. G. Ymbert, *L'Art d'obtenir des places* (1817), and *Des employés* etc., 21–9, for other aspects of the debate on security and freedom from political intervention.

⁸ Savoye, 'Quelques aspects de l'œuvre de L.-A. Macarel', 47–9, and Fougère, *Le Conseil d'état*, 672–6, deal with administrative law. Cf. also Sautel, *Histoire des institutions publiques*, 438–59, and A. Darbel and D. Schnapper, *Le Système administratif* (The Hague, 1972), 60–1.

⁹ G. Thuillier, *La Vie quotidienne dans les ministères au XIXᵉ siècle* (1976), 213–31, and, for a fuller account of the assault on the first ENA, V. Wright, 'L'École nationale d'administration 1848–49', *RH*, cclv/1 (1976), 21–42.

¹⁰ Van Berkel, op. cit., v, 623–4, and, on the development of new services, Dawson, *L'Évolution des structures du gouvernement déconcentré*, 83, 99, and 117–18.

¹¹ The period is conveniently discussed in general by G. Bertier de Sauvigny, *La Restauration* (1963), and by A. Jardin and A. J. Tudesq, *La France des Notables*, 2 vols. (1973), while P. Bastid, *Les Institutions politiques de la monarchie parlementaire française, 1815–1848* (1954), provides a guide to the institutions of the period.

¹² Ibid., 6 and 16–19. M. Brugière, in *Histoire de l'administration . . . Problèmes et Méthodes*, 40–1; D. Resnick, *The White Terror and the Political Reaction after Waterloo* (Cambridge, Mass., 1966), 108–9; Cusson, *Origines et évolution du Ministère de l'Agriculture*, 265–9, and Vidalenc, in both *Les Préfets*, loc. cit., and *Les Épurations administratives*, 63–7 (together with Tulard, ibid., 49–54), are among secondary works dealing with this period. Amongst archival sources are *AHG*, Xˢ 116 (Dossier 1814), and 117 (Dossier 1816), and especially *AD*, Haute-Marne, 9 M 2, for Jerphanion's letters of spring 1815 which reflect attempts to purge the administration.

¹³ Legendre, *Histoire de l'administration*, 502–5, and Poutier, op. cit., ii, 4–111. Cf. also Fougère, op. cit., 202–19.

¹⁴ Sauvigny, op. cit., 68–74 and 288–93, and Jardin and Tudesq, op. cit., 18–20. Cf. also *De l'influence des directeurs généraux sur l'administration du royaume* (1818).

¹⁵ Gousset, 'Evolution historique de l'administration centrale du Commerce', 134–5; Durand-Barthez, *Histoire des structures du Ministère de la Justice*, 37–51, and Outrey, *L'Administration française des Affaires Étrangères*, Appendix I. For Dennié's letter of 27 March 1823 see *AHG*, Xˢ 118 (Dossier 1823).

¹⁶ A good example of this, albeit from the July Monarchy, is that in

the Ministry of Public Instruction, described by L. Trenard, *Salvandy en son temps, 1795–1856* (Lille, 1968), 343–5. For Cabinets see Thullier, op. cit., 181–2, and on Directors General, Vidalenc in *Les Directeurs* 14–26.

[17] V. Crabbe, 'Balzac et l'administration', *Revue internationale des sciences administratives*, xx (1954), 293–9, and J. H. Donniol, *Les Réalités économiques et sociales dans le Comédie Humaine* (91961), 366–9.

[18] Sauvigny's estimate (op. cit., 274–6) of 5,000 in the Administrations Centrales, of whom 3,000 were in the financial bodies, is probably too high, though 120,000 may well be right for the civilian administration as a whole in France. Malouet is quoted by Richardson, op. cit., 154. Cf. also C. H. Pouthas, 'La Réforme administrative sous la Restauration', *Revue d'histoire moderne*, i (1926), 329–34, and F. Ponteil, *Les Institutions de la France de 1814 à 1870* (1966), 30–6 and 60–1.

[19] Fougère, op. cit., 239–96, and Chevallier, *L'Élaboration historique du régime de séparation*, 103–5 and 122–3.

[20] Richardson, op. cit., 23–6 and 124–35, and Spitzer, op. cit., 391–2.

[21] Cited in Legendre, *L'Administration du XVIIIe siècle*, 49–51. Cf. also J. G. Ymbert, *La Bureaucratie* (1825), 5 and 10–14.

[22] *Le Cri de la justice et de l'humanité en faveur des employés réformés* (c.1814); *Les Employés vengés* (s.d.); *Des employés des réformes*, (1818); C. Farcy, *Les Commis ou l'intérieur d'un bureau* (1818); 'Refléxions sur l'organisation du personnel des employés du Ministère de la Guerre' (*AHG*, X^s 148, of 4 December 1822); *De la possibilité de réduire les charges de l'état* (1823); and J. G. Ymbert, *La Bureaucratie, Mœurs administratives* and *La cri des employés*.

[23] A. Daumard, *La Bourgeoisie parisienne* (1964), 80–4 and 101–2, and J. Lhomme, *La Grande Bourgeoisie au pouvoir* (1960), 25.

[24] Thuillier, op. cit., 40–59, and J. Vidalenc, *La France de la diligence au Concorde* (1975), 40–3.

[25] Sautel, op. cit., 380–1, together with Meininger, 'D'Hauterive et la formation', 51–2 deal with training schools and 'objective' recruitment patterns. The latter sees these as fading with the July Monarchy, so that not till the 1850s did diplomats need diplomas again. Cf. also J. P. Bury, 'La Carrière diplomatique au temps de Second Empire', *Revue d'histoire diplomatique* xc (1976), 277–99.

[26] Tranchant, *De la préparation aux services publics;* Ponteil, *Histoire de l'enseignement,* 169 and 181, and Thuillier, *Témoins de l'Administration,* 99–110. Against this most be set the evidence of M. Kessler 'Historique de système de formation et de recrutèment des hauts fonctionnaires', *Revue française d'administration publique,* i/1 (1977), 12–13, and the backwardness of the Universities *pace* T. Zeldin, 'Intellect, Taste and

Anxiety', *France 1848–1948* (Oxford, 1977), ii, 141 and 317–18.

[27] The following discussion is based on a sample of 73 entrants under the Restoration, analysed by the same computer program as for the Empire. Their date of birth was 1760–9, 6.2%, 1770–9, 20.6%, 1780–9, 13.4%, 1790–9, 19.4%, and 1800–9, 17%. .

[28] The precise figures are 1814–15: 31.8%; 1816–19: 17.6%; 1820–4: 12.6% and 1825–30: 16.7%.

[29] In their previous jobs 30.1% were soldiers; 13.7% had been in private life; 12.3% had been students; 6.8% came from the field services; and 5.5% from the professions.

[30] Thuillier op. cit., 132–6. He is also right to note the blockages to promotion but not, 146, to imagine dismissal and reappointment were rare.

[31] D. Pinkney, *The French Revolution of 1830* (Princeton, NJ, 1972), 288–93, although T. Beck, *French Legislators, 1800–1834* (Berkeley, Cal., 1974), 133, argues that this is a slightly limited view. Cf. also Julien-Laferrière, *Les Deputés–Fonctionnaires sous la Monarchie de Juillet*, 86–8, and Chaussinand-Nogaret, op. cit., 283.

[32] On the purges of 1830 see Tulard, Gerbod, and Sandevoir in *Les Épurations* 57, 90–1, and 106–12 together with P. Pilbeam, 'The Emergence of opposition to the Orleanist Monarchy', *EHR*, lxxxv, (1970), 12–28, and Pinkney, op. cit., 55, 277, and 283. On the 'ruée vers les places' see Vte de Guichen, *La Révolution de Juillet et l'Europe* (1916), 53, and, for a successful case of promotion from a partly clerical level, R. Bied, 'La Vie quotidienne d'un fonctionnaire préfectoral', *RA*, xxviii (1974), 328–38.

[33] C. Pouthas, 'La Réorganisation du Ministère de l'Intérieur et la reconstitution préfectorale', *RHMC*, ix (1962), 242–4.

[34] See the proclamation urging the Orleanist candidature in Pinkney, op. cit., 159. For reforms see *AHG*, X^s 118 (Dossiers 1830–2) and for complaints Thuillier, *Témoins de l'administration*, 170–4, 180–5, 198–9, and 248–50.

[35] Pouthas, loc. cit., and Legendre, op. cit., 177–80.

[36] Julien-Lafferrière, op. cit., 14, 42, 46, 51, and 106, and on the problem of estimating the size of the civil service, 19–22. Tudesq in *Directeurs*, 27–37, and P. Birnbaum, *Les Sommets de l'État* (1977), 27–30, discuss politicization further. Cf. also S. Kent, *Electoral Procedure under Louis Philippe* (New Haven, Conn., 1937), 135, and H. H. Finer, *Theory and Practice of Modern Government* (1961), 710.

[37] The Budget of 1830 (as detailed in *AHG*, X^s 128) showed Justice with 87 staff, Affaires Étrangères with 88, Affaires Écclesiastiques 48, Instruction Publique 71, Intérieur 199, Commerce et Manufactures 192, Guerre 397, Marine 143, and Finances 723, a total of 1928.

[38] Julien-Lafferrière, op. cit., 88–9, and, for the contrary view,

Donniol, op. cit., 369–75, and A. Dansette, *Louis Napoléon à la conquête du pouvoir* (1961), 196.

[39] Van Berkel, op. cit., v, 654–61 and 690–709, and the evidence of Haute-Marne, 7 M 1 and 7 M 3 on prefectoral administration. On the ministries, Ponteil, *Histoire des institutions,* 137–8, and Jardin and Tudesq. op. cit., 137–8. For the field services T. Shinn, 'From "Corps" to "Profession". The Emergence and definition of Industrial Engineering in Modern France', unpublished paper contributed to a forthcoming Parex volume on 'The Organisation of Science and Technology in France, 1815–1914'.

[40] On the Ministry of War see *AHG,* X^s 128 which has many estimates of staff strengths and Pensions civiles, i, 49, Lamée, and i, 69, Potier for the cases invoked here. Cf. also J. Tulard and G. Thuillier, 'Pour une histoire des directeurs du ministère en France au XIXe et XXe siècles', *Revue internationale de science administrative,* i (1974), 227–9.

[41] O. Pirotte, *A. F. A. Vivien de Goubert, Contribution à l'étude d'un libéral authoritaire* (1972), 98 and Chevallier, *L'Élaboration historique,* 105–6. Cf. also H. Deray, 'L'Inspection des Finances', *Revue des deux mondes,* xxvii (1958), 459–60; V. Silvera, 'Une Vieille institution originale: le Conseil d'Administration du Ministère de la Justice', *RA,* xxvii (1972), 297–8, and G. Thuillier, 'Le Droit disciplinaire dans les Ministères au XIXe', *RA,* xxx/1 (1977), 26–37.

[42] Legendre, *Histoire de l'administration,* 66–8 and 532–45, together with Daumard, op. cit., 80, 216, and 228.

[43] Trenard, op. cit., 349 and 651, shows how Salvandy light-heartedly brought in outsiders to his ministry and sought to promote them rapidly, until checked by the Budgetary Commission of the Chamber of Deputies. Cf. also Tudesq in Chaussinand-Nogaret, op. cit., 360–8.

[44] J. Delbousquet, *De l'organisation des administrations centrales des divers ministères* (1843); Anon., *Examen critique de la brochure de M. Delbousquet* (1843); and Patience, *Pétition à MM. les membres de la Chambre des Deputés* (1847). Cf. also A. Vivien, *Études administratives* (1845), 59, 95, 163–5, and 212.

[45] Thuillier, *La Vie quotidienne,* 53, 61, 70–2, and 100–7 etc.

[46] Kessler, op. cit., 12–13, and A Lanza, 'Étude sur le statut de la fonction publique' in C. Durand, *Études sur les rapports entre la loi et le règlement gouvernmental'* (Aix, 1976), 257–318. Cf. also A. Lefas, *L'État et les fonctionnaires* (1913), 213; W. Sharp, *The French Civil Service* (New York, 1934), 51 and 247; Grégoire, *La Fonction publique,* 48, and Gournay *et al., L'Administration publique,* 236.

[47] Savoye, op. cit., 189 et seq., and Ponteil, *Histoire de l'enseignement,* 163–4. Cf. also A. G. Bellini, *Des avantages des concours* (1846).

⁴⁸ Van Berkel, op. cit., v, 661–90, and Duval, cited in Thuillier, Témoins, 234–9.

⁴⁹ This discussion is based on a further sample of 93 analysed as before. 15.8% are known to have come from the country and 66.3% from the town compared to 71.2% and 11.0% in the Restoration sample.

⁵⁰ Their date of birth was 1770–9, 2.1%; 1780–9, 2.1%; 1720–9, 5.2%; 1800–9, 10.3%; 1810–19, 35%; and 1830–9, 28.8%.

⁵¹ The precise figures were 1830–9, 41.2%; and 1840–8, 53.6%.

⁵² Some 27.4% had been students, 20% came from commerce, 8.4% from private life; 6.3% from the professions, 5.3% had been notarial clerks, and 1.1% came from the field services and local government respectively.

⁵³ To be precise 14.7% had had a private tutor (as against 8.2% in the Restoration); 11.6% had been on a University Arts course (2.7%), 5.3% on a Law course (4.1%), and 2.2% (—) on a Science course. 5.3% came from a *Grande école* (2.7%) and 1.1% from a *lycée* without any Tertiary education (1.4%). Cf. also G. Thuillier, 'La Gestion du personnel des ministères au XIXᵉ. L'Exemple de la Guerre, 1830–1880', *RA*, xxxi/3 (1978) 261–73.

⁵⁴ Pouthas, loc cit., and see also Strauss, *The Ruling Servants*, 193–9.

⁵⁵ T. Zeldin, 'Ambition, Love and Politics', *France 1848–1945* (Oxford, 1973), i, 113–30, is a useful guide to this process.

⁵⁶ Fougère, op. cit., 397–460, and Chevallier, op. cit., 101–10 and 197–8. Other aspects of the effect of 1848 on the administration are discussed by Chardon, *L'Administration de la France;* C. Gabolde, 'Un projet de création des Tribunaux Administratifs en 1848', *RA,* viii (1954), 247–50, and Poutier, op. cit., ii, 324–44.

⁵⁷ *AD,* Haute-Marne, 7 M 2, a series of 'Petitions des employés, 1848–52', shows a nation-wide campaign to create a proper corps for prefectoral employees.

⁵⁸ Thuillier, op. cit., 212–19.

⁵⁹ V. Wright and G. Thuillier, 'Pour un histoire du coup d'état', *Le Mouvement social*, 94 (1976), 106.

⁶⁰ Savoye, op. cit., 288–9; M. Saurin, 'L'École d'administration en 1848', *Politique,* viii (1964–5), 105–95; G. Langrod, 'L'École d'administration française, 1848–9', and *Annali della Fondazione Italiana per la Storia Amministrativa* (1965), 487–523, together with Thuillier, op. cit., 204–11. Unfortunately the latters monumental *Bureaucratie et bureaucratés en France au XIXᵉ siècle* (Geneva, 1980) was published too late for it to be used here.

NOTES TO CHAPTER X

[1] Hayward, *The One and Indivisible French Republic*, 8–17, and V. Wright, 'Politics and Administration', *Political Studies*, xxii/1 (1974), 63–5.

[2] A. Plessis, *De la fête impériale au mur des fédérés* (1973), 28, and 38–48.

[3] Marx, *The Eighteenth Brumaire*, 132.

[4] This process of adjustment, which involved above all the fragmentation of the Ministry of the Interior is admirably demonstrated by the diagram which accompanies Darbel and Schnapper's *Le Système administratif*. Cf. also Birnbaum, *Les Sommets*, 30–47.

[5] Ridley and Blondel, *Public Administration in France*, 156, and J. Sallois (ed.) *L'Administration*, 68–70, 285–6, and 330–40, together with M. Baratier, *L'Administration publique en France* (1885), cover this period. Cf. also Wright, op. cit., 61.

[6] The various drafts of a *Statut* can be conveniently found in *AN*, (Archives Économiques et Sociaux), F^{30} 248. Commentaries include G. Demartial, *Le Personnel des Ministères* (1906), 7–8; Sharp, *The French Civil Service*, 51–69, and Zeldin, *Ambition, Love and Politics*, loc. cit., Cf also J. Siwek-Pouydesseau, 'Élaboration du Statut Général', *Annuaire internationale de la fonction publique* (1971), 13–14, together with Kessler, 'Historique du système', 27–38. Lanza, 'Étude sur le statut', 257, and Braibant and others in *Les Épurations administratives*, 78, 114, and 116.

[7] J. F. Godfrey, 'Bureaucracy, Industry and Politics in France during the First World War', unpublished Oxford University D. Phil. thesis (1974), 57–60, and 114–21.

[8] Legendre, *Histoire de l'administration*, 373–433, together with A. Lanza, *Les Projets de réforme administrative en France de 1919 à nos jours* (1968), and R. F. Kuisel 'The Legend of the Vichy "Synarchy" ', *FHS*, vi (1970), 384–96.

[9] A. Mignot and B. Orsay, *La Machine administrative* (1969), and J. Duperrier, *L'Organisation administrative de la France* (1973), are useful guides to the present-day situation.

[10] R. Mousnier, *Louis XIV* (Historical Association, 1974), 19.

[11] M. Walzer, *Regicide and Revolution* (Cambridge, 1974), 8, 25, and 27. This view has also been largely upheld by two recent studies of the subject which appeared too late for full consideration here: G. Aylmer, 'Bureaucracy', in P. Burke (ed.), *New Cambridge Modern History Companion Volume* (Cambridge, 1979), xiii, 167–8 and 180–1, and M. Krygier, in E. Kamenka *et al.*, *Bureaucracy—The Career of a Concept* (1979), 5.

[12] Legendre, op. cit., 46–59 and 494–502. Wright, loc. cit., makes a similar differentiation between the phases and traditions of French

administration as that advanced here.

[13] The most recent histories of administration in general are those of E. N. Gladden, *A History of Public Administration* (1972), and S. F. Romano, *Breve storia della burocrazia* (Bologna, 1969), while something can still be gleaned from Finer, *Theory and Practice of Modern Government*, B. Chapman, *The Profession of Government*, and E. Barker, *The Development of Public Services in Western Europe* (Oxford, 1944). P. Legendre, *Jour du pouvoir* (1976), 66 and 157, argues that French administration is inextricably linked to French legalism.

[14] This deduction was erroneously drawn from a lecture by the present writer by one 'A. Mr.' in *La Nation* of Lausanne, 967 of 17 January 1975, 1.

[15] Girard, in *Problèmes et méthodes*, 15.

[16] V. Wright, *The Government and Politics of France* (1978), 84–106.

[17] Bloch-Lainé, *Profession: Fonctionnaire*, 233, and J. Armstrong, 'Old Regime Administrative Élites in France, Prussia and Russia', *Revue internationale des sciences administratives*, xxxviii/1 (1972), 33.

[18] On the need see J. R. Suratteau in *AHRF*, xlix/1 (1977), 151–3, who also calls the methodology 'pointillisme tout Britannique', a criticism perhaps better reserved for the Tulard–Thuillier approach to administrative history, cf. G. Thuillier and J. Tulard, 'L'Histoire de l'administration du dix-neuvième siècle depuis dix ans', *RH*, 524 (1977), 441.

[19] E. N. Gladden, 'Public Administration and History', *Revue internationale des sciences administratives'* xxviii/4, (1972), 379–84. Cf. Baecheler, *Les Phénomènes révolutionnaires*, 23.

[20] Ridley and Blondel, op. cit., 58.

[21] W. Delaney 'The Development and Decline of Patrimonial and Bureaucratic Administraitons', *ASQ* vii (1963), 470–1, and Sallois, op. cit., 55–89.

[22] P. Legendre, *L'Amour du Censeur* (1974), esp. 219–24.

[23] S. Weil, *L'Enracinment* (1950), iii, 165.

[24] Quoted in Savoye, 'Quelque Aspects . . . de Macarel', 110.

[25] Balzac, *Les Employés*, 314.

BIBLIOGRAPHY

A. PRIMARY SOURCES

I. *Manuscript.* The titles for the primary sources have been drawn from those given in the various *État Sommaires* but it should be noted that in many cases these are misleading and do not give a satisfactory description of the contents. Where necessary additional information has been supplied within square brackets. Certain items appear to have no recognized catalogue numbers and these have therefore been marked as '*hors de séries*'. A considerable amount of material is either subject to certain difficulties of access or needs ministerial permission before it can be consulted. In certain cases the number of cartons in a series has been noted to give some guidance as to the extent of the material.

ARCHIVES NATIONALES

a. *Secrétariat d'État: Papers relating to the Directory: cartons.*
(Cf. the not completely reliable *inventaire* (no. 748) drawn up in 1875 by Felix Rocquain (MS).)

AF III	
20^a	Employés des bureaux du Directoire.
20^b	États des Appointements des employés.
21^d	Organisation intérieure du Directoire.
24	Serments des employés [des bureaux du Directoire].
28–9	Personnel des diverses Ministères; Commission des Dix-Sept; Appointements.
31	Prestations de Serments [des bureaux des Ministères].
37	Dépenses judiciaires.
52–5	(one carton) Rapports du Ministre [des Relations Extérieures au Directoire].
91–2	Prestations de Serments des employés [du Ministère de l'Intérieur].
114	Correspondance du Ministre des Finances avec le Directoire.

118   Dépenses des Ministères.

136–142   Prestations de Serments [des employés du Ministère des Finances].

144[a]   Guerre: Objets divers.

146   Correspondance relative aux armées.

169–172   Prestations de Serments [des employés du Ministère de la Guerre].

202   Prestations de Serments [des employés du Ministère de la Marine et Colonies].

203[a–b]   [Ministère de la Marine et Colonies] Administration générale.

b. *Secrétariat d'État: Papers relating to the Directory: registres*

AF[x] III 1–17   Procès-Verbaux des séances du Directoire Exécutif.

18–19   Actes du Directoire Exéctif: ressortissant du Bureau Particulier du Secrétariat-Général.

20   Délibérations secrètes du Directoire.

26   Arrêtés et correspondance: matières diverses.

29–34   Correspondance du Secrétaire Général.

117–38   Délibérations, arrêtés, et messages du Directoire concernant l'Intérieur.

148–56   Délibérations, arrêtés, et messages du Directoire concernant l'Intérieur.

157   Lettres du Directoire au Ministre de la Justice.

158–66   Délibérations, arrêtés, et messages du Directoire concernant la Justice.

175   Lettres du Directoire au Ministre [des Relations Extérieurers].

176–8   Délibérations, arrêtés, et messages du Directoire concernant les Relations Extérieures.

179   Pièces remises en bureau diplomatique.

181–90   Délibérations, arrêtés, et messages du Directoire concernant les finances.

202–3   Lettres du Directoire au Ministre de la Guerre etc.

204–6   Délibérations, arrêtés, et messages du Directoire relatifs à la Guerre.

218–22   Arrêtés et lettres du Directoire au sujet de la Guerre.

245–8   Délibérations, arrêtés, et messages du Directoire concernant la Marine.

c. *Other papers in the collection of the Secrétariat d'État*

AF II	20–24	Organisation du Comité de Salut Public, des Ministères, et des Commissions Exécutifs.
AF^x II	284	Organisation intérieure du Comité du Sûreté Générale.
AF^x IV	47–8	Secrétaire Général des Consuls: Correspondance.
AF IV	1065	Administration Générale et Correspondance.
	1326^b	Secrétaire d'État. [Affaires diverses.]
	1387^b	Secrétaire d'État: Appointements des Employés.

d. *Miscellaneous papers in the Archives Nationales*

C	226–32	Papiers de la Commission des Onze.
	355–6	Commission des Seize.
	360	[Comité des Inspecteurs de la Salle de la Convention.]
	364	[Employés des Comités de la Convention.]
D III	360	Employés du Comité [de Législation]: demandes de places.
	381	Organisation du Comité [de Législation] etc. (1792–an III).
D^x XXV^{a-c} 5		Comité des Inspecteurs de la Salle [de la Convention].
D XLIII 1		Comité de Sûreté Générale et Survillance: lettres etc. (esp. pièces 94–124).
O^1	747	Charges et déspenses de la Maison du Roi.
27 AP	13	François de Neufchateau
117 AP		Treilhard
210 AP		Reubell
216^1 AP		Thibaudeau
138 AP 2 + 6		Daru

MINISTERIAL DEPOSITS IN THE ARCHIVES NATIONALES

e. *Papers of the Ministry of the Interior*

F	3053	Enregistrement de la Correspondance envoyée par le sixième bureau de la première division (personnel administratif) du Ministère.
F^{1a}	1–5	Organisation du Ministère etc. (1791–1835).
	63	Circulaires au sujet du personnel.
	76	Arrêtés du Comité de Salut Public [et du Directoire].
	634–5	Organisation des Bureaux.

F^{1ax} 249 Relations du Ministère avec le Directoire etc. (an IV–1815).

F^{1b1} 1 Ministres, Secrétaires Généraux, et Directeurs du Ministère (1791–1828).

2–6 Personnel du Ministère: Organisation des Bureaux (1790–1807).

11–14 Personnel du Ministère etc. (1792–1820).

15 États des Traitements.

82 Traitments.

105–6 Commissaires du Pouvoir Exécutif dans les départements. (The État Général of the size of the bureaucracy in 1796 referred to on page 164, n.1, seems by rights to belong in F^{1b1} 122/3).

261^1–86 Dossiers individuels des fonctionnaires de l'administration centrale du Ministère, an VII–1890 (c.60 cartons).

F^{1b1x} 531 Organisation des bureaux etc. (1792–1811). (One of a series of catalogues drawn up in the mid-nineteenth century).

F^4 1016 Appointements et salaires des fonctionnaires etc.

F^4 2848–53 État des traitements des employés du Ministère etc.

F^{17} 1012, 1032–4, 1045, 1245 Instruction Publique.

f. Papers of the Ministry of Finance (Archives Économiques et Sociaux)

F^{30} 112 Trésorie Nationale etc.; Ministère des Contributions Publiques: personnel. (Previously numbered F^{30} 1004^x–6^x.)

F^{30} 2424 Catalogue analytique de l'organisation du Personnel du Ministère (1769–1926).

g. Papers of the Ministry of Justice

BB^4 1 Organisation du Ministère etc.

2 Dépenses Intérieures du Ministère.

7–9 Personnel de l'Administration centrale etc. (1773–an VI).

BB^{25} 21–3bis États des Pensions et retraites des employés etc. (1808–27).

BB^{30} 30 Organisation des bureaux de la Commission des Administrations Civiles, Police, et Tribunaux. an II etc.

497–500   Ministère de la Justice: Personnel et appointements.

509–10   Agence puis bureau des lois: Personnel et appointements.

512^1 Chancellerie etc.; Organisation des bureaux, 1791–1875.

516^1 Fonctionnaires du Ministère etc., 1806–37.

516^{1-2} Pensions et secours, 1824–9.

761^{1-2} Imprimerie Nationale: personnel et appointements. (an IV—1810)

h. *Papers of the Ministry of Police.* Besides the items recorded below a certain amount of information relating to the functionaries of the Ministry of Police can be found among the papers of the Ministry of the Interior, with which the former was amalgamated after 1822.

F^{7x} 2228   Serment de fidelité à la Constitution, an IX.

F^7 3007–7   Organisation du Ministère de la Police Générale, an IV–1815.

        4229   Personnel du Ministère de la Police.

        12249–50   États financiers, ans IV–XIII.

        12253   Comptabilité du Ministère etc. (personnel etc.) an V–1807.

        12278   Travail des pensions de retraite et secours, 1814–28.

i. *Papers of the Ministry of Marine and Colonies.* These are still in the process of being deposited in the *Archives Nationales* and thus there is no adequate printed catalogue of the modern archives of the Ministry. Moreover, the reference numbers clash with those of the Ministry of Justice in several cases and it is best to prefix the *côtes* of either with the name of the deposit.

bb^8 110   Secrétariat Général: Service intérieure. Decisions, an IV–1859.

        269–78   [Bureaux de la Marine: matières diverses] an V–1873.

C^7I 1–355   Personnel: dossiers individuels. This is the first of three series and its 355 cartons cover the period up to 1790. They are not restricted to administrative officials.

ARCHIVES OTHER THAN THE
ARCHIVES NATIONALES

j. *Service Historique de la Marine*

C^7 II   Personnel: dossiers individuels. This is the second series and covers the perion 1790–1870. It runs to just over 2,500 cartons for which there is no *inventaire*.

k. *Archives des Affaires Étrangères*

Fonds France: 335 Affaires intérieures et extérieures, 1795–1814

             518 1744–1800; Personne diplomatique etc.

       1413–5 Affaires intérieures, 1794–1805.

Dossiers du Personnel: these run to 70 volumes for which there is
(*hors de series*)   a typescript *inventaire* in the Quai d'Orsai. Dossiers dealing with employees who served after 1814, together with ministerial accounts later than 1839, are not open for consultation. The personnel dossiers cover both diplomats and *fonctionnaires* of the administration.

l. *Archives de la Guerre*

X^s 1–3   Administration.

     115–8   Administration Centrale, 1792–1802.

     128   Organisation de l'Administration Centrale.

     129–30   Attributions de l'Administration Centrale.

     148   Administration Centrale: Historique, ans III–XI.

     228   Pensions civiles: bureaux de la Guerre.

A^1 1886   Les Bureaux de la Guerre sous l'Ancien Régime

     3208   Correspondence

     3579   Correspondence

Mémoires 1790   Various

       2015   Various

Y^a 23–25   Documents sur les bureaux: États de personnel, 1711–89.

     26–32   Personnel de l'administration centrale.

S^{12} 12^x Correspondance du Ministère avec le Directoire.

Fonds Préval 2014–5   Ministère de la Guerre etc.

            2018   Organisation jusqu'en 1820 etc.

Hors de Series.   (a) 2 cartons relating to the organization of the Ministry from 1789–1896. (b) A series of cartons relating to the *Dépôt Général de la Guerre*, of which numbers 1–4 were used.

                                 Pensions civiles, à partir de 1806, (*c*.90 cartons).

m.   *Bibliothèque Nationale*

Fonds Français 700   Recueil de pièces historiques sur la Révolution etc.;

                                V: Documents divers etc.

Nouvelles Acquisitions Françaises:

          323   Recueil de pièces sur la Révolution et la Restauration, 1782–1815.

     3568–71   Recueil de lettres de ministres etc., 1794–1804.

       3574   Recueil de lettres originales addressées par divers à Barras.

(In addition the Bibliothèque Nationale holds several collections of papers of Directors and other personalities of the regime, such as NA 23643, Papiers de Reubell.)

n.   *Departmental Archives:* cartons—variously titled—on local bureaux *c*. 1780–1820.

Eure	9 L 13 and 30 L 9
Eure-et-Loir	L 40–43
Loir-et-Cher	L 276
	L 1021
Loiret	L 56
Haute-Marne	L* 106–111
	L 126–7
	L 233–7
	L 375–8
	L 472–4
	F 60 and F 153
	7 M 1–4
	9 M 12
Oise	L 1 13–15
	L 1 21
	L 1 60–65
Seine-et-Marne	L 115–118
Pyrennées, Basses	IL 18–21.

II. *Printed Sources*

a. *Archives Nationales:* Collection Rondonneau.

AD I	60	Le Directoire.
AD I	76–8	Les Ministres.
AD XVIII^f 7–22		Budgets et Comptes Rendus.
AD XIX F 45		Finances.

b *British Library:* Croker Collection.

FR	89–92	Constitution de l'an III.
	94–98	Les Ministres.
	471	Finances XII: 1795–1801.
	551–3	Dépenses des Ministères etc.
	575	Pensions, II.
F	763–4	Livre Rouge.
	1102–9	Gouvernement.
	1120	Le Directoire.
F	55^{xx}	Le Directoire.
R	114–5	Le Directoire.
	143–5	Les Ministres I–III: 1788–1817.
	434	Police.
	563–5	Les Ministres.
	624–5	Finance II–III: 1792–1815.

Some reference was also made to FR 68, 478, 506, 566–72; F 643–6; and R 479 and 499.

c. *John Rylands University Library, Manchester*

Adolphus Tracts (27 vols.).
Rowan Tracts (24 vols.).
Some use was also made of the as yet uncatalogued Crawford collection of pamphlets.

d. *Newspapers*

Some numbers only of the following journals have been consulted, depending on their availability in England. Local papers have not been consulted. On the whole newspapers carried little information on the processes of government apart from rumoured changes among the governing élite.

L'Accusateur public
Les Actes des Apôtres.
Le Bulletin décadaire.
Le Censeur des journaux.

La Clef du cabinet des souverains de l'Europe.
Le Conservateur.
Le Courrier universel.
Le Défenseur de la verité et des principes.
L'Historien.
Le Journal des débats et décrets.
Le Journal des défenseurs de la patrie.
Le Journal d'économie publique, de morale et de politique.
Le Journal des hommes libres.
Le Journal de Paris.
Le Journal des patriotes de '89.
Le Journal du Petit Gaultier.
Le Gazette nationale ou *Le Moniteur universel.* (This is a prime source for the period mainly because of its reports of debates. The original edition has been consulted throughout, in preference to the *Réimpression de l'Ancien Moniteur* since the latter has only the briefest of entries for the period after the spring of 1796.)
Le Publiciste.
Le Rédacteur. (This paper, which was the Directory's main propaganda organ was at first entitled Le Bulletin politique, then Le Bulletin official and finally, a few days ater after the dismissal of Antonelle, the *Rédacteur.* It kept this title until it closed down under the Consulate.)
Le Sage Observateur.

e. *Modern Collections of Official Sources*[1]

Aulard, F. A. (ed.)   *Recueil des actes du Comité de Salut Public.* 28 vols. (Collection de documents inédits sur l'histoire de France, 1889–1923.)
Paris pendant le réaction thermidorienne et sous le Directoire. (Collection de documents relatifs à l'histoire de Paris pendant la Révolution française, 1898–1902.)

Debidour, A. (ed.)   *Recueil des actes du Directoire exécutif.* 4 vols. (Collection de documents inédits sur l'histoire de France, 1910–17.) [This collection covers only the period from Brumaire an IV to Pluviose an V, and for the later part of the period one

[1] Unless otherwise stated the place of publication of French books is Paris and of English ones, London.

must have recourse to the MS registers of the Directorial sessions.]

Mautouchet, P. *Le Gouvernement révolutionnaire* (1911).

f. *Other Printed Sources*

R. David d'Angers, *Mémoires de la Revellière Lépaux*, 3 vols. (1895).

Almanach national, etc. (1789–1804).

Anon., *De l'influence des Directeurs Généraux sur l'administration du royaume* (1818).

Anon., *Des employés, des reformes* (1818).

Anon., *Examen critique de la brochure de M. Delbousquet* (1843).

Anon., *Le Cri des employés du gouvernement* (1828).

Anon., *Des employés, des reformes et du régime intérieur des bureaux* (1817).

Arnna, J. (ed.), *Napoleon Ier: Lettres au Comte Mollien* (1959).

D'Argenson, R. L. Voyer de Paulmy, Marquis, *Considérations sur le gouvernement ancien et présent de la France*, 2nd ed. (Amsterdam, 1784).

Aulard, F. A., *Paris pendant la réaction thermidorienne et sous le Directoire* (1901).

Babeau, A. *La France et Paris sous le Directoire: Lettres d'une voyageuse anglaise, suivies d'extraits des lettres de Swinburne 1796–1797* (1888).

Barthelemy, F. de, *Mémoires* (1914).

Baudot, M. A., *Notes historiques sur la Convention Nationale* (1893).

Bégis, A. (ed.), *Conduite politique de Lejeune* (1896).

Bonnasieux, P., *Conseil de Commerce et Bureau de Commerce, 1700–1791: Inventaire analytique des procès-verbaux* (1900).

Bourdon, J., *Napoléon au Conseil d'État: Notes et procès-verbaux inédits de Jean Guilliaume Locré, Secrétaire Général du Conseil d'État* (1963).

Buchez, P. J. B., and Roux, P. C., *Histoire parlementaire de la Révolution française* (1833).

Bulletin des loix 15 vols., an II–an VIII.

Chronolgie des lois, décrets, ordonnances, etc. relatifs à l'organisation . . . du Ministère de l'Intérieur (1790–1835) (1835).

Delbousquet, J., *De l'organisation des administrations centrales des divers ministères, des droits et des devoirs des employés* (1843).

Dossion, E. A., *Le Cri de la justice et de l'humanité en faveur des employés réformés* (1817).

Driault, E., *Napoléon: Pensées pour l'action* (1943).

Duguit, L., Monnier, H. and Bonnard, R., *Les Constitutions de la France* (1952).

Dumouriez, C. F. D., *La Vie et les mémoires du Général Dumouriez* (Berville et Barrière, 1823).

Durand de Maillane, P. T. *Histoire de la Convention Nationale* (1825).

Duruy, G. (ed.), *Mémoires de Barras, membre du Directoire* (1895).

Duval, G., *Souvenirs de la réaction thermidorienne* (1844).

Duvergier, J. B., *Collection complète des lois, décrets, ordonnances et règlements* (1834).

Fabre, J. P. (de l'Aude), *Histoire secrète du Directoire* (1832).

Fabre, A.U.D.P. (de Narbonne), *Le Directoire* (1830).

Fauvelet du Toc, *Histoire des secrétaires d'Etat*, etc. (1668).

Godechot, J., *Les Constitutions de la France* (1970).

d'Huart, S. (ed.), *Lettres, ordres et apostilles de Napoléon, extrait des Archives Daru* (1965).

Jourdan, Isambert, Decruisy, *et al.*, *Recueil général des anciennes lois françaises*, (1822–33).

Lebrun-Tossa, J. A., *Portefeuille politique d'un ex-employé au Ministère de la Police* (1800).

Legendre, P. (ed.), *L'Administration du XVIIIe à nos jours. Textes et documents* (1969).

Long, M., Braibant, G., and Weil, P. (eds.), *Les Grands Arrêts de la jurisprudence dministrative*, 5th ed. (1969).

Lois et actes du gouvernement (1806).

Massin, J. (ed.), *Napoléon Bonaparte, l'œuvre et l'histoire* (1971).

Senac de Meilhan, G., *Du gouvernement. Des mœurs et des conditions en France avant la Révolution* (1799).

Mercier, L. S. G., *Le nouveau Paris* (1861).

Mercier, L. S., *Paris pendant la Révolution* (1882).

Milet-Mureau, L. M. A. D., *Compte rendu de l'administration de ce département Ventôse VII–Messidor VII*, 28 Brumaire VIII (1800).

Bertrand de Moleville, A. F. *Mémoires secrètes pour servir à l'histoire de la dernière année du regne de Louis XVI* (London, 1797).

Monnier, J., *Mœurs administrative dessinées d'après Nature* (1828).

François de Neufchâteau, *Recueil des lettres, circulaires et autres actes du Ministère de l'Intérieur* (1821).

Patience, *Petition à MM. les membres de la Chambre des Deputés* (1845).

Procès-verbaux des séances du Conseil des Anciens (1796–1800).

Procès-verbaux des séances du Conseil des Cinq Cents (1796–1800).

Procès-verbaux de la Convention Nationale (1792–6).

Puraye, J. (ed.), *Ce 10 Germinal An V. Lettres de Gilbert Claes* (Bruges, 1957).

Roserot, A (ed.), *Mémoires de Madame Chastenay* (1896).

Royau, F., *La Bureaucratie maritime* (1818).

Soudet, P. (ed.), *L'Administration vue Par les siens . . . et par d'autres* (1975).

Thibaudeau, A. G., *Mémoires* (1824).

Thuillier, G., *Témoins de l'administration de St. Just à Marx* (1967).

Tulard, J., *L'Anti-Napoléon* (1963).

Usteri, P., and Ritter, E. (eds.), *Henri Meister: Souvenirs de mon dernier voyage à Paris* (1910).

Vox, M. (ed.), *Correspondance de Napoléon* (1943).

Ymbert, J. G., *L'Art d'obtenir des places* (1816).

Ymbert, J. G., *La Bureaucratie* (1825).

Ymbert, J. G., *Mœurs administratives* (1825).

B. SECONDARY SOURCES

Since the potential and actual sources for this study are vast, this list must necessarily be selective. In fact it is doubly so since it includes only works which made a major contribution to the study and can therefore be fairly counted as sources. Other works which are merely illustrative or which relate to specific points can be found in the notes.

1. Reference and related works

D'Amat, R., *et al.*, *Dictionnaire de biographie française* (1933 on). For earlier publications of this kind see Church, 'Organisation and Personnel', 396–7.

Bardin, E. A., *et al.*, *Dictionnaire des armées de terre* etc., (1941–51), 16 parts.

Bodiguel, J. L., and Kessler, M. C., *L'Administration française* (1971).

Boulet-Sautel, M., Sautel, G., and Vandenbossche, A. (eds.), *Bibliographe en langue française d'histoire du droit* (IVe s–1875) (Montchrestien, in theory annual since 1961).

Caron, P., *Manuel pratique pour l'étude de la Révolution française* (1947).

Cheruel, A., *Dictionnaire historique des institutions, mœurs et coutumes de la France* (1855).

Church, C. H., 'Bibliographie pour l'histoire administrative: Travaux de langue anglaise sur la France', *Bulletin de l'Institut Internationale d'Administration Publique*, 30 (1974), 369–84.

Eisenstadt, S. N., 'Bureaucracy and Bureaucratization: A Trend Report and Bibliography', *Current Sociology*, vii 2 (1958), 129–63.

Eisenstadt, S. N., 'Bureaucracy, Bureaucratization and Debureaucratization', *ASQ*, 4 (December 1959), 302–21.

Eisenstadt, S. N., 'The Study of Organizations—A Trend Report and Bibliography', *Current Sociology*, xiii 3 (1965), 95–119.

Fougère, L., *et al.*, *Histoire de l'administration* (1972).

Gérard, A., *La Révolution française. Mythes et interprétations 1789–1970* (1970).

Gilissen, J. (ed.), *Introduction bibliographique à l'histoire du droit et à l'ethnologie juridique*,

1. M. Boulet-Sautel *et al.*, 'France (Avant 1789)' (1967).

2. G. Sicard, 'France (Depuis 1789)' (1967).

Gladden, E. N., 'Public Administration and History', *International Review of Administrative Sciences*, xxxvii/4 (1972), 379–84.

Godechot, J., *Les Révolutions, 1770–1799*, Nouvelle Clio (ed. R. Boutruche et P. Lemerle) (1963).

Godechot, J., *L'Europe et l'Amerique à l'Époque napoléonienne 1799–1815*, Nouvelle Clio (1967).

Gournay, B., *et al.*, *L'Administration française*, 2 vols. (1961–7).

Legendre, P., 'Studi di storia dell'ammistrazione nella Francia moderna', *Quaderni storici* (18) (Ancona, 1971), 609–40.

Legendre, P., 'L'Administration sans histoire. Les Courants traditionnels de recherche dans les Facultés de Droit', *RA* (1968), 427–32.

Legendre, P., 'La facture historique des systèmes', *Revue internationale de droit comparé* (1971), 5–47.

Legendre P., 'La Royauté du Droit Administratif', *RHDFE*, lii/4 (1974), 140–176.

Lepointe, G., and Vandenbossche, A. (eds.), *Éléments de bibliographie sur l'histoire des institutions et des faits sociaux 987–1875* (1958).

Mandrou, R., *La France aux XVIIᵉ et XVIIIᵉ siècles*, Nouvelle Clio, 33 (1967).

Marion, M., *Dictionnaire des institutions de la France aux XVIIᵉ et XVIIIᵉ siècles* (1923).

Puget, H. (ed.) *et al.*, *Bibliographie de la fonction publique et du personnel civil des administrations publiques* (1948).

Darbel, A., Dubost, F., and Schnapper, D., 'La Condition du fonctionnaire: Bibliographie historique critique (1870–1914)', *Annuaire international de la fonction publique 1970–71* (1971), 386–92.

Sheriff, P., 'Sociology of Public Bureaucracies, 1945–1975', *Current Sociology*, xxiv/2 (1976), 1–195.

Spuler, B., *Rulers and Governments of the World* (NY, 1977).

Suleiman, E. N., 'French Bureaucracy and its students: towards the desanctification of the state', *World Politics*, 23 (1970), 121–43.

Thuillier, G., and Tulard, J., 'L'Histoire de l'administration du dix neuvième siècle depuis dix ans. Bilan et perspectives', *RH*, 524 (1977), 441–56.

Villat, L., *La Révolution et l'Empire* (1936).

2. *General studies*

Albrow, M., *Bureaucracy* (1970).

Anderson, E. N. and P. R., *Political Insitutions and Social Change in Continental Europe in the Nineteenth Century* (Berkeley, 1968).

Anderson, P., *Lineages of the Absolutist State* (1975) (3rd imp. 1977).

Anon., *Notice sur le Ministère de la Guerre* (1879).

Antoine, M., *Le Secrétariat d'État de Bertin, 1763–80* (École des Chartes) (1948).

Antoine, M., *Les Comités des ministres sous Louis XV* (1957).

Antoine, M., *Le Conseil d'État sous Louis XV* (Geneva, 1970).

Antoine, M., *Le Conseil Royal des Finances au XVIIIᵉ siècle et le registre E 3659 des Archives Nationales* (Geneva, 1973).

Antoine, M., 'La Notion de subdélégation dans la Monarchie de l'Ancien Régime', *Bibliothèque de l'École des Chartes*, cxxxii (1974), 267–87.

Antoine, M., 'Les Subdélégues Généraux des Intendances', *RHDFE*, liii/3 (1975), 395–435.

Ardant, G., *Histoire de l'impôt*, Les Grands Études historiques (1972).

Armstrong, J., 'Old Regime Administrative Élites in France, Prussia and Russia', *Revue internationale des sciences administratives*, xxxviii/1 (1972), 21–40.

Armstrong, J., 'Old Regime Governors: Bureaucratic and Patrimonial Attributes', *CSSH*, xiv/1 (1972), 2–29.

Armstrong, J. A., *The European Administrative Élite* (Princeton, NJ, 1973).

Artaud de Montor, A. F., *Histoire de la vie et des travaux politiques du Comte d'Hauterive* (1839).

Aulard, F. A., *Histoire politique de la Révolution française* (1901).

Baecheler, J., *Les Phénomènes Révolutionnaires* (1970).

Baecque, F. de, *L'Administration centrale de la France* (1973).

Baecque, F. de, *et al.,Les Directeurs de Ministère en France (XIXᵉ–XXᵉ siècles)*, (Centre de recherches d'histoire et de philologie de la IVᵉ section de l'École Pratique des Hautes Études) (Geneva, 1976).

Baker, R. J. S., *Administrative Theory and Public Administration* (1972).

Balzac, H. de, *Les Employés, Œuvres complètes*, vol. 17 (Société d'Éditions Littéraires et Artistiques, 1912).

Barker, E., *The Development of Public Services in Europe* (Oxford, 1944).

Barker, R. J., 'The "Conseil Général des Manufactures" under Napoleon 1810–14', *FHS*, vi/2 (1969), 185–213.

Beaud, M., 'Le Bureau de la Balance de Commerce', *Revue d'histoire économique et sociale*, xlii (1964), 357–77.

Belloni, G., *La Comité du Sûreté Général de la Convention Nationale* (1924).

Belloni, G., 'Les Douze Commissions Exécutives', *La Révolution française*, lxvii (1924), 104.

Belorgey, G., *Le Gouvernement et administration de la France* (1970).

Bénoit, F. B., *Le Droit administratif français* (1968).

Berenger, J., 'Pour une enquête europééne. Le problème du Ministériat au XVIIᵉ siècle', *AESC*, xxix (1) (1974), 166–92.

Bergeron L., *Banques, négociants, et manufacturiers parisiens. Du Directoire à l'Empire* (Lille, 1975).

Bernadin, E., *Jean Marie Roland, Ministre de l'Intérieur; Essai sur l'administration révolutionnaire, 1792–3*, Bibliothèque d'histoire révolutionnaire, IIIe serie, no. 2 (1964).

Bertaud, J., *La Révolution française* (1976).

Berthaut, J., *Les Ingénieurs–Géographes militaires* (1902).

Bezard, Y., *Fonctionnaires maritimes et coloniaux—Les Bégon* (1932).

Bienvenu, J., 'L'Organisation du conflict administratif: Recherches sur la pratique contentieuse des Conseils de Préfecture', *RHDFE*, lii (1974), 12–37.

Billy, A., *Les Technocrates* (1975).

Birnbaum, P., *Les Sommets de l'États. Essai sur l'élite du pouvoir en France* (1977).

Blanc Gonnet, P., *La Réforme des services extérieurs du Ministère de l'Agriculture* (1969).

Blau, P. M., *The Dynamics of Bureaucracy* (1957).

Blau, P. M., and Scott, W. R., *Formal Organisations—A Comparative Approach*, International Library of Sociology and Social Reconstruction (1963).

Blondel, J., *The Government of France* (1975).

Bluche, F., 'L'Origine sociale du personnel ministériel français au XVIIIe siècle', *Bulletin de la Société d'Histoire Moderne*, 12e serie, Jan–Feb 1957.

Bon, F., and Burnier, M. A., *Classe ouvrière et révolution* (1971).

Bordes, M., *L'Administration provinciale et municipale* (1972).

Bosher, J., *Jacques Necker et l'État moderne*, Réimpression de la Société Historique du Canada, Rapport 1963 (of annual meeting, Quebec 5–8 June), contenant les communications historiques, ed. J. P. Heisler and F. Ouillet).

Bosher, J., 'Le Comité Contentieux des Finances près le Conseil du Roi (1777–91) A review and a document', *Annali della Fondazione Italiana per la Storia Amministrativa*, iv (1967), 598–607.

Bosher, J., *French Finances 1770–1795—From Business to Bureaucracy*, Cambridge Studies in Early Modern History (1970).

Bourdon, J., 'Le Mécontentement public et les craintes des dirigeants sous le Directoire', *AHRF*, xviii/2 (1946), 215–37.

Bouloiseau, M., *Le Comité de Salut Public*, Que Sais-Je? (1962).

Bouteron, M., 'Le Fonctionnement du Conseil du Roi du Roi Louis XVI, Expliqué par l'un de ses Secrétaires', *Revue d'histoire moderne*, xii (1937), 325–37.

Boyer de Saint-Suzanne, E. V. de (Baron, *Le Personnel administratif sous l'Ancien Régime* (1868).

Brecht, A., 'How Bureaucracies Develop and Function', *Annals of*

American Academy of Political and Social Science, ccxcii/2 (1954).

Buisson, H., *La Police: Son Histoire* (1958).

Buot de l'épine, A., *Du Conseil du Roi au Conseil d'État, le Comité Contentieux des Départements (9 viii 1789–27 iv 1791)* (1972).

Buot de l'épine, A., 'Les Bureaux de la Guerre à la fin de l'Ancien Régime ', *RHDFE*, liv (1976), 533–58.

Burns, T., and Stalker, G. M., *The Management of Innovation* (1961).

Busquet, J., *Les Fonctionnaires et la lutte pour le droit* (1910).

Calvert, P., *Revolution* (1970).

Cameron, I. A., 'The Police of Eighteenth Century France', *ESR*, vii/1 (1977), 47–76.

Caritey, J., 'Pour un histoire des ministères du XIXᵉ Siècle', *RA* (1959), 216–19.

Caritey, J., 'Politique, administration et administrateurs', *RA*,

xii (1959), 69 pp. 260–7
         70   367–73
         71   476–83
         72   609–19

Caritey, J., 'Note sur le personnel des ministères en 1793', *RA*, Jan–Feb 1960, 24–7.

Caron, P., *et al.*, 'Les Commissaires du Conseil Exécutif—Les origines du Comité de Sûreté Générale: Les douze Commissions Exécutifs de l'an II', *Revue d'histoire moderne*, xix (1914), 5–23.

Caron, P., 'Conseil Exécutif Provisoire et pouvoir ministériel, 1792–4', *AHRF*, x/1 (1937), 4–16.

Casinelli, C. W., *Total Revolution* (Santa Barbara, Cal., 1976).

Chapman, B., *The Profession of Government: the Public Services in Europe* (Manchester, 1954).

Charbonneau, S., 'Mutations des structures ministérielles et théories modernes des organisations bureaucratiques', *Esprit*, 38/1 (1970), 121–32.

Chaunu, P., 'L'État' in Labrousse and Braudel, *Histoire économique et sociale* i/1 (1969) 11–228.

Chaussinand-Nogaret, G., *Une Histoire des élites* (1975).

Chenot, B., *et al.*, *Histoire de l'administration française depuis 1800. Problèmes et méthodes* (Geneva, 1975).

Chevallier, J., *L'Élaboration historique du principe de séparation de la juridiction administrative et de l'administrative active* (1970).

Chevallier, J. J., *Histoire des institutions et des régimes politiques de la France moderne 1789–1958*, 3rd ed. (1967).

Church, C. H., *The Organization and Personnel of French Central Government under the Directory*, Ph.D. (London 1963).

Church, C. H., 'The Personnel of French Central Government under the Directory, 1795–1799', *Past and Present*, 36 (1967), 59–71.

Church, C. H., 'Bureaucracy, Politics and Revolution: The Evidence of the "Commission des Dix-Sept" ', *FHS*, vi/4 (1970), 492–516.

Church, C. H., 'In Search of the Directory' in J. F. Bosher (ed.), *French Government and Society 1500–1850. Essays in Memory of Alfred Cobban* (1973), 261–94.

Church, C. H., 'Du Nouveau sur les origines de la Constitution de 1793', *RHDFE*, liii (1974), 38–71.

Cobban, A. B. C., 'Local Government during the French Revolution', *EHR*, lviii (1943), 13–31.

Cohan, A. S., *Theories of Revolution: An Introduction* (1975).

Contamine, H., 'Les Conditions du travail de Chateaubriand', *Revue d'histoire diplomatique*, lxix/3 (1955), 193–206.

Cruickshanks, E. G., *Factions at the Court of Louis XV and the Succession to Fleury, 1737–45*, Ph.D. London, 1956.

Cusson, G., *Origines et évolution du Ministère de l'Agriculture* (1929).

Dagnaud, E., 'L'Administration de la Marine et Colonies sous l'Ancien Régime', *Revue maritime et coloniale* (1912).

Dakin, D., *Turgot and the Ancien Régime in France* (1939).

Damien, A., 'Le Personnel révolutionnaire', *Souvenir Napoléonien*, xxiii/256 (1970), 28–35.

Darbel, A., and Schnapper, D., *Les Agents du système administrative* (The Hague, 1969).

Darbel, A., and Schnapper, D., 'Le Système Administratif', *La Morphologie de la haute administration française II*. Cahiers du Centre de Sociologie Européene (The Hague, 1972).

Dawson, G., *L'Évolution des structures de l'administration locale déconcentrée en France* (1969).

Day, R. C., and Hamblin, R. L., 'Some effects of close and punitive Supervision', *American Journal of Sociology*, lxix/5 (1964), 499–510.

Decoufle, A., *La Sociologie des Révolutions* (1970).

Dejoint, G., *La Politique économique du Directoire*, Bibliothèque d'Histoire Économique et Sociale (1951).

Delany, W., 'The Development and Decline of Patrimonial and Bureaucratic Administration', *ASQ*, vii (1963), 458–501.

Demartial, G., *Le Personnel des ministères* (1906).

Desgranges, E., *La Centralisation républicaine sous le Directoire* (Poitiers, 1954).

Detton, H., *L'Administration régionale et locale de la France* (1972).

Deutscher, I., 'Les Racines de la Bureaucratie', *L'Homme et la Société*, xi, 1969, 63–81, trans. from the English.

Deville, G., 'Thermidor et Directoire' in J. Jaurès, *Histoire socialiste*, vols. 5–6 (1900).

Dogan, M. (ed.), *The Mandarins of Western Europe*, (NY, 1975).

Doucet, R., *Les Institutions de la France au XVI siècle* (1948).

Downs, A., *Inside Bureaucracy* (Boston, 1967).

Duchêne, A., *La Politique coloniale de la France—Le Ministère des Colonies depuis Richelieu* (1928).

Dunan, M., *Histoire intérieure du Directoire*, Cours de la Sorbonne (1951).

Dunn, J., *Modern Revolutions* (Cambridge, 1972).

Dunsire, A., *Administration, The Word and the Thing* (1973).

Dupriez, L., *Les Ministres de l'Europe et l'Amerique* (1892–3).

Durand, C., 'Conseil Privés, Conseil des Ministres', *RHMC*, xvii (1970), 814–17.

Durand, C., and Lanza, A., 'Études sur les rapports entre la loi et règlement gouvernemental au XIXe Siècle', *Travaux et mémoires de la Faculté de Droit et de Science Politique d'Aix-Marseille*, no. 26 (Aix-Marseille, 1976).

Durand-Barthez, P., *Histoire des structures du Ministère de la Justice, 1789–1945* (1973).

Edwards, L. P., *The Natural History of Revolution* (NY, 1927).

Eisenstadt, S. N., *The Political Systems of Empires* (Glencoe, Ill., 1963).

Eisenstadt, S. N., *Essays in Comparative Institutions* (New York, 1965).

Eisenstadt, S. N., *The Comparative Analysis of Historical Political Systems* (NY, Committee on Comparative Politics of the Social Science Research Council, 1958).

Ellul, J., *Histoire des institutions*, 5 vols., (1969–70).

Evans, H., *L'Administration locale* (Edinburgh, 1973).

Fesler, J. W., 'French Field Administration—The Beginnings', *CSSH*, v (1962), 76–111.

Finer, H., *The Theory and Practice of Modern Government*, 4th ed. (1961).

Fougère, L., *et al.*, *Le Conseil d'État—Son histoire à travers les documents d'époque 1799–1974* (1974).

Friedrich, C. (ed.) 'Revolution', *Nomos*, viii (NY, 1966).

Furet, F., et Richet, D., 'Du 9 Thermidor à 18 Brumaire', *La Révolution française*, ii (1966).

Gaxotte, P., *Le Directoire*, Cercle historique (1957).

Gerbod, P., *et al.*, *Les Épurations administratives XIX–XXe siècles* (Geneva, 1977).

Gladden, E. N., *A History of Public Administration* (1972).

Godechot, J., *La Vie quotidienne sous le Directoire* (1977).

Godechot, J., 'L'Origine des institutions françaises de l'époque révolutionnaire', *Revue internationale d'histoire politique et constitutionelle*, i (1951), 92–9.

Godechot, J., *Les Institutions de la France sous la Révolution et l'Empire* (new ed. 1970).

404　BIBLIOGRAPHY

Goncourt, E. and J., *Histoire de la société française sous le Directoire* (1863).

Goodwin, A., 'The French Executive Directory, A Revaluation', *History*, xxii (1927), 201–18.

Gortner, H. F., *Administration in the Public Sector* (NY, 1977).

Goubert, P., *L'Ancien Régime:* II, Les Pouvoirs (1973).

de Gournay, B., *et al*, 'La Politisation de l'administration', *Res Publica*, xiii/2 (1971), 161–242.

de Gournay, B., Kessler, J. F., and Siwek-Pouydesseau, J., *Administration Publique* (1967).

Gousset, P., 'L'Évolution historique de l'administration centrale du commerce et de l'industrie', *RA*, lxxx (1961), 132–7.

Greene, T. H., *Comparative Revolutionary Movements* (Englewood Cliffs, NJ, 1974).

Grégoire, R., *La Fonction publique* (1954).

Gros, J. P., *St. Just. Sa Politique et ses missions* (1976).

Gruder, V. R., *The Royal Provincial Intendants—A Governing Élite in Eighteenth Century France* (Ithaca, NY, 1968).

Grusky, O., and Miller, G. A. (eds.), *The Sociology of Organizations: Basic Studies* (New York, 1970).

Guenée, B., 'L'Histoire de l'État en France à la fin du Moyen Âge, vue par les historiens français, etc.', *Revue historique*, ccxxxii/4, (1964), 331–60.

Hall, R., 'The Concept of Bureaucracy: An Empirical Assessment', *American Journal of Sociology*, lxix (1963), 32–40.

Handmann, M., 'The Bureaucratic Culture Pattern and Political Revolution', *American Journal of Sociology*, xxxix (1933), 301–13.

Hauterive, E., *Napoléon et sa Police* (1943).

Hayward, J., *The One and Indivisible French Republic* (1973).

Henry, P., *Histoire des Préfects* (1950).

Herlaut, A. P. (le Général), *Le Colonel Bouchotte, Ministre de la Guerre en l'An II*, 2 vols. (1946).

Hill, M. J., *The Sociology of Public Administration* (1972).

Holtman, R. B., *The Napoleonic Revolution* (Baton Rouge, La., 1967).

Izdebski, H., 'Direction collégiale de personnelle: vers un perspective pour l'histoire comparative des administrations centrales en Europe', *RHDFE*, lii (4) (1974), 752–4.

Jacques, E., *A General Theory of Bureaucracy* (NY, 1976).

Jalouniex, J., 'Le Journal de la Meurthe de 1798 à 1830', *Thèse en droit* (Nancy II, 1974.)

Josal, J., *Le Ministère des Finances* (1882).

Joussain, A., 'Le Directoire et Nous', *Les Libertés françaises*, xxi (1957).

Jouvencal, H., *Le Contrôleur Général des Finances sous l'Ancien Régime* (1901).

Julien-Laferrière, F., *Les Deputés-Fonctionnaires sous la Monarchie de*

Juillet, Travail et recherches de la Faculté du Droit et des Sciences Économiques de Paris. Série Science Administrative 4 (1970).

E. Komenka *et al.*, *Bureaucracy. The Career of a Concept* (1979).

Kessler, M. C., 'Historique de système de formation et de recrutement des hauts fonctionnaires', *Revue française d'administration publique*, i/1 (1977), 9–52.

Kircheimer, O., 'Confining Conditions and Revolutionary Breakthroughs', *American Political Science Review*, lxix (1965), 964 et seq.

Kitchen, J., *Un Journal 'Philosophique': La Décade 1794–1807* (1965).

Kollefrath-Laprat, C., Madame, *Les Modalités de l'organisation et de l'activité du Ministère de l'Intérieur*, D.E.S. Mémoire (Paris II, 1977).

Kumar, K., *Revolution. The theory and practice of a European idea* (1971).

Labrousse, E., and Braudel, F. (eds.), *Histoire économique et sociale de la France* (1969 on).

Laferrière, J., 'La Raison de la proclamation de la règle de la séparation des autorités', *Mélanges Paul Negelesco* (Bucharest, 1935).

Lafon, J., 'Le Contrat de Fonction Publique—la naissance de l'état fonction', *RHDFE*, lii/4 (1974), 658–95.

La Palombara, J. (ed.), *Bureaucracy and Political Development* (1963).

Latreille, A., *L'Ère napoléonienne* (1974).

Le Clère, M., 'Comment opérait la police de Fouché', *Revue de criminologie et de police technique* (1951), 33–6.

Lefèbvre, G., *Les Thermidoriens* (1937).

Lefèbvre, G., *Le Directoire* (1938).

Lefèbvre, G. *La France sous le Directoire* ed. J. Suratteau (1979).

Lefort, C., *Éléments d'une critique de la bureaucratie* (Geneva, 1971).

Legendre, P., 'Le Régime Historique des bureaucraties occidentales, remarques sur le cas français', *Revue internationale des sciences administratives*, xxxviii/4 (1972), 361–78.

Legendre, P., 'Prestance du Conseil d'État', *RHDFE*, liii/4 (1975), 630–5.

Legendre, P., *Jouir du pouvoir. Traité de la bureaucratie patriotique*, Coll. Critique (1976).

Legendre, P., *Histoire de l'administration de 1750 à nos jours*, Thémis, (1968).

Legendre, P., 'La bureaucratie: science et rendement, au sommaire d'une recherche', *Bulletin de l'Institut International de l'Administration Publique*, xxviii (1973), 7–15 and 551–9.

Leguin, C. A., 'An Anti-Clerical Bureaucrat in Eighteenth Century France—J. M. Roland', *Catholic Historical Review*, li/4 (1966), 487–542.

Leguin, C. A., 'Roland de la Platière—Public Servant', *Trans. am. Phil. Soc.*, lvi (6) (1966).

Lelong, P., 'Trois attitudes du fonctionnaire en face de l'activité politique', *RA*, vii (1954), 486–91.

Leroy, M., *Les Transformations de la puissance publique* (1907).

Logette, A., *Le Comité Contentieux des Finances près le Conseil du Roi, 1777–1791*, (Nancy, 1964).

Logette, A., 'Quelques nouvelles sources pour l'Administration des Finances à la Fin du XVIII', *RHDFE*, xlvii/3 (1969), 408–40.

Lot, F., and Fawtier, R., *Histoire des institutions française au Moyen Âge* (1958).

Lucas, C., 'The First Directory and the Rule of Law', *FHS*, x/2 (1977), 231–60.

de Lucay, H., *Des origines du pouvoir ministérial en France: Les Secrétaires d'État depuis leur institution jusqu'a la mort du Louis XV* (Paris, 1881).

Lyons, M., *France under the Directory, 1795–99* (Cambridge, 1975).

Marion, M., *Histoire financière de la France* (1922).

Markoff, J., 'Governmental Bureaucratization: General processes and an anomalous case', *CSSH*, xvii (1975), 479–503.

Marx, K., *The Eighteenth Brumaire of Louis Bonaparte*, Trans. D. de Leon (NY, 1898).

Bessand Massenet, P., *De Robespierre à Bonaparte—Les Français et la Révolution* (1970).

Masson, F., *La Ministère des Relations Extérieures sous la Révolution, 1787–1804* (1877).

Mathews, G. T., *The Royal General Farms in Eighteenth Century France* (NY, 1958).

Mathiez, A., *La Réaction thermidorienne* (1929).

Mathiez, A., *Le Directoire*, Armand Colin, edited by J. Godechot (1934).

Mead, G. J. de C., *The Administrative Noblesse of France During the Eighteenth Century*, London University Ph.D. Thesis (1954).

Meininger, A, A., 'D'Hauterive et la formation des Diplomates', *Revue d'histoire diplomatique*, lxxxix/1–2 (1975), 26–69.

Menon, P. L., 'La Fonction Publique d'hier et d'autrefois', *Bulletin de l'Économie et des finances*, no. 72, (1975), 135–48.

Mercier, S., 'Les bureaux politique du ministère des Affaires Étrangères à l'époque de Vergennes, 1774–1787', *Revue historique de Versailles et de Seine-et-Oise*, lv (1965), 115–50.

Merton, R. K. (ed.), *Reader in Bureaucracy* (Glencoe, Ill. 1952).

Methivier, H., *L'Ancien Régime* (1968).

Meynier, A., *Les Coups d'État du Directoire*, 3 vols. (1928).

Michaud, H., *La Grande Chancellerie et les écritures royales au XVIe siècle (1515–1589)*, Mémoires et documents publiés par la Société de l'École des Chartes, 17 (1969).

Michaud, H., 'Aux Origines du Secrétariat d'État à la Guerre: les

"Règlements" de 1617–19, *RHMC*, xix (1972), 389–413.

Mignot, G., et d'Orsay, P., *La Machine administrative* (1968).

Monnerot, J., *Sociologie de la Révolution* (1969).

Morange, J., *L'Idée de municipalité de Canton, de l'An III à nos jours* (1971).

Morstein Marx, F., *The Administrative State: An Introduction to Bureaucracy* (Chicago, 1957).

Mousnier, R., *État et société sous François Ier et pendant le gouvernement personnel de Louis XIV*, Cours de la Sorbonne (1966).

Mousnier, R., *État et société en France XVIIe et XVIIIe siècles I: Le Gouvernement et les corps*, Cours de la Sorbonne (1968).

Mousnier, R., *Le Conseil du Roi de Louis XII à la Révolution* (1970).

Mousnier, R., *Les Institutions de la France sous la monarchie absolue, 1598–1789*, i, 'Société et État' (1974).

Mousnier, R., with Tapié, V.-L., Goubert, P., Bluche, F., and Corvisier, A., 'Serviteurs du Roi: Quelques aspects de la fonction publique dans la société française du XVIIe siècle', *XVIIe Siècle*, 42–3 (1959).

Mouzelis, N., *Organisation and Bureaucracy: An Analysis of Modern Theories*, International Library of Sociology (1967).

Nanteuil, Colonel de, *Le Comte Daru ou l'administration militaire sous la Révolution et l'Empire* (1966).

Noell, H., *L'Administration de la France: Les Ministères* (1911).

Olive, H., *L'Action exécutif exercé par les Comités.de la Convention Nationale, 1789–1795* (Marseilles, 1912).

Ording, A., 'Le Bureau de Police du Comité de Salut Public', *Skifter ut gett au Videnkaps Akademi i Oslo*, Hist. Filos. Klasse II, 6 (Oslo, 1930).

Outrey, A., *L'Administration française des Affaires Étrangères* (1954).

Pagès, G., 'Essai sur l'évolution des institutions administratives en France', *Revue d'histoire moderne*, vii (1932), 8–57, and 113–37.

Pallain, J., *Le Ministère de Talleyrand sous le Directoir* (1891).

Pappalardo, J., *Étude sociologique du personnel d'un centre de tri* (1969).

Pariset, G., 'L'Administration, les affaires et le pays sous le Directoire' in *Études d'histoire moderne et contemporaine* (Strasburg, 1929), 79–133.

Parker, H. T., 'Two Administrative Bureaux under the Directory and Napoleon', *FHS*, iv/27, (1965), 150–69.

Parsons, T., and Henderson, J. (eds.), *The Theory of Social and Economic Organization* (NY, 1946).

Perrot, J. C., 'L'Âge d'or de la statistique régionale (an IV–1804)', *AHRF*, lviii/2 (1976), 181–214.

Pertué, M., 'Les Luttes de Classe et la Question de la dictature au début de 1793', *AHRF*, lix/3 (1977), 454–62.

Petot, J., *Histoire de l'administration des Ponts et Chaussées 1599–1815*

(1958).

Piccavet, G. C., 'Les Commis des Affaires Étrangères au temps de Louis XIV (1660–1715)', *Revue d'histoire moderne*, i (1926), 103–20.

Piccioni, C., *Les Premiers Commis des Affaires Étrangères aux XVIIe et au XVIIIe siècle* (1928).

Pietri, F., *La Réforme de l'État au XVIIIe siècle* (1935).

Pinaud, P. F., 'L'Administration des Cultes de 1800 à 1815', *Revue de l'Institut Napoléon*, 132 (1976), 28–36.

Pirotte, O., *Alexandre-François-Auguste Vivien de Goubert (1799–1854). Contribution à l'étude d'un liberal autoritaire* (1972).

Poggi, G., *The Development of the Modern State. A Sociological Introduction* (1978).

Ponteil, F., *Napoléon et l'organisation autoritaire de la France* (1956).

Ponteil, F., *Les Institutions de la France de 1814 à 1870* (1966).

Poullet. P., *Les Institutions françaises 1795–1815* (1907).

Poutier, C., 'L'Évolution des structures ministérielles de 1800 à 1944', *Thèse droit*, (Paris, 1960).

Pouthas, C. H., 'Les Projets de Réforme Administrative Sous la Restauration', *Revue d'histoire moderne*, i/5 (1926), 321–67.

Pouthas, C. H., 'Les Ministres de la monarchie de juillet, *RHMC*, New Series i/2 (1954), 102–30.

'Pouvoir Politique et Administration', *Rapport de la 84e promotion L'École de Guerre* (1972).

Rabony, C., 'Les Types sociaux—Le Fonctionnaire', *Revue générale de l'administraiton*, xxix (1907), 5–28.

Racinet, A., 'De la spécialisation ministérielle en France', *Thèse droit* (Paris, 1910).

Ranum, O., *Richelieu and the Councillors of Louis XIII* (Oxford, 1963).

Raulin, G. de, 'Fonctionnaires de la Marine sous la Révolution', *Revue maritime*, ii/1 (1921), 501–17.

Regnault, H. de, *La Royaume de la France et ses institutions* (1942).

Reinhard, M., *Le Département de Sarthe sous le régime directoriale* (Saint-Brieuc, 1936).

Reinhard, M., *La France du Directoire*, 2 vols., Cours de la Sorbonne (1956).

Resbecq, H. de Fontaine de, 'Administration Centrale de la Marine et Colonies avant 1793', *Revue maritime et coloniale*, xvi (1879), 148–54.

Resbecq, H. Fontaine de, 'L'Administration de la Marine et Colonies', *Revue maritime et coloniale*, xxv (1886), 5–20.

Richet, D., *La France moderne: L'Esprit des institutions* (1974).

Richardson, N., *The French Prefectoral Corps, 1814–1830* (Cambridge, 1966).

Ridley, F., and Blondel, J., *Public Administration in France* (1964).

Robin, P., *La Compagnie des Secrétaires du Roi (1351–1791)* (1933).

Romano, S. F., *Breve Storia Della burocrazia Dall'antichità all'età contemporanea* (Bologna, 1965).

Rule, J. and Tilly, C., 'Political Process in Revolutionary France, 1830–32' in J. M. Merriman (ed.), *1830 in France* (NY, 1975).

Sallois, J. (ed.), *L'Administration. Les Hommes, les techniques, les rouages* (1974).

Samoyault, J. P., *Les Bureaux du Secrétariat d'État des Affaires Étrangères sous Louis XV* (1971).

Sandevoir, P., *Études sur le recours de pleine juridiction* (1964).

Sautel, G., *Histoire des institutions administratives* (1971).

Sautel, G., *Histoire des institutions publiques depuis le Révolution française*, 3rd ed. (1974).

Sauvel, T., 'L'Empereur et le Conseil d'État statuant au contentieux, 1806–15', *Revue du droit public*, lxxxix (1973), 1402–3.

Sauvigny, B. de, *La Restauration* (1963).

Sauvy, A., *La Bureaucratie*, Que Sais-Je? no. 712 (1961).

Sauvy, A., *Bureaux et Bureaucratie*, 2nd ed. (1967).

Savoye, J., *Quelques Aspects de l'œuvre de Louis-Antoine Macarel (1790–1851), contribution à l'étude de la naissance des sciences politiques et administratives* (Lille, 1970).

Schnerb, R., 'La Dépression économique sous le Directoire', *AHRF*, xi (1933), 27–49.

Sharp, W. R., *The French Civil Service* (New York, 1934).

Siffin, W. J. (ed.), *Toward the Comparative Study of Public Administration* (Bloomington, Ind., 1957).

Siwek-Pouydesseau, J., *Le Personnel de Direction des Ministères* (1969).

Siwek-Pouydesseau, J., 'Les Conditions d'élaboration du statut général des fonctionnaires de 1946' in *Annuaire international de la fonction publique* (1970–1), 12–39.

Silvera, V., 'Une vielle institution originale: le conseil d'administration du ministère de la justice', *RA*, xxv (147) (1972), 297–8.

Soboul, A., *Le Directoire et le Consulat* (1967).

Soemardjan, S., 'Bureaucratic Organization in a Time of Revolution', *ASQ*, ii (1957), 182–99.

Sorokin, P., *The Sociology of Revolution* (New ed., NY, 1967).

Spitzer, A. B., 'The Bureaucrat as Pro-Consul—the Restoration Prefects and the Police Générale', *CSSH*, vii (1965), 371–92.

Strayer, J. R., *On the Mediaeval Origins of the Modern State* (Princeton, NJ, 1970).

Sturgill, C. C., 'The Relationship of French General Officers to the Civil Government of France, 1715–1730', *Transactions of the Conference Group for Social and Administrative History*, i, 38–52 (Madison, Wisc., 1971).

Strauss, E., *The Ruling Servants. Bureaucracy in France, Russia and Britain* (1961).

Suleiman, E. A., *Politics, Power and Bureaucracy in France—the Administrative Élite* (Princeton, 1974).

Les Superstructures des administrations centrales, Cahier de l'Institut Français des sciences Politiques (1973).

Suratteau, J.-R., 'Fonctionnaires et Employés', *AHRF*, xxix/2 (1958), 71–2.

Suratteau, J.-R., *Les Élections de l'An VI et la 'Coup d'État du 22 Floréal' 11 Mai 1798. Étude documentaire, statistique et analytique. Essai d'interpretation* (1971).

Suratteau, J.-R., 'Le Directoire d'après des travaux recénts', *AHRF*, xlviii/2 (1976), 181–214.

Sutherland, N., *The French Secretaries of State in the Age of Catherine de Medici* (1962).

Sydenham, M. J., *The First French Republic, 1792–1804* (1973).

Tarrade, J., 'L'Administration Coloniale en France à la fin de l'Ancien Régime', *RH*, 1963 (229), 103–22.

Tersen, H., *Origines et évolution du Ministère de l'Intérieur* (Montpellier, 1913).

Tilly, C. (ed), *The Formation of nation States in Western Europe* (Princeton, 1975).

Thuillier, G., *La Vie quotidienne dans les bureaux au XIX siècle* (1978).

Thuillier, G., 'La Gestion du personnel des ministères au XIXe. L'Exemple de la Guerre 1830–80', *RA*, xxxi/3 (1975), 183, 261–73.

Thuillier, G., 'Le Droit disciplinaire dans les ministères au XIXe', *RA*, xxx/1 (1977), 175, 26–37.

Thuillier, G., and Tulard, J., 'Pour une histoire des Directeurs de Ministère en France au XIXe et XXe Siècles, *Revue internationale des sciences administratives* i (1974), 227–9.

Thuillier, G., 'Comment les français voyaient l'administration en 1789—Jacques Peuchet et la Bureaucratie', *RA*, xviii (1962), 373–83.

De Tocqueville, A., *L'Ancien Régime et la Révolution* (ed. G. W. Headlam, Oxford, 1965).

Tourdes, C., 'Une Étude de sociologie historique: Administration et décisions sous la Convention et le Directoire en matière d'enseignement', *DES* Paris II, Histoire des Institutions (1973).

Trenard, L., *Salvandy en son Temps, 1795–1856* (Lille, 1968).

Trenard, L., 'Les Intendants et leurs enquêtes', *L'Information historique*, xxxviii/1 (1976), 11–23.

Tulard, J., *La Préfecture de Police sous la Monarchie de Juillet . . . suivi d'un inventaire ds sources de l'histoire de la police aux Archives Nationales* (1964).

Tulard, J., *Paris et son Administration 1800–1830* (1976).

Tulard, J., *Napoléon ou le Mythe du Saveur,* 2nd ed. (1977).

Udy, S. H. Jnr., 'Bureaucracy' and 'Rationality' in Weber's 'Organization Theory: An Empirical Study', *American Sociological Review,* xxiv (1959), 791–5.

Van Berkel, R., 'Recherches sur le centralisme français. L'Exemple de l'administration locale dans le Nord 1750–1850', *Thèse droit* (Lille, 1973).

Van Berkel, R., 'Produit du droit par les bureaux', *RHDFE,* lii/4 (1974), 742–51.

Vauthier, G., 'Le Directoire et le Garde Meuble', *Annales révolutionnaires,* vii (1914), 533–6.

Vedel, G., *et al., Traité de Science administrative* (The Hague, 1966).

Vial, J., 'L'Administration Centrale de l'Instruction Publique en France de 1792 à 1855, *Paedagica Historica,* 916 (1969), 120–8.

Vidalenc, J., *et al., Préfets en France, 1800–1900* (Geneva, 1978).

Viollet, P., *Le Roi et ses ministres pendant les trois derniers siècles de la monarchie* (1912).

Waldo, D., 'Public Administration in an Age of Revolution', *Public Administration Review,* xxviii (1965), 366–7.

Waline, M., *Droit administratif* (9th ed. 1963).

Wallace-Hadrill, J., and McManners, J. (eds.), *France: Government and Society* (1957).

Warnotte, D., 'Bureaucratie et Fonctionnairisme', *Revue de l'Institut de Sociologie,* xvii (1937), 218–60.

Warwick, D., *Bureaucracy* (1974).

Werthman, M. S., and Dalby, M. (eds.), *Bureaucracy in Historical Perspective* (Glenview, Ill., 1971).

Whitcomb, E. A., 'The Duties and Functions of Napoleon's External Agents; *History,* lvii (1972), 189–204.

Whitcomb, E. A., 'Napoleon's Prefects', *American Historical Review,* cxxvx/4 (1974), 1089–1118.

Woloch, I., *Jacobin Legacy: The Democratic Movement during the Directory* (Princeton, 1970).

Woronoff, D., *La République bourgeoise, de Thermidor à Brumaire, 1794 à 1799,* Nouvelle Histoire de la France contemporaine: 3 (1972).

Wright, V., 'Politics and Administraiton under the French Fifth Republic', *Political Studies,* xxii/1 (1974), 44–65.

Wright, V., 'L'École Nationale d'Administration de 1848–1849: un échec révélateur', *RH,* cclv/1 (1976), 21–42.

Wright, V., *The Government and Politics of France* (1978).

Wright Mills, E., and Gerth, H. (eds.), *From Max Weber, Essays in Sociology* (1957).

Zeldin, T., *France 1848–1945* (Oxford, 1973–7).

Zivy, H., *Le Treize Vendémiaire An IV* (1898).

INDEX